ROEL STERCKX

Chinese Thought
From Confucius to Cook Ding

A PELICAN BOOK

PELICAN
an imprint of
PENGUIN BOOKS

PELICAN BOOKS

UK | USA | Canada | Ireland | Australia
India | New Zealand | South Africa

Penguin Books is part of the Penguin Random
House group of companies whose addresses can
be found at global.penguinrandomhouse.com.

First published 2019
001

Text copyright © Roel Sterckx, 2019
The moral right of the author has been asserted

Book design by Matthew Young
Set in 11/16.13pt Freight Text Pro
Typeset by Jouve (UK), Milton Keynes
Printed and bound in Great Britain by
Clays Ltd, Elcograf S.p.A.

A CIP catalogue record for this book is available
from the British Library

ISBN: 978-0-241-38590-6

For En-En

Contents

Preface

China has emerged onto the world scene wielding economic and political power and influence as never before. When the thirteenth-century Venetian traveller Marco Polo reported on the riches of this vast empire, its people and its cities, his stories were bundled together in a book that announced itself as describing the 'marvels' of the world (*Le Livre des merveilles du monde*). Today our encounters and fascination with China are more sophisticated and multifaceted. To an increasing number of students and professionals, China no longer represents that quintessentially 'other' civilization, that place where each and every habit, virtue and vice seems to turn upside down everything held dear by a loosely self-identified 'West'.

The direction of human travel, too, has turned irreversibly. Gone are the days when a handful of missionaries fuelled European curiosity about China during the eighteenth-century Enlightenment, or when, a century later, accounts of the achievements and tribulations of a waning Chinese empire were funnelled to Europe by a select group of traders, diplomats and preachers. Today, every respectable university campus in the world recruits and plays host to highly talented Chinese students and researchers. China trades visibly, and invisibly, in every corner of the world. Its goods, services and cultural capital are discernible, audible or edible in every household. Young people explore the Chinese language at school, university or in evening classes with the same curiosity that drew foodies to Chinese cuisine before noodles and Peking duck went global.

Yet our schools, colleges and media have barely begun putting together the elementary curricula needed to introduce aspiring global citizens to the basic outlines of Chinese civilization and Chinese ways of thinking. China, so far, tends to creep into our narrative only from the time it appears on the imperial horizons of the West, or when it enters the international politics of the twentieth century, or when its economy seems unresistingly relevant (or threatening) to us. In university departments, philosophy still sounds mostly Greek; neither does one-fifth of the world's population appear to have a religion, judging by many course syllabi. Beyond its moments of encounter with the West, to many China remains a land of tea and calligraphy, poetry and porcelain, and the odd imposing emperor. For those still comfortable with intercultural conversation in terms of 'we' versus 'them', the knowledge that the average Chinese teenager or college student knows much more about 'us' than 'we' know about 'them' should be a gentle wake-up call. To understand China, we need to learn to think Chinese.

This book requires no knowledge of China. Its thematic organization reflects my personal digest as it has grown in conversation with students and audiences over the years. Like myself at the age of eighteen, many of my students did not know what to expect or where to begin when they came to college to study China, its history, language(s) and thought.

I hope this book will give readers some useful vantage points from which to begin their own dialogue with Chinese thinkers. Readers who wish to jump straight into the world of ideas can consider skipping the first chapter, which offers background information on Chinese history, geography, the classical Chinese language and the nature of the sources at hand. Busy readers should be able to turn to individual chapters in no particular order.

Historians short of ideas tend to become historians of ideas. A good way to characterize Chinese thought is to spell out what it is not. In the pages that follow, you will find little theoretical reflection on how the human mind works, or whether there exists a world or reality beyond this one. Nor will you be told how matter relates to spirit, what truth is (let alone logic) or whether there exists such a thing called mind or knowledge. Why? Because such questions (known among professional philosophers as epistemology and ontology) did not figure highly on the agenda of Chinese thinkers. The classical Chinese language did not have a term for 'philosophy'; the modern Mandarin term (*zhexue*) was imported from Japan in the late nineteenth century (and initially only referred to Western philosophy).

Chinese thought is predominantly human-centred and practice-oriented. The great questions that have occupied China's brightest minds are not about who and what we are, but rather about how we should live our lives, how we relate to others, how we should organize society and how we can secure the well-being of those who live with us and for whom we are responsible. Human conduct, human nature and the politics of human society will form the bulk of the story here.

When comparing philosophical traditions, it is easy to get lost in the many different answers various thinkers give to the enduring questions of life. A more fruitful way into a culture is to focus first on the questions that are asked, before worrying about the answers. In China these questions included: what makes a good person; what type of person is fit to govern and lead others; how can we create order in society; how can past traditions inform the present; what can we learn from those who came before us; what strategies will enable us to outmanoeuvre our enemies and competitors; how do we persuade others; does social engagement make for a fulfilling life, or is it better to retreat from society altogether?

Ancient China's masters of philosophy – the protagonists of this book – rarely engage in intellectual debate for its own sake. Most ideas are offered as guidance to be lived, experienced and practised. (Ironically, China's most influential thinker, Confucius, was a failure in office and unable to find a ruler willing to put his ideas into practice.) They reflect on how to live, function better and find harmony with the world. Yet in putting lived experience above theoretical knowledge, their teachings touch the entire person, the brain as well as the emotions. That is why they are as relevant today as they are interesting for their past.

Timeline

Legendary ages and Xia dynasty

Shang dynasty c.1600–c.1045 BCE

Zhou dynasty c.1045–256 BCE

Western Zhou period c.1045–771 BCE
Eastern Zhou period 770–256 BCE
Spring and Autumn period 770–481 BCE
Warring States period 481–221 BCE

Qin dynasty 221–206 BCE

Han dynasty 206 BCE–220 CE

Western/Former Han 206 BCE–9 CE
Xin interregnum 9–23 CE
Eastern/Later Han 25–220 CE

Six Dynasties period 220–589 CE

Sui dynasty 581–618

Tang dynasty 618–907

Five Dynasties period 902–979

Song dynasty 960–1279

Northern Song period 960–1127
Southern Song period 1127–1279

Yuan dynasty 1271–1368

Ming dynasty 1368–1644

Qing dynasty 1644–1912

Republican period 1912–49

People's Republic of China
1949 to present

Principal Figures

Table showing the principal Chinese thinkers and other historical figures covered by this book, arranged in approximate chronological order. A comprehensive list of names is included in the index. In Chinese names, the surname appears first, followed by the given name (e.g. in the case of Sima Qian, Sima is the surname and Qian the given name).

	Confucian	Daoist
Zhou (*c.*1045–256 BCE)		
	Confucius (551–479 BCE)	Laozi (*fl. c.* sixth century BCE?)
		Yang Zhu (*fl.* fourth century BCE)
	Mencius (*c.*372–289 BCE)	Zhuangzi (*c.*369–286 BCE)
		Xu Xing (*fl. c.*315 BCE)
	Xunzi (*c.*335–*c.*238 BCE)	
Qin (221–206 BCE)	Lu Jia (*c.*228–*c.*140 BCE)	
Han (206 BCE–220 CE)	Jia Yi (201–169 BCE)	
	Xu Gan (171–217 CE)	
Song (960–1279 CE)	Zhu Xi (1130–1200 CE)	

Legalist	Other	Historical
		Duke of Zhou (*fl.* 1046–1036 BCE)
		Guan Zhong (d. 645 BCE)
	Mozi (*c.*479–381 BCE)	
Shang Yang (*c.*390–338 BCE)	Sun Bin (?378–?301 BCE)	
Shen Buhai (d. 337 BCE)	Hui Shi (*c.*370–300 BCE)	
Shen Dao (*c.*360–*c.*285 BCE)	Gongsun Long (b. *c.*320 BCE)	
Han Fei (*c.*280–*c.*233 BCE)	Zou Yan (306–?240 BCE)	
	Lü Buwei, patron of *Lüshi chunqiu* (d. 235 BCE)	Qin Shihuangdi, the First Emperor (r. 221–210 BCE)
	Dong Zhongshu (*c.*179–104 BCE)	Emperor Han Wudi (r. 141–87 BCE)
	Liu An, patron of *Huainanzi* (?179–122 BCE)	Sima Qian (*c.*145–*c.*86 BCE)
		Liu Xiang (79–8 BCE)
	Wang Chong (*c.*27–100 CE)	Ban Gu (32–92 CE)
	Wang Fu (*c.*90–165 CE)	Ban Zhao (*c.*48–116 CE)
	Ying Shao (*c.*140–204 CE)	

China in Time and Space

What do we mean by China? Who are the Chinese? At first sight, you may think these are somewhat superfluous questions (like asking Socrates if Athens is located in Greece). But the issue merits some consideration. The history of China, like that of Europe, is not a linear story of one static, everlasting and stubbornly uniform continent. An oft-repeated line in history books, travel and museum guides and in television documentaries runs: 'What sets China apart from the rest of the world is the fact that it boasts a continuous civilization running through at least two and a half millennia' (and preferably longer). It is no surprise to see such cultural pride invoked on occasions by Chinese politicians, diplomats and other public figures. And, yes, many things have an admirably long history in China. But, as the social historian Wolfram Eberhard once pointed out, the greatness of a civilization is established by its achievements, not by claims to the longest history. To be sure, China has achieved a great deal. But claims to being the 'oldest living civilization' on the basis of a 'longest continuous history' can also offer a licence for veiled or misplaced cultural exceptionalism.

We could, and probably should, be open to alternative views. One would be to point out that the history of China consists of moments of political and geographical union interspersed by centuries of division. In the period from the early third to the mid tenth century CE alone, more than forty-five dynasties ruled over parts or all of its territory. Further back in time, more than ten centuries had already elapsed before China would emerge for the first time as an empire in 221 BCE. China's historical continuity, therefore, is marked by a striking measure of discontinuity. For large swathes of time, China has been ruled by regimes whose leading elites and officials were not ethnically Chinese. On that account, the Mongols and Manchus alone already take up nearly four centuries on China's historical chronology (the Yuan and Qing dynasties).

To counter this image of China as a uniform giant – either sleeping, restless or rising – it is more useful to think of its history as a history of regions, to imagine its people as regionally and often ethnically diverse, and to look at those in power as agents charged with the challenging task of keeping the regions in line with the demands of the political centre. The last has been the single most pressing mission of any ruling house that has governed China, be it the imperial courts of the past or the Communist Party and those at the helm today. Throughout China's long history, a pronounced regional consciousness has never really disappeared. The division between north and south is one of its constants. The gradual southward expansion of the Han Chinese from their place of origin in the Yellow River basin was of key importance. In the north, political, social and economic developments were shaped against the threat of invasions by non-Chinese nomads. The much more scarcely populated western regions were a corridor to Central Asia. At certain stages, these outlying edges of the Chinese empire ranked among the most multi-ethnic and multilingual areas anywhere in the pre-modern world. In today's China, regionalism continues to be high on the political agenda, reflected, for instance, in renewed interest in local heritage and state-sponsored approaches to the study of local cultures. In short, when we speak of 'China', or of people and things as 'Chinese', these are to some extent terms of convenience we use to refer to the peoples and geography within the evolving political borders of what has come to correspond roughly to the People's Republic of China today.

The origins of the term 'China' itself remain disputed. One widely held view has been that it is related to Qin, the name of the state that founded the first unified empire. But a Sanskrit term, *Cīna*, already appears in Indian sources that may go back two centuries earlier. Before the unification of the Chinese empire in 221 BCE and the first long-lasting Han dynasty, few would have identified themselves as 'Chinese'. If you hailed from the region corresponding to present-day Shandong, for instance, you would have introduced yourself as a person from Qi, or, in the case of Confucius, a person from Lu. As a southerner you would be known as coming from Chu, Ba or Yue. If you were born in the region around today's Beijing, you came from Yan (the name still figures in the brand name of a popular Beijing beer). As in China today, there is plenty of evidence in ancient texts that people were aware of linguistic diversity. Sources mention the peculiar nature of different dialects and the use of translators. Anecdotes survive that turn multilingualism and speech confusion into a source of entertainment or moral counsel. One story tells of a man from Zhou who tried to sell some freshly dressed rats to a merchant from Zheng. The latter politely declined the offer once he realized that he had mistaken the Zhou word for 'rats' for the similar-sounding Zheng word for 'unpolished jade' (*Zhanguo ce*, Qin 100). What you hear is not always what you get. You cannot eat jade (unless you are an immortal), and a rat would make an odd addition to the jewellery box. At the time when China's major thinkers began to formulate their ideas, the state of Zhou and some of its immediate neighbours in the middle and lower reaches of the Yellow River came to be identified as *Zhongguo*, translated in the plural as the 'Central Kingdoms'. The use of the same toponym to refer to China as the 'Middle Kingdom' or nation state would have to wait until Ming, Qing and modern times. More often, the known civilized world that was within reach of the monarch was known as 'All under Heaven' (*Tian xia*). So while philosophers and statesmen often spoke of human nature and human behaviour in a more or less universal manner, there was a sense in ancient China that the region, its soil and local climate influenced not only the way people looked, but also their character. To be born in the Central Kingdoms, according to some at least, came with temperamental advantages:

> People who live in regions of hard soil are hard and unyielding; people who live on easily worked soil are fat. People who live on lumpy soil are large; people who live on sandy soil are small. People who live on fertile soil are beautiful; people who live on barren soil are ugly. People who live on level ground are clever ... People in

the east are tall and large, they become knowledgeable
early but are not long-lived ... People in the south mature
early but die young ... People in the west are daring but
not humane ... People in the north are stupid as birds
or beasts but are long-lived ... People in the centre
are clever and sage-like and are good at government.
(*Huainanzi* 4.9, 4.13)

With these caveats in mind, I refer to the plurality of peoples
and the protagonists in this book as Chinese and to the continent on which they lived and live as geographical China.

Historical setting

Chinese civilization began in the loess highlands around
the great bend of the Yellow River and the Wei river valley.
The Shang dynasty (*c*.1600–*c*.1045 BCE), which produced the
oldest forms of writing in the shape of oracle bone inscriptions on turtle shells and animal bones, marks the point where
history departs from prehistory. The formative phase for the
development of Chinese thought starts slightly later, during
the Zhou period (*c*.1045–256 BCE). It culminated in the six or
so centuries traditionally referred to as the Warring States
and early imperial periods (fifth century BCE to second century CE).

Throughout this book I refer to 'ancient China' using a
broad brush to cover the period extending from about the
ninth century BCE to the second century CE. This thousand-
year stretch of history was marked by various stages of state
formation. It was a time when China gradually evolved from
a confederacy of feudal states into a unified empire, a shape

it retained until 1911 (and which, in some spheres of political life, arguably still holds sway over China today). In accounts of Chinese history, this period is also referred to as the 'classical' age, because scholars who first studied China compared its influence on Chinese civilization to that of the Graeco-Roman period in the history of the West. In the world of ideas, the Warring States and early imperial period runs parallel to the classical age of Plato, Aristotle and Alexander the Great in ancient Greece. It ends at the time of the Late Republic and the dawn of the Augustan period in Rome.

China's classical age has exerted a lasting influence on the socio-political and intellectual development of the Chinese world. It witnessed the birth of popular and anecdotal literature, the development of historiography and the growth of administrative record-keeping. It was the time when China produced some of its greatest philosophers, and when a canon of texts came together that would directly, or indirectly, shape the thinking of every person of influence in China for centuries to come. This was also the age when a number of renowned political figures took centre stage to instigate policies and inaugurate institutions that would leave an indelible mark on Chinese history. Another label that has been used to describe the centuries during which these ideas emerged is the Axial Age, a term coined by the German philosopher Karl Jaspers (1883–1969) to refer to a period of four or five centuries during which philosophical ideas exploded simultaneously, and without direct contact, from the Graeco-Roman world, across Eurasia, to India and China.

Ancient China produced a chain of ideas that was to inform the way in which the Chinese have viewed the world ever since. Some of the individuals we will encounter survive as enduring figures in China's intellectual and cultural heritage. But to present Chinese thought simply as a history of significant figures, their works and their influence upon the world of ideas would not do justice to its richness. Nor would we be able to account for its diversity and productivity if we relied only on those texts later generations and scholars have dubbed 'philosophical' (a term even philosophers fight over!). Much is to be found between the cracks of scholastic philosophy.

When, during the late second century BCE, the historian Sima Tan (d. *c*.110 BCE) looked back at ancient China's philosophical landscape, he divided it up into six schools or lineages: the School of Yin-Yang, the Confucians, Mohists, Legalists, the 'School of Names' (sophists or logicians) and the Daoists. Together with other masters and specialists, including military strategists, the world of thought in ancient China came to be known as that of 'One Hundred Schools' (*bai jia*) of thought ('one hundred' being a common term for 'many'). Most textbooks, in both the East and West, remain deeply influenced by this paradigm. As a term, the 'One Hundred Schools' took on a life of its own. Mao Zedong drew on the image of ancient China's roaming debaters to launch his Hundred Flowers Campaign in 1956 ('let a hundred flowers bloom, let a hundred schools of thought contend'), only to abort the short-lived movement when he concluded that the criticism offered was unhealthy and damaging to his authority.

Mao aside, the 'one hundred' label acknowledges the wide variety of thinkers that were dotted across China during the classical period. And it is correct to identify Confucianists, Daoists and Legalists as the most influential among them.

Yet reducing ancient Chinese thought into a neatly defined world of 'schools' is problematic. It suggests that ideas are appropriated by one individual or can be attributed exclusively to one particular thinker or text. In recent years, scholars have questioned the very concept of a 'philosophical school' as a useful means of understanding how ideas were spread and made part of the canon in ancient China. Ideas tended to be transmitted through lineages of masters and disciples who gathered together around the study of certain texts and commentaries. But, as we shall see, in reality both the ideas and the texts in which they are preserved are messier and, at times, even a hybrid mixture of different concepts. Ideas can bounce off and back into each other in an innovative and unpredictable way. Attributing them to one school rather than another often does little to help us appreciate what they mean. We also need to keep in mind that the historical information we have on the lives and deeds of many, if not most, of ancient China's key thinkers is very limited. Explaining ideas as direct accounts from the mouth or brush of one particular person often proves problematic.

Nevertheless, some thinkers and strands of thought were clearly reacting to opposing views. In that sense, it is fine to think of a 'school' as a retrospective way of grouping together people who have a common stance on certain issues or who draw on the same figures, concepts or texts. The dialogue was one of the main formats in which ideas were transmitted. These could be real or imaginary interchanges between a master and a disciple, a ruler and a minister, a court official and his superior, or between a commentary and a prior version of a text. Dialogues were also choreographed between fictional characters, culture heroes, or figures from the distant and legendary past. Thus ideas in ancient China seem to move like oil patches on the surface of water: they appear cohesive at one moment, only to be pulled in different directions, forming new outlines, until they are scattered around, or bubble up and reconnect to form a new patch. To understand the social and political background that shaped much of this intellectual landscape, a brief review of certain key facts, individuals and events may help by way of historical context.

THE SHANG

The oldest written records available in China today are divination inscriptions (formulas seeking to predict the outcome of events) incised onto cattle bone and turtle shell. These brief inscriptions date mostly from the twelfth to the mid eleventh century BCE. Well over two hundred thousand fragments have been attested since they came to the attention of scholars in the late nineteenth century. Oracle bone inscriptions are very short and not reflective in nature, but they do tell us something about the religion of the Shang people and their view of the world. The Shang kings revered as their supreme power a spirit named Di, who presided over a host of nature spirits. The Shang pantheon included spirits that would come to occupy an important role in Chinese religion in later times, such as powers linked to the soil, mountains or rivers. The topics of the oracle bone inscriptions are wide-ranging. They show how the Shang kings sought guidance on all sorts of issues, from the weather, war, hunting and the health of the king and his consorts to the timing of sacrifices to ancestors, the issuing of commands and the offering and receipt of gifts. Priests would crack the turtle shells and cattle scapulae using a hot poker and interpret these cracks, while answers to the questions they posed were written down on the bone.

The Shang people had a ten-day week. Large amounts of livestock (including prisoners of war who were counted by the heads or ears) were set apart to maintain ritual sacrifices to the spirits and the royal ancestors. These meats were offered together with ale. Royal ancestors carried much weight in the scheduling of sacrifices to which their spirits were invited. Tablets that represented their souls were used to receive offerings during rituals. These spirit tablets were housed in temples. The Shang conceived of the world as a central square around which lay four areas or 'lands' (east, south, west and north). By the time of the oracle bones, Shang society was primarily agricultural with people living in small settlements surrounded by fields. The Shang could mobilize troops of around three to five thousand warriors, commanded by officers that travelled the battlefield in light horse-drawn chariots. Chariots, along with ceremonial bronzes – vessels that held offerings – and oracle bone inscriptions, continue to be found today.

Several elements that would become important in Chinese thought in the following centuries are already evident in the Shang world. One is the notion that nature is inhabited by spirit powers that need to be placated or beseeched to secure a good outcome for future events. Another is the vital role of ancestors in bridging the gap between the human world and a seemingly distant and whimsical supreme spirit force. Then there is the key role played by the offering of sacrifices to forge relationships with ancestral and other spirits. Shang religion already illustrates that the economic resources needed to sustain such rituals were substantial: soothing the spirits did not come cheap. The need for rituals, paired with calls to justify or moderate ritual expenditure, would become one of the threads that run through ethical discussions of many thinkers in the classical period. At some point during the ninth century BCE, there were already calls for greater austerity on sacrificial occasions. (We must assume that some turned into extravagant feasts.) Bronze ceremonial vessels made to hold alcohol become less prominent in the archaeological record. We can be grateful to the Shang for keeping archives of their inscribed bones. Indeed, Shang diviners may have been China's first bureaucrats. Record-keeping would emerge as a central activity in China's courts of power, as would the manipulation of records. After all, by the end of the dynasty the Shang king appears as virtually the sole diviner to consult the spirits. Those who commanded mantic powers in order to solicit the spirits in a way that might elicit the disapproval of the king were unlikely to have a long career.

THE ZHOU

Around 1045 BCE, the Shang kings were overthrown by their western neighbours, the Zhou, who established their power base along the Yellow River in north-west China (present-day Gansu) but soon moved east towards the fertile lower Wei river valley (in present-day Shaanxi). They developed agricultural skills and made advances in irrigation technology.

The Zhou identified Heaven (*Tian*), the powers of the sky, as their supreme authority. Heaven was not a transcendent or personified deity but an overawing force that governed all. Trying to gauge the mood and follow the will and powers of Heaven would become a major theme in Chinese political thought. Being abandoned by Heaven became a euphemism for meeting one's political demise.

The first three centuries following the fall of the Shang are known in Chinese historiography as the Western Zhou period. The Zhou realm was a network of city states and the term feudalism is often mooted to describe Zhou society on the basis of parallels that can be drawn with medieval Europe, such as the central role of a hereditary warrior nobility, and a system of patronage and protection in return for labour and service. Crucially, the Zhou king acted as the nominal and ritual head of the entire polity and kinship determined succession. The Zhou nobility, together with the king, topped the social hierarchy. Members of the Zhou royal family received fiefs. Great noble families supplied warriors drawn from domains they had been granted and where they kept vassals and retainers. It was a world governed by alliances between aristocratic lords and overlords, based on a duty of allegiance to the Zhou house, and sealed by means of rituals.

In addition to retrospective accounts written during later periods, our main sources for the early Zhou period are its inscriptions cast in bronze vessels. The earliest parts of what later became known as the Five 'Confucian' Classics (parts of *The Book of Changes* and *The Book of Documents*, and most of the *The Book of Odes*) can also be dated to the earliest centuries of the Zhou dynasty. The Shang people produced magnificent bronze vessels (I recommend a visit to the Shanghai Museum or the Palace Museum in Taipei), but only a few of these bronzes are inscribed. The Zhou, however, produced thousands of vessels with commemorative inscriptions on the inside. These record the investiture of kings, sacrificial ceremonies and royal donations, or they commemorate significant events. The vessels vary in size and shape depending on their intended use (the largest known vessel weighs over eight hundred kilograms). Unsurprisingly, most inscriptions end with a wish that the Zhou king and his offspring will be blessed and will reign for many more generations. The volume of surviving bronzes is staggering, with some twelve thousand Zhou-period vessels still in existence today. Every year, vessels hidden from view in China's soil for over two millennia keep turning up.

Politically, the early Zhou period is known for three figures who would become the subject of countless historical analogies, and the focus in equal measure of praise or blame in later times. King Wen (*fl.* 1056–1050 BCE), the 'civil' king, ruled Zhou during the last days of the Shang. He is regarded as a ruler of high moral calibre for having made the case that the last drunk and debauched kings of the Shang could be rightfully unseated. King Wen would become known as a paragon of wisdom and benign administration. The second figure was the founding King Wu (*fl.* 1045–1043 BCE), the 'martial' king, who conquered the Shang at the Battle of Muye and built a new capital. The third figure, and the one that gained the widest renown as a wise statesman, was King Wu's brother, the Duke of Zhou (Zhou Gong; *fl.* 1046–1036 BCE). The Duke of Zhou epitomizes the height of enlightened statecraft. As regent over the inexperienced crown prince, King Cheng, he developed Zhou institutions and would become known in later times as the model of the sage-ruler, adviser, overseer and trusted confidant. His decision to step aside when his young nephew came of age played to an ideal that was much discussed in later Chinese political history, namely the notion that ceding power to a more legitimate, and hence more virtuous, ruler was the right thing to do. The early Zhou period would be invoked, most notably by Confucius (551–479 BCE), as a golden age during which the world ('All under Heaven') was united under the governance of an enlightened ruler (the 'Son of Heaven'): 'The Zhou dynasty modelled itself on the example of two preceding dynasties. What a splendid civilization; I am a follower of Zhou!' (*An.* 3.14).

The year 771 BCE is usually presented as a second phase in the history of the Zhou. This is when the royal capital was moved from west to east, from Hao (near present-day Xi'an) to the area of present-day Luoyang in Henan province. Traditional historiography divides the Eastern Zhou period into the Spring and Autumn (Chunqiu) period and the era of the Warring States (Zhanguo). The Zhou world continued to be a delicately balanced confederacy of local powers, a world of multiple interests and at times conflicting identities, as the following anecdote drives home:

Once there was a man from Wen who migrated to Zhou, but Zhou would not let him in. 'Are you a foreigner [literally, a guest],' they asked him. 'No, I am a native [literally, a host],' he replied. Then he was asked what lane he lived in, but he appeared not to know. So an official took him off to prison. The ruler sent someone to question him: 'Why did you call yourself a native when you are in fact a foreigner?' The man replied: 'When I was young and studied *The Book of Odes*, I chanted the following verses from it: "All land underneath Heaven is the king's land. To the far shores of the Earth every person is the king's servant." Since Zhou today rules All under Heaven and I am a servant of the Son of Heaven, how then can I be considered a foreigner? That's why I said that I was a native.' The ruler of Zhou thereupon ordered his officer to set the man free. (*Zhanguo ce*, Zhou 42)

This Zhou version of 'all men are brethren' did not last, however. Increasingly, the Zhou kings held on to their position as overlords only nominally. As they failed to control local rulers, Zhou territory disintegrated into a patchwork of hundreds of territorial units and mini-states. For nearly five centuries, contending states and their professional armies engaged in a relentless and endlessly complex sequence of rivalries, annexations, battles, treatises and alliances. It is therefore fitting that the two and a half centuries (481–221 BCE) during which seven major states (Yan, Qi, Wei, Zhao, Hann, Qin and Chu) contended for supremacy should be known as the Warring States period.

As cohesion between the Zhou city states and their networks of allied vassal states broke down, in its place emerged the warring state: 'warring' because warfare and gaining military supremacy became a core mission; 'state' because new rulers proclaimed the territorial state as their ambition. Thus the warring state's goal was to gain supremacy over its rivals by any means – strategic, military or otherwise. The opening lines of the most famous military classic from the period, *Master Sun's Art of Warfare* (*Sunzi bing fa*), sum it up with chilling conviction: 'Warfare is the greatest affair of state, it is the basis of life and death, and the way to survival or extinction. Therefore it is a subject of inquiry that cannot be left un-investigated.' China's masters of philosophy were a product of this age of profound political and military turbulence. The chaos around them must have felt like the end of the world. Many thinkers were descended from the now jobless ranks of lower-level aristocratic families. As travelling scholar-knights and men of service, they roamed from court to court to sell their ideas to whoever would grant them sustenance and patronage. 'Surely, old man,' a king in the opening passage of the *Mencius* states, 'you haven't come all this way without wanting to tell me how I can benefit my state?' (*Mencius* 1A.1).

Instead of a feudal confederation of city states and hegemons bound together through kinship and ritual obligations, China had now become a conglomerate of states that each had their own army, institutions, borders and registered population. Power came to be concentrated in the hands of a single monarch who surrounded himself with advisers and ministers. Even more than during the preceding aristocratic age, the state and its politics were entirely ruler-centred. Society was thought to fare best under monarchic rule: a single and unique ruler. Virtually all statesmen and philosophers of the time brooded over what would become a central tenet in Chinese political thought: political regimes operate most efficiently when power is concentrated in the hands of a single ruler and

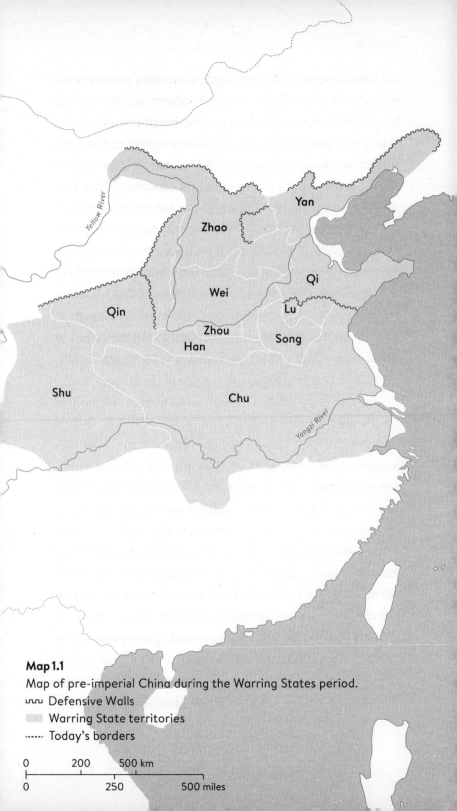

Map 1.1

Map of pre-imperial China during the Warring States period.

꒜ Defensive Walls

▨ Warring State territories

···· Today's borders

0	200	500 km

0	250	500 miles

his court, and when this ruler is assisted by a salaried official-dom that implements the will of the centre across the land.

This notion that ultimate power should issue from and reside in one individual or institution reverberates up until today. The Chinese language of the time had a rich assortment of words touching on the idea of unity (terms such as one-ness, harmony, uniting, bringing together, regarding as one, making similar, unify, etc.). Whatever the differences in em-phasis or rhetoric that successive Chinese ruling elites have been keen to promote, underpinning them all is an unwaver-ing conviction that institutions ought to support one strong and sole leader. From its inception the state in China conceived itself as autocratic, one in which strong rulers, assisted by professional armies and a bureaucracy of administrators, held sway over the populace.

Warring States political thought centred on a desire to break up the interests of great families whose power base derived from the control of local human and economic resources. Qin, a state on the western edges of the Zhou polity, had under-taken to restrain hereditary landholders by dividing parts of its territory into counties that were administered by a magistrate appointed directly by the central government. Several other states had started to curb the powers of their internal fief hold-ers. Yet despite these measures, throughout the Warring States period and into the early empires, the central government never managed to eradicate hereditary landownership completely. Ancient China remained a patchwork of centrally controlled territory coexisting with hereditary land.

After a gruelling series of military campaigns that lasted two decades, the state of Qin emerged as the dominant player. In

221 BCE, it brought to an end centuries of division and warfare by turning a multi-state world into a unified empire for the first time. Just as states and cities had built defensive walls around them to guard against attacks by rival armies, so China's most formative thinkers had carved out their own philosophies and theories of government. An age of unrelenting political upheaval and rampant warlordism had concentrated minds in a way that the comforts of peace and tranquillity might never have done. The philosophers of ancient China had little time to dabble with abstract theories or toy with questions to which there was no immediate answer. They had to address a pressing demand of their time: how does one cultivate and educate people and organize a state to gain advantage over its rivals? These historical circumstances explain why so much of Chinese thought is focused on the social and political, on ethics and etiquette. By the time the state of Qin had joined up large sections of its rival states' defensive walls into the Great Wall of imperial China, the battle of ideas on how human beings should conduct themselves and how to run society had largely been waged. Its core ideas would remain in place, to be tested for centuries to come.

THE QIN

When in 221 BCE King Zheng of Qin proclaimed himself the 'First August Emperor of Qin [Qin Shihuangdi]', he adopted the title of the superior deity of the Shang people (Di). The First Emperor saw himself as semi-divine, a ruler who acted not just as a link between higher powers and the human world, but who embodied the highest powers in person. As the sovereign over all rulers and kings that had come before, Qin

Shihuang aspired to join the ranks of the legendary and immortal gods. The historian Sima Qian (*c.*145–*c.*86 BCE) portrays him as a physically imposing figure, with a prominent nose, a chest like a bird of prey and the voice of a jackal. The man who unified China is depicted as a character of little compassion, with the heart of a tiger or a wolf.

The First Emperor rolled out a series of reforms for which he would be both admired and despised by posterity. They were inspired by the ideas of Shang Yang (*c.*390–338 BCE), the foundational figure of a philosophical tradition later known as Legalism. (We will return to Lord Shang in more detail in Chapter 3.) The names of the entire population would be recorded in household registers to facilitate efficient taxation. This would also allow the state to draw on forced labour for massive building projects. Its subjects would be deployed as peasant-warriors; farming was singled out as the backbone of the economy, but in times of expansionist warfare, the state would mobilize the people into a highly effective military machine. All hereditary titles were to be abolished and personal achievement was to replace hereditary privilege. A draconian criminal justice system that meted out harsh punishments was put in place.

The Qin unified weights and measures and introduced a standard currency. This circular bronze coin with a square hole through the middle (known as the *banliang* or 'half of sixteen grams') replaced different currencies that had been in use in other states (coins in the shape of shells, knives and spades, among other things). The new coins could be strung together for easier accounting. The emperor introduced new standards for carts and chariots, including specific axle widths, to ensure

Map 1.2
China during the Qin dynasty.
ᴖᴖ Great Wall
░ Qin territory
...... Today's borders

Xianyang

Yellow River

Yangzi River

South China Sea

0   250   500 km
0   250   500 miles

access to roads throughout the empire. A network of imperial highways ran across the empire, believed to have covered as much as six thousand eight hundred kilometres – rivalling the Roman road system. One of these highways, constructed by the general in charge of building the Great Wall, was known as the 'Straight Road'. It extended eight hundred kilometres north of the Qin capital Xianyang into Inner Mongolia; parts of it can still be seen today. Roads, however, did not mean free movement of people or goods. All travel and migration was subject to police control. Checkpoints were in place, tolls were levied and travellers (including their horses!) needed permits or passports. The new road system allowed Qin Shihuang and later emperors to embark on tours of the empire. These gigantic processions, combined with ritual mountain ascents, were a symbolic way for an emperor to assert his power and vitality to both the population and the spirits. Imperial tours might require years of preparation. During a series of such excursions, the First Emperor left a record to posterity in the form of inscriptions cut into stone stelae (columns or slabs with commemorative inscriptions) which he had placed on mountains in the eastern part of his empire. They leave a telling imprint of how he wanted future generations to remember him: as a tirelessly dedicated and devoted monarch who broke with the past and whose influence extended everywhere and to everyone, 'even to the oxen and horses' (*Shiji* 6).

One of the most significant measures initiated by Qin Shihuang was the unification of the Chinese character script. This reform, overseen by prime minister Li Si, created the basis of a universal Chinese writing system (in existence up until 1949), which would become one of the most important tools in running an efficient bureaucracy. Prior to the Qin's effort to regularize the form, meaning and sound of Chinese characters, the different states each had their own standards of orthography. These regional variants were the main target of the reforms. Known as the Small Seal script as it simplified the older, variable Large Seal script, the new script allowed for faster and easier writing with brush and ink, which led in turn to more efficient record-keeping. But we should not imagine the script reforms as a process in which new characters were devised from scratch. In reality, 'unifying' the script involved suppressing the use of a significant number of previously used and local characters. Many pre-Qin characters may have been censored. Alongside the ban on the use of certain characters, complex writing forms such as those found on the Zhou ritual vessels were simplified.

Like most events associated with the First Emperor, his reform of the Chinese character script has been idealized. There is no evidence that the script of an empire was unified overnight. The standardization was a gradual process that continued for several centuries after Qin Shihuang. Yet, as for many learners today, mastering Chinese characters must have seemed a daunting task. To work as an official clerk at the Han court, you had to memorize no fewer than nine thousand characters and master several calligraphic styles (a comprehensive Chinese dictionary that includes all variants contains between fifty and sixty thousand characters). Strict accuracy was required as writing characters in an irregular way was not tolerated. Orthography purportedly reflected the moral character of an official (much in the way that graphologists today claim to be able to assess your personality from your style of handwriting). One mistake with the brush could potentially be costly, as the following story illustrates:

> Once when Shi Jian was chief of palace attendants, he had the occasion to submit a report to the emperor. Later, after the report had been returned to him, he was reading it over, when he exclaimed in great alarm, 'A mistake in writing! The character for "horse" should have five lines for the feet and tail, but this has only four lines. One of the feet is missing! The emperor could have had me put to death for such an error!' He was very frightened. He was just as cautious and meticulous as this in whatever he did. (*Shiji* 103)

Nevertheless a degree of variability never disappeared from Chinese writing. It hardly ever does in any language. If Shakespeare can be forgiven for spelling his own name in different ways, the relative continuity of the Chinese character script over the course of nearly three millennia stands out as nothing short of remarkable. Without the reform of the character script instigated by Qin Shihuang, efficient official communication would have been severely hampered and political unity may never have lasted.

Two public works initiated by the First Emperor still catch the eye today: the Long or Great Wall and the emperor's tomb complex known for its terracotta army. Walls were constructed to protect the imperial heartland from incursions by nomadic tribes, most notably the Xiongnu, who operated from the northern and north-western steppes. While the Great Wall as it can be seen today dates from the fifteenth, sixteenth and seventeenth centuries, the Qin had set an important

帝 皇 始 秦

Figure 1.1
The First Emperor
Facsimile reprint from
Sancai tuhui, 1609.

precedent by connecting several existing walls together into a continuous structure (of around three thousand kilometres). The works lasted over five years and involved moving several hundred million cubic metres of stone and earth, and a labour force of perhaps as many as three hundred thousand men. The reputation of the Great Wall as an imposing, uninterrupted structure is not free from suspicion, however. Historical records make less of its actual grandeur than many past and contemporary Chinese historians have led us to believe. As the American historian Arthur Waldron points out, one should not conceive of the Great Wall as a single age-old structure that can be documented continuously and coherently through the sources. Qin Shihuang's wall may be more myth than historical reality, not because it did not exist, but because the image of a continuous Great Wall has been invoked throughout history as an ideological tool to praise the achievements of Chinese civilization against those of its neighbouring peoples ('us versus them'). Perhaps history has accorded the First Emperor's wall building a greater reputation than its original brickwork could have hoped for. Nevertheless, it does illustrate the megalomaniac ambitions of a man who was not to know that astronauts today still dispute whether the wall is visible from the moon.

Since excavation works began in 1974 in Lintong county (Shaanxi province; some thirty kilometres outside the city of Xi'an), millions of people have visited or seen selections of the First Emperor's mausoleum and its terracotta warriors. Fearing death and obsessed with assuring his own immortality, he ordered its construction as soon as he came to power as king (in 246 BCE). Circumnavigating today's hill of rammed earth takes a brisk walk just short of one and a half kilometres. The original mound may have been over one hundred metres high. All childless concubines followed the emperor into his grave. To keep things secret, those who had worked on the tomb were imprisoned and sealed within it too. Trees and grass were then planted over the mausoleum to make it look like a natural hill. Today the tomb at Mount Li remains clad with evergreen cypresses and pines, symbolizing long life. Archaeologists have yet to excavate the tomb itself. Perhaps they never will. Who would want to release the unpredictable spirit of the First Emperor? And what lies beneath may not live up to the description of the tomb by Sima Qian: a coffin of molten copper; a burial chamber filled with models of palaces, towers and official buildings; the waterways of the empire recreated using mercury and made to flow mechanically. Above, in the vault, heavenly constellations lit by whale-oil lamps. The First Emperor intended his tomb to be a microcosm of the entire world. The area around the actual tomb was surrounded by buildings and by several pits containing an entire terracotta army of thousands of life-size figurines aligned in battle array. These were the henchmen of the warring state that had chewed through the map of pre-imperial China like an army of caterpillars.

Another story concerning the First Emperor lives on with some persistence. In 213 BCE, he allegedly commanded that all books be burnt except those on medicine, divination and tree-planting. A year later, he ordered the death of four hundred and sixty Confucian scholars (all buried alive, according to his detractors). Those who failed to burn their privately owned books within thirty days – books that praised models of the past that could be used to criticize him – were tattooed as convicts and sentenced to hard labour. But scholars have questioned this perception of the First Emperor. Throwing political opponents in a pit, and destroying texts that can be used to slate your regime, is precisely the sort of propaganda those who succeeded Qin Shihuang might have used to demonize him as a one-sided brute and uncultured despot. Indeed, it was in the Han's interest to depict their immediate predecessors in a bad light. Vilifying those who have come before you provided succeeding dynasties with a highly effective means of justifying their own ascent to power. The burning of the books may have some historical basis, but its impact was minimal, possibly limited to books within the capital. There is no evidence to suggest that the First Emperor ever undertook a purge of culture and tradition on the scale of Mao's Red Guards during the Cultural Revolution. On the contrary, Qin literati appeared to master the language and style of past writings. This is clear from the very few surviving texts closely associated with the emperor himself, such as the stone inscriptions erected on sacred mountains during his imperial processions.

Throughout history, China's First Emperor has carried a dual legacy: praised as an empire builder, but denounced for being a harsh despot; hailed as a great reformer of the Chinese script, but blamed as culturally ignorant; admired for imposing efficiency and a sense of meritocracy, but condemned for the human suffering his policies caused; applauded for his Legalist determination, but reviled for stamping on Confucian sensibilities. As the historian Yuri Pines puts it: 'The ongoing debate over the Qin Empire concerns not just the past, but, primarily, the present: it is the debate about how China is to be governed, how much autonomy is to be accorded to each of its parts, what role intellectuals should have in society, and what means are legitimate in restoring China's glorious position as a powerful and awe-inspiring nation.' The Qin dynasty did not last. It is known as much for its rapid collapse as it is for its impressive rise. The First Emperor died only eleven years after the foundation of his remarkable empire.

THE HAN

In 206 BCE Liu Bang, born into a peasant family, established the Han dynasty following a series of battles against aristocratic factions seeking to restore some of their old noble privileges. He served as its first emperor, Gaozu. After an initial period of internal strife, the Han would endure for nearly four centuries, marking the first long-lasting and relatively stable chapter in the history of imperial China. Politically, Han rulers continued to implement many of the reforms set in place by the Qin. The unification of currency, weights and measures, and of the Chinese character script, was carried on and consolidated. The Han devised a smaller coin (known as a *wuzhu*) that weighed just over three grams. To avoid forgeries, the Han government tried hard to monopolize the minting of coins.

The figure of the emperor as the ultimate model of sovereignty became firmly established over the course of the Han period. New rituals and symbols, along with new religious cults, were established at state level to back up imperial authority and legitimacy. Henceforth, the emperor became a cosmological figure. As the 'Son of Heaven', he no longer ruled primarily by military force and awe alone. Instead, he was the link between Heaven and Earth and acted as the symbolical pivot on which hinged the stability of the world at large. Han thinkers insisted that the cosmos, the human world and the human body were intimately linked and that everything operated according to similar moral and physical laws. I will discuss this form of correlative thinking (in Chapter 2) and explore how it influenced Chinese views of nature (in Chapter 7).

The Han expanded and consolidated the bureaucratic state that had developed under its predecessor. It set up institutions run by a hierarchy of officials and it mapped out the empire in administrative units known as provinces and commanderies, some of which still exist in name today. Parts of the territory were granted to members of the imperial family as royal domains. The Han also expanded the empire's territory. For the first time, mechanisms were put in place to handle foreign policy. Neighbouring states and local chieftains symbolically submitted to the Han court by exchanging tribute (gifts to show one's obedience or dependence on another ruler). Han princesses were married off to barbarian rivals.

Keeping the peace, however, came at a cost. In the north and north-west, constant battles waged against the nomadic Xiongnu confederation exhausted the treasury coffers of Emperor Han Wudi (r. 141–87 BCE). Nevertheless, significant inroads were made into Central Asia through a corridor corresponding to present-day Gansu and Xinjiang provinces. It stretched as far as Ferghana in eastern Uzbekistan, the land of swift and blood-sweating 'heavenly horses'. In the north-east, the Han pushed up as far as the area surrounding present-day Pyongyang in North Korea. In the south, they annexed the region of Yue, corresponding to present-day Fujian and Guangdong, and the Han's influence extended all the way to the kingdom of Champa in Vietnam.

In the Han expansion of the Chinese empire, was there any interaction with the Romans? There is no evidence of direct contact with Rome, but both civilizations sat at opposite ends of the Silk Road and were indirectly aware of each other's existence. The Romans spoke of a country where silk was produced. The Chinese spoke of a mythical place known as 'Great Qin'. Somewhere around the first century CE, the first vestiges of Buddhism, a philosophy and religion that originated in India, reached the Han empire, mostly via central Asian merchants. But we must wait until 166 CE for the first recorded instance of an imperial sacrifice to the Buddha. The story of

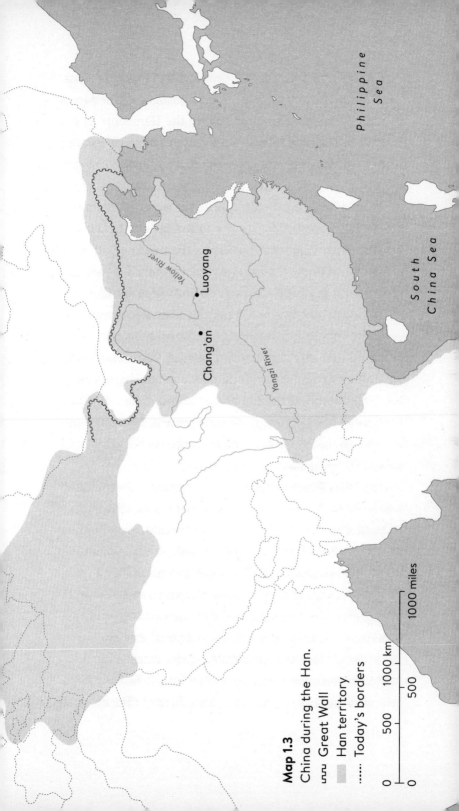

Map 1.3
China during the Han.

᠕᠕᠕ Great Wall

░░ Han territory

...... Today's borders

the entrance and adaptation of Buddhism in China would largely take place during the centuries following the period that forms the background to this book.

For a brief period (between 9 and 23 CE), Wang Mang, who had seized power from the Liu family, established an interregnum known as the New or Xin dynasty. Wang initiated a series of reforms, mostly focused on the equal redistribution of land, and he modelled his reign on *The Rites of Zhou* (*Zhouli*), a text that portrayed the ideal state as resembling that of the golden age of Zhou. His utopian reforms proved to be short-lived, however, as did his reign. Great landed families took back control and, like the Roman Empire, Han became increasingly dominated by powerful aristocratic families that undermined the authority of the court and the capital. A combination of natural disasters and millenarian peasant rebellions finally brought the dynasty to its knees in 220 CE. China was about to undergo nearly four centuries of disunion before a second great moment of imperial unity would arrive in the form of the great Tang dynasty in the early seventh century CE.

The Han dynasty heralded a golden age of Chinese culture. For the first time, the court and state sponsored a literary canon and actively encouraged the study of classical texts. While it would be incorrect to label this new wave of state-supported classicism as 'Confucianism', Confucius himself was the main focus in the transmission of, editing of and commentaries on several classical works. A set of five canonical texts were categorized collectively as 'classics' (*jing*). They became part of the curriculum at the Imperial Academy established in 124 BCE. Within one century, more than thirty thousand students attended the academy to study with master interpreters of the so-called Five 'Confucian' Classics. These comprised *The Spring and Autumn Annals (Chunqiu)*, a historical chronicle set in Confucius's native state of Lu for the period 722–481 BCE; *The Book of Odes (Shijing)*, a collection of 305 poems, folk songs, eulogies and temple hymns allegedly compiled by Confucius; *The Book of Documents (Shangshu)* containing speeches on governance by the early Zhou rulers; *The Ritual Records (Liji)*, a compendium of ceremonies and rules of etiquette; and *The Book of Changes (Zhouyi)*, a divination text with sections on cosmology.

Each of these texts had been added to over time and contained parts that stretched back to the early Zhou and Warring States periods. But during the Han they took on the format and shape that would define them as a canon for the next two millennia and as the basis for the civil service examination until the fourteenth century. From the outset, the Five Classics were cited by scholars and literati to make political and moral arguments. To the modern reader at least, their literary quality is sometimes underplayed. Once the value of a poem appears to derive predominantly from the moralizing commentary or political interpretation of its verse and imagery, its lyrical delights are all too easily erased from the reading experience. Fortunately for those who feel the ancients fettered their literary Muse with too much dull political commentary, the Han also gave rise to the new genre of the rhapsody or prose poem, and China went on to produce works of lyrical and literary genius on an impressive scale during the centuries to come.

Two major works of history compiled during the Han would establish a model for official historiography (the study of the writing of history and of written histories) in China up until the twentieth century. The writing of history was not simply an exercise to gather facts and inform posterity. More importantly, imperially commissioned historians acted as spin doctors, depicting previous regimes in a way that would appear to legitimize the rule of their pay masters. The notion that one should use the past to explain and justify the present became a motto deeply ingrained in Chinese moral and political thinking. The first main account of the history of China is *The Historical Records (Shiji)* compiled by Sima Qian (whose official position was that of court astrologer) and his father. It contains a history of China from the mythical past up to his time (second century BCE). A second major work of history, *The Book of Han (Hanshu* – also translated as *The Dynastic History of the Former Han)* was compiled by Ban Gu (32–92 CE) and his father and sister. It covers the history of the first two centuries of the Han, the so-called Western or Former Han period.

The Han set an important precedent in that, for the first time, the court actively sponsored the cataloguing of texts held at the palace library. This painstaking work, shouldered by Liu Xiang (79–8 BCE) and his son Liu Xin (46 BCE–23 CE), included gathering, restoring and editing all known manuscripts and transmitted texts from the past, and classifying them into subject categories or genres. The cataloguing work of Liu Xiang and his son formed the basis of a bibliographical chapter in *The Book of Han.* This catalogue of the imperial library lists over six hundred titles of which three-quarters are no longer extant. Throughout imperial times, court-based dynastic histories would regularly include such a bibliography.

Ruling the world required mastering and controlling the texts (and authors) that described it.

The Han established a system of civil service exams. In principle, this aimed at selecting individuals on a meritocratic basis; in reality, personal connections and recommendations proved equally important. But the concept of a civil service examination system as a funnel for upward social mobility was born. What originates during the Han is the idea that officials should also be scholars and that public administrative duty and skill should go hand in hand with a private pursuit of literature, the arts and philosophy. Cultivating the self, in other words, was a precondition to being an efficient public servant. This ideal of the scholar-official would take hold for most of Chinese history. Even in the twentieth century, and indeed even today, prominent Chinese officials have not been averse to being seen to experiment with a spot of calligraphy, poetry or landscape painting. The civil service examinations, in one form or other, were the main pool for the recruitment of officials until 1905.

The court also sponsored the patronage of the arts, and the state was actively engaged in the layout and construction of imperial cities, parks and monuments, including funerary art. Highlights in the fields of science and technology included improved schemes for irrigation and conserving water (such as wells and canals). By this time, iron and iron tools were increasingly used. Han was also the age of great advances in mathematics and astronomy; new agricultural methods (a seeding machine, the nose ring for oxen); the invention and spread of paper; new glazing techniques in ceramics; developments in textile technology (the loom) and the production of bricks and tiles; advances in nautical technology (the axial rudder); and the compilation of medical classics.

In the meantime, the population had grown. Statistics are moving targets when it comes to population figures for ancient China and it is best to interpret them with caution. Local officials or those wishing to dodge the intrusive hand of central government had an interest in under-reporting population numbers in good times to avoid taxes and labour duties. Under-reporting the number of adult males or recording a false age (above sixty) might be linked to the evasion of military service. In times of crisis, such as natural disasters or bad harvests, local bureaucrats could have an interest in inflating population numbers (or acreage) to ensure a good share of relief provisions or seeds. We know that China's population in those early centuries already fluctuated substantially, subject to natural disasters, emerging conflicts or changes in the economic climate. The first official empire-wide census, dating to the year 2 CE, records a population just short of sixty million individuals, distributed over twelve million households. Population growth in ancient China may seem tardy in comparison with today – during the time it takes you to read this page, there will have been twenty new births in the People's Republic. Yet cities during the Western Han could be sizeable communities. Well over a dozen of them had populations of between thirty and one hundred thousand residents. The metropolitan region around Chang'an (present-day Xi'an) had a registered population of nearly seven hundred thousand people.

Time: thinking in cycles

One can think of time as either cyclical or linear. The Chinese did both. Like us, they noticed that time passed each day from dawn to dusk and that events succeed one another chronologically from point alpha to omega. To understand how events related to each other one had to 'thread' together what came before with what was happening in the present, like a filament of silk that links together other fibres in a piece of fabric. To explain who you are, linear chronology also allowed you to trace your ancestry to a point of origin, from one generation to the next. Indeed, the word that translates 'thread' (*ji*) in ancient China also refers to a period of time or a chronicle giving a year-by-year account of events and significant actors over the course of a ruler's reign or dynasty. From the earliest times, rulers kept genealogical tables. To legitimize one's accession to the throne, a monarch or dynasty needed to be able to insert itself into a line of unbroken succession linked to those who came before, preferably going back to the mythical times of the legendary Three Sages and Five Emperors. These were culture heroes (they included, among others, the Yellow Emperor, Fu Xi, Yao and Shun) who were credited with the invention of the core tools of civilization, such as writing, the calendar, weaving and agriculture. In terms of claiming your stake in the ranks of those who hold political power in China, knowing (or being seen to know) the past appeared more important than speculating about what the future might hold.

The idea that the essence of all we need is already embedded in the past and that these truths are worth drawing out and preserving unites almost all Chinese thinkers. A verse in *The Classic of the Way and Virtue* (*Daodejing*) runs: 'Hold on to the way of antiquity, in order to keep in control the world of today. The ability to know the beginning of antiquity is called the thread running through the Way' (*DDJ* 14). Confucius too insisted that he did not create new ways but merely transmitted ancient ones (*An.* 7.1). And the same motto is echoed in imperial times: 'If you do not know what is to come, observe what has gone before' (*Chunqiu fanlu* 5.7). To be innovative one has to be conservative. China's great thinkers, writers and statesmen were praised not so much for their ability to offer innovation that radically broke with the past, but for the genius that stemmed from an ability to master tradition.

More importantly, the Chinese also saw time as a cycle and noted how a sequence of linear events (what you do between breakfast and bedtime) can repeat itself over and over again (you get up and go to bed each day). They saw this cyclical passage of time as a track (*li*), along which successive cycles of rising and falling, birth and death, could be charted. 'Archiving a recurrent scale of events' freely translates the modern Mandarin word for history (*lishi*). The notion of time as a cycle is central to the way the Chinese have viewed and described history since ancient times. Chinese historiography traditionally divides the past into a succession of dynasties. In its strictest sense, a dynasty is nothing more than a clan or family that gains and maintains influence and control during any given period of time. To qualify as a dynasty requires the presence of family genealogy and power. But a dynasty more broadly also stands for a collective idea (sometimes a fiction), rather than a real fact. One can nominally proclaim to rule as a dynasty while people other than the imperial family pull the strings (for example, consort families, influential ministers, palace eunuchs). So when one speaks of a Chinese dynasty, one might draw a comparison with an American-style presidency or a British premiership. A presidency hinges on the person of the president and those who surround an administration, but it is about much more: ideology, policies, scandal and intrigue, or simply any significant event that takes place during a period in office, even if events bear no direct connection with those who govern.

In Chinese thought, the concept of the dynastic cycle was based on the presumption that there is a formal pattern underlying the progression of each dynasty. History repeats itself, if not in factual details, then certainly in the course it takes. When one ends, to paraphrase the historian Sima Qian, another must begin (*Shiji* 8). Thus a ruling dynasty would always see itself as the latest descendant in a series of preceding dynasties. It would acknowledge its deeply rooted origins by venerating or sacrificing to earlier dynastic founders, rulers or culture heroes while at the same time presenting itself as the natural inheritor of this lineage for 'ten thousands of generations' to come. The parallel fate of many Chinese dynasties is striking. Once a new dynasty is founded, often on the back of popular rebellions against central authority, the court strengthens its military grip and implements economic reforms, while borders are expanded or consolidated. At some point this initial period of prosperity, state-building and peace gives way to disruption and disintegration. Rulers overreach themselves and become too self-assured, corruption poisons the court, governments fail to collect taxes and revenues, rebellious and dissident voices are heard across the land. Lacking the charisma of the dynastic founders, the court wilts away and is besieged both from within and by external players. Child emperors are put up. Last emperors in a dynasty are weak or even powerless. Finally, a natural disaster such as a drought or plague of locusts adds fuel to the already boiling discontent. The dynasty falls prey to rebellion from either inside or outside the court. It has run its course. It is time for a new cycle to begin, as *The Book of Documents* states: 'Heaven's Mandate is not granted for ever!' (*Shangshu*, 'Kang gao').

Thus the course of history was seen to evolve in a cycle in which moments of order alternated with periods of chaos, and moments of military violence (*wu*) alternated with periods of peace and civility (*wen*). In this view of history, the founding rulers of a dynasty are always competent and morally good, while the final rulers are invariably weak, incapable or both. The fate of a ruling house is thus analogous to a life cycle: it inevitably comes to an end. Regimes were said to be at their best when the ways of the great sages and kings prevailed. Without them, according to the philosopher Mencius (372–289 BCE), 'lords become arbitrary and intemperate, and unemployed scholars indulge in unreasonable discussions' (*Mencius* 3B.9). Yet it is important to remember that the concept of the dynastic cycle was nothing more than a model used by political actors and court-based historiographers to analyse the past and legitimatize claims to power. It does not of course represent how actual historical events unfolded. To churn the course of Chinese history exclusively through a string of dynastic cycles would result in a narrow, court-based and highly biased narrative of history. Much to their credit, modern historians have taken a more nuanced approach in analysing China's past, drawing on sources, archives, figures and locations far removed from the brush and inkstone of official court historians.

When the Zhou unseated the Shang, they did so on the basis that they had gained the 'Mandate of Heaven' (*Tian ming*). Heaven had now transferred the licence to rule to its more virtuous successors. As indicated previously, Chinese Heaven (*Tian*) is not a place or creating force as in the Judeo-Christian tradition. It represents the force of all that exists and exerts a power that covers everyone and everything (what you see when you look upwards at the sky). As such, Heaven was seen as a supreme moral arbiter. The Mandate of Heaven is a political concept that is part of the vocabulary of all thinkers and statesmen in traditional China. Receiving the Mandate of Heaven was essential to claim legitimate succession. It was used as an ideology to explain and legitimize the transfer of political power up until 1911, when China's last emperor abdicated and a republican system replaced the imperial model.

Think of the Mandate of Heaven as a form of cosmic investiture: Heaven selects those who are capable and of good moral standing and it grants them the authority to rule. As the supreme power, Heaven charges credit to the account of a prospective ruler, who is entrusted with discharging that credit to the best of his ability for the benefit of the people and the country. But the Mandate of Heaven is the sole licence that grants legitimacy to a ruler. Having it taken away or transferred to someone else means that Heaven has dismissed the ruler, and the ruling house, because he failed to discharge its moral credit appropriately. The concept of the Mandate of Heaven, combined with the principle that power should be transferred in a hereditary way among members of the imperial family, are the two cornerstones of how the court legitimized its power base.

How then did the Chinese record time? They did so in various ways. The main way was to record time by the year of a particular reign period or a part thereof. *Yuanfeng*, year two, for instance, refers to the second year in the reign period entitled 'Original Phoenix', and hence corresponds to 79 BCE. This system remained in place until the end of the Qing dynasty in January 1912, when the Republic was inaugurated. (In Japan, year designations based on an emperor's reign survive until today.) Another way of recording time involved counting according to a sexagenary cycle – one of two main counting systems used in traditional China (the other being the decimal system). It derives from the combination of two sets of counters: a set of ten units known as 'Heavenly stems' and a set of twelve known as 'Earthly branches'. From these may be derived a total of sixty exclusive combinations that can be used to count days or years. The sexagenary cycle may be familiar to readers through the Chinese zodiac, and the twelve patron animals associated with the Earthly branches (rat, ox, tiger, rabbit, dragon, snake, horse, sheep, monkey, rooster, dog and pig). The origins of the Chinese zodiac remain disputed, although there is evidence of the use of animal cycles in the late Warring States period. Some scholars claim the zodiac entered China through Central Asia and was possibly Turkic in provenance.

From at least the fifth century BCE, Chinese astronomers related the movement of the sun to that of the other heavenly bodies according to a yearly circuit ('zodiac') of twenty-eight (uneven) divisions. But measuring the phases of the moon dictated the acceptance of twenty-nine temporal divisions. This led to a year that was roughly divided into twelve equal segments or 'lunar mansions'. While it is relatively straightforward to base a calendar on the phases of the moon, it is much harder to base it on those of the sun because the succession of months quickly ceases to correspond with the sun's apparent movement and the seasons. Normally, a year consisted of twelve months (following the lunar cycle), but in order to synchronize the cycles of the Earth, sun and moon, an extra month (known as an intercalary month) had to be inserted once every thirty-three months. Since a lunar month is somewhere between twenty-nine and thirty days, and the solar year of 365 days is not precisely twelve lunar months, a calendar was needed to ensure the cycles matched and to show how many days there were in each month.

The Chinese were meticulous in recording time. They had good reason for doing so. Agriculture was the main form of economic subsistence and necessitated accurate timekeeping, although we must assume that farmers knew their own local circumstances best. The calendar also facilitated other activities, such as military conscription, the collection of taxes and the registration of the population. In order to impose curfews after dark in cities, officials needed an accurate way to measure the hours of the day. As in other parts of the world, nights were divided into 'watches' often indicated by the sounding of a bell or drumbeats from watchtowers. The water clock (or clepsydra) already existed in pre-imperial times. This consisted of a jar of water with a small hole at the bottom. Units of time were measured by a float that dropped down as the water leaked out.

Over and above the various techniques and systems in use to calculate time, timekeeping itself was essential to exert political control, both in reality and on a symbolical level. Controlling time through issuing a calendar was the prerogative of those who ruled. Even today, calendars are not simply tools that help us organize our diaries. To issue a calendar is to claim control over the organization of time. It enables one to steer the activities of those over whom one has authority. Illustrated diaries and calendars are still a favourite gift to mark the New Year at embassies and companies around the world. And most of us, often subconsciously, think of time in the way it has been institutionalized for us: as a student you are likely to divide up time in units corresponding to teaching terms or semesters (not to forget reading weeks and examination periods); for a salesperson the notion of quarterly returns will mark the organization of time; for a farmer the start of the harvest will be a major temporal signpost. Just as those who ruled China insisted that their subjects subscribed to time in the way it was organized in the agricultural calendar, so today employers, universities and sports federations issue calendars to broadcast their own schedule. Underlying the attention devoted to timekeeping in ancient China was a conviction that human activities were not just a matter of private interest. On the contrary, they were to be planned, executed and inspected in accordance with the movements of the heavenly bodies and the patterns of Heaven. The calendar was a key to maintaining both the cosmic balance and control over one's subjects. A ruler or emperor had the power to determine which month of the year could be nominated as the first in the annual cycle. This meant that the calendar also conveyed a sense of ritual time in that important ceremonies could dictate the start of the New Year and the seasons.

Space: thinking in circles

Geography in the ancient world, as it is today, is about much more than a description of one's physical environment and is rarely totally objective. The ancient Chinese developed a moral geography of their world. Most civilizations, empires or colonial powers like to locate themselves at the centre of the known world, and China was no exception. Although texts and archaeological findings are replete with data that show up ethnic and cultural diversity, the overtone in sources linked to the courts and those who acted as their advisers remains unquestionably one of cultural centrism (remember the passage above: central terrain breeds people skilled for good government!). Foreigners and their lands, their foods and medicines, products and customs sparked curiosity, but, morally speaking, the world beyond the civilized court, the Central Kingdoms or the empire at large tended to be denigrated in contrast with Chinese achievements.

One way to understand the worldview that emerged is to think of a set of concentric circles in which the centre is seen to radiate its influence into the periphery, materially, physically and ethically. The word scholars sometimes use to describe this process is 'sinicization' (whereby groups of non-Chinese people come under the influence of Chinese culture). Although, in reality, regionalism and local identities were complex issues, deeply embedded in Chinese thinking was the idea that China's interior operated according to different social and economic laws than those of its border zones. The further away you are from the centre, the more you relinquish direct control, not only over the economic and military resources of the people, but also, and more importantly, over their minds, their culture, their customs and behaviours.

Those in the employ of rulers at the courts of the central states or the imperial capital saw the world outside as a graded zone of waning degrees of civilization. Confucius notes how the 'Yi and Di barbarian tribes with their rulers are not as viable as the various Chinese states without them' (*An.* 3.5). Better to be a headless Chinese than a barbarian with a brain, in other words. Meanwhile, the Confucian philosopher Xunzi (*c.*335–*c.*238 BCE), who came from Zhao and served in Qi and Chu, spoke of a 'Great Divine Order' in which the central states would put to good use the indigenous products of the barbarian periphery: 'That way, all that Heaven shelters and Earth supports is brought to its ultimate refinement and its fullest utility; so that the refined is used to adorn the worthy and good, and the useful is employed to nourish the Hundred Clans [all the people in the Central Kingdoms], and peace and contentment are brought to them' (*Xunzi* 9.14). The tribes and nomadic people that surrounded the Chinese heartland were sometimes compared to animals: they belonged to a biosphere where creatures ate raw meat instead of cooked grains, they dressed in animal hides and spoke in strange tongues that resembled the calls of the birds and beasts.

The implication is that those who refuse to be transformed by the civilizing influence of Chinese power are bound to fall off the map. Many Chinese thinkers defined civilization, culture (and later empire) and what it meant to be fully human by distinguishing the heartland from its outer periphery. This bipolar view conceived of the world as consisting of a division between 'inner' and 'outer'. To be sure, much of this was a matter of perception or political rhetoric. The symbolic reach of empire, 'All under Heaven', and its actual powers and influence rarely coincided. Already by Han times, imaginary geographies were presented in imperial parks or depicted in poetry. Here the mind could travel far beyond the edges of the world one had physically experienced. One gets a taste of some of the geographical imagination at play from *The Classic of Mountains and Seas (Shanhaijing)*. This curious work guides the reader on a journey of the world, recording the unknown creatures and sites the legendary Yu the Great was believed to have encountered when he toured the continent that was to become China after having saved it from the Yellow River floods. Each corner of the realm offers a melange of people, spirits, animals and other oddities together with actual and mythical landmarks:

> In the middle of the Great Wilderness there is Mount Notstraight. The River Glory comes to an end in it. There are people with three bodies on this mountain. Sublime Grace, who is the wife of the great god Foremost, gave birth to this Country of Threebody. The people here took the family name of Charm. They are millet-eaters. They control the four birds. Here there is a gulf; its four sides and four corners all join up together. The north forms part of the River Black. The south forms part of the Great Wilderness. The name of the north side of the gulf is Minorblend Gulf.

The name of its south side is Trailer Gulf. This is where the great god Hibiscus bathes. (*Shanhaijing* 15)

While these imagined locations derived from myths and legends, merely describing strange lands and creatures could be seen as an important way of controlling them. Naming meant explaining, even if one was unlikely ever to catch sight of these distant curiosities and creatures oneself.

An older geographical account of China is featured in a text known as *The Tribute of Yu* (*Yu gong*), which claims to originate in the legendary times of emperors Yao and Yu, but probably dates from around the fourth century BCE. It divides all known lands into nine provinces or territories and paints a diverse tableau of the people who inhabited them and the products they sent in as tribute to the court. By the third century BCE, yet another version of China's geography emerged in the theories of the naturalist philosopher Zou Yan (305–?240 BCE). According to him, the territories referred to as the Central Kingdoms constituted one of eighty-one regions that made up the entire world. The region occupied by the Central Kingdoms was part of the 'Spirit Continent of the Vermilion District', which itself comprised 'nine regions'. Beyond this lay nine other continents, each encircled by a small sea, which meant that people and animals could not cross from one continent to another. China thus formed the ninth part of one of nine large continents.

After reading these early geographical accounts, one comes away with a sense that order, in the Chinese worldview, ultimately issues from the centre and that all regions, goods and people naturally flow towards a civilized heartland. The world is organized in a radial or circular pattern of zones surrounding the royal domain or centre. In practice, however, the actual geography of China during the classical period, as shaped by socio-political, cultural and economic factors, was less fanciful. The map of the Yellow River valley essentially divided China into two main spheres of influence. West ('within the [mountain] passes') was the area traditionally dominated by the martial state of Qin. The states dotted across the eastern parts of the Yellow River basin nurtured China's most significant philosophical, literary and administrative talent. To the south lay the Yangzi drainage basin, where a distinctively southern culture had developed. As in China today, where household registration is required, free movement of people and goods was very limited. Travellers needed tallies and passports to pass through internal and external border posts. So, overall, during the centuries that were most significant in the development of Chinese thought, China was geographically confined to a relatively small area corresponding roughly to the zone between the Yellow River in the north and the Yangzi in the south.

Language, writing and script

Today, more than ever before, the Chinese character script has gone global. It permeates our image of China. Chinese characters come to us in neon-lit shopping malls, on restaurant menus, through pop-ups on the World Wide Web, on stadia billboards and the shirts of major football teams or as tattoos on trendy teenage shoulders. Ever since the script became more uniform, the written character has been an identity marker. Written Chinese has operated as a lingua franca for centuries up until today: it has enabled Chinese communities, separated by geography, social station or local dialect, to communicate with each other. Oral and written Chinese operate in different registers. The written language allows you to read without necessarily being able to speak and communicate orally; on the other hand, for those who only speak without mastering written characters, an entire sphere of meaning remains inaccessible. Throughout China's history, the use and mastery of writing have represented a feat of power. In no other culture is the role of writing so deeply ingrained at the heart of social, intellectual and religious life.

Historians take the invention of writing as a starting point to define historical origins. If the longevity of a culture is to be measured against the age of its writing system, then China would rank among the less senior members of world civilization. After all, the Shang oracle bone inscriptions appeared only around 1200 BCE – that is, about two thousand years after the appearance of writing in Egypt or Mesopotamia. Chinese civilization is of course much older than its written record, with a Neolithic ancestry that can be traced back to the fifth millennium BCE. To appreciate the power and prestige wielded in Chinese thought by writing and the written character, we need to understand that, for the ancient Chinese, written signs were not simply an invented code.

Writing was instead thought to derive from the natural world. The written character was something organic, as legends about its origin illustrate. According to one account, preserved in a commentary connected with *The Book of Changes*, the mythical sovereign Fu Xi looked up at the images in Heaven and then observed the tracks of birds and beasts in the earth.

This inspired him to invent a set of line diagrams known as trigrams – sets of three broken or unbroken lines which could be combined to form sixty-four hexagrams that were used to prognosticate future events (we will encounter these again in the next chapter). Another story concerns Cang Jie (see Figure 1.2), a scribe at the court of the legendary Yellow Emperor. He too is said to have invented the script by imitating bird tracks. A later commentator notes that unfriendly ghosts feared the invention of the written word, as it could be used to impeach or expel them (a superstition that persists today in the use of amulets and talismans for repelling ghosts.) We are told that even rabbits lived in fear as they foresaw how their fur would now be used to make writing brushes! The unfortunate fate of bunnies aside, these myths convey a sense that

Figure 1.2
Cang Jie, legendary inventor of the Chinese character script. Facsimile reprint from *Sancai tuhui*, 1609.

writing reproduced the structure of reality and the universe at large. Thus mastering texts and the written word was about more than simply bookish learning or being literate; it provided you with a vital key to life with which you could unlock a deeper meaning. It gave you power over the world and its history.

Chinese writing has a continuous history of more than three thousand years. Most sources available to us today are written in classical Chinese (*wenyan*). From the Han period up until the last days of the Qing dynasty a relatively uniform version of classical Chinese was used. Until the early twentieth century, classical Chinese was the main language of official written communication across East Asia. As a universal written and administrative language among administrators and the educated classes, its impact and reach can be compared to that of Latin and French during long periods of European history, or perhaps even English today. Naturally, languages never remain static; they evolve as a result of internal and external influences. The introduction of Buddhism from the third century CE onwards represented the first major external influence on the classical Chinese language. From the Yuan dynasty onwards the classical language also increasingly absorbed vernacular – that is, spoken or non-literary – elements.

There is a direct link between the linguistic structure of the language on Shang oracle bones and classical Chinese. Some characters as they are used today still resemble their oldest forms, such as those representing the heart, the sun, the moon, a door, a human being or a demon. Such characters are formalized direct representations of objects, sometimes called pictograms. In addition to pictograms, the Chinese language also combines two or more graphic signs into one character to express more abstract concepts or ideas (for example, a sun plus moon forms the graph for 'bright, intelligent, clear'; two trees indicate a forest; a person leaning against a tree makes up the graph for 'resting, relaxing'). China's first etymological dictionary, *Explaining Graphs and Analysing Characters* (*Shuowen jiezi*), compiled by Xu Shen (30–124 CE), groups characters according to 540 graphic classifiers or 'radicals'; modern Mandarin dictionaries use around two hundred. The dictionary also classifies characters into six types: graphs that symbolize ideas; graphs deriving from pictograms; graphs consisting of a form and a sound element; graphs with a combined meaning; graphs that are sounded differently but which have a similar meaning; and loan characters. In modern Mandarin (which contains around 420 different syllables), 90 per cent of characters are phonograms – that is, they are made up of a semantic element indicating their meaning and a phonetic element indicating the sound. In order to be literate in the Five Classics and able to write, a scholar had to rely on an active knowledge of around five thousand characters. But in practice one would have to master many more as one had to be able to recognize variants and borrowed characters and to decipher commentaries.

Chinese as it appears in our sources was not fundamentally a spoken language. The fact that classical Chinese can be read but is ineffective as a spoken medium largely explains its success as a shared tool for written communication. Most official documents and works of literature prior to the early twentieth century in China are recorded in one or other version and style of classical Chinese. It was the language used by philosophers, poets, officials and those who wrote scriptures and commentaries. To capture more accurately the sense of its widespread use into the twentieth century, it would be more precise to speak of 'literary' Chinese. But since many important canonical texts and their key thinkers emerged in the classical period, scholars and students today tend to refer to all formal ways of writing in Chinese prior to the early twentieth century as 'classical Chinese'.

The influence of classical Chinese on modern Mandarin is pervasive, especially in literary and formal expression. The ability to write and read texts written in classical Chinese continues to be a defining feature of the educated person in Chinese societies today. Reciting, memorizing and quoting from famous texts remains common practice in schools. Chinese politicians will throw in the occasional quote; some attempt to put brush to paper to copy out quotes from classical texts, others (most notably Mao Zedong) compose verse in the style of the ancients. In both its spoken and written form, modern Mandarin is awash with vocabulary – proverbs, analogies and anecdotal references – borrowed from classical Chinese. From our modern point of view, classical Chinese is a language that is primarily to be seen and read, not heard (with poetry as a possible exception). As a primarily written language, classical Chinese is therefore much more than a transcription of the spoken language. For this reason, good university courses include training in classical Chinese to help students probe beneath the surface in their understanding of Chinese civilization. Despite attempts by the New Culture Movement during the May Fourth period (c.1915–21) to abolish the official use of the classical language in favour of a more vernacular Chinese, it continues to permeate China's linguistic and textual landscape.

One way in which the distinction between modern Mandarin and the pre-modern language is sometimes made is by suggesting that modern Mandarin uses simplified characters whereas the ancients used traditional or more complex characters. However, it is inaccurate to associate simplified characters with the modern world and complex ones with the traditional past. The simplification of Chinese characters, instigated in the 1930s and driven through after the foundation of the People's Republic in 1949, did not affect the writing system used in Chinese communities beyond the reach of communist China, such as Hong Kong and Taiwan. Simplification sought to promote mass literacy and education. It served a political purpose by associating the new communist regime with an official script deemed more efficient and accessible across the social divides; it was intended to close the gap that had separated the highly educated elites of imperial China from the uneducated and largely illiterate masses. Not unlike the First Emperor, the Chinese State Council's introduction of writing reforms combined pragmatism with symbolism. Yet simplifying complex characters was not in fact a twentieth-century invention: most of the vulgar forms behind today's list of twenty-two hundred or so officially approved simplified characters can be traced to handwriting culture dating back as far as the Tang and Song periods. Chinese manuscript culture illustrates that ease of use and accessibility to writing was not an exclusively modern concern.

Ideas are intricately linked to the structure of a language. Classical Chinese is what linguists would identify as elliptical in nature. This means that the language, which is mostly monosyllabic, tries to express a great deal through a relatively sparse number of characters. In other words, one of the tricks in reading classical Chinese is to handle omission. Readers need to learn how to infer what is not said, which they may do on the basis of word order, the parallel occurrence of certain words and phrases, the use of function words and rhyme, among other things. Classical Chinese has no inflection in the form of word endings to indicate tense, case, voice, person or number. It has no declensions. The grammatical function of words is largely derived from word order or syntax. Most words therefore can adopt multiple functions depending where they occur within a phrase or sentence. For instance, a character with the basic meaning of 'goodness' can operate as an intransitive verb (as in 'she is good'), a noun (as in 'goodness means ...'), an adjective ('a good person') or a transitive verb ('to regard something as good'). Except for some basic rules of syntax and a set of particles or function words, the reader of classical Chinese therefore does not have to master a complex set of grammatical rules. Instead, unlocking the language requires mastering a large vocabulary and learning how to deal with the semantic gymnastics of characters. This involves, especially in the initial stages, a fair amount of rote learning combined with developing a creative feel for the workings of the language. These capricious habits of the classical Chinese language no doubt partly account for what sometimes appear as significant differences in translation among Western translators, especially in the case of a text rich in abstract or figurative language. In addition to writing, memorization and oral transmission also served as an important means of conveying ideas. Many recorded texts are economical with words or use a box of stylistic tricks that aid memorization (such as rhyme, parallelism, quotes, repetition). Thus the texts attributed to China's masters of philosophy are unlikely to be direct transcriptions of what was said.

Finally, another significant feature of the language in which Chinese thinkers expressed themselves is that it is not heavily analytical. This is one of the reasons why a Western readership may not immediately identify a Chinese text as 'philosophical'. Classical Chinese is wedded to the use of analogy, metaphor and allusion to get ideas across. Now, you might argue that a straightforward and distinct analytical vocabulary should be the hallmark of a mind that thinks clearly. But should it? One could equally claim that the use of catchy imagery, analogies and metaphors conjures possibilities that could not be evoked by the dry language of logic and definition. As Feng Youlan (1895–1990) once remarked: 'The sayings and the writings of the Chinese philosophers are so inarticulate that their suggestiveness is almost boundless.' Figurative language is by no means less efficient for conveying abstract concepts. Often the use of images and metaphors expands the horizon of how we interpret ideas. It can soften the edges of abstract or very theoretical language. Being told that you are in the spring or autumn of your life offers possibilities other than having your age spelled out or being called a teenager or a person of pensionable age.

Primary sources

The nature of many texts from ancient China is that they are open-ended and invite commentary, interpretation and reinterpretation. Rather than thinking of a text as a stable or final product, it is more useful to see it as organic and evolving. Many of our sources are texts that have accreted over time. Like a sandwich cake, one often needs to eat through layers of sponge and icing to get a taste of the creamy core. There are of course ways and techniques one can use to stake out a claim that a particular text or version is final and authoritative. For instance, one could write a commentary to accompany the text, and thereby shape the identity of what should be considered as the definitive version of it. Or one could carve a version of the text in stone to ensure that it becomes more or less unalterable. More often than not, a Chinese text becomes a classic not so much because an original or primary version (a so-called 'urtext') can be identified with certainty but, rather, because the editorial arrangements and commentary by a particular scholar have come to be accepted as commanding and definitive. Texts in ancient China often derived their authority from being associated with one authoritative figure or lineage of commentaries. To be linked with a towering figure such as Confucius could provide a text with an intellectual trademark for generations to come.

In addition to textual sources that have been transmitted through the ages (so-called received texts) and material evidence gathered by archaeologists, scholars who study ancient China also rely on a growing body of newly excavated texts. Partly as a consequence of rapid modernization and construction, China has been the scene of unprecedented manuscript finds in recent decades, in particular texts written on bamboo slips, wooden slats and silk. The work conducted today by philologists and paleographers (specialists

Figure 1.3
Writing on bamboo from
the state of Chu.

in ancient handwriting and manuscripts) on this vast body
of material illustrates what a puzzle an ancient Chinese text
can prove to be.

Before the age of paper or printing, the most common way
to record a text was by handwriting characters on bamboo
slips (and wooden plaques). Scribes might also scrape off the
bamboo slats or make corrections to the text, as indicated
by the knives and whetstones found in tombs. Bamboo slips
were tied together with cord or string and rolled up in a bundle.
When uncovered centuries later from the tomb, the cords
that held together the text in sequence will have disintegrated.
Depending on the nature of the soil and moisture levels, the
characters themselves may have partially vanished or become
illegible. Joining and restoring these slips into their original

order, then, can be akin to trying to gather up a bundle of un-cooked spaghetti that has spilled from the packet onto the kitchen floor, with pieces scattered everywhere. Imagine a text, consisting of tens of scrolls of strung-together bamboo slips piled up on an ox cart and transported from one location to another. It may have taken no more than a few potholes in a cobbled road for a 'roll' (still translated as 'volume' in modern Mandarin) to be jolted off the wagon and fall by the roadside to be forgotten. An army of philologists and histor-ians might debate for centuries how many slips were lost or, conversely, what larger work the misplaced roll that fell off the cart might have belonged to. Tomb robbery and a lucra-tive black market for antiquities do not help. Some manu-scripts remain unfortunately without certain provenance.

We tend to think that texts are shaped only by the ideas they contain. This is clearly not the case. The physical history of a text is equally important. Take graffiti, for instance. Their location and the object on which they are painted can tell us as much about the intent of the artist (or vandal) as does the actual text or the spraying technique employed. Likewise, the site where an ancient text has been found, the items buried with it, the arrangement of the actual text across the medium on which it is written, and even the position of a text in rela-tion to its immediate surroundings can teach us a great deal. Archaeologists and philologists of the future will no doubt find it equally challenging to make sense of the phones, com-puters and other devices in use today and the cryptic texting and messaging vocabulary left behind on them. The Chi-nese have produced a prodigious volume of textual criti-cism themselves through the ages. And while the science of textual criticism has advanced a great deal in modern times, scholars will no doubt continue to mull over the composition and meaning of many sources. One remarkable departure from the past in recent years is that China has been at the forefront of efforts to digitize old texts. In terms of the sheer volume of digitization, China is now leading the way in producing electronic versions of primary sources. This means that many more materials are now easily accessible. Today, newly discovered manuscripts are first discussed in scholarly notes on the internet. The wealth of archaeologically recovered texts from ancient China in recent decades has been a tremendous boon to modern scholars. It permits them to revise their previous understandings of texts that have been transmitted virtually unchanged for centuries. It also allows philologists to see where their predecessors got it wrong in their interpretation of received sources.

Texts are also prone to misconstruction and manipulation. When we study texts from ancient China, it is therefore crucial to separate the historical personalities associated with certain texts from the ideas reflected in them. The authorship of some of the most foundational texts in the Chinese tradition is either unknown, only partly attested or heavily disputed. For many of the key thinkers we will encounter, including Confucius and Laozi, little or no reliable biographical information is available. Nevertheless, their names have been associated with multiple texts and wide-ranging ideas, sometimes on very tenuous grounds. Confucius is the best example of a figure that has been reincarnated, selectively and strategically, throughout Chinese history up to the present. In the introduction to his translation of the Confucian

Analects (*Lunyu*), one of many that have appeared in recent years, the Belgian-Australian sinologist and essayist Simon Leys makes that point succinctly when he states that 'Confucius was certainly not a Confucianist', by which he means that the imperial powers-that-were tended to pick out and magnify only those statements by the Master that supported submission to authority. Confucius's insistence on a duty to evaluate rulers critically, or even dissent from them when they lose their grip on the moral rudder of society, was conveniently ignored.

Many governments would be delighted to be able to fall back on a booklet such as the *Analects* to broadcast their support of such universally prized values as harmony, equality, equal distribution of wealth, universal education, social mobility, sustainable development, respect for the elderly and a devotion to learning and service to the community. This does not, of course, mean that those texts do not also contain ideas that could be less palatable to the same governments or interpreted as critical of the established order.

Sinologists

The academic study of China, especially text- and philology-based studies focusing on literature, history, religion and philosophy, is the terrain of scholars sometimes referred to as 'sinologists' (not to be confused with psychologists). The term is mainly used in Europe, where it appears in university curricula and on degree certificates, and by scholars of pre-modern China in particular. Scholars in the West have been fascinated by ancient China for some time. Dominican and Jesuit missionaries took the lead in translating and

interpreting Chinese texts during the seventeenth and eighteenth centuries. But it was not until 1814 that the first professional chair of sinology in Europe was established, at the
Collège de France in Paris. It was occupied by Jean-Pierre
Abel Rémusat (1788–1832), a scholar of medicine who taught
himself Chinese after becoming captivated by a Chinese
herbal treatise. His successor, Stanislas Julien (1797–1873),
translated a large body of works of literature and history
over nearly four decades. Following in their footsteps, several other giants in Chinese philology, bibliography and
manuscript studies emerged in France, including Edouard
Chavannes (1865–1918) and Paul Pelliot (1878–1945). Other
first-generation French sinologists viewed ancient China
through a more historical and anthropological lens. These
included Henri Maspero (1883–1945) and Marcel Granet
(1884–1940).

It was a German, Georg von der Gabelentz (1840–93),
who pioneered the systematic study of Chinese and Chinese
grammar, and two Scottish Protestant missionaries, Alexander Wylie (1815–1887) and James Legge (1815–1897), who put
British sinology on the map in the nineteenth century (see
Figure 1.4). Legge is known for his landmark translation of
the Confucian Classics. In 1876 he was appointed to the first
chair of Chinese at Oxford. By 1888, a chair of Chinese had also
been created at Cambridge. Its first two holders, Sir Thomas
Wade (1818–95) and Herbert A. Giles (1845–1935), turned to
academic work after careers as diplomats and consular officials in China. Despite their personal dislike of each other,
they are twinned for ever as creators of the 'Wade–Giles' romanization system for Chinese that was widely used in the

Anglo-Saxon world to transcribe Chinese. It is still in use today, although pinyin, developed by Zhou Youguang (1906–2017) and the Chinese government during the 1950s, has largely superseded it as the most widely used romanization system.

In North America and the wider Anglo-Saxon world, the study of China has been propelled onto university curricula in the wake of the new geopolitical order established since the Second World War. John K. Fairbank (1907–91) at Harvard was a key figure in steering research on China towards interdisciplinary area studies. This brought the study of China, and Chinese thought, within the orbit of social and political scientists. The academic study of China will undoubtedly continue to bob along with changing trends in the disciplines and will respond to new demands on educational curricula. But it is worth reminding ourselves that, with an innings of a mere two hundred years, the study of Chinese civilization, language and culture in the West remains a relatively young discipline, certainly when compared with the study of Western languages and of the history of many other parts of the world. Those who pioneered the translation of many of China's most important texts embarked on this painstaking work without the help of basic tools such as dictionaries or other reference works. Often they had to work without informants. In the 1865 preface to his translation of *The Book of Documents*, James Legge put it prophetically: 'When a dictionary shall have been made on true principles by some one who understands the origin of the characters, and has pursued the history of every one through the various forms which it has assumed, the interpretation of the [Confucian] Classics will be greatly simplified.' But for all the frustrations

Figure 1.4
James Legge, translator of the Confucian Classics, and his Chinese assistants.

those pioneering scholars had to endure, the relative youth of Western studies of ancient China, combined with ongoing discoveries of new texts and artefacts, make it a truly exciting pursuit. Few intellectual pastimes can be more rewarding than studying a civilization that constantly throws up new historical sources, manuscripts and archives, and a society that continues to change at the rapid pace China does. On that note, it is now time to familiarize ourselves with some of the basic concepts in Chinese thought.

The Way (Dao) and Its Ways

Picture yourself lost in the middle of a busy city. As much as you might admire and want to spend time enjoying the architecture of the buildings and squares in front of you, it is secondary to your wish to find a way out of the city. To feel at ease amid this bewildering labyrinth of streets and buildings, you are searching for a way that will lead you from the centre to the outskirts. You try out various routes and search for landmarks. But at no point can you be absolutely certain that the streets and alleyways along which you are walking will take you in the right direction. You check street maps and ask a policeman and a traffic warden the way. But they each have their own view about the best route and send you in opposite directions. For a while, you begin to wonder whether you will ever get out of the city. But as you navigate through the maze of streets and buildings, marvelling at what you see around you but also apprehensive about what might be around the corner, you gradually realize that you quite like this idea of wandering about. As you explore, new vistas open before you and your anxiety about whether you will ever get out gradually dissipates. It's still early in the day and you can take your time, after all. Among the streets, squares and passageways, you discover that the city around you is endlessly fascinating.

What began as a burning need to find a way out has given way to a realization that trying different routes, without knowing where they might lead, has transformed the city from what seemed an oppressive trap into a beguiling pleasure ground. The only way you will ever know where the road you are on will lead to is by walking along it. But you have finally realized that the fun lies in the walking, not in analysing the map or even following the road to the end. You have become a traveller no longer intent upon arriving at one particular destination.

Dao

'Road', 'path' or 'course' is one of the primary meanings of the Chinese word *dao*. Arguably the most important and frequently recurring term in the Chinese philosophical vocabulary, all Chinese thinkers speak of the Dao. Yet the word *dao* is not easily defined. The Chinese character for it is composed of two graphic elements: one representing a head, and one representing the idea of 'moving' or 'leading through'. In its older forms, you might be able to detect a picture of a crossroads. One of its earliest usages is in the context of guiding a river to prevent it from flooding the banks. So, what does it mean? Dao can be understood only as an aggregate of its various meanings: it is a road, a way, a method, a formula, an art; it refers to teachings, the act of explaining, or a doctrine. It is a noun as well as a verb; a path as well as the process of treading a path; a way of life as well as advice on how to conduct one's life; a discourse as well as a practice.

As the guiding principle behind all that exists and the path along which everyone and everything travels, the Dao governs the course of all things. It embodies the natural and

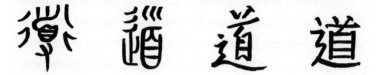

Figure 2.1
Various forms of the Chinese character for *dao*.

spontaneous processes that regulate the cycle of the universe. But when you look for the Dao, you won't be able to see it; when you listen out for it, you won't hear it. It is formless, yet it shapes everything. The moment you think you can identify or name the Dao, it escapes you. In that sense, the Dao is mysterious without being mystifying, fundamental without being elementary. It is beyond the world of language and rational thinking. *The Classic of the Way and Virtue (Daodejing)* opens with the lines: 'The Dao that may be spoken of is not the constant Dao; a name that may be named is not a constant name' (*DDJ* 1). You can of course try and express in words what the Dao is, as many Chinese thinkers and poets have done in the elegant texts they have left behind. But language will always be an imperfect vehicle to express what is inexpressible. You cannot split up the Dao into several components or ingredients, since it is 'one'. It is a wholeness, a unity that permeates everything and ties everything together: humans, the heavens, Earth. So you could think of it as a sort of ultimate reality or process, a force that keeps everything moving. As such it is not accessible by means of words. The more I continue writing about it, the more its essence will escape me: 'One who knows does not speak about it, one who speaks about it does not know' (*DDJ* 56).

The art of getting closer to the Dao therefore lies in discarding judgement. We need to quieten our minds and leave language behind: 'Truthful words are not beautiful, beautiful words are not truthful. Good words are not persuasive, persuasive words are not good. He who knows has no wide learning, he who has wide learning does not know' (*DDJ* 81). *The Classic of the Way and Virtue* contains several similar aphorisms that describe the nature of the Dao. The text itself is short and consists of eighty-one brief chapters. It is associated with the quasi-historical figure of Master Lao (Laozi), who is alleged to have lived in the sixth century BCE. From excavated manuscript versions of the text we can infer that *The Classic of the Way and Virtue* may have come together at least two centuries later. But we do not know who wrote the book, where it was written or why. It would perhaps be against the anti-intellectualism of the text itself for scholars to probe any further.

The term 'Dao' may have come to prominence in the West predominantly through *The Classic of the Way and Virtue*, but it is important to note that nearly every other philosophical text offers one or more descriptions of how the Dao operates. The following extract from a long poem entitled *Inner Training (Nei ye)*, transmitted as a chapter in *The Master Guan (Guanzi)*, explains:

> As for the Dao,
> It is something of which the mouth is incapable
> of speaking,
> The eyes are incapable of seeing.
> The ears are incapable of hearing.

It is the means whereby we cultivate our heart
    [mind] and align our body.
When people lose it, they will die.
When people gain it, they will live.
When our affairs are without it, they will fail.
When they gain it, they will succeed.
In all cases, the Dao has neither root nor trunk,
It has neither leaves nor flowers.
The ten thousand things [i.e. 'all things'] are
    generated by it,
The ten thousand things are completed by it.
We designate it 'the Dao'. (*Nei ye* 6)

De, the second Chinese character in the title *Daodejing*, trans-lated here as 'virtue', is the inner potency or power inherent in each of us. People possess a certain amount of free and in-dividual energy which enables them to accomplish particular actions and to live according to the patterns of the Dao with greater efficacy. *De* represents the power to tailor the prin-ciples of the Dao to the individual, or, alternatively, it may be thought of as the way in which the Dao operates in individual things. For instance, in order to get from point A to point B, some form of locomotion is needed, and animals and people have different means and amounts of energy at their disposal to make that journey, whether crawling, walking, jumping, running, swimming, flying, riding, driving, cycling, and so on. What distinguishes human beings, then, from other species is that we have that little bit extra free energy that enables us to be creative and not bound entirely by the patterns of nature. If we were to live entirely according to the Dao of the seasons, we would get up at sunrise and turn in when the sun sets, giving us very short days in winter and long ones in summer. But electricity, or candlelight in the past, allows us to prolong the days in winter, while window blinds or curtains help us shorten daylight during the summer. So our free energy permits us to manipulate natural daylight patterns. However, we should only do this in a measured way to keep pace with the Dao: individual free energy needs to align with the natural order. Once we block out sunlight for days on end or spend the night living under a lightbulb, we have breached the Dao of the seasons and this lack of harmony with nature could harm our physical and emotional well-being.

The point made in these portrayals of the Dao is that we may not understand everything about the world that surrounds us, but that we can at least see that it operates according to certain patterns. There seems to exist an overarching order that governs the world and the cosmos. Our own lives and the physical world in which we live appear to follow an underlying road map. Why exactly this map radiates out in an infinite number of directions, with endless twists and turns, we cannot know for certain. Admitting human ignorance therefore is key. Do not ask what the Dao 'is'; the Dao is something you 'do'. By following one particular route, we might get closer to finding out where we are heading, but even if we do not, we will have gained experience along the way and hopefully even appreciated this quest for no answer. If the answer to the question 'What is life?' eludes us, the Chinese philosopher would argue that it is better to ask the question 'How should I lead my life?' Western philosophy (and science) is very much interested in the 'what' question. It allows us, for instance, to define water as dihydrogen monoxide (H_2O). But water is also wet, it flows, is drinkable (at times) and vital for the hydration of all living things. Someone who is dehydrated and craves a drink will derive little comfort from being able to recite the molecular formula for water. Farmers or engineers in charge of diverting a river to prevent it from flooding a city, or to irrigate the paddy fields, will conceive of water first and foremost as something that moves and flows. When you take a shower, water feels wet and cleansing; when it rains, water drops down on you, soaking you through; when you swim, water, unlike air, keeps you afloat. Water is what water does; a thing is what it does. For Chinese thinkers, what truly matters is explaining how things 'thing' (try to read this as a verb).

The term Dao is often immediately linked to a philosophy known as Daoism. In ancient China, Daoism is usually associated with two enigmatic texts from the Warring States period: the aforementioned *The Classic of the Way and Virtue* and *The Master Zhuang (Zhuangzi)*, a masterpiece of Chinese literature attributed to Zhuangzi (Zhuang Zhou; *c.*369–286 BCE). But in its broader meaning as a method or path, Dao is not just used in the cosmological sense outlined above, and the term is by no means exclusive to so-called Daoist thinkers. The Dao of life is nothing more than the track one needs to follow to get from birth to seniority in a physically and psychologically fulfilling manner. Chinese thinkers propose multiple 'Daos' or methods, each providing different answers to the 'how' question. Each tradition proposes its own road map. As we shall see, for Confucians, who emphasize the importance of human ethics and social engagement, Dao mostly refers to the 'way of humans'. Human beings, they argue, can devote their efforts to making the journey along the path more interesting than the path itself: 'Humans can broaden the Dao; it is not the Dao that broadens humans' (*An.* 15.29). For Daoist thinkers, the good life is best lived by retreating from society, and so their Dao tends to stand for the fundamental rhythm of nature or a primordial oneness to which everything belongs and returns. The Dao of the Legalist thinkers who inspired the First Emperor is adherence to the rule of law by means of a system of reward and punishment. In sum, as a concept Dao is elastic. Its meaning stretches from describing the underlying pattern that governs the universe to the way people should live their lives and, in a narrower sense, a method: the way of warfare, the way of the sage, the way of the gentleman, the way of the ancients, the way of governing, the way of the body.

But let us return once more to the Dao as a cosmic force. Where does the Dao come from? The answer is that it has always been there and continuously regenerates itself. There is no other reality hidden beneath the world in which we live. There may be many different road maps and theories to help us navigate the path, but there is only one path. Unlike the Judeo-Christian tradition, Chinese thinkers appear generally content with this explanation without having recourse to an omnipotent power, a universal lawgiver or a divine god. Thus the Dao is not created or designed, nor does it have external forces working on it, such as a first cause or big bang: 'People model themselves on the Earth, the Earth models itself on Heaven, Heaven models itself on the Dao, the Dao models itself on that which is naturally so [*zi ran*]' (*DDJ* 25). The last term in this quote fittingly covers how the ancient Chinese conceived of the workings of the Dao. *Zi ran* may be translated as 'to be so of itself' or 'to be so of one's own accord'. It is still used in modern Mandarin to refer both to spontaneity and nature (as in natural science, the natural environment, the natural world). Yet its core meaning in ancient times was the first sense, 'spontaneity', rather than a physical and objectifiable reality. 'To be so of itself' describes a state of being rather than an essential quality or a physical world that exists of itself and by its own laws.

In short, the Chinese universe is dynamic and organic. It finds its order of itself. Try to think of it as a field of energy. Things behave in a particular way, not because of the prior actions or impulses of other things, but because they do so spontaneously. The difference is as subtle as that between claiming that a football rolls across the pitch because it is kicked there by a player, or because it is the nature of a ball to roll. Chinese thought follows the latter: the world functions by its own internal spontaneity; it generates and processes itself. It is 'of itself so'. Rather than claiming that the world was created out of nothing, the Chinese conceive of the world and its complex structures as something that evolved out of a prior state of simplicity or non-differentiation: 'The Dao gave birth to the one; the one gave birth to the two; the two gave birth to the three; the three gave birth to the Ten Thousand Things; the Ten Thousand Things carry *yin* and embrace *yang*, and create harmony through the blending of *qi*' (*DDJ* 42). But what exactly is this *qi* that needs blending?

Qi

The basic stuff out of which all things are configured is known as *qi*. *Qi* is translated variously as vapour, vital energy, essential energy, material energy, life force, breath, fluid, ether. The pictographic origins of the Chinese character have been explained as dew turning into steam, or a cloudy vapour or damp rising from heated sacrificial offerings (variant forms of the character show the recurring element or radical for 'rice' or 'to feed').

The idea that *qi* represents the 'breath of life' explains why it has been likened to concepts in other cultures that are related but not quite equivalent (such as Greek *pneuma*, Sanskrit *prajñā*, Latin *spiritus* or Hebrew *neshamah*). *Qi* is perhaps best left untranslated. Derived from its original sense of 'vapour', *qi* came to mean the primal stuff of the

Figure 2.2
Early variants of the Chinese character for *qi*.

universe, a substance that permeates everything in the living world. The comparison with climate conditions or the atmosphere comes to mind (the modern Mandarin word for 'weather' literally translates 'the *qi* of Heaven'). In cosmological terms, one may think of *qi* as a sort of fluid that is present in the atmosphere, out of which everything condenses and into which all things dissolve. *Qi* is not some sort of dualistic counterpart to substance (like energy to matter); that is, you cannot just take a thing and then add some *qi* to it. It is nothing like a stable atom. *Qi* is energetic and constantly on the move, like the steam that surrounds you when you take a hot shower in a cubicle. It can condense into water drops again or evaporate when you open the door, but it never really disappears. In medical terms, *qi* is the life force which, together with blood, animates the body, flows through the vessels, veins and arteries, and provides the physical substrate for our organs, skin, flesh and muscles, as well as our emotions.

Qi informs every aspect of our behaviour: from movement and actions to thoughts and temperament. It can be both a physical and a moral force. In one passage from *The Analects*, Confucius suggests that the condition of our 'blood and *qi*' changes with age, and he makes a direct link with moral conduct: 'There are three things a gentleman should guard against; when he is young, and when his "blood and *qi*" are still unsettled, he should guard against the temptation of female beauty; when he reaches the prime of life and when his "blood and *qi*" have become unyielding, he should guard against being contentious; when reaching old age and when the "blood and *qi*" have declined, he should guard against acquisitiveness' (*An.* 16.7). Another main Confucian philosopher,

Mencius (fourth/third century BCE), speaks about nourishing his own 'vast, flowing *qi*'. By this he means that when a person conducts him- or herself with a sense of rightness, he or she accumulates morally good *qi* that 'will fill the space between Heaven and Earth' (*Mencius* 2A.2). Thus *qi* can take control of our senses, leading us to live ethically. It can be channelled in a good or a bad way. When refined and in flow, it can ensure physical and moral well-being, but when depleted, blocked, entangled or configured in the wrong way, it can cause illness or lack of moral wit and emotional intelligence. *Qi* is present in everything, including items we might perceive as more or less inanimate: rocks, trees, a painting.

Qi manifests itself in various forms and degrees of consistency. It can be rough or refined, light or heavy, coarse or pure. It can expand or congeal, become concentrated or dissipated. *Qi* may be murky and muddy or clear and distilled. Coarse or heavy *qi* can settle to become the earth. Light and refined *qi* can rise to become the sky, clouds, stars, sun and moon.

> When Heaven and Earth were not yet shaped, all was
>   amorphous,
> Vague, blank, a blur. This was called the Grand Beginning.
> The Dao began in a nebulous void.
> This nebulous void produced space and time,
> Space and time produced *qi*.
> Then there was a boundary that divided *qi*.
> What was pure and bright spread out to become Heaven.
> What was heavy and muddy congealed to become Earth.
> The concentration of the pure and bright is easy,
> But it is difficult for the heavy and muddy to congeal.

> Therefore Heaven was completed first and Earth was
> fixed afterwards. (*Huainanzi* 3.1)

In order to live, we need *qi*. As *The Master Zhuang* states, 'Human life is nothing but an accumulation of *qi*. When it comes together, we live; when it scatters, we die' (*Zhuangzi* 22.1). In terms of the condition of our *qi*, as human beings we are somewhere in the middle. We use rough energy such as physical force but also operate on the basis of more subtle or concentrated forms: our wit, intelligence, senses. The quality of our *qi* sets us apart from other creatures: 'coarse *qi* forms animals, and refined *qi* forms humans' (*Huainanzi* 7.1). All living creatures are made up of the same stuff, with physical and behavioural differences emerging from the way in which a creature's *qi* is structured. The cosmos therefore generates itself from a formless state through a process in which *qi* is refined to produce everything in the universe.

Change and transformation

With the universe consisting of constantly changing vital energies, change is also what defines the life and world of human beings. The classical Chinese language is rich in verbs and phrases for describing changes, transformations and alternations of some kind. Most thinkers in ancient China held that what unites people in their view of the world around them is the incontrovertible law that everything is in a state of constant flux. The only stable point of reference is the knowledge that everything is subject to change. But rather than being anxious about it, endeavouring to keep things as they are, or trying to transcend it, our aim should be to align ourselves with these constantly changing circumstances, be they the physical changes in nature or changes in society. Living and understanding the world, in essence, mean managing change. *The Master Zhuang*, the late fourth-century BCE Daoist classic that we will encounter again throughout the book, is full of anecdotes and parables illustrating the world in flux:

> Once upon a time Master Zhuang dreamed that he was a butterfly, flitting around and happily enjoying himself. He did not know that he was Master Zhuang. Then suddenly he woke up and was Master Zhuang again. He did not know whether he was Master Zhuang who had dreamed of being a butterfly or a butterfly dreaming that he was Master Zhuang. However, there must be a difference between Master Zhuang and the butterfly. This is called the transformation of things. (*Zhuangzi* 2.14)

But how do you handle change and cope with it? The first step is to understand what types of changes we experience and observe around us: the passing of the seasons, the growth and decay of crops and other plants, ageing and its effect on the body, the ebb and flow of emotions, and so on. The second step is to try and guide our actions so that we adapt ourselves to this world of flux. For instance, we can attempt to predict what will change and try to mitigate the outcome of events in the future. The Chinese developed many mantic techniques to divine what might lie ahead. Nearly all of them continue to be popular today: consulting the stars; making numerological calculations; interpreting patterns on the body, the palms or face (physiognomy); interpreting dreams (oneiromancy); casting yarrow stalks; or interpreting omens and freak events in nature. Once we have identified the patterns of change around us, we can attempt to fall into line with them and thereby exercise some sort of control over our constantly changing environment. This guards us against the negative effects that can result from not responding to change but it also enables us to turn it to our advantage, as a farmer does when he adapts his activities to the seasons. We can take charge of time, and devise a schedule or calendar to plan our activities throughout the year with greater efficiency. Psychologically, we might even draw comfort from the idea that change is the only form of permanence in the world.

The famous *Book of Changes* (also known as the *Zhouyi* or *Yijing*), some parts dating as far back as the tenth to eighth century BCE, provides the classic example of a guide aimed at helping the user navigate his or her way through a perpetually changing world, giving guidance on how to respond to newly emerging situations. The text is organized around sixty-four variations of six solid or broken lines, known as hexagrams. (For examples, see Figure 2.3.)

Each hexagram has a name that is followed by a string of formulaic phrases that make up a statement. The statement captures the meaning associated with the hexagram as a graphic symbol for the purpose of divination (such as 'It is beneficial to establish a lord and move troops', or 'It is beneficial to decide about difficulty'). Next follow statements for each of the six lines in the hexagram with different layers of commentary. The images used in the core text are cryptic and ambiguous. This allowed diviners, using yarrow stalks, to offer different interpretations of

Qian Creativity	*Kun* Receptivity	*Heng* Constancy

Figure 2.3
Hexagrams for *Qian*, *Kun* and *Heng*.

their meaning. This abstract and cryptic language, with its range of possible meanings, is no doubt responsible for the industry the book has sparked as a type of wisdom manual that has been used (and abused) for multiple purposes, from self-healing to gambling and computer games. The changing lines in the hexagrams were seen to capture the constancies within the changing dynamics that underlie each emergent situation. In this way, the diviner could predict what future outcomes would result.

Leaving aside the technical complexities of *The Book of Changes* as a diviner's handbook, the underlying question the text aims to address is clear: how do I make sense of a world in constant flux? More telling than the numerology and oblique language associated with the hexagrams and the core text are the commentarial portions that accompany the hexagram statements. These are known as the 'Ten Wings'. The most important of these, the so-called 'Great Treatise' or 'Appended Statements', narrates the cosmology of change represented by the hexagrams in more generous, but no less difficult, prose. It tells of the ancient sages who detected graphic symbols and signs in nature which inspired them to invent the tools for creating society and human civilization and the institutions that underpin them. It registers how everything emerged from a primal state of formlessness and undifferentiated *qi*. It almost presents *The Book of Changes* itself as an incarnation of these deep cosmic patterns and suggests that in order to unlock the mysteries of this changing universe, you need to turn to this book and master it. The commentaries are full of metaphors and images that portray the concept of change, the most expressive of which is one of China's most iconic symbols, the dragon. Take, for instance, the following passage from a silk manuscript associated with *The Book of Changes*, discovered in 1973 at Mawangdui near Changsha (Hunan province), in which Confucius describes this most versatile of creatures:

> The dragon is great indeed. The dragon's form shifts. When it approaches the Lord in audience, it manifests the virtue of a spiritual sage … Into the deep currents the fishes and reptiles surround it and of those beings of the watery currents there is none that does not follow it; perched up high, the god of thunder nourishes it, the wind and rain avoid facing it, and the birds and beasts do not disturb it. [Confucius said]: 'The dragon is great indeed. While the dragon is able to change into a cloud, it is also able to change into a reptile and also able to change into a fish, a flying bird or a slithery reptile. No matter how it wants to transform itself, that it does not lose its basic form is because it is the personification of spiritual ability.
>
> (*Ersanzi wen*)

What makes the dragon sacred is its ability to preserve itself by changing with and transforming itself into every other species that exists. Just as the dragon is the ultimate shape-shifter, so humans need to develop a knack of responding to the perpetual changes the world throws at them. But to do so, we need a blueprint to help us follow the rules or codes according to which this world-in-change operates, and understand how all of us in the system relate to one another.

Correlation, *yin* and *yang*

The Chinese developed several cognitive systems to show how change works and how everything is correlated. Correlation is not an abstract concept, nor is it uniquely Chinese. In many aspects of our daily lives, we analyse and spontaneously think about the world in correlative terms or binary oppositions. For instance, we define role expectations for men against those of women; we identify something as beautiful by comparing it with something we find ugly; we measure hot against cold, young against old, energy against fatigue, day versus night, peace versus war, good versus bad, water versus fire, pain versus gain, high versus low, sweet versus sour.

Although there are traces of correlative thinking that go back to earlier times, it is from about the fourth century BCE that the Chinese started to view the world as operating through a binary set of forces that they termed *yin* and *yang*. The standardization of *yin–yang* thinking has been attributed to the philosopher Zou Yan (fourth/third century BCE) and his followers. No writings by Zou Yan have survived, but his influence is apparent in other texts. The system and cosmology he devised gained wide influence. By Han times, 'correlative' thought was pervasive. It would leave a lasting imprint on the ways in which the Chinese analysed the world.

Figure 2.4
The yinyang symbol.

Let us first go back to *yin* and *yang*. Contrary to what is suggested by some books that make up the vast self-help industry that has developed around them, there is nothing mystical or mysterious about the concept of *yin* and *yang*. The original meaning of the character *yin* is the shady side of a mountain, while *yang* represents its sunny side. And this image sums up the principle in a nutshell: you can't have a shadow without light, and vice versa; *yin* and *yang* are complementary opposites and are correlated. You can define one only in relation to the other. The idea is captured graphically in a version of a well-known diagram (also known as the 'Diagram of the Great Ultimate') that has taken on iconic status since Qing times (but goes back to the fourteenth century at least).

The universe is a sphere divided along two planes, with a curved division separating them. One side is *yang*, on the other is *yin*. Each side contains within it the seed or core of the other. What is *yang* now will produce *yin*, and *yin* will change into *yang* again (you can picture the diagram in a constantly spinning motion). Ideally, both need to coexist in harmony or compensate each other to prevent sickness, death or natural and man-made disasters. Too much *yang* 'heat' will give you a fever; too much *yin* 'cold' will freeze over the crops. One of the earliest descriptions of the relationship of *qi* to *yin* and *yang* comes from a collection of historical anecdotes, *The Zuo Tradition* (*Zuozhuan*), compiled in the fourth century BCE. The description is given by a physician named He:

> Heaven has six kinds of *qi*. They descend to generate the five flavours; radiate to make the five colours; are called forth to make the five sounds. If there is excess they produce the six illnesses. The six *qi* are *yin* and *yang*, wind and rain, dark and light. They separate to make the four seasons; form a sequence to make five pitches [of sound]. When there is excess [in one of these] they will cause calamity. (*Zuozhuan*, Lord Zhao 1)

So far so good. But what is really important is not to think of *yin* and *yang* as a 'thing'. Each event, person, object or process has a *yin* and a *yang* side, but they interact with varying levels of one or the other. *Yin* and *yang* describe functions, stages in the processes of a constantly changing world. 'One *yin* and one *yang* are called Dao,' the 'Great Treatise' states. In essence the *yin–yang* pair is a means of making sense of the world and what surrounds us in terms of complementary opposites (light–dark, fire–water, noise–silence, male–female, husband–wife, and so on). Yet nothing is *yin* or *yang* of itself. Take the example of male and female: they each procreate and possess a measure of physical strength and mental agility. But these are functions by which we all exist and conduct our lives, so who is *yin* and who is *yang*? The answer to this depends entirely on what function or activity we are trying to describe.

When we compare physical strength, the male body tends to be stronger than that of the female, so when we are relating men to women on the basis of physical strength, men can often be said to be *yang* and women *yin*. Yet the nature of this relationship can change depending on the function we are describing. Indeed, when it comes to reproduction women clearly shoulder the greater share of the process. Inseminating requires less time and energy than gestation and nourishing a baby in the early stages, hence one can argue that here the classification is reversed. The biological mother clearly takes on the *yang* role, with the biological father operating in the shadow. He has become *yin*. Water is *yang* to fire (it extinguishes it), but *yin* to the sun (which evaporates it).

Every phenomenon, in other words, can be either *yin* or *yang* depending on the function in question. Any situation in the human or natural world can be made to fit this framework. You can be active and enterprising (*yang*) during certain stages of your life, while feeling more unadventurous or contemplative (*yin*) during other periods. But neither *yin* nor *yang* can exist by itself: mountains require valleys, teachers require pupils, harvesting requires planting, hard needs to be measured against soft, speech requires silence, movement requires stillness. In this way, the Chinese universe presents itself as one big correlative network, wherein everything is linked to everything or, at least, wherein each element requires the presence of another for it to be able to function. It operates like a living organism, much like the natural world and its climate regimes. On this basis, small causes may lead to large effects, something that Chinese thinkers would have deduced long before Edward Lorenz (1917–2008) famously coined the phrase 'butterfly effect' – the idea that a butterfly flapping its wings in one part of the planet could over time cause a hurricane elsewhere.

With this invisible connective tissue between us and everything that surrounds us, humans must attempt to understand and manage the relationships between what appear at first sight to be separate events or entities. By Han times a more complex system for explaining the correspondence between everything in the world had become deeply embedded. In addition to viewing the interplay between things as a dynamic between *yin* and *yang* forces, correlative thinkers used a model known as the Five Phases (*wu xing*). The Five Phases system employs five vital resources (water, fire, wood, metal, earth) to explain the mutual relationships between phenomena in the world, including space and time. They are first mentioned in the 'Great Plan' ('Hongfan'), a text compiled sometime before 400 BCE and included as a chapter in *The Book of Documents*:

> The first is water, the second is fire, the third is wood, the fourth is metal, the fifth is earth. The nature of water is to moisten and flow downwards; the nature of fire is to blaze and ascend; the nature of wood is to be bent and straight; the nature of metal is to yield [liquefy] and change [solidify]; the nature of earth is to be seeded and produce harvest. (*Shangshu*, 'Hongfan')

These Five Phases can be arranged in a 'conquest' cycle (*wood* digs soil; *metal* cuts through wood; *fire* melts metal; *water* extinguishes fire; *earth* conquers water by damming it). Or they can be arranged in a sequence in which they produce or generate each other (*wood* produces fire; *fire* becomes ash; the *soil* harbours metals; *metal* melts into a liquid; *water* feeds wood). Regardless of the order in which they are used, the important thing is that these Five Phases or agencies act as coordinates that can help explain the sequence of things. As well as all things alternating between *yin* and *yang*, this pattern of alternation itself was thought to go through five successive stages. Note that I have used the word 'phases' and not 'elements'. When the ancient Greeks spoke of the elements (earth, fire, water, air, ether), they conceived of these as substances or building blocks that make up everything. They were driven by the question 'What is it – what are we made of?' The Chinese model of the Five Phases is different. A phase is not a thing; it is a process and a stage. The assumption is that all natural and cultural phenomena are closely interrelated, and that these correlations between the human body, nature, time and space can be described as passing through a (production or conquest) cycle of five phases. From the third century BCE onwards, *yin–yang* thinking and the use of the Five Phases model were so pervasive that it can be seen in almost every branch of intellectual inquiry in China, from medicine to the writing of history, from the speculative arts of fortune-telling and astrology, to Confucian political thought. Today these concepts continue to be used in Chinese medicine, in the martial arts, feng shui (Chinese geomancy) and even in Chinese cooking.

But how should we think of life according to the Five Phases model? What were the practical implications of ordering the world according to this set of five? It is hard for us today to imagine how these theories were put into practice beyond the level of symbolism or outside the study quarters of intellectu-als and scholars. Cosmology is not easily linked to actual be-haviour, let alone to practices that can be dated to a particular time and place. The trick for Chinese thinkers was to ensure that everything could be fitted into the model. Correlative thinkers were obsessed by the search for equivalences be-tween the world of Heaven (nature) and the world of man. They attempted to map all aspects of life against the order of the Five Phases: seasons, directions, colours, flavours, sounds, the weather, numbers, sacrifices, rituals, diet, organs, animals, grain crops, human emotions, and even the succession of dy-nasties and the course of history itself (see p. 91).

A practical example of cosmological thinking according to the models of *yin–yang* and the Five Phases can be seen in a particular type of calendar that had emerged by the third cen-tury BCE. It gave instructions as to what to do when – hence its name, 'Monthly Ordinances' – and specified what activities were permitted in each season. It also warned that acting out of season would result in disaster. The 'Monthly Ordinances' divided the year into five seasons, with the hot midsummer inserted as a fifth season corresponding to the phase of earth. According to these ordinances, the killing of living things was to be avoided during the growth phases of the year (wood and fire; spring and summer), for instance, while criminals had to be executed under the patronage of the metal phase – that is, in autumn through to early winter, the seasons associated with death and *yin*. Since the Son of Heaven was charged with main-taining the link between Heaven (that is, the force that granted him power through the Mandate of Heaven) and his subjects, he had to try to maintain the cosmic balance. The calendar

	Seasons	Directions	Colours	Flavours	Emotions	Organs	Animals
Wood	spring	east	green	sour	anger	liver	scaly
Fire	summer	south	red	bitter	joy	heart	feathered
Earth	mid-summer	centre	yellow	sweet	pensive-ness	spleen	naked
Metal	autumn	west	white	acrid	sorrow	lung	hairy
Water	winter	north	black	salty	fear	kidney	armoured

Table 2.1
Mapping out the world according to the Five Phases

thus prescribes how a ruler should organize his life according to the model of the Five Phases. He has to adapt his diet according to the seasons, for instance, change the colour of his robes and the decorations on his chariot, perform key rituals at each important node in the calendar, adapt court music and even change his living quarters in the palace according to the time of year. Like a dragon (the shape-shifter encountered above), the ruler becomes master of the world by adapting himself constantly. Those who governed had to represent the passage of time in the proper manner. Failure to uphold this order and acting in an untimely manner would have adverse consequences, according to this passage from *The Spring and Autumn Annals of Mr Lü (Lüshi chunqiu)*:

> If the ordinances for the summer are put in place in the first month of spring, winds and rains will not be seasonable, grasses and trees will wither early; and the state will thereupon become alarmed. If the ordinances

for autumn are put into effect [in spring], the people will suffer a great plague, severe winds and violent rains will frequently occur, and briars, darnel, brambles and artemisia weeds will flourish together with the crops. If the ordinances for winter are put into effect [in spring], floods and heavy rains will cause ruin, frost and snow will do great damage, and the first-sown crops will not ripen for the harvest. (*Lüshi chunqiu* 1/1.7)

The implication of this example is that natural disasters are at least partly caused by people. In this way of thinking, physical and moral categories are linked to each other. Some scholars have argued that correlative thinking, because of its basic premise that the natural world is deeply implicated in human affairs, has prevented the Chinese from seeing nature as a separate sphere of knowledge (which, in turn, the argument goes, has hampered the development of the natural sciences in China). We will return to this question at greater length in Chapter 7. It is certainly the case that in many writings the Five Phases model becomes highly mechanistic and speculative. Thinking based on *yin–yang* and the Five Phases is, of course, not set up to prove anything, but merely to establish a sequence between things and events. As long as everything finds a place in the model, the relationship is explained. But trying to explain everything – from the workings of the human body to government institutions – through a system divided into five categories can often be more inhibiting than helpful. At times it requires an inventive mind to come up with the analogies and metaphors that link things together. For example, the association of fire with the summer, brightness, the south and the colour red seems self-explanatory. For all those *yang*-generating reasons, the Chinese emperor was seated on his throne facing south, with his back turned to the shadowy north. But to then link birds to the fire phase requires a greater leap of the imagination. One could say that birds rise up like fire or fly towards the sun, for instance. Or, if the feeling of joy corresponds to fire and sorrow corresponds to metal, then overcoming sorrow with joy can be explained as the natural order of things, since fire melts metal. Too much fiery joy, however, can produce a heart full of ponderous thoughts (fire produces earth). If one associates different dynasties with different phases in the cycle (as Zou Yan did), the logic of the conquest cycle dictates that political regimes must naturally replace each other. When cooking, a good balance between the five flavours prevents one from overpowering the other. And so we can extrapolate endlessly.

Let us conclude by looking at how we as human beings figure in this model of the Five Phases. As is illustrated in the table above, animal species are classified according to their external shape, more specifically the covering of the skin. The Five Phases model divides creatures into scaly, feathered, naked, hairy and armoured. In most versions of this scheme, human beings represent the central class of naked animals. So not only were humans seen as creatures generated by a more refined residue of *qi*, the Five Phases model also portrays them as somehow central to the balance of the system. However, it does so not by granting them biological superiority as part of an evolutionary hierarchy – that is, in a scale of perfection with man at the top (as Aristotle or Charles Darwin did) – but by locating them at the centre, where the *yang* energies are at their highest, and from where they can most easily adapt to and transform the world around them. As humans, we have more free energy to change habitat and adapt our bio-rhythm according to changing circumstances. What sets us as human beings apart from other creatures (or from people who behave like animals!) is our capacity to move, act and adapt confidently in response to the ever-changing situations in which we find ourselves.

The interconnectedness that Chinese philosophers detect-ed in the cosmos and nature at large was not simply a game of abstract or speculative thinking. As we will see in the next few chapters, a strong concern with defining relationships between members of a greater entity or group also defines the Chinese social world. At the heart of Chinese ethics are two central questions: how we should define the role of human beings in their interdependent relationship with the world and each other; and what strategies are most helpful in order to govern and control the human situations that are played out in this world of change.

CHAPTER 3

The Art of Government

Much of early Chinese thought is elitist. It is ruler- rather than people-centred. Chinese philosophers devoted most of their time to thinking about those who occupied leading roles in society: the ruler, the general, the sage, the worthy, the scholar, the noble person, the authentic person, the king, the sovereign, the lord, the duke or the emperor. Defining the art of rulership, therefore, stood high on the agenda of ancient China's 'Hundred Masters', a term used to refer to the collective of thinkers of the fourth and third centuries BCE. There is virtually no Chinese philosopher from this period who does not have a view on how to manage people and rule society, and that includes those who preferred to withdraw from the lure of statesmanship rather than engage with the world.

What makes a person powerful? Is it personality, inborn talent or the ability to spot potential and persuade others to work for you? Is it charisma, simple intelligence, or are power and authority merely the product of the position or institution you inhabit (teachers always get to speak first, even if they have nothing important to say)? How then do you inspire others or stave off your opponents, protect yourself and assess the loyalty of those around you? Should you be invisible or get out among the people? Should you appear assertive, inspire by example, or is it better to hide behind high walls or deep inside a palace so others will have to imagine how potent you might be? Why not simply get rid of those who disagree with you (subtly, if needed) and reward those willing to be the echo to your shout and arm to your torso? How do you reprimand people for not doing their job, and what tone and language do you adopt when firing off orders and directives? Should you offer chapter and verse about what you wish to achieve, or is it better to shut up (even if you have something worth saying) and channel your communication through the voice of others? What works best to get your point across? Do you jump in with a confident and direct 'I think that ...', 'I say that ...', 'It is my contention that ...', 'In my opinion ...'? Or how about a more indirect 'It is said that ...', 'I have heard that ...', 'The ancients tell us that ...' (three of the most common formulas of speech in classical Chinese dialogue)?

These are the types of questions that preoccupied Chinese thinkers when they tried to identify the characteristics that distinguish those who rule from those who are ruled. They were united in their fascination with the question of how one should position oneself in order to govern or lead with the greatest efficiency. There was no disagreement on the basic premise that power must be monarchical – that is, concentrated in the hands of a single ruler or figurehead. Yet each thinker proposed a different strategy for empowering those who had to discharge the Mandate of Heaven to good effect. Some argued that society could best be run by a person of moral authority who ruled by example. Others claimed that nothing short of total and absolute power would do. For some, 'to be in or to be out' was the question. There were those who insisted that the best way to govern is not to govern, and others who made the case that ruling by indirect means was most effective. Idealists dreamed up theories of what they thought society ought to be; realists looked at the hard realities of the Warring States world in which they lived and conceived of politics as the art of what was possible there and then.

Positioning oneself

The easiest route into Chinese political philosophy is to start from where it originated: the battlefield. As the philosopher and sinologist Roger Ames points out, Chinese military texts are themselves 'applied philosophy'. Nearly every ancient Chinese philosopher or theorist reflects on warfare or draws analogies from it. Alongside Confucian, Legalist and other masters, military experts were just another group among the men of service that peregrinated from state to state offering advice. Since warfare was the currency of the day, the cross-fertilization that took place between Chinese military tactics and political strategies is no surprise.

China's most important surviving treatise on military strategy is *Master Sun's Art of Warfare* (*Sunzi bing fa*), also known as *The Art of Warfare*. It is a text that can be read simply as a technical and psychological guide to military tactics (as such, it continues to be studied in military academies around the world). But *The Art of Warfare* is much more powerful if read as a treatise on strategy in general. The book says as much about how to manage people as it does about how to use weapons, for it contains stratagems, images and metaphors that can be extended into many aspects of life.

The Art of Warfare (surviving in a received version of thirteen chapters, to which a manuscript find in 1972 added another five), deals with methods of waging war. It discusses the economics of war, the psychology of conflict, and gives advice on reconnaissance and intelligence-gathering. Historically, there may have been more than one Master Sun: Sun Wu, a contemporary of Confucius, and his descendant, Sun Bin, who lived about a century later. But the text is most likely the product of several hands, compiled sometime during the mid fifth to early fourth century BCE. Master Sun came to represent the archetypical paragon of military genius alongside other military masters whose names are associated with similar treatises (such as *The Master Wu* or *The Methods of Sima*). A famous anecdote in Master Sun's biography recounts how he persuaded the King of Wu to employ him by bossing around a troupe of palace ladies as if they were soldiers. He divided them into regiments, and, when the women knew no better than to giggle in response to their drill orders, Master Sun executed the king's two favourite concubines who had been assigned the role of unit commanders. Orders must be obeyed. Like the exemplary general who aspires to lead a harmoniously operating troop of warriors, the ultimate aim for those who lead society is to achieve social discipline, order and harmony reminiscent of that of a well-drilled army.

The core message of *The Art of Warfare* is that clever strategic thinking should make actual battle avoidable. Victory ought to precede battle. War represents a loss: 'If one is not fully cognizant of the disasters of waging war, one cannot be fully cognizant of how to turn war to one's best advantage' (*Sunzi bing fa* 2). But if having to cross swords is a form of defeat, what, then, is there to be learned? The genius of Master Sun lies in the strategies he devises to get to the point where battle can only be the final resort. Rather than being forced to fight, the good commander tries to achieve his goal by strategic positioning: 'To gain a hundred victories in a hundred battles is not the highest excellence. The highest excellence is to subdue the enemy's army without fighting at all' (*Sunzi bing fa* 3). Instead of confronting an opponent head on, it is better to start by attacking his plans first, and drive a wedge through any alliances he might have forged with others. Attempting to scale a walled city should be the very last option.

So the perfect battle is won before a single clash of arms has occurred or a single soldier has given his life. Only when these strategic battles of the mind have been tested to the full does a commander order an attack on an actual army. Rather than relying on brute and reactive force, the aim is to gain strategic advantage over your enemy through intelligence and anticipation. The exemplary commander shows restraint and self-control. He remains hidden and invisible, and is highly adaptable to changing circumstances. He is a master in the art of dissimulation. In the end, the Dao of warfare is nothing but a game of deception: 'Although you are capable, show your enemy that you are incapable. When you commit to deploying your troops, pretend to be inactive. When nearby, make it appear as if you are at a distance; when far away, seem near' (*Sunzi bing fa* 1). The aim is to make the enemy move rather than be moved by him (*Sunzi bing fa* 6). In addition, a commander should not crave fame, reputation or reward for bravery; instead, he should seek victory where it is easily gained (*Sunzi bing fa* 4).

'Circumstance', 'position', 'power base', 'potential', 'strategic advantage', 'positional advantage' all translate the Chinese term *shi*. A commander derives his courage and physical strength from his vital *qi*, but he is not tempted to engage in full-on battle from the word go. In order to control a situation and eventually gain victory, he develops ways to assess his strategic advantage. Like someone playing the stock market or setting out a football team on the pitch, the good commander manipulates and responds to circumstances. He hedges his options and manoeuvres himself in such a way that, when he is forced to act, he will always start from a superior position. Thus he takes into account all factors that could influence the outcome of his decisions and actions: topography and terrain, timing, psychology of the enemy, logistics, military intelligence. One of several images used in *The Art of Warfare* to illustrate this notion of 'advantage-derived-from-positioning-yourself' is that of a crossbow that has been drawn and stretched to the maximum such that it would require only one effortless pull of the trigger to shoot and kill from a distance. The victim would have no time to see where the arrow came from or even register what had happened. But for this shot to be efficient, the bow needs to remain at maximum stretch. The sense of power and threat conveyed by not having to pull the trigger depends on the crossbow being kept fully drawn.

The tactical key is the ability to react to changing circumstances: new troop configurations, new weapons, adaptable strategic manoeuvres, up-to-date intelligence. Paired with this is learning how to anticipate: knowing when to act or fight, and knowing when not to. One's effectiveness in reaching one's final goal depends on self-knowledge and being fully informed: 'He who knows the enemy and himself will never be at risk in a hundred battles. He who does not know the enemy but knows himself will sometimes win and sometimes lose. He who knows neither the enemy nor himself will be at risk in every battle' (*Sunzi bing fa* 3). The strength of an army thus lies not in its capability to attack but in its ability to defend and preserve itself: 'He who is expert at defence hides himself in the deepest recesses of the earth; he who is expert at attacking strikes from out of the highest reaches of the heavens. Thus he is able to protect both himself and to take the complete victory' (*Sunzi bing fa* 4). Put differently, the aim is to provoke your opponent into showing his vulnerabilities while hiding and covering up your own weak points. It is this knack to seemingly act without acting that needs to be nurtured in those who lead. Like the martial arts fighter, the strategy is to avoid being hit. Appearing aimless will prompt the opposing party to reveal its aims. Thus by focusing on those factors over which you have control, you can lure your opponent into a position of vulnerability: 'Invincibility lies with yourself; vulnerability lies with the enemy' (*Sunzi bing fa* 4). To conquer the world and be competitive, it is of the essence to keep yourself intact and preserve your moral and physical health.

But let there be no mistake about the end game in *The Art of Warfare*. There is no middle ground on which to meet your opponent: no handshakes, no compromises, no ceasefire. The ultimate goal must be nothing less than total victory – quick rather than protracted – and the total annihilation of the enemy: by all means possible, but preferably by minimal means and non-confrontation. Hit your opponent by evening when his *qi* or morale is at its lowest (*Sunzi bing fa* 7). Avoid head-on or direct confrontation. Victory should be the necessary and predictable outcome of skilful planning. It need not depend on a soldier's martial talents, brute physical force or sophisticated weaponry (though you must make sure all is in perfect working order, nevertheless). Victory results from the way a commander has manipulated circumstances and his troops' position. Master Sun recommends methods we would associate with modern guerrilla warfare. If he lived in the twenty-first century, drones directed via satellites from distant control rooms would no doubt be part of his arsenal.

What emerges in *The Art of Warfare* is a portrait of the exemplary commander as someone who possesses all the character traits, intelligence and other virtues required by anyone in charge of a large group of people. The Chinese ruler can be seen as the political double of the general (who, according to the text, acts like the people's Master of Fate, deciding their lot and overseeing their security). Just as an army requires one single voice of command to operate harmoniously, so society requires one leader or sage-ruler at its helm. Master Sun insists that skilful command means being able to lead and reward the army 'as if it was one person'. The relationship between the general and his troops is parental, but for it to be effective the general must be strict and not overly lenient towards his military dependents:

> Because he regards his men as if they were his own infants, they will advance with him into the deepest valleys.
> Because he regards his troops as if they were his own

beloved sons, they will be willing to die by his side. If they are well treated but can't be deployed, if he loves them but they don't heed his commands, or when they are so undisciplined he cannot control them, they are like spoiled children that cannot be put to good use. (*Sunzi bing fa* 10)

Many of the principles that render a troop formation operational and victorious can be weapons in the armoury of those tasked with a leading role in society: clear instructions, consistency in following through on one's orders, clear-cut and efficient organizational hierarchies, unquestionable dedication, courage, energy, aspiring to be the best. Small wonder, then, that *The Art of Warfare* has become one of the world's most read and interpreted classics. Its theories and stratagems have been applied to many domains of life: from social relationships to political manoeuvres and the art of conducting business negotiations.

Ruling by example

Like an army with an enlightened general at its helm, society should be ruled by a vanguard of morally accomplished people. This ideal of society as a harmonious (*he*) community led by an exemplary elite is at the forefront of the philosophy of China's most enduring and influential thinker: Confucius. The personality traits that make up the authoritative Confucian person converge around a set of values that permeate Chinese social and political thought. These so-called Confucian virtues include a sense of righteousness (*yi*), sincerity (*cheng*) or trustworthiness (*xin*), benevolence or humaneness (*ren*), ritual propriety (*li*), filial devotion (*xiao*), and a desire to be loyal (*zhong*), considerate (*shu*) and knowledge-able (*zhi*). But let us look first at what we know about the person and the work associated with him.

Confucius is the Latinized form of Kong Fuzi (Master Kong, meaning that he was born into the Kong family). His official name was Kong Qiu, his courtesy name (a name given when one reached adulthood) was Zhongni. Our knowledge of Confucius's life is patchy. For a biography we have to skip three or four centuries to a chapter in Sima Qian's *Historical Records* (Chapter 47). But reconstructing a historical and chronological account of Confucius's life would have been difficult. The only vaguely reliable information Sima Qian had to hand were fragments from the *Analects*, a text notoriously devoid of historical context. The mass of oral and written information linked to Confucius that circulated in the four centuries after his death proved hard to organize into a cohesive biography. Moreover, as with all biographies of famous figures, biographers have their own agenda. Having lost favour with Emperor Han Wudi, who had condemned him to the cruellest punishment of castration, Sima Qian saw himself as a shadow double of Confucius: an unrecognized and 'uncrowned' king, whose ideas failed to gain the ear of those in power. In short, his biography of Confucius coalesces around a series of facts and incidents sourced from other texts in what almost certainly is an anachronistic account. It is therefore best to think of Confucius as an eponymous figure – that is, someone embodying a set of ideas and ideals not clearly traceable to a specific time or place. His name has been used as a foot to fit many an authorial shoe. As early as the fourth and early third centuries BCE, he was typecast in various ways: mythologized and credited with superhuman perspicacity, caricatured or depicted as a hero with unnatural physical features (a protruding lump on his head). A quasi-hagiography developed around him in later times, including a tale of his miraculous birth that tells how his mother was impregnated by a spirit in a dream.

The main source of Confucius's thought and related biographical information are the *Analects* (*Lunyu*). *Analects* translates 'selected' (*lun*) 'sayings' (*yu*). Scholars have dated the compilation and completion of the text a little before, or around, 400 BCE, but debates still abound as to its provenance. Since the text is unattested before the Han dynasty, some have labelled it as a Han text. Yet some of its language appears to belong to an older stratum than the classical Chinese used in Han times. So the text is almost certainly layered: the first fifteen of its twenty chapters are accepted as coming close to Confucius's own words; the final five probably contain additions from later times. A version of the *Analects* was engraved in stone, alongside other classics, during the latter part of the second century CE. Once the text was 'petrified', the stone permitted multiple impressions, in the form of ink rubbings, and hence wide circulation. The *Analects* is best regarded as an assortment of brief statements, anecdotes and dialogues between Master Kong and his disciples which over time evolved into a book. It is not informed by one historical Confucius.

Confucius emerges as a relatively ordinary person – neither a political activist nor a religious leader claiming divine status of any kind. He was born in 551 BCE in the small state of Lu, in a town near Qufu on the Shandong peninsula. His ancestors were members of the lower aristocracy, office holders who found themselves experiencing economic and social hardship by the time of his birth. Confucius was educated by his mother and lost his father at a very young age. For most of his life, he was active in the private domain as a clerk and minor official, before spending the rest of his days fulfilling his vocation for public service. He took no interest in the military – a brave career choice given the belligerent times in which he lived. Instead, he devoted himself to learning about the culture and rituals of the long-gone Zhou kings, whom he idealized as models of moral rule. He is said to have had a son who predeceased him, as well as a daughter. Not much else is known about his private life. A circle of disciples gathered around him, perhaps as many as three thousand. The *Analects* feature just over two dozen named disciples, each with their own character, strengths and foibles. The poor and frugal Yan Hui is Confucius's favourite and most gifted disciple. On several occasions Confucius laments his untimely death. Zigong, a merchant, is a more statesman-like figure, admired but also criticized for his stubbornness. When his master died (in 479 BCE) and the prescribed three-year mourning period had ended, Zigong built a hut beside the grave mound and stayed for an extra three years. Another disciple, Zengzi, is known as a staunch advocate of filial piety. Confucius's teachings take shape through this master–disciple relationship. Together with them, he roamed from state to state offering his teachings to a string of local lords and rulers.

Not surprisingly, the biographical narrative of Confucius prefigures some of the values he is associated with. As a child, he likes to play with ritual vessels (why bother with a football if you can play with a missal?). He is interested in music, craves being called to office but has no desire to serve unworthy rulers. Frustration and a fear of political failure resonate throughout. A sense of perpetual rootlessness informs his thinking about trust, loyalty and family. But there is a touch of resignation, too, in his belief that people of talent will always be on the move, either by force or by volition. The discomfort of upping sticks inspires him: 'A gentleman who is attached to a settled home is not worthy of being a gentleman' (*An.* 14.2). He is chronically anxious about being misunderstood. When he is in office, all is said to run smoothly. In the presence of women, he appears uneasy and cold, even sexist: 'Only women and petty persons are hard to manage. If you draw them close, they become insolent; if you keep them at a distance, they become resentful' (*An.* 17.25). Greeted with respect and courtesy at each port of call, Confucius eventually is always forced to leave either because his advice falls on deaf ears or because he deems his patron morally unworthy. Sima Qian's biography has the Master end up back in his small home state of Lu, not to work in government but to edit and write. His talents neglected and unrecognized, he dies in his early seventies, little realizing that he would go down in history as China's 'Supreme Sage'.

Confucius's philosophy is first and foremost a code of conduct for the ruling class (he was after all of noble descent himself). The term he uses to describe the morally accomplished person who inspires by example is *junzi* (literally, 'son of a lord'). *Junzi* is somewhat awkwardly translated into English as 'gentleman'. This accurately reflects the fact that Confucius himself probably did not have women in mind when

Figure 3.1
Confucius sculpture by Wu Weishan at Clare College, Cambridge.

analysing the human condition (although a tradition describing virtuous women would emerge later). Yet the *junzi* is more than someone who is simply polite, courteous or honourable. Originally it referred to a person of good stock who commanded some social standing. Over time it came to mean a person with good moral credentials, someone whose pedigree was not merely measured by blood and descent but by deeds and behaviour. Pre-Confucian texts already identify several core personal qualities required to deserve the accolade of being a 'superior person' (my less literal translation of *junzi*): to uphold ritual norms; revere, respect and emulate one's ancestors; to radiate self-confidence; to possess insight, foresight and wisdom; to be courageous, trustworthy and loyal; to be able both to serve and command the service of others.

For Confucius, leadership means moral leadership before all else. A ruler's authority is grounded in his gift to inspire others by example. Confucius has little to say about institutions. He has an almost blind (and at times naïve) belief in the idea that good and positive role models will inspire good and positive behaviour in others. In the Confucian perspective, power derives almost entirely from moral character. Leaders are there to be looked up to, not because they have the power to put you down if you refuse to do so, but because people will spontaneously crane their necks to emulate someone who displays praiseworthy conduct: 'The virtue of the gentleman is like wind; the virtue of the small man is like grass. Let the wind blow over the grass and it is sure to bend' (*An*. 12.19). Ruling by good example should put the ruler in a position that 'can be compared to the pole star: it commands the respect of the multitude of stars, without leaving its place' (*An*. 2.1). But in order to avoid others messing up your firmament, you have to shine and work at it. Leading is about cultivating character, knowing that the rest will follow, according to the Confucian philosopher Xunzi (Xun Qing; fourth/third century BCE), who uses the image of a sundial and a bowl to illustrate this: 'The ruler is the sundial; the people are the shadow. If the form is upright, then the shadow will be upright. The ruler is the bowl; the people the water. If the bowl is round, then the water will be round; if it is square, then the water will be square' (*Xunzi* 12.4).

Leading, for Confucius, also requires positioning oneself, or, more specifically, cultivating an awareness of one's station in society. Although it is possible to climb up through the ranks on the basis of merit and diligent study, Confucian society is inherently hierarchical (which is not always the same as unequal). The power and efficiency with which you perform your tasks is intimately related to the role you inhabit in a community. Role consciousness, or being aware of your job description, is key. 'Let the ruler be a ruler, the minister a minister, the father a father, the son a son' (*An.* 12.11). You should only engage in government, therefore, if that is within the remit of your role: 'Do not concern yourself with matters of policy unless they are the responsibility of your office' (*An.* 8.14, 14.26). If members of a group know what is expected of them, something resembling harmony will result. Social order can ultimately only be guaranteed when its members develop an internal moral compass. The argument here is not that we are predestined to occupy (or are manacled to) a particular position in society from which there is no chance of escape; the point made is that, when inhabiting a certain role, we must make sure we understand the expectations, obligations and etiquette that come with it. A ruler who behaves like a child in constant need of advice from others will lose his authority. A head of state who feels it necessary to act as if she is simply one of the people will see her power wane. While president, be presidential. While a servant, be subservient.

The aspiration is to rule by promoting harmony. Dissonance and conflict can be overcome by relying on moral prompting and persuasion. This also implies that those who control other people should be able to control their own emotions too. A balanced society requires balanced individuals at its helm. The opening section of *The Doctrine of the Mean* (*Zhongyong*), a chapter in *The Ritual Records* (*Liji*), speaks of the gentleman as someone who 'centres himself':

> The moment at which joy and anger, grief and pleasure have yet to emerge is called the [internal] equilibrium. Once the emotions have emerged, that they are all brought into proper measure is called harmony. 'Centring' is the great root of the world; 'harmony' is advancing the Dao ... The gentleman upholds the golden mean; petty people distort it ... Upholding the mean is a task of the highest order. It is rare among the common people to be able to sustain it. (*Zhongyong* 1/2/3)

'Centring' of course can be read in more than one way. The most important consequence (intended or not) of the need to maintain an equilibrium in society is that the ruler must be or ends up at the centre of attention. Programmed into the moral consciousness of the Confucian ruler is the belief that the common people require good leadership as they are inherently incapable of providing it themselves: 'The common people can be made to follow a path but not to understand it' (*An.* 8.9). In other words, there is no expectation that all members of society are political animals, as long as the ruler commands the trust of the people he is 'shepherding' (a term that was used sometimes to mean 'ruling'):

> Zigong asked about government. The Master said, 'Give them enough food, give them enough arms, and make sure the common people have trust in you.' Zigong asked, 'If I had to give up one of these three, which should I give up first?' 'Give up arms.' Zigong said, 'If one had to give up one

of the remaining two, which should one give up first?' 'Give up food. Death has always been with us since the beginning of time, but when there is no trust, the common people will have nothing to stand on.' (*An.* 12.7)

Conversely, there is an obligation on those who have skills and moral integrity to serve in society and work on behalf of others. Confucius has little respect for those wishing to keep their talents hidden and not putting them to good use. He turns his back on female beauty and other 'gifts' and distractions that detract from serving the state. But the climate for service needs to be right. The men holding the reins of power in his days he decries as folk 'of such limited capacity that they hardly count' (*An.* 13.20), yet one should not govern at all costs, nor serve incompetent rulers: 'When the Dao prevails in the world, show yourself; when it does not, hide yourself' (*An.* 8.13).

It is imperative, therefore, for the ruler to be able to select a group of talented people. This requires playing out against each other those with potential and exposing those who have already acquired status and position to competition: 'You can tell those who are above average about the best, but not those who are below average' (*An.* 6.21). The aim should be to 'raise those who are straight and set them over the crooked' (*An.* 2.19, 12.22). The good ruler is thus a master at scouting around for the best, and conscious that there is competition: 'Promote those you do recognize. Do you suppose others will allow those you fail to recognize to be passed over?' (*An.* 13.2). The same applies to personal relations. Here the Confucian gentleman combines professional discernment with emotional intelligence. He picks his friends carefully: 'To befriend those who are upright, true to their word and well informed will benefit you; to befriend those who are ingratiating in action, pleasant in appearance and glib in speech will cause you a loss' (*An*. 16.4).

Ruling by personal example is the only way to gain credence and credibility. Politics is not simply about functions, roles and offices, it is about the personalities who inhabit them: 'To govern means to be correct. If you set an example by being correct yourself, who will dare to be incorrect?' (*An*. 12.17). Competent and inspiring rulers exude a radiance that attracts good people to them: 'Ensure that those who are near are pleased, and those who are far away are attracted to you' (*An*. 13.16). To draw people near, the Confucian gentleman must at all times set standards for himself that are more stringent and exacting than what is expected of others: 'If you demand much of yourself but make allowance for others when making demands on them, you will keep ill will at bay' (*An*. 15.15). To be in power also requires a knack of adjusting oneself to changes in the world and acknowledging that no ruler is ever wholly capable of controlling and mastering everything society throws up.

Is there a space in which one may reprimand or criticize someone with 'pole-stellar' qualities? Again, contesting authority or showing disagreement requires correct positioning. Rather than confronting your superior head on or slicing through an argument with open confrontation, Confucius suggests assuming an attitude of passive aggression. One should remain silent or contrite in the presence of people of authority. Instead of expressing openly that someone is wrong, remain compliant and suggest that there are alternative views or methods. Here is how Confucius speaks of his most intelligent disciple: 'I can speak to Yan Hui all day long without him disagreeing with me in any way, as though he were stupid. But then when I take a closer look at what he does in private after he has withdrawn from my presence, I discover that, in fact, it throws light on what I said. Indeed there is nothing slow about Yan Hui!' (*An.* 2.9). Contradiction and disagreement must be allowed to exist, but instead of attempting to debunk or expose an argument through confrontation it is better to wrap up dissent and present it as an alternative: 'For a man quick with a retort there are frequent occasions on which he will incur the hatred of others' (*An.* 5.5). Direct results require indirect methods. The core question for Confucius is not whether you are for or against, but whether something is moral or not: 'In his dealings with the world the gentleman is not invariably for or against a person. He is on the side of what is right' (*An.* 4.10). He therefore makes a distinction between genuinely agreeing with someone's point of view, and absorbing its essence, and merely appearing to agree with someone in a position of authority: 'The gentleman seeks harmony with others without being an echo. The petty man echoes without being in harmony' (*An.* 13.23). Safer than trying to secure universal approval is to create the conditions in which those who are morally upstanding are drawn to you and those who are not avoid you (*An.* 13.24).

Confucius was not the only thinker who believed that leadership required skill and moral worth. We find similar echoes in a work associated with Master Mo (Mozi or Mo Di; *c.*479–381

BCE), whom we will encounter at greater length in the next chapter. On the issue of who should be a leader, Mozi and his followers, known as Mohists, asserted that one should always aim to 'elevate worth and employ ability', as the ancients had done: 'Even if someone worked as a farmer, craftsman or merchant, if they had ability they were promoted, given high rank and a generous salary; they were entrusted with responsibility and provided with executive power' (*Mozi* 8.5). If the worthy and able are selected for the job, favouritism, factionalism and destructive rivalries can be forestalled. Master Mo paints a sanguine picture of capable and utterly dedicated officials and administrators, 'leaving early and coming back late, ploughing and harvesting, planting trees and gathering pulses and grain' (*Mozi* 9.2).

But who will guarantee that rulers (or parents, or teachers) get it right? Unlike Confucius, for whom any person of virtue may rise through a family-based hierarchy to take on the role, Mozi trusts only one force, Heaven, as the ultimate source of moral authority. For Mozi, Heaven provides the sole and non-negotiable standard against which everything should be measured. Allowing any lesser agent to make that judgement (such as one's family, one's acquaintances, associates or other contacts) would mean giving in to bias and partiality. Good rulers, Mozi claims, model themselves on Heaven. That is how they know how not to discriminate between 'poor and rich, noble and base, those far removed and those near at hand, or close and distant relatives' (*Mozi* 9.8). Mozi's Heaven is the supreme moral guarantor policing those who rule. Thus those who gain power and are competent at wielding it draw on Heaven.

The Mohist Heaven is impartial and generous. It is object-ive, imposes uniform standards and distributes benefits to all. But there is a snag. Submitting to the will of Heaven must also mean that, ultimately, the ruler can fall short and may rightfully be ignored: 'There are many in the world who are rulers, but only few that are humane. So if everyone took their own rulers as a standard, then this would mean one would take the inhumane as a standard. This is not acceptable as a benchmark' (*Mozi* 4.2). The thrust of his argument is that moral standards cannot be negotiated, nor can the bar of what is morally acceptable be moved at the whim of ordinary mortals. This cascades from the top downwards. Once the best individuals are in position at every level, and appointed on a meritocratic basis, absolute obedience to one's superi-ors should be the rule: 'If your superior considers something to be wrong, you too must consider it wrong.' If everyone, from the village head up to the Son of Heaven, reports up-wards on things good or bad, order will prevail. The ruler at the top should be no exception. At the same time, everyone, from top to bottom, should have their moral antennae tuned to Heaven: 'If the people of the world all obey their supe-riors up to the Son of Heaven but the people do not obey Heaven, heavenly calamities will still not be avoided' (*Mozi* 11.4). In the end, then, power for Mozi consists in having your subjects pass on information and conform upwards in total confidence, or, to put it differently, secure blind submission to capable superiors. Mozi's Heaven feels almost human: it sees everything, it can love or hate and it has a will. It also has a sense of justice: 'The will of Heaven to me is like the compass to the wheelwright, or the square to the carpenter. The wheelwright and carpenter take their compass and square to measure what is round and square in the world, saying: "What fits is right, what does not fit is wrong"' (*Mozi* 27.10). Those who rule, then, ought to replicate these moral standards within themselves, and those who fail to live up to Heaven's standards merit punishment.

Mozi also takes a firm stand against offensive warfare, which he considers the gravest of crimes. Failing to condemn aggression, lauding war as a necessary means to a greater end, or not recognizing the fundamental injustice in warfare, is wrong. There should be no difference morally between rejecting a small crime and rejecting warfare: 'If you kill one person, you are branded as unrighteous and should pay for this crime with your own life. Reasoning along these lines: if you kill ten persons, you are ten times as unrighteous and should pay for these crimes with ten lives; and if you kill a hundred people, you are a hundred times as unrighteous and should pay for these crimes with a hundred lives' (*Mozi* 17.2). Yet Mozi does not advocate all-out pacifism. He allows for the possibility of attacking rogue states, if needed, or defending oneself against aggression by others. The human and economic cost of warfare, however, never validates what might be gained by conflict: 'If you send officers and men to certain death and aggravate the misfortunes of superiors and inferiors, with the sole purpose of capturing a town in ruins, you waste what you do not have enough of to gain what you already have in excess. To govern like this is a disservice to the state' (*Mozi* 18.2). Warfare not only harms the people, it can also violate the will of Heaven and the spirits who, ultimately, are the only objective arbiters to judge whether a state has lost the mandate to rule or even exist.

The belief in the force of moral power is repeated ad nauseam by Confucius and Mozi, to the extent that one wonders how much they were men of the world, taking stock of what was happening around them at the time. The mantra that only the talented, morally cultivated and worthy should be put forward is largely inspired by looking back to the past and the ancient and former kings. In their eyes the ancients are the future, and Confucius and Mozi are idealists. They find comfort in the past and concentrate on the prospect of what the world could look like. Confucius was a teacher and philosopher, not a man of practical politics. However, some snippets from the *Analects* hint that even the Master had a human side. A life exclusively dedicated to service and flawless moral conduct proved a tough sell, and he understood this: 'I have yet to meet the man who is as fond of virtue as he is of female beauty' (*An.* 9.18, 15.13). Confucius also acknowledged that the incentive of material reward is part of the psychology of many who seek power. Unlike most other main philosophers of his time, Confucius valued pleasure and a modicum of luxury and enjoyment, as long as such comforts did not detract from the gentleman's mission to rule by example.

Doing nothing

There was a counter-current to the proactive moral leadership proposed by Confucius and Mozi. Some thinkers argued that the best way to run society and master the world was to be passive. In the Daoist view, ultimate power resides in non-action and non-intervention. The core concept here is *wu wei*, which means something like effortless action, non-action, minimal intervention or passive achievement. *The Classic of the Way and Virtue* sets out the position with poetic eloquence: to rule you need to not rule; to learn it is better to not learn. Like the general whose final aim is not to fight, the sage-ruler does not try to be proactive. Instead, he maintains the peace by interfering in a minimal way. He nips things in the bud, and addresses problems when they are in their germinal stage. In that sense, he does nothing yet nothing is neglected: 'The Way never acts yet nothing is left undone. Should lords and princes be able to hold fast to it [the Way], the myriad creatures [all living things] will be transformed of their own accord' (*DDJ* 37). The greatest efficacy is achieved by minimal effort and energy. If one sets targets the population can spontaneously identify with, the state should run itself; an overload of laws, regulations, doctrines, schemes and new technology unbalances the natural order in society. The assumption here (as with Confucius) is that society is naturally harmonious.

Daoists take this idea to extremes by suggesting that, instead of micromanaging affairs through an army of busy, ant-like officials, the ruler should be blind to his immediate surroundings. That way he will avoid being distracted and can concentrate on the really important and essential tasks. Powerful are those who know what goes on in the world without having to witness it personally: 'Without going out the door, one can know the whole world; without looking out from the window, one can see the Way of Heaven. The further one goes, the less one knows. Therefore the sage knows without having to stir, identifies without having to see, accomplishes without having to act' (*DDJ* 47). The Daoist take on governance is as sceptical of the power of government through top-down diktat as it might today denounce government-by-tweet, because dictator and instigator alike remain shackled by their wish to micromanage or their compulsion to have a view on everything. The best way to govern, therefore, is hands off: 'Whoever gains the world and wishes to do anything to it, I see that they will have no respite. The world is a sacred vessel and nothing should be done to it. Whoever wants to do something to it will ruin it; whoever wants to grab hold of it will lose it' (*DDJ* 29). Craving power will naturally result in being deprived of it.

Unsurprisingly, a common theme in Daoist texts is the refusal to take up office. There is virtue in not getting involved in government and having less ambition, or none at all. Given the political circumstances in an age of warfare or conflict, there were bound to be thinkers whose philosophy would revolve around variations on the theme of 'how to say no'. The most famous snub to a job offer in early China occurs in a story in *The Master Zhuang*:

> Master Zhuang was fishing in the Pu River. The King of Chu dispatched two high-ranking officials to go before him with this message: 'I wish to trouble you with the administration of my realm.' Without turning around, Master Zhuang just kept holding on to his fishing rod and said: 'I have heard that in Chu there is a sacred tortoise that already has been dead for three thousand years. The

king stores it in his ancestral temple inside a hamper wrapped with cloth. Do you think this tortoise would rather be dead and have its bones preserved as objects of veneration, or be alive and dragging its tail through the mud?' 'It would rather be alive and dragging its tail through the mud,' said the two officials. 'Begone!' said Master Zhuang. 'I'd rather be dragging my tail through the mud.' (*Zhuangzi* 17.5)

From the Daoist perspective, then, there are occasions when being useless and worthless to society, or living in a way that is beyond normal social expectations, constitute an act of self-preservation. A tree with warped and twisted branches is more likely to escape the axe of the lumberjack than a straight one. Being blind or deaf can be a serious impediment to your career in public office, but it will save you from being conscripted into the army and, in the Warring States period, almost certain death on the battlefield. Several stories in *The Master Zhuang* parody the Confucius figure for not appreciating the vanity of the ambition to accumulate knowledge, put oneself through an arduous education and training, and aspire to public office. In one of the more colourful anecdotes, Confucius ends up sending away his disciples and retires to a marsh. Dressed in animal skins and happy to live on acorns and chestnuts, he moves among the herds of animals and flocks of birds without disturbing them: 'If even birds and beasts were not afraid of him, how much less were men!' (*Zhuangzi* 20.4).

One can argue that the Daoist does not have much to offer in the form of a viable guide to practical power and politics. In many ways, it is the antithesis to Confucius's call for service and social engagement. Or perhaps not entirely? The Chinese term for 'acting effortlessly' (*wu wei*), discussed earlier, occurs once in the *Analects* (*An.* 15.5). And remember that the pole star is fixed and does not move at all. In several passages, Confucius insists that rulers should be so charismatic in their own conduct (and astute in selecting followers who are good role models) that people will submit to them spontaneously and without needing to be forced. In reality, however, there are fundamentally different expectations here. Whereas Confucians conceive of society as an intricate social network operated by an educated elite, Daoists argue that the good society is one that does not aspire to rise above the level of a simple and self-contained unit. Here is how *The Classic of the Way and Virtue* pictures the ideal community:

> Reduce the size of the state and its population. Make sure that, even though the people have labour-saving tools, they are never used. See to it that they take death seriously and they will be reluctant to move to distant places. Even when they have boats and carts, they will have no use for them. Even when they have armour and weapons, they will have no reason to make use of them. See to it that the people return to the use of the knotted rope [i.e. keep records by making knots in a cord rather than writing them down], that they will find their food savoury, their clothes fine, their houses comfortable, their lives happy. Then even if adjoining states are within sight of each other, and even when they can hear each other's dogs bark and cocks crow, the people will grow old and die without ever having had dealings with one another. (*DDJ* 80)

What comfort can be derived from knowing that the dog barking in your neighbourhood is a terrier or Dalmatian? Trying to find out will merely frustrate you in the end as you scramble across the fence only to be met by an irate neighbour. Curiosity can be stimulating but also damaging. The message is to stay at home, content with your lot, instead of turning yourself into a travelling salesman of ideas, always on the move and with doors constantly slammed in your face. Happy are those who know less:

> In the pursuit of learning, one knows more every day;
> in the pursuit of the Dao, one does less every day.
> One does less and less until one does nothing at all,
> and when one does nothing at all there is nothing
> that is undone. It is always through not meddling
> that the world is won. As soon as you actively meddle
> with it, you will fall short of winning the world.
> (*DDJ* 48)

The ideal Daoist ruler is in control, not because he is fully hands off or does nothing at all, but because he does as little as possible and times his actions to take place at the most opportune moments. He possesses instinctive ability, rather than socially endorsed intellect. Like planning victory before being dragged into battle, non-intervention implies tackling problems at their most manageable stage:

> What is stable is easily upheld, what has yet to begin is
> easily planned for. What is brittle is easily broken, what
> is faint is easily dispersed. Do things before they become
> something. Bring order before they become disordered.

A tree with a span of two arms embraced is born from
the tip of a hair. A terrace nine stories high rises from a
layer of dirt. A journey of a thousand miles begins with
one step. (*DDJ* 64)

Effortless action as proposed in texts such as *The Classic of
the Way and Virtue* and *The Master Zhuang* hardly provided
the most practicable guide for handling the challenges and
complexities of a society that was undergoing profound social
transformation. During the Western Han period, there was a
moment when a faction at court that advocated minimalist
government gained some influence (it included an empress
who was besotted with *The Classic of the Way and Virtue*).
Known as adepts of Huang-Lao thought (a composite of the
names of the legendary Yellow Emperor and Laozi), they included several individuals with a background in the military,
hostile to the idea that scholars and bureaucrats should run
government. They proposed withdrawal and retirement from
active politics as the best means to preserve life (which, for
one of them, alas, meant giving in to drink). However, this
brief romance with Daoism as an ideology at court soon ebbed
away when Emperor Han Wudi elevated Confucian scholars
to office.

Governing the world by dragging one's tail through the mud
may not be the best formula for pragmatic politics. Yet underneath a philosophy of withdrawal, deeply cynical of the power
of proactive leadership, lay a hidden means of facilitating absolute power. Circumstances do exist when non-intervention
and a distrust of education, social rules and codes of conduct
can play to the advantage of those in power: 'In ancient times,

those who excelled in practising the Way did not use it to enlighten the people, but rather to keep them in the dark. The reason why people are hard to govern is because they know too much. So to rule a state by cleverness will be the detriment of the state. Not to rule the state by cleverness will be a blessing to the state' (*DDJ* 65). Keeping people in a state of ignorance can embolden those who covet power; here passive and spontaneous Daoist non-action contains echoes of a political philosophy that offers the polar opposite to government by moral example.

Total power

In contrast to Confucius and Mozi, one set of thinkers, known as Legalists, profoundly distrusted the idea that moral worth makes good government. 'Legalist' is an imperfect translation deriving from the Chinese term *fa*, 'law' or 'standard'. It resonates with our understanding of law in the West but does not coincide with it. At the heart of Legalist thought is the claim that each and every action must be measured against clearly articulated standards issued by a supreme authority:

> The clear-sighted ruler is attentive to laws and regulations. He does not heed words that do not conform to the law; he does not esteem behaviour that does not conform to the law; he does not undertake a task that does not conform to the law. If words conform to the law, they are heeded; if behaviour conforms to the law, it is esteemed; if a task conforms to the law, it is undertaken. (*Shangjun shu* 23.4)

To achieve total power, one must create the total state. A recipe for how this may be achieved can be found in the foundational text of Legalist thought, *The Book of Lord Shang* (*Shangjun shu*). Like many texts from early China, this book accreted over time and comprises more than one voice. But at its core are the crystallized ideas of Shang Yang (Gongsun Yang; fourth century BCE), or Lord Shang, the statesman whose ideology and political reforms bolstered the power of the state of Qin, which ultimately delivered China's first unified empire. After a period in the employ of Lord Wen of Wei (r. 446–396 BCE), Shang Yang became an adviser and chief minister to Lord Xiao of Qin (r. 361–338 BCE).

Lord Shang argues that the ruler should have total control over the human and material resources in his state (there is no point in having rules if there is no ruler to enforce them). People benefit from strict hierarchies and order, hence distinctions between a ruler and his subjects, as well as those between a ruler and his ministers, should be unambiguously clear. Those who take liberties with the law and deviate from prescribed standards must be punished. Instead of judging government by the moral worth of those who govern, Legalists believe that harsh and impersonal policies, detached from human 'likes and dislikes', are, on balance, more effective: 'The True Monarch prohibits through rewards and encourages through punishments; he pursues transgressions and not goodness; he relies on punishments to eradicate punishments' (*Shangjun shu* 7.6).

The Book of Lord Shang starts from the premise that human beings are intrinsically selfish. You can teach people to live their lives by a moral compass, but only up to a point. When populations grow and resources are scarce, education is not enough. People will do anything to pursue wealth and status, even if it means breaking the rules and endangering themselves or others. To prevent social turmoil, the state needs to empower itself: 'When the people are weak, the state is strong; when the people are strong, the state is weak. Hence the state that possesses the Way devotes itself to weakening the people' (*Shangjun shu* 20.1). It is not possible to change people and alter their basic instincts, but one can manipulate people's selfish desires and use them for the benefit of the state and the common interest. That is why the state needs a supreme monarch, and why this supreme leader needs a system of laws and regulations, prohibitions and punishments, to incentivize his people – either positively or negatively – to follow his orders:

> Human beings have likes and dislikes; hence the
> people can be ruled. The ruler must investigate likes
> and dislikes. Likes and dislikes are the root of rewards
> and penalties. The disposition of the people is to like
> ranks and emoluments and to dislike punishments and
> penalties. The ruler sets up the two in order to guide
> the people's will and to establish whatever he desires.
> (*Shangjun shu* 9.3)

Lord Shang asserts that the essential business of the state is to develop a deadly efficient military machine funded by resources drawn from the land. Yet he readily acknowledges that nobody enjoys fighting or labouring in the fields. He proposes, therefore, that the ruler should grant rank and office only to those who are fully devoted to the pursuit of warfare and agriculture, at the exclusion of all other activities. Benefits can only issue from a 'single opening': 'The gates of riches and nobility are exclusively in the field of war' (*Shangjun shu* 17.4). Fighting and farming thus become the sole objective of the state and the sole avenue for social mobility: 'within the borders, everyone among the people first devotes himself to tilling and warfare and only then obtains whatever pleases him' (*Shangjun shu* 25.5). By clamping down aggressively on any alternative routes to acquiring income and status besides those that serve the interests of the state, the ruler can turn tasks that people intuitively eschew into a benefit for the state. If, let's imagine, the state is in need of vinegar, it should execute those who devote their energies to producing choice ale. By doing so, people will come to believe that vinegar is the norm of the day. You know when people are ready to be deployed 'when they look at war in the same way as a hungry wolf stares at meat' (*Shangjun shu* 18.3). Lord Shang thus postulates that people will be glad to be used because they know no better.

The Legalist ruler is a brutal social engineer. He eradicates all activities or occupations that compete with warfare and agriculture, and this includes banning the free movement of people. The universal registration of the population is essential to this end: it allows strict control over military service and taxation; prevents anyone from absconding from their post and duties; and it facilitates (mutual) surveillance. Allocating the right number of people to the land available is key: when too many people inhabit a strip of land, the ruler should open up new territories. If there is a shortage of people in one part of the state, he should attract immigrants. Only then can one fully exploit the natural resources in a given area (*Shangjun shu* 6.1). Lord Shang and the state of Qin devised policies that offered tax exemptions to attract immigrant workers. Here we find one of the earliest and most outspoken arguments in favour of immigration: immigrants help you make the most of the land and its resources and (when managed well) they provide supplies and sustenance for the army.

To improve one's lot in the Legalist state, an individual or his unit should have only one ambition: to achieve the required quota of severed heads on the battlefield and meet the quota for grain yields on the land. Those who peddle goods, or lose themselves in books and theories, are a loss to the state. (In *The Book of Lord Shang* they are vilified as 'villains' and 'caterpillars' – gnawing away what others produce.) Whereas Confucius felt that no state can be governed without an intellectual elite, the Legalist ruler sees intellectuals as the most serious threat to the state. Every minute wasted in glib talk and conversation is a minute lost to farming and fighting; conversation can only lead to subversion.

The ruler therefore must keep his people simple and ignorant. It is fine to celebrate with your subjects once something has been accomplished, but never 'discuss beginnings' with them (*Shangjun shu* 1.2) – that is, never involve them in decision-making and planning. 'If the mind turns to farming, the people are simple and can be rectified; if they are ignorant, they can be easily employed; if they are reliable, they can be used in defence and fighting' (*Shangjun shu* 3.7). The Legalist ruler seeks to repress intellectuals; his power feeds off organized ignorance. For the people, not knowing is better than knowing something: 'If ignorant peasants do not become knowledgeable or fond of learning, they will strenuously devote themselves to agriculture. If knowledgeable peasants have no way to abandon their original occupation, then wastelands will surely be cultivated' (*Shangjun shu* 2.14).

Lord Shang's language and theories are harsh and jarring to the senses, but one of his greatest achievements and lasting reforms was the introduction of a system in which ranks of merit replaced aristocratic pedigree. Downright revolutionary in his own time – Warring States China of the fourth century BCE – it remains perhaps even the most significant social reform ever introduced in Chinese history. *The Book of Lord Shang* does not advocate mind control or suggest that the ruler should brainwash his people. The idea is simply to promote or demote individuals on the basis of (mostly military) merit. The flip side is that the state is entrusted with unlimited powers to control people socially and economically. As for punishments, Lord Shang insists on the principle that everyone (below the ruler, that is) should be equal before the law, with no regard to rank. Mitigating circumstances, such as a history of good behaviour, must be ignored. The punishment is to reflect the actual error that has been committed (*Shangjun shu* 17.3).

The authoritarianism with which the Legalist ruler enforces his will on the people is reminiscent of the military commander achieving his aim on and off the battlefield. As *The Art of Warfare* notes: 'If commands are consistently enforced in the training of men, they will obey; if commands are not enforced in their training, they will not obey. The consistent enforcement of commands promotes a complementary relationship between the commander and his men' (*Sunzi bing fa* 9). Likewise, the idea that obedient and productive people are those who have been pushed to extremes echoes life on the battlefield:

> Confer extraordinary rewards and post extraordinary orders, and you can command the entire army as if it were but one person. Give the troops their charges, but do not reveal your plans; get them to face the dangers, but do not reveal the advantages. Only if you throw them into life-and-death situations will they survive; only if you plunge them into places where there is no way out will they stay alive. Only if the rank and file have plunged into danger can they turn defeat into victory. (*Sunzi bing fa* 11)

Sinologists have perhaps been too quick to condemn Legalism as a doctrine that lacks any sense of morality. Yuri Pines, the most recent translator of *The Book of Lord Shang*, suggests that for Lord Shang and his followers 'violence and oppression are the necessary evil en route to universal good'. After all, the aim of harsh punishment is to create a deterrent that will make punishing redundant. A later Legalist, Shen Dao (*c.*360–*c.*285 BCE), even claimed that 'if the laws/standards are not good, they are still better than having no laws/standards' (Shen Dao *Shenzi* 23). There is of course some truth in this. Given the environment of conflict and warfare in which they operated, most Chinese thinkers presented their views as a way out of a prevailing state of affairs and saw ideal society as a utopia yet to come. Yet it is hard to imagine that those at the receiving end of Legalist wrath could afford the luxury of the long-term view. Coercion as a strategy for government only lasts as long as the state apparatus that implements it functions efficiently and operates under tight control. The history of the rise and fall of the Qin shows the limits to the moral ends that can be achieved by immoral means. As the scholar-official Jia Yi (201–169 BCE) remarked only a few decades later: 'The power to conquer and the power to preserve what one has won are not the same' (*Shiji* 48).

Brutal philosophers meet brutal ends. Back in the state of Qin, the ruling lineages soon grew to resent Lord Shang's far-reaching power. Once his patron, Lord Xiao, had died, they did not wait long to accuse and execute him. They tore his body to pieces with chariots pulling in different directions and executed his entire family. The architect of an authoritarian streak that would embed itself into the fabric of Chinese political culture fell by the sword of his own making. During the long centuries of imperial China that followed, Lord Shang and his legacy would by turns be vilified, ignored or painted with a negative brush. It is only in the early twentieth century that some started to (re)appraise Lord Shang's thought as an anti-conservative (for which read anti-Confucian) ideology to strengthen the state. During the 1970s, Mao Zedong quietly acknowledged and admired the Legalists and the First Emperor. Despite these moments of tacit approval among academics and politicians that continue up to today, Lord Shang has not managed to shake off his image as the statesman who gave China a doctrine for oppressive despotism, or, as the sinologist Angus Graham has called it, 'an amoral science of statecraft'.

Other thinkers have elaborated or refined existing concepts or introduced new ideas to the Legalist tradition. One core issue is whether it is possible for a single ruler to hold exclusive decision-making and executive powers. Some have proposed that a ruler can be empowered to make decisions by himself. This is a view expressed in a fragment associated with Shen Buhai (Shenzi; d. 337 BCE), a thinker about whom we know next to nothing: 'One who sees things independently is called clear-eyed. One who hears things independently is called sharp-eared. He who can reach decisions independently is therefore able to be ruler of the whole world' (*Shenzi* 19). For Lord Shang, too, the ideal monarch rules without officials or advisers and avoids having to rely on layers of intermediaries. The people themselves ought to serve as the eyes and ears of the ruler; they should control (that is, spy) and oversee (that is, report on) one another. Again, the tactics are reminiscent of the military treatises: 'Only the most sagacious ruler is able to employ spies; only the most humane and just commander is able to put them into service; only the most sensitive and alert person can get the truth out of spies. So delicate! So secretive! There is nowhere that you cannot put spies to good use' (*Sunzi bing fa* 13).

But how do you protect the absolute monarch from his own entourage, his ministers, his advisers and all those desperate to curry favour with him? Of key importance to the Legalist ruler is his ability to play his ministers off against each other so that no single person gains the upper hand. Shen Buhai compares this to a husband refusing to give preferential treatment to any of his wives (Chinese elites in his time were polygamous):

> When one wife gains exclusive influence over the husband, all wives are thrown into disorder; when a single minister

monopolizes the ruler, the whole body of ministers will be overshadowed. Thus a jealous wife has no difficulty in breaking up a family, and a troublemaking minister finds it easy to disrupt the state. For this reason, the clear-sighted ruler causes all his ministers to advance together, like the spokes of a wheel that converge in the hub. That way no one minister can gain the ascendancy with the ruler.

(*Shenzi* 1)

Securing total power and maintaining it requires positioning oneself in such a way that one's power base does not become diluted. So out goes the Confucian ruler, who acts as a moral stakeholder, and in comes the emotionless master manipulator, able to pull the strings and control the self-interest of those who surround him.

The most sophisticated theory on how to keep an absolutist leader in power through astute positioning appears in a work known as *The Master Han Fei* (*Han Feizi*). Han Fei (*c.*280–*c.*233 BCE) was an aristocrat born into the family that ruled the state of Han (in modern-day Shanxi and Henan). For a brief period, he was a pupil of the Confucian philosopher Xunzi, together with Li Si, the man who was to become prime minister of the state of Qin and the driving force behind Qin's ambition to conquer and unify China. When dispatched as an emissary to the Qin court, Han Fei died a tragic death at the hands of his former fellow student, who now saw him as his rival. Slandered in front of the king and horrified at the prospect of the brutal execution that awaited him, he accepted self-poisoning instead (permission to drink poison provided the same gracious 'get-out' for Socrates). Han Fei had a bad stutter, which prevented him from presenting his ideas in court with the eloquence that characterized the wandering persuaders of his time, so he channelled his energy into writing. Most of the fifty-five chapters in the received text that carries his name are believed to be by his own hand. In many ways, Han Fei is the theoretical architect of the ideology that shaped China's first empire.

Han Fei radically rejects the idea that government should depend on the moral character of those in power, let alone that it should be modelled on the way of the ancients: 'past and present have different customs'. The good ruler does not wait for people to be good and full of esteem for him. He creates a situation in which they will find it impossible to do wrong (*Han Feizi* 50). You may be fortunate and have one rabbit break its neck on a stump in the field right next to you, all ready for the pot, but dropping your plough to go stump-watching until another rabbit comes crashing along is a waste of time (*Han Feizi* 49). The point he makes is that only very few leaders have the capacity to be moral exemplars. The vast majority of people will not yield to a ruler simply because he displays moral rectitude (look at Confucius, Han Fei sneers: for all his moral integrity, only a handful of disciples followed him!). Instead it is your position of power, not your personality, that makes people submit to you. Efficient government therefore requires an acknowledgement that there are no 'permanent standards of what is acceptable'. The monarch should take stock of the circumstances of the day and operate accordingly.

To get a firm grip on government, the ruler should use a system of reward and punishment. Han Fei calls these the 'two

handles of government', and he recommends no half measures. No appreciative pat on the back, no gentle telling-off:

> When handing out rewards, there is nothing better than
> to make them substantial and credible, so that people
> will really consider them beneficial. When meting out
> punishments, there is nothing better than to make them
> severe and inescapable, so that people really fear them.
> When devising laws, there is nothing better than to
> make them unmistakable and firm, so that the people
> will understand them. Therefore if a ruler bestows
> rewards and does not transfer [i.e. repeal] them, if he
> administers punishments without granting pardon, if
> he supports his rewards with praise and accompanies
> his punishments with scorn, then both the worthy
> and the unworthy will do everything they can for him.
> (*Han Feizi* 49)

Elsewhere he makes an analogy with parental love. Love of
itself will not teach a child how to behave; it needs to be
backed up by the whip of the local magistrate – that is, the
state: 'A mother's love for her son is twice that of the father,
but when the father gives orders to his son they are ten times
more effective than the mother's. The magistrate has no love
for the people, but when he issues orders to them they are
ten thousand times more effective than the father's' (*Han Feizi*
46). Good Legalist rule therefore means that the law always
supersedes any form of bias. This prioritizing of procedure
over favouritism is also described in 'Reliance on the Law',
a chapter in *The Master Guan* (*Guanzi*), a text named after
Guan Zhong (d. 645 BCE), a famous minister to Duke Huan

of Qi, but containing later material dating to Han Fei's time: 'No matter whether people are close or distant, near or far, high or low, beautiful or ugly, the good ruler uses procedures and measurements when judging them. When he executes people, they bear no resentment; when he rewards them, they have no feeling of gratitude. By using the law to regulate them, he becomes like Heaven and Earth in having no self-interest' (*Guanzi* 45).

Power is not shared; it must be exclusive and therefore rest solely with the monarch. Instead of dividing his power, Han Fei's ruler divides those who vie for his power. He develops 'methods' or 'techniques' (*shu*) to control and manipulate his officials and protect himself against treason. There is a public and a private side to Legalist despotism. When both are managed skilfully, it allows the sovereign 'to command openly and manipulate secretly', as the French philosopher François Jullien puts it. While the ruler draws on clearly visible and well-defined norms to which everyone must comply, there is a concealed or hidden aspect to his power base. Through a clever system of intelligence-gathering and secret manoeuvring, he manages to keep himself intact and controls those who make up the immediate machinery of government. He gets his officials to work for him as his eyes, ears and limbs.

Han Fei acknowledges that very few individuals possess the astuteness, perseverance and energy to rule as an absolute monarch, especially when ministers with conflicting interests surround him like a pack of ambitious wolves. In reality, power tends to be eroded and split between the competing factions that orbit the monarch. It is therefore very important, Han Fei argues, that the monarch is protected from his ministers and the monarchy from the monarch. The institution must be immunized against the potential cancers that can erode it when an incompetent person inherits and occupies the throne. So Han Fei overturns Confucius's confidence in the power of personality: absolute rule can survive only if the office transcends those who inhabit it. In contemporary language, the party must survive, regardless of who represents its outward face at any one time.

What to do, then, when the ruler in place at the time makes a mess of it? One way to protect the throne against its incumbent is to wipe out his human personality and turn him into a pure symbol of authority. Han Fei strips the sovereign of everything associated with normal human behaviour. He is an emotionless figure who has no knowledge or desires, a mute hologram that does not engage in debate. With his true character concealed and his power base hidden, the ruler can protect himself against conspiracies directed at him by his officials. Like Master Sun's good military commander, he is unpredictable and keeps his motivations and intentions secret, even from his own people and soldiers: 'He is calm and remote, correct and disciplined. He is able to blinker the ears and eyes of his officers and men and to keep people ignorant. He makes changes in his arrangements and alters his plans, keeping people in the dark' (*Sunzi bing fa* 11).

Han Fei wants the ruler to manipulate and eliminate his rivals, like a puppeteer pulling the strings of his puppets from the shadows. The art of government lies in knowing how to exploit the power of being unknown: 'to see others without being seen, hear others without being heard, know others without being known' (*Han Feizi* 5). The goal is to achieve a political version of the Banksy effect: ministers are prevented from guessing the monarch's intentions: 'A ruler should never reveal what he desires. For if he reveals what he desires, his ministers will cut and polish themselves accordingly' (*Han Feizi* 5).

But here is the dilemma: Han Fei's ruler is caught between a rock and a hard place. In order to appear absolutely powerful and outwit his rivals, he needs to transform himself into a seemingly distant and enigmatic figure, cut off from the daily running of society. This means that he must delegate executive power to minister-advisers who can be judged loyal and competent. To create an aura of invulnerability, he needs to distrust each and every one around him. Yet to be effective, he has no choice but to entrust responsibility to capable officials who inherently mistrust him. So, ironically, when the person who inherits the throne turns out to be inept, incompetent or obstinate, his power and stature depend entirely on the good services of those wise ministers he wants to keep at bay. When the ruler is short-sighted, his minister needs to be far-sighted. But neither party wants its own objectives to be visible to the other.

Unfortunately, complete and undivided ministerial loyalty rarely exists; self-interest and the temptation to deceive lurk in all officials, according to Han Fei. This is why anyone who oversteps the bounds of his office, even if it is to please the ruler, must be punished. One's office and title correspond to a reality that cannot be confused:

> Once the Marquis Zhao of Han [358–333 BCE] was drunk and fell into a nap. The crown-keeper, seeing that his ruler

was exposed to the cold, put a coat over him. When the Marquis awoke, he was glad and asked his attendants: 'Who covered me with my coat?' 'The crown-keeper did,' they replied. Consequently, the Marquis put both the coat-keeper and the crown-keeper to death. He punished the coat-keeper for neglect of his duties and the crown-keeper for overstepping his position. It was not that the Marquis did not dislike the cold but rather that he felt that the harm that follows from ministers straying beyond their assigned duties was worse than him catching a cold.

(*Han Feizi* 7)

Thus, in the end, what binds the absolutist ruler and his ministers together is a mutual distrust and potential for betrayal (recall Master Sun's maxim: for an arrow to be deadly, the bow has to remain tensely drawn at all times). In each and every circumstance, the Legalist ruler needs to assess, re-assess and reposition himself in a landscape of constantly shifting loyalties and rivalries. If he decides to reveal the person behind the façade, become 'human' and abandon the protective screen of high office, he could be at risk. And since the monarch inherits rather than merits his position, he might find himself in a permanent limbo of distrust and paranoia. Logic dictates, then, that for government and bureaucracy to operate effectively, it is better to have a mediocre leader than one that is either too wise or too stupid.

Being mandated to reign supreme in ancient China was something of a poisoned chalice. The First Emperor moved incognito among the crowds and between his palaces, sleeping in different quarters at night out of fear of assault. For the custodians of the monarch, the task proved no less taxing. When the First Emperor died in 210 BCE on a tour away from the capital, such was the fear for an uprising that his body had to be smuggled back into the city hidden under a cartload of rotting fish. The despot was dead; long live despotism. The Legalists' theory of power may have vanished in name, but the question they put before us still holds true: is it better to trust in the wisdom of those who rule, or should society place its trust in the institutions by means of which it is ruled? Is it possible to take the person out of politics? In the end, the Legalist ideology that propelled the state of Qin and the First Emperor proved too radical and repressive. It generated laws but was too short-lived to transform these into lasting political institutions. During the Han dynasty, barely four decades after the death of Han Fei, Confucianism emerged as the dominant ideology of imperial rule. But the influence of Legalist thought on Chinese political culture would remain invisibly pervasive. As one saying goes, those who commanded power in China were 'Confucian on the outside, and Legalist on the inside' (*wai Ru nei Fa*).

Hidden and invisible

In one passage in the *Analects*, someone suggests to Zigong, the entrepreneurial disciple of Confucius, that he might be worthier than the Master himself. Zigong replies:

> Let us take a residence surrounded by outer walls as an analogy. My own walls are shoulder high, so that it is possible to peer over them and see the beauty of my house. But the Master's walls are twenty or thirty feet

high, so that, unless one gains entry through the gate, one cannot see the magnificence of the ancestral temples or the sumptuousness of the estate inside. Those who have been able to gain entry through the gate though are rather few. (*An.* 19.23)

Zigong reminds his appraiser that, for all his own personal wealth and flair, Confucius's inner power and charisma are far superior. The official career of Zigong, who eventually served as a high-ranking minister in two different states, dwarfed that of Confucius himself. Yet, he suggests, it is extremely testing and demanding to gain access to the unfathomable depths of Confucius's mind. Note how Zigong uses the image of a wall (though not a Great Wall). Behind high walls accessible only through a single gate lie powers exclusive to one individual, but inaccessible to and elusive for most. Attempting to climb the walls is futile. What is unseen will remain unknown except to those select few who are deemed worthy enough to enter through the gate.

From Master Sun's strategy on the battlefield to the secretive monarch of Han Fei, there is a fascinating dynamic at work in the political thought of ancient China: one that associates power and authority with the art of remaining unknown and invisible. The Romans lauded the achievements of their rulers through public display: muscular statues, sculpted busts of their heroes (senators, writers and philosophers) and lavish ceremonies celebrating their political and military triumphs. No similar tradition of portraiture or sculpture existed in ancient China. Napoleon is depicted crossing the Alps in triumphalist neo-classical style on the back of his rearing horse, while the great Qing emperors perch quietly on the dragon throne, deep in the palace, draped in yellow silk robes that conceal all but the face: 'The Son of Heaven does not look yet sees, does not listen yet hears, does not think yet knows, does not move yet accomplishes: rather, like a clod of earth, he sits alone on his mat, and the world follows him as though it were of a single body with him, just as the four limbs follow the dictates of the mind' (*Xunzi* 12.7). The palace architecture was designed to hide the Chinese ruler: walls and screens sheltered him from public view. Trees lined the roads along which official convoys or imperial processions travelled. Chariots concealed important passengers from view. Tombs and mausoleums sealed away the deceased from the eyes of the living. Today the Communist Party's leadership and much of its government machinery are still hidden within the walled compound of the former imperial garden complex known as Zhongnanhai, adjacent to the Forbidden City. Much like the inner court in imperial times, the world within those walls operates on its own terms. Walking along the long maroon western wall that separates it from the outside world, it is hard not to sense the power that radiates from the inner sanctum it conceals.

For ancient China's thinkers, power and authority derive from being able to keep a good balance between deliberate ostentation (showing off who you are, what you have and what you are able to do) and strategic concealment (hiding your talents and possessions). When visibly weak, the ruler is at risk of being overthrown by more able pretenders. Yet public displays of ability and supreme confidence risk exciting the envy of lesser figures who pine for his position.

What emerges is a vision of power and authority that can be generated by being passive and receptive, by facing inward rather than outward. The sage-ruler knows the world without having to look out of his window, but to protect and safeguard his power, his senses should not be exposed to each and every matter, which would cloud his judgement and prevent him from seeing the bigger picture:

> The kings of antiquity hung a veil of pearls in front
> of their caps to prevent them from seeing too clearly;
> they had yellow silk plugs stuck in the ears to suppress
> a hearing that would be too keen. The Son of Heaven
> was surrounded by external screens in order to separate
> himself off ... If his eyes were to see in a disorderly
> fashion, that would lead to excess; if his ears were to
> hear in a reckless way, that would lead to confusion; and
> if his mouth would speak foolish words, that would lead
> to disorder. These three (sensory) gateways were to be
> carefully guarded. (*Huainanzi* 9.1)

The Chinese ruler thus sees all and hears all without having to look or listen. This passive-receptive image turns the sovereign into an almost mysterious and transcendent figure. Alternatively, he may be seen as a powerful operator who commands and orchestrates the world from his hidden power base – an inaccessible silhouette whose true identity is impenetrable. Think of the ruler as a shadow without a body, a voice without a mouth, a persona without a personality. The enlightened sovereign rules by yielding. The best chief executive officer does not execute policies but is able to delegate in such a way that he or she appears almost redundant and people fail to notice how, all along, he/she is pulling the strings in the background: 'The clear-sighted ruler avails himself of an appearance of stupidity, establishes himself in insufficiency, places himself in a posture of timidity, and conceals himself in inaction. He hides his motives and conceals his tracks. He shows the world that he does not act. Therefore those who are near him will cherish him' (*Shenzi* 1.5).

There is a Daoist hiding within each Legalist. An absolutist ruler who conducts his government through his officials should be able to sit back and let his ministers do the work. He invites proposals, checks whether what is being done accords with the agreed plan, and rewards or punishes on the basis of whether performance matches expectations. China's historical circumstances no doubt influenced this concept of passive power. In the turbulent world of the Warring States, visibility could quickly equate with vulnerability. We are back on the battlefield again, where the most accomplished general stays out of the sight of the enemy and lies low in a valley instead of posing in glittering armour on top of a hill.

Spoken and unspoken

The power of language is a subject that spins like a merry-go-round through Chinese philosophy and political thought. What's in a name? For some Chinese thinkers, names and language meant everything; to others language was futile, a worthless means to no end. For Confucius, the use of language is an important issue. He insists that it matters greatly how you speak and choose your words. To lead and persuade others, things should be correctly named. The theory is known as 'the rectification of names' (*zheng ming*). In order to avoid misunderstandings or false expectations, a person of authority should call a spade a spade. To administer (*zheng*) a state, you need to rectify or correct (*zheng*) the language you use:

> When names are not correct, what is said will not sound reasonable. When what is said does not sound reasonable, affairs will not culminate in success. When affairs do not culminate in success, rites and music will not flourish. When rites and music do not flourish, punishments will not fit the crimes. When punishments do not fit the crimes, the common people will not know where to put hand and foot. Thus when the gentleman names something, the name must be usable in speech, and when he says something, this must be practicable. The thing about the gentleman is that he is anything but casual where speech is concerned. (*An.* 13.3)

In the Confucian perspective, correct terminology and transparent language is of the utmost importance. Names and titles are powerful tools in this regard as they create clear role expectations. We have all experienced occasions when the incorrect use of names, titles or forms of address shocks us out of our social comfort zone: shall I address my line manager by his title or his first name? Is my friend's mother Mrs Smith or just Angie? When, during a medical emergency, you shout out for a doctor in the room, the last thing you need is a doctor of philosophy to stand up, oblige and medicate. Or how about the medley of terms on offer to encourage you to pay your taxes: charge, rate, levy, tariff, toll, cost, contribution, duty, due. If people are to pay up, call a tax 'tax' and be clear about what it applies to. As Confucius would argue, vocabulary matters. The more tortuous and drawn out the small print on the back of your sales receipt or tax return, the less respect you will have for those extracting payment from you.

For Confucius, names are performative – that is, the words you use are like the act itself. Names are norms. When you call someone 'boss', this comes with the expectation that the person you are addressing is actually fulfilling that role. As the sinologist Benjamin Schwartz puts it, Confucius implies that titles 'do not refer simply to bare biologic or political facts' but that 'every role is the bearer of its own role-norms'.

'It is enough that the language one uses conveys the point' (*An.* 15.41). Once language becomes too florid – when glib rhetoric and fancy terminology overshadow the substance of what is being said – knots appear in communication and, as a consequence, in the gentleman's reputation. Confucius is adamant that those in power are assessed 'to the bone' by the language they use. As one of his disciples notes: 'The gentleman is judged wise by a single word he utters, he is judged foolish by a single word he utters. That is why one really must be careful of what one says' (*An.* 19.25). One should also be judicious in evaluating language: 'The gentleman does not recommend someone solely on the basis of his words, neither does he dismiss words simply on account of the person who utters them' (*An.* 15.23). The distance between speech and action can be such that words become empty and cannot be trusted. Words must stand for actions, and actions must correspond to words. A proper use of names and titles is all about establishing clear role expectations in communities: we expect those we call teachers to teach us and those we call soldiers to fight for us. It follows that we must be highly critical of those who put teachers on the battlefield or soldiers in the classroom. Calling your girlfriend 'wife' or your wife 'girlfriend' can lead to friction. So effective rule depends on the correct use of names. Names are more than labels; they are functions. They mark out social and political distinctions: calling someone a father is an implicit order to that person to behave like a father. Thus for a ruler to be known as the 'father of the people', this is a charge, not a privilege.

There was a group of philosophers who took reflection on language, and how words relate to things, to a more abstract and theoretical level. They were lumped together as the so-called 'school of names' (*ming jia*), also known as 'sophists' or 'dialecticians'. Their main concern was how, and if, language can represent reality. Its most famous proponents are Gongsun Long (*c.*325–250 BCE) and the slightly older Hui Shi (Huizi; *c.*370–300 BCE). The former's ideas survive in a text known as *The Master Gongsun Long* (*Gongsun Longzi*). Hui Shi appears in dialogues and passages throughout other texts, and often acts as a debating companion to Zhuangzi. Building on the Confucian premise that one name should stand for one thing, Gongsun Long is well known for his proposition that 'a white horse is not a horse' ('horse' and 'whiteness', shape or colour, are two different things). Hui Shi is known for formulating a set of ten paradoxes reminiscent of Zeno (such as: 'Simultaneously with being at noon, the sun declines; simultaneously with being alive, a thing dies'). Questions of epistemology (how we know something) also figured on the agenda of the Later Mohists, who are known to us through a set of debates and logical puzzles preserved in six chapters in the received version of *The Master Mo*. But the sophists' theoretical horseplay never really gained much traction in the Chinese tradition. Such is the verdict of Xunzi: 'Although formulated with extreme exactness, their propositions concern matters of no urgency ... Though they treat many topics, their results are meagre, and they cannot be considered to have provided any guiding rules or ordering norms for government' (*Xunzi* 6.6). Theories that do not translate into practice – debate for the sake of debate – are a pastime the Confucian gentleman would rather do without.

But what about the words themselves? What makes good and functional language? Here the Confucian thinker Xunzi elaborates. Words, he acknowledges, are arbitrary and nothing but a convention. They do not represent something inherently:

> Names have no intrinsic appropriateness. They are
> bound to something by agreement in order to name it.
> The agreement becomes fixed, the custom is established,
> and it is called 'appropriate'. If a name differs from the
> agreed name, it is then called 'inappropriate'. Names
> have no intrinsic object. They are bound to some reality
> by agreement in order to name that object. The object
> becomes fixed, the custom established, and it is called
> the name of that object. Names do have intrinsic
> good qualities. When a name is direct, easy and not
> at odds with the thing, it is called a 'good name'.
> (*Xunzi* 22.2g)

Any name could be appropriate. You can call an apple 'blue'. But words can be deemed correct only when there is agreement by a group (that is, when we agree 'apple' refers to the fruit and 'blue' is a colour). For practical purposes, names should be uncomplicated and direct. To avoid confusing our senses, words should be chosen in such a way that they do not contradict what they are trying to name. It helps to name a region or continent that is covered by ice 'Iceland' rather than 'Arizona' or 'Greenland'; Blacky the dog, ideally, has a tinge of black somewhere. For Xunzi, language is pragmatic. We process the world through our sensory organs, notice that there are similarities and differences between the things we sense around us, and settle on words to express and demarcate those. Sometimes we want to refer to things collectively (and call them 'things'); on other occasions, we want to drill down and draw distinctions between them (Xunzi gives the terms 'birds' and 'beasts' as an example). Once we have fixed our language and agreed what names to assign, it is important to stick to the convention. Only then is communication effective. Therefore people with authority are those who are able to take in a wide-ranging topic and see right to its essence. They present things simply and concisely. The gentleman makes sure his propositions fit the facts; he does not labour the point. He is crystal clear about what he means and what his intentions are (*Xunzi* 22.4c). To be wise, you have to be easy to understand. A white horse, after all, is a horse.

As much as Confucians underline the importance of language, in Zhuangzi they find their harshest critic. *The Master Zhuang* offers the most dazzling deconstruction of the value of words and language preserved in any text from ancient China: 'Saying is not just blowing air; saying says something. The only trouble is that what it says is never fixed, so do we really say anything? Or have we said nothing? We think speech is different from the peeping of fledglings. But is there really any difference between them?' (*Zhuangzi* 2.5). Language, Zhuangzi claims, is a code that splits up the world. Whereas Xunzi insists that we must prevent words from being arbitrary by establishing a clear consensus on usage, Zhuangzi suggests there exists no good use for words. Language fragments. Words create an illusion as they force us to divide reality into components that alienate us from the world – that is, the Dao – as a lived experience. Language programmes us into thinking 'this' is different from 'that'. It trains us to reason in terms of opposites, of affirmatives and negatives: right versus wrong, true versus false, beautiful versus ugly, me versus you (or you versus me). Language creates knots and tangles that clutter rather than free up our existence. Moreover, since our choice of language is entirely arbitrary, it is never an accurate reflection of reality. Once we carve up the world into categories by means of language, we can no longer experience it as an undifferentiated whole: 'To split something up is to create something else; to create something is to destroy something else. But nothing is created or destroyed when they are understood as one' (*Zhuangzi* 2.6).

Language thus conceals rather than reveals; it prevents us from grasping the bigger picture and complicates what is not complex: 'Once upon a time there was a monkey keeper passing out nuts. "I'll give you three in the morning and four at night," he told them. The monkeys were all angry. "All right, then," said the keeper, "you'll get four in the morning and three at night." The monkeys were all happy with this arrangement' (*Zhuangzi* 2.6). Without changing the name or amount of the food he gives them, the monkey keeper solves the problem. Using language is like being given nuts in varying portions while failing to understand that it does not affect the overall quantity. Trying to bring things together without realizing that they already are the same makes us prone to accepting 'four in the morning'. So Zhuangzi does not believe that words order the world. The sage allows his words to order themselves and issue spontaneously as he goes along. Ultimately, language and speech should be redundant. It is perhaps ironic that those who questioned the value of language did so through texts that rank among China's masterpieces of literary expression. But they were of course making an important point: some truths are inexpressible in words: 'A fish-trap is for catching fish; once you have caught the fish, forget about the trap. A snare is for catching rabbits; once you have caught the rabbit, forget about the snare. Words are for catching ideas; once you have caught the idea, forget about the words' (*Zhuangzi* 26.13). I do not disagree, but remain grateful for the words!

Beyond the insistence that language should be used correctly, or as little as possible, Confucians and Daoists both share a distrust in the power of words when they merely serve the purpose of rhetoric and persuasion, when they are used as arguments for argument's sake. In one passage in the *Analects*, an exasperated Confucius even seems to sympathize with the idea that the world can do without clever talk, glib speech and the hypocrisy that comes with it: 'The Master said, "I am thinking of giving up speech." Zigong said, "If you do not speak, what would there be for us, your disciples, to transmit?" The Master said, "What does Heaven ever say? Yet there are the four seasons going round and there are the hundred things coming into being. What does Heaven ever say?"' (*An.* 17.19). When it comes to questioning the use of language, even the Legalist joins in: 'It is only the clear-sighted ruler who knows that being fond of words will neither strengthen the army nor expand the territory' (*Shangjun shu* 3.10). For the Daoist, words are inadequate to describe the Dao and a distraction to experiencing the world around us; for the Legalist, words are an excuse for action. For Confucians, words are inadequate unless they are tightly controlled by convention.

We cannot assume, therefore, that those involved in political and philosophical argument in ancient China always either spoke clearly or not at all. In a fragmented world where wandering philosophers had to gain the ear of potential patrons, the art of persuasion was never far away. If anything, the philosophers' distrust of rhetoric and cleverness of speech suggests that there existed a strong and living tradition of oral artistry, albeit perhaps not as developed as the art of discourse in ancient Greece and Rome. To be sharp of mind and tongue was important for courtiers seeking patronage. Without it, life at court, or life altogether, could be short. Anecdotes and records of court speeches, such as those collected in *The Stratagems of the Warring States* (*Zhanguo ce*), offer a telling insight into the verbal equivalent of the art of war with which we began this chapter. Several of the texts associated with the masters of philosophy, most notably *The Master Han Fei*, also contain advice on how to get one's point across to the ruler, using anecdotes that often revolve around factually dubious events or set in the didactic depths of the past. The aim is to make a political point through historical and literary allusions and thereby persuade, or criticize, those in power by indirect means.

The Stratagems of the Warring States (after which the historical period it covers is named) feature an array of clever and witty characters who gain advantage through the sort of manipulation, intrigue and trickery of which a good Confucian would thoroughly disapprove. The collection reads almost like a historical novel. Some of its stories may have been written as scenarios to train disciples in the art of persuasion. Figures such as the wandering persuader Su Qin (d. 284 BCE) – noted for having convinced other major warring states to form an alliance against Qin – go down in Chinese history as master tricksters and rhetoricians. Here is how he managed to hoodwink two rulers at the same time:

> East Zhou wished to sow its land with rice, but West
> Zhou refused to open the river sluices. East Zhou was
> troubled over this. Su Qin spoke to its ruler and said: 'May
> I have your permission to persuade West Zhou to open
> its sluices?' He went on his way and in an audience with
> the ruler of West Zhou, he said: 'My Lord, your strategy
> is faulty. By withholding water from East Zhou you are
> making East Zhou wealthier! At present, all the people
> there have sown wheat and nothing else. If you would
> really like to harm them, you should open your sluices
> immediately so you can damage their [dry] seeds! Once the
> sluices are opened, East Zhou will be forced to replant with
> rice. And when they plant rice, you can again deny them
> water so they must come as supplicants to West Zhou and
> receive orders from your majesty!' The King of West Zhou
> agreed and released the waters. Su Qin pocketed the gold of
> both states. (*Zhanguo ce*, Zhou 24)

Many of these stories gave rise to idioms that survive in the Chinese language to this day. To achieve your goal, better not 'paint legs on a snake', a stock saying for overreaching, changing your answer, offering unnecessary detail or enjoying too much of a good thing. Taking advantage of someone else's strategic position makes you a 'fox availing himself of the tiger's fearfulness' (the sly fox tricks the tiger into walking behind him and believing that all the animals they encounter scatter away out of fright for the fox). 'Travel by night yet hide by dawn'; waiting to pounce once 'two tigers have quarrelled each other' to exhaustion; 'while mussel and heron clamp on to each other (and do not let go), a fisherman catches them'. Aphorisms such as these plucked from the rhetorical battlegrounds of ancient China's wandering persuaders illustrate the enduring virtue of the political art of positioning oneself.

We have seen how strategies and techniques deployed by those who rule, lead and administer form part of the bedrock of Chinese thought. Yet without the other constellations that surround it, no pole star can shine by itself. Similarly, rulers cannot rule alone but require subjects that need or wish to be ruled. They require institutions by which to implement their strategies. In one way or another, it is hard to conceive of society as anything other than an assemblage of individuals, even if they are nameless. So how did Chinese thinkers conceive of human nature and the ways in which human identity is shaped? How do human beings become persons – that is, agents with a self? How do individuals relate to the larger community? That is the story of the next chapter.

The Individual and the Collective

Gaozi said:

> Human nature is like swirling water. Open a channel for it to the east, and it will flow east; open a channel for it in the west, and it will flow west. Human nature does not distinguish between good and bad, just as water does not distinguish between east and west.

Mencius replied:

> It is true that water does not distinguish between east and west, but does it fail to distinguish between up and down? Human nature is good just as water tends to flow downwards. There is no human being lacking in the tendency to do good, just as there is no water lacking in the tendency to flow downwards. Now, water, if you make it jump by splashing it, you may cause it to rise above your forehead. By damming and channelling it, you can force it to flow uphill. But is this the nature of water? It is so because of the situation in which it is placed. Although people can be made to do what is not good, their nature remains as it was. (*Mencius* 6B.2)

Thus runs one exchange in the most famous dialogue on human nature from ancient China. Its interlocutors are Mencius (Mengzi or Master Meng; fourth/third century BCE), the most influential thinker in the classical Confucian tradition after Confucius, and Gaozi, who is known to us only from his debates with Mencius. We have seen how China's masters of philosophy had much to say about how to be a ruler. But there was another important question under discussion: how to be a person. In describing his ideal of the *junzi* or gentleman, Confucius defined human character mostly in terms of a public personality: human beings ought to cultivate themselves and aspire to social engagement. As we have seen, his chief aim was to clarify the rituals and rules that help people navigate social relationships and function appropriately in society. But is it possible to think of a person merely as someone engaged in social role play? Do we all share the same human nature and underlying character? And how do human beings act as individuals?

Most Chinese thinkers acknowledged that humans are primarily social animals. Even those who claimed that to lead a good life one must hide oneself away from the world were questioning a shared sentiment: human nature is shaped, or shapes itself, in relation to its environment and the people and institutions that constitute it. Generally, Confucian thinkers held that every human being was perfectible: 'It is only the most wise and the most stupid that cannot be changed' (*An.* 17.3). The issue was not so much whether or not it is possible to train and educate someone to be a fitting member of society, but how this is best done. A dominant view was that human character should be formed through a regime of study and learning, and in the context of the family. Some insisted that apprenticeship to a master and thoughtful nurturing required a firm disciplinary hand, and that education in the rituals of the ancients was indispensable in controlling human desire. Mozi and his followers questioned whether the family should be the context in which to socialize and educate human beings. Radical Daoists saw no point at all in refining people within the context of the family or the state. Instead of life in harmonious association with others, they proposed, the priority should be to turn inwards and live in harmony with the self. Yet from these conflicting views on how individuals may best thrive in their surroundings, one shared reality emerges: without others there is no self; without a self there is no other. Whether human beings are seen as part of a social or a natural order, they become (or cease to become) persons while standing in relationship to others and other things.

Human nature

Confucius had little to say about human nature. He stressed the importance of benevolence or humaneness (*ren*), which he explained as a sense of compassion and love for one's fellow man (*An*. 12.22). A person of moral standing should reach out and extend his human-heartedness to others, even if this is not reciprocated: 'Do not be concerned about whether or not others know you; be concerned about whether or not you know others' (*An*. 1.16, 14.30). Carefree about his own reputation, the *junzi* empathizes with others and sets out to help. And so Confucius formulates his version of the Golden Rule: 'Do not impose on others what you yourself do not desire' (*An*. 15.24).

Alongside this sense of humaneness, Confucius insists that people should develop a sense of rightness (*yi*). Certain things must be done because it is morally right to do so. One should never shun responsibilities that come with one's social position: a father should look after his family; a ruler should care for his people; the young should look after the elderly; students must respect their teachers. Confucius does not elaborate much on why we should uphold these moral virtues or how the human mind arrives at making the right decisions. Rather than seeking to dissect human psychology and address the question 'Who are we?', he theorizes mostly about human conduct as it appears on the outside: where do we stand in relation to others? Confucius's primary focus is on social roles, not hearts. Yet his only significant comment on human nature set the stage for the debate: 'Human beings are by nature similar, but they vary greatly from each other as the result of practice' (*An.* 17.2). Human behaviour, for Confucius, tends to go with the flow. It is only particular habits that shape us into good or bad human beings. The riverbanks determine the course of a stream. This can turn out to be good (when irrigating the fields) or bad (when flooding a neighbourhood). In the three centuries following his death, Confucius's neutral stance on how our natural tendencies are oriented turned into a topic of debate among his followers, most notably Mencius and Xunzi.

Mencius (the Latinized form of 'Mengzi'; or Meng Ke) was the first major intellectual descendant of Confucius, which is why he is also known as the 'Second Sage'. He was a native of the state of Zou, in southern Shandong province. An apocryphal story tells how his mother moved residence three times in order to ensure young Mencius was exposed to the right environment. After living near a cemetery and a marketplace, she decided that the sight of tombs and haggling salesmen were no good for a child, so she set up home next to a school. There 'the boy played at arranging sacrificial vessels and the rituals of bowing, yielding, entering and withdrawing' (*Lienü zhuan* 1.11). Mencius studied with Confucius's grandson, Zisi (or one of his disciples). For most of his life, he travelled from state to state. For a while, he held an honorary office in the state of Qi, where he may have spent time at the so-called Jixia Academy ('The Academy below the Westgate'). At this centre of learning in the Qi capital, Linzi, intellectuals enjoyed the patronage of the kings of Qi, most notably kings Wei (357–320 BCE) and Xuan (319–301 BCE). For a period of about a hundred and fifty years, scholars gathered here and were given generous stipends and accommodation to devote their time to thinking, teaching and learning. The text that carries his name, the *Mencius* (*Mengzi*), is closely linked to the historical figure. Sinologists generally agree that the received version (seven books, each divided into two parts) was put together by Mencius himself and his disciples. Like the *Analects*, the *Mencius* consists of dialogues and collected sayings presented in a random order. But unlike the *Analects*, several of its exchanges are more analytical, with a succession of arguments that run on for considerable length.

Mencius is the first major Chinese philosopher to elaborate on the ethical disposition that is innate to human beings and articulate a theory of human nature (*xing*). All species and kinds, he argues, have their own nature. Human nature is universal to all human beings: the same natural abilities are present in each of us. As we go through life, we display constant behaviours that are common to us all (such as wanting to feed ourselves, keep warm or procreate). However, what sets people apart are external circumstances and environment. To borrow the metaphor from his dialogue with Gaozi: we can use our hands to splash water across our face and make it run against its natural course. For Mencius, there exists a natural equality in people, one which only external circumstances can disrupt:

> In years of abundance, most young people have the
> wherewithal to be good, while in years of adversity, most of
> them become violent. This is not a matter of a difference
> in the native capacities sent down by Heaven but rather
> of what overwhelms their minds. Now, let barley be sown
> and covered by earth; the soil being the same, and the time
> of planting also being the same, it grows rapidly, and by
> midsummer, it all ripens. Though there may be differences
> in the yield, this is because the fertility of the soil, the
> nourishment of the rain and the dew, and the human effort
> invested are not the same. Things of the same kind are thus
> like one another. Why should one doubt this when it comes
> to human beings alone? The sage and we are of the same
> kind. (*Mencius* 6A.7)

There is a moral impulse that is nascent within each of us, which Mencius calls the four 'sprouts of virtue' (also known as 'beginnings'). Each of these emerging shoots sparks the development of four cardinal virtues: sympathy or pity gives birth to humaneness (*ren*); a feeling of shame leads to a sense of rightness (*yi*); modesty and deference foster a sense of propriety (*li*); and a sense of right and wrong is the sprout of wisdom (*zhi*). These four sprouts are like our four limbs: there is no excuse for not developing them. But these ethical impulses must be stimulated and nurtured to reach their full potential. Humaneness (*ren*) and rightness (*yi*) are highest on Mencius's agenda: 'The five kinds of grain are the finest of all seeds. But if they are not mature, they are not even as good as the tares or weeds. With humaneness, too, maturity is everything' (*Mencius* 6A.19). Mencius takes this development of our innate moral potential as a sacrosanct ambition. Living unethically is worse than not living at all: 'I desire fish, and I also desire bear's paws [a delicacy at the time, it seems]. If I cannot have both of them, I will give up the fish and take bear's paws. I desire life, and I also desire rightness. If I cannot have both, then I will give up life and take rightness' (*Mencius* 6A.10).

But which way does the human temperament tilt? Mencius believed it tends towards goodness. If presented with a choice, humans have a natural tendency to do the right thing. They possess a moral autonomy that is lodged within and spurs them on to do what is good: 'All human beings have a mind [heart] that cannot bear to see the suffering of others' (*Mencius* 2A.6). This sense of rightness sits within us; it is not an external standard that is imposed from the outside. The Chinese term translated as 'mind' here is the character for 'heart' (*xin*). In ancient China, it is the heart (and not the brain) that functions as the thinking organ that makes judgements; the heart is the seat of both affection and cognition (hence the composite translation 'heart-mind', which has no equivalent in the main Western languages).

CHAPTER 4

To prove that compassion is innate, Mencius sets a test:
'If anyone were suddenly to see a child about to fall into a
well, his mind would be filled with alarm, distress, pity and
compassion.' Mencius is adamant that you would immediately
jump after the child to rescue it, but why? After all, you might
drown yourself, or fail to save the child, in which case you
could even be blamed for its death. Mencius argues that, by
nature, anyone would jump after the child, instantaneously
and without giving it a second thought. You jump because it
is part of your moral make-up; inborn moral sprouts are activated instinctively, not as the result of a process of rational
deliberation. There is no external motivation that prompts
you. You do not save the child because it belongs to your own
family; you need not be educated or instructed to feel for a
fellow man or woman. The prospect of a reward or social rec-
ognition is not on your mind.

This is all well and good, but if all humans have the same
natural tendencies, why do some develop into good individuals and others not, why do some achieve and do well in life
and others fail to do so? Here Mencius acknowledges that
there is a potential within each of us to do wrong. People
can be led astray, but they will only do so if their natural tendencies have been violated, obstructed or left undeveloped.
The task is to make the right sprouts flourish (water the
flowers, not the weeds). Hence his reply to Master Gongdu
(Gongduzi): 'Those who follow the part of themselves that
is great become great persons, while those who follow the
part that is small become small persons' (*Mencius* 6A.15). A
desire for material wealth and physical comforts such as food
and sex are part of human nature. But Mencius warns that

they should not be allowed to overshadow our internal moral compass. In political terms, the implication is that the ruler should share these material pleasures with his people. The heart-mind is there to reflect on the impulses of the senses. It judges whether or not desires (the smaller part of ourselves) violate the inborn moral propensity (the greater part of ourselves): 'The ears and the eyes do not think and they are obscured by things. When one thing comes into contact with another, it is led astray. But the function of the heart-mind is to reflect. If it thinks, it apprehends; if it does not think, it fails to apprehend. This is what Heaven has given us' (*Mencius* 6A.15).

Mencius is conscious that there can be many reasons that prevent people from making the right moral judgements. The will can be weak, people can be psychologically damaged or insufficiently trained to develop a moral sense that enables their shoots to appear above ground. To many, humaneness is a halfway station. We are happy to extend feelings of compassion to those in our immediate surroundings (family, friends, the local neighbourhood), but reaching out beyond our familiar circles is more challenging. Anyone who donates to charity will recognize the feeling. To illustrate this, Mencius uses the story of King Huan of Qi, who sets free a sacrificial ox, as he could not stand the sight of the innocent and frightened animal on its way to be slaughtered. The king's impulse of compassion had clearly set in. 'Your heart is ready to be a genuine king,' Mencius tells him. However, next the king orders the ox to be substituted by a sheep. His people assume the king is merely being mean, swapping a large offering for a smaller one. 'What was there to choose between an ox and a sheep?' Mencius asks. King Huan then explains that his compassion did not extend to the sheep because he had not seen it while it was alive. The king had failed to show humaneness to the sheep. Mencius uses the incident as a veiled criticism to point out how the king failed to acknowledge and remedy the suffering of his people. His compassion extended to animals, but not to his people. He was sensitive to the suffering he could see before him, but not to that which took place out of sight (*Mencius* 1A.7).

Yet, despite the obstacles and impasses that prevent our moral shoots from branching out to others, Mencius has an unswerving confidence in the prospect that people's innately good tendencies will always spontaneously re-germinate. Human nature repairs itself, over and over again. He describes this with a beautiful allegory (one that has not escaped the attention of contemporary environmentalists!):

> The trees on Ox Mountain were once beautiful. But being situated on the outskirts of a large state, the trees were cut down by axes. Could they remain beautiful? Given the air of the day and the night, and the moisture of the rain and the dew, they did not fail to put forth new buds and shoots, but then cattle and sheep came along to graze upon these. This accounts for the barren appearance of the mountain. Seeing this barrenness, people suppose that the mountain was never wooded. But how could this be the nature of the mountain? So it is with what is preserved in a human being: could it be that anyone should lack the mind of humaneness and rightness? (*Mencius* 6A.8)

Ox Mountain represents a powerful and positive vote of confidence in the capacity of humans to bounce back against all odds and do what is right.

Yet, while Mencius urges us to tend to the moral potential in others, his idealism also contains a touch of realism. One cannot force human nature to blossom overnight; it requires gradual and staged growth from within. The human character needs to be cultivated at the right pace; it warrants a delicate balance between nature and nurture:

> There was a man from Song who, worried that his seedlings were not growing, pulled them up. Having done so he returned home wearily, telling people: 'I am tired today; I have been helping the seedlings to grow.' When his sons rushed out to have a look, they found that all the seedlings were withered. There are few in the world who do not try to help the seedlings to grow. Those who believe there is no way to benefit them neglect the seedlings and do not weed them. Those bent on helping them to grow pull them up, which is not only of no benefit but, on the contrary, causes them injury. (*Mencius* 2A.2)

Mencius's view of human nature also drives his political philosophy. If compassion and humaneness can encourage people to pull towards each other, then this should also apply to those in power. True, a ruler who displays a sense of humaneness and does the right thing will inspire everyone to follow him (*Mencius* 4B.5). But Mencius puts the onus on the people to hold the ruler to account. Rulers and states are there to serve the welfare of the people. Support by the people is a moral measure of legitimacy. Mencius is the first philosopher to openly state that bad rulers should be unseated (in which case, killing the ruler is not regicide). It is a failure of highly placed ministers not to point out the flaws in their superior's character and urge him to change: 'If the ruler has great faults, they should remonstrate with him. If, after they have done so repeatedly, he still does not listen, they should depose him' (*Mencius* 5B.9). A consequence of putting the people's well-being first is that the ruler should avoid waging war whenever possible. Mencius does not believe there is such a thing as a just war: it only happens 'that some [wars] are better than others' (*Mencius* 7B.2). Aggressive warfare can only be justified if it is punitive – that is, if it is inflicted by a superior on an inferior to redress a transgression (like an individual being punished for a crime by the authorities). When other rulers exploit their people, 'were you to go and punish them, who would oppose you?' (*Mencius* 1A.5).

The counterargument to Mencius's theory of human nature was set out by Xunzi, the third major representative of the Confucian lineage in pre-imperial times. Born in the state of Zhao, Xunzi also travelled to Qi, where he spent time at the Jixia Academy. He was also active at the court of Chu and visited Qin. Xunzi lived a very long life and died sometime after 238 BCE, possibly well into his nineties. In his work, known as *The Master Xun* or *Xunzi* (transmitted in 32 chapters), he defends Confucian values against what he perceives to be internal and external intellectual threats (most notably the Mohists, but also Legalist and Daoist thinkers), including the theories proposed by Mencius, whom he takes on in a chapter entitled 'Human Nature is Bad' (*Xunzi* 23).

Xunzi refutes that humans possess a strong inborn moral

guide, claiming instead that people have a tendency to do what is bad. This does not mean that human nature *is* evil, or that people delight in doing the wrong thing. Rather, Xunzi argues that humans are naturally selfish and will put their own desires first, above all else: 'People's nature is such that as soon as they are born, they begin to depart from their original simplicity and their childhood innocence; they are certain to lose these things' (*Xunzi* 23.1d). If Mencius's cup of inborn moral potential is half full, Xunzi's is half empty.

Xunzi opens his chapter with the statement: 'Human nature is bad. What is good in them is acquired through conscious exertion.' To get people to do what is good, Xunzi suggests, you need to institute a programme of deliberate effort and actions (*wei*). Humans must be subjected to a regime of learning and education. They require guidance from teachers who instil a clear set of standards. Unless people are directed by a code of rituals and rules, they will make the wrong choices. Being a good person does not come naturally; rather, it requires training and artificial means. Turning humans into sociable and moral individuals requires more than nurturing saplings to grow into beautiful trees (as Mencius would have it). It takes the job of a carpenter to steam, bend and straighten a crooked piece of wood into shape. Human nature is like a piece of blunt metal that requires a whetstone to sharpen it (*Xunzi* 23.1b).

The premise for Xunzi is that humans are born with a love for profit, which causes aggression and greed. They harbour feelings of envy and hate that lead to violence and crime. Lust for beautiful things (he calls it 'the desires of the ears and eyes') leads to licentious behaviour. Humans (like animals) are driven by primal desires that would lead to anarchy and disorder if left uncurbed. Nevertheless, these characteristics are part of our inborn nature which is granted by Heaven and cannot be undone. Xunzi's Heaven is not the ethical guardian of the human world; it does not respond to human concerns or assist us to act morally. In short, inborn nature needs to be shaped and fashioned by other forces:

> The part of man that cannot be gained by learning or mastered by application is called 'inborn nature'. What must be learned before a man can do it and what he must apply himself to before he can master it is called 'acquired nature'. This is precisely the difference between 'inborn' and 'acquired' nature. (*Xunzi* 23.1c)

In other words, Xunzi believes that the source of morality is not lodged within people, but exists beyond them, namely in the teachings and rituals of the sages. Only their guidance and models can restrain natural impulses and lead to orderly behaviour. An example: you are hungry. If left to your own instincts, you would try to satiate your desire for food instantaneously and without regard for others. However, having acquired a second nature through being taught the principles of deference and moral duty, you have learned that elders should be fed first before you tuck into your bacon and eggs (or rice, or noodles), and leave the most savoury parts of a dish to them. Inborn human nature thus needs corrective moral direction. This can only be gained through education and learning rituals. Xunzi compares it to the work of a potter who turns clay into a pot, or a craftsman who turns wood into tools. Ironically, it is as if he is telling us that, in order to become good, one has to be bad in the first place:

> In general, the fact that humans desire to do good is precisely because their nature is bad. Those with very little think longingly about having much; an ugly man longs for beauty; those in cramped conditions long for spacious surroundings; the poor long for wealth; those who are humble desire eminence. Indeed, whatever a man lacks within himself he is sure to seek outside. Thus those who are already rich will not long for wealth, nor do the eminent wish for high position. What a man already possesses within he will not bother to look for outside. From this we can see that man's desire to do what is good is the product of the fact that his nature is bad. (*Xunzi* 23.2b)

In essence, the difference of view between Mencius and Xunzi is one of emphasis rather than substance. Both share a belief that all human beings can be perfected; every person in theory can become a sage. We all have a heart-mind that selects and guides our impulses. Both philosophers also recognize the need for human beings to be socialized through learning. Where they differ is in their confidence in the role of nature versus nurture. Mencius believes inborn goodness merely needs a stimulus and is therefore largely a spontaneous product; Xunzi thinks a more concerted human effort is needed to civilize humans and turn them away from their inborn self-centredness. Mencius comes across as an idealist, believing that our ethical inclinations are already structured in an appropriate way. Xunzi appears more of a realist: we possess the raw materials but they need shaping and polishing; hence the distinction he makes between inborn nature (which yields to basic desires) and acquired nature, which is man-made through education.

In the battle for Confucian minds, centuries later during the Song period (960–1279 CE), the Mencian view of human nature would prevail and become accepted as orthodox, while Xunzi was discredited for having obscured the authentic tradition of Confucius. Since its compilation in the thirteenth century, the most popular primer used to educate the young at home was *The Three Character Classic* (*San zi jing*). At just over five hundred characters in length and made up of three-character lines in alternating rhyme, the text could be easily memorized. For over seven hundred years, its opening lines were incised into the minds of countless generations of children and students:

> People from birth
> have a nature that is good.
> By nature people closely resemble each other,
> but through habit they become distant from each other.

Nurturing the sprouts

The Three Character Classic continues: 'If a child does not study, this would not be appropriate. If a child fails to learn while young, what is there to be done when he is old?' Whether it takes carpentry tools to cleave and fashion wood into a useful shape or a farmer's knack to encourage a tree to grow straight, Mencius and Xunzi shared an unshakeable conviction that human character is a work in progress. Confucians insist that, whatever the state of their inborn nature, people need to be educated to become fitting members of an orderly society. The implication is that those who are already morally accomplished (the sages among us) should respond to the call to teach and instruct others. Integral to living as a Confucian is the obligation to transmit their knowledge to others (I teach, therefore I am). Here Confucians fall back on one of the primary images associated with the Master and his major followers: they present themselves as master teachers, keen to continuously learn, and eager to formulate clear expectations for others to study and improve themselves.

In the *Analects*, Confucius emerges first and foremost as a teacher who takes every opportunity to emphasize the importance of learning. He describes himself as so absorbed in his studies that he forgets to eat, worry about other things or notice the onset of old age (*An.* 7.19). With uncharacteristic immodesty, he proclaims that his love of learning is equalled by no one (*An.* 5.28, 7.2). Today Confucius continues to enjoy this status as the first person in Chinese history to devote his entire life to teaching. For centuries he has been acclaimed as China's 'First and Supreme Teacher'. His birthday (28 September) is still celebrated as Teachers' Day in Taiwan. In official publications in mainland China, he is referred to as a 'thinker' and 'educator'. Promotion of the image of Confucius as an effective teacher reflects an unwavering belief through the ages that all human beings can be perfected through learning. Each situation can be turned into an occasion to learn: 'When I walk in the company of two other people, I will always find a teacher among them. I select what is good in my companions and follow it. I pick out their weaknesses, and reform myself accordingly' (*An.* 7.22). Confucius is also an advocate of lifelong learning, which he sees as an accumulative process: 'At fifteen, my heart was set upon learning; at thirty, I had become established; at forty, I was no longer perplexed; at fifty, I knew the Mandate of Heaven; at sixty, I obeyed; at seventy, I could follow my heart's desires' (*An.* 2.4).

He expects a high degree of commitment from his students. They must be able to think and solve problems for themselves:

> I do not open the door for someone who is not already driven to understand; I do not supply words to someone who is not already trying hard to find a language for his ideas. If I hold up one corner of a problem and a student does not come back to me with the other three, I will not try again to teach him. (*An.* 7.8)

Mencius concurs: 'There are many arts in teaching. If I decline to teach someone, I am teaching him all the same' (*Mencius* 6B.16). Yet Confucius is also portrayed as accommodating and inclusive. When selecting his students, he makes no distinction according to economic background or social standing. He accepts whatever payment students can offer for his services, even 'if they could only afford a strip of dried meat' (*An.* 7.7). His best and most admired student, Yan Hui, was poor. Yet in the context of his time, Confucius's open invitation to come and study regardless of their background rested on a false demographic. Only elite families could spare young or adult males from working the fields. Teaching and tutoring in ancient China were largely a privately funded affair.

The need for gifts and honoraria to secure a teacher deprived most commoners from the opportunity to study.

In the opening lines of the *Analects*, Confucius promotes a very specific view of learning: 'To learn and then repeatedly apply what you have learned, is that not a source of delight?' (*An.* 1.1). Learning should not be a purely theoretical, abstract or intellectual endeavour (although, in practice, studying the Confucian Classics does involve a fair amount of rote recitation). Learning has a practical dimension: it consists of understanding and replicating, theory and practice. 'If you learn without reflecting on what you have learned, you will be lost. If you reflect without learning, you end up in perilous circumstances' (*An.* 2.15). Above all, studying is a moral undertaking: 'The Master instructs under four headings: culture, conduct, doing one's utmost and making good on one's word' (*An.* 7.25). Teachers ought to be moral exemplars who practise what they preach. Ultimately, it is by imitating and emulating exemplary teachers that one can elevate oneself to be an example to others. (This also means that the values that students hold in high esteem echo those qualities they value in their teachers.) Confucius has an almost blind confidence in the autonomous desire of people to study and seek moral self-cultivation, though he is equally critical about the motivation behind it: 'The scholars of old only studied for their own sake, those of today do so to impress others' (*An.* 14.24). Nevertheless, as much as one should delight in the process of learning itself, absorbing knowledge without putting it to practical use is to be avoided. Confucius was in this respect a realist: 'It is not easy to find someone who can study for three years without thinking about earning a salary' (*An.* 8.12). Here his outlook reflects the much-expressed concern among students today who wonder what occupation a degree course might lead to.

Confucian education for the elites consisted of a curriculum that covered history, literature, ritual and music, with an emphasis on texts said to contain wisdom passed on by the ancients. In the *Analects*, Confucius repeatedly flags up the merits of studying the poems in *The Book of Odes*: 'Why is it, my friends, that none of you study the *Odes*? Reciting from the *Odes* can stimulate your imagination, strengthen your powers of observation, improve how to live in a group with others, and help vent your misgivings' (*An.* 17.9). Mencius for his part likes to quote from *The Book of Documents*, among others, to back up his arguments. Yet Confucian learning aims to go beyond the intellectual mastery of traditional texts and rituals. Learning is to equip the student with values and skills that can be put into practice in daily life. The so-called 'six arts' to be mastered – ritual, music, archery, charioteering, writing and mathematics – were aimed at character building. Confucius questions the value of studying the martial arts. The purpose of archery, by contrast, is not to create warriors, but to perfect an inner equilibrium that allows one to hit the mark. For those who aspire to become gentlemen, study involves not only refining the mind but the entire body, its movements and postures, its full range of emotions. The *Xunzi* reiterates this in its opening chapter, 'Exhortation to Learning', which quotes several of the dictums on learning from the *Analects* and elaborates on their importance:

> The learning of the gentleman enters through his ears, is stored in the mind, spreads through his four limbs, and

manifests itself in his activity and repose. His softest word, his slightest movement, in one and all he can be taken as a model and pattern (for others). The learning of the petty person enters through his ears and comes out of his mouth. Since the distance from mouth to ear is no more than four inches, how could it be enough to refine the seven-foot body of a person! In antiquity students learned for the sake of self-improvement, today they learn for the sake of others. (*Xunzi* 1.9)

The ideal that learning should instil moral values was often no more than just that: an ideal. In practice, Confucian education often turned into competitive bookish learning and the pursuit of antiquarian and literary knowledge. Memorization, the reproduction of information, and rote learning were never far away. Ironically, Confucius is his own best critic here: 'If people can recite all of the three hundred *Odes* by heart, yet, when given a job in government, are unable to carry it out, or when sent to distant quarters, are unable to engage of their own initiative, then no matter how many [poems] they have mastered, what good are they to them?' (*An.* 13.5). In imperial times, among the countless candidates who submitted themselves to the pressures of the civil service exams, with an official post as the ultimate reward, many must have wondered what had happened to Confucius's motto that one should not study to impress others. And while the subject matter on the curriculum may have changed, a similar atmosphere of pressure and competition still surrounds school and university entrance exams across the Chinese world today. China may not be unique in this respect, however: many institutions of learning in the West have replaced a culture of education with a culture of examination.

In the Confucian perspective, learning necessitates outside assistance from a master or teacher: 'In learning, no method is of more advantage than to be near a man of learning' (*Xunzi* 1.10). The master–disciple relationship is central in the education of the pupil. Instruction takes place not simply by verbal means, but by observing the behaviour of the teacher among his circle of disciples. Learning should be empirical rather than theoretical. Mencius mentions various types of schools the ancients had set up (*Mencius* 1A.3, 3A.3). Ritual texts such as *The Ritual Records* describe in detail how the student should show deference and respect to his teacher during the learning process: he should be dressed properly, keep quiet, listen respectfully and not interrupt: 'When requesting instruction on the subject of his studies, the student should rise; when requesting further information, he should rise again' (*Liji*, 'Qu li').

Some questioned whether all this devotion to studying the words of the ancients was worth the effort. Does it really turn people into better individuals? For the authors of *The Master Zhuang*, it certainly does not. The argument here is that the best things in life are not acquired as the result of bookish learning or studied erudition. Talent, skill and the knack of overcoming life's obstacles, they claim, are transmitted spontaneously; there is no wisdom worth pursuing in books. Zhuangzi and his adherents deplored the relentless Confucian insistence on education and moral cultivation as nothing but a drag. He illustrates this with the story of Duke Huan and the wheelwright. While the duke is reading, his wheelwright interrupts him and asks what he is reading. 'The words of the sages,' the duke replies. 'Are they still alive, then?' asks the wheelwright. 'No, they are already dead,' responds the duke. 'In that case,' the wheelwright continues, 'all my lord is reading are merely the dregs of the ancients.' The ancients have taken their wisdom to the grave, he argues. 'Look at my own profession,' he says. 'I have learned to adjust the spokes in a wheel by sensing it in my hand and feeling it in my heart. But I cannot put into words how I do it, I have not been able to teach it to my son, and he has not been able to learn it from me. It simply is a knack' (*Zhuangzi* 13.8).

Thus against the Confucian insistence that intervention and effort (either more or less of it) are essential for shaping human nature, and for imparting values and skills, may be set the Daoist claim that leaving things untouched is the best way to develop a spontaneous sensitivity to the world and acquire skills. Teaching requires no explanations or intellectual analysis. The authors of texts such as *The Master Zhuang* succeeded magisterially in launching sharp-witted challenges to the value of study and intellectual pursuit as a means of developing personhood. However, they failed to emasculate what would become a core tenet of Confucian(ized) societies, past and present: the obligation to better oneself through untiring study and hard work.

Living in the plural

In Confucian thinking, the belief that humans need to be acclimatized to ethical norms through education and ritual starts from the premise that we live in the plural: not only do we dwell and act in groups with others (Xunzi uses the term 'flocking together'), but within this social setting we also wear multiple hats. Imagine a person as an aggregate of multiple roles, rather than an individual with a specific, one-dimensional personality. So instead of seeing John as a single (and unique) individual with a particular set of character traits (shy, compassionate, intelligent, self-centred at times, but modest), there is John the father, the teacher, the son, the student, the husband, the lover, the taxpayer, John the employee, the line manager, the poet, the joker, etc. In order for John to be functional in society, then, he needs to be mindful of his role and place in any given situation. Changing circumstances prompt us to adapt our role. To be effective as a person requires us to master the art of putting on the right hat in any given circumstance. Failing to do so will short-circuit the network of relationships that link us to those around us, professionally and socially. During office hours, John may well be a distinguished university professor used to commanding the (more or less interested) ear of an auditorium of students. However, should he choose to lecture his wife and children around the dinner table every evening in a similar fashion, he is likely to provoke an adverse reaction. In sum, it is our relationship to others, more so than our character as an individual, that should guide our actions.

The core five relationships are described as follows in *The Doctrine of the Mean* (*Zhongyong*), a text attributed to Master Zisi (483–402 BCE), a grandson of Confucius:

In the world there are five methods to reach the Dao and three ways by means of which to put them into practice:

> ruler towards minister, father towards son, husband
> towards wife, older brother towards younger brother, and
> interactions between friends. These five are the method
> to reach the Dao. Wisdom, benevolence and courage are
> the three ways in the world to reach virtue. The manner
> in which they are put into practice is one and the same.
> (*Zhongyong* 20)

The same text also trumpets the virtue of integrity (*cheng*). People possess sincerity in graded quantities (the sages have it from birth, other mortals acquire it through learning) and so one needs to work hard at developing it.

Of paramount importance in the Confucian make-up of society is the family. The family forms the unit in which children and adults are conditioned to acquire the social skills and obligations that can then be projected to the level of the state. (The ruler regards his people as his own kin; his people display a sense of loyalty and obligation to him that is similar to what is expected within the family.) Instead of making the state and its institutions the primary force for regulating human behaviour, Confucians delegate this authority to the patriarchal family and the kinship relations that rule it (patriarchal meaning that authority issues from and flows through the male line: male ancestors, the father figure, sons). Ruled by customs, conventions and rituals as much as by externally imposed laws, the family exerted a major influence on Chinese legal thought, as will be shown in the next chapter. Within the family, each member must fulfil designated role obligations.

Let us begin with the child. There are at least two ways to

define childhood. It may be seen, first of all, in terms of the natural child – that is, a person of specific age at a certain stage of his or her physiological and psychological development. Secondly, it can be defined as a social station, a stage in life corresponding to certain normative behaviours displayed within the context of the family, local community, school, and so on. Traditionally, the interest in China has been mostly in the social definition of childhood.

In ancient China, infants were not considered full persons. Chinese thinkers show little curiosity about infancy or the developmental process of infants. Only when the child can walk and talk does it appear on their radar. But even then, childhood tends to be presented as a transitory stage to adulthood. To be sure, the masters of philosophy are keen to use the image of the child for the sake of philosophical argument. For Laozi, a vulnerable baby is proof that apparent weakness should be seen as a source of strength: 'One who possesses virtue in abundance is comparable to a newborn baby. Poisonous insects will not sting it, wild animals will not pounce on it, birds of prey will not swoop down on it. Its bones are weak and its sinews supple yet its hold is firm' (*DDJ* 55). Confucius notes that the young should be respected: 'How are we to know that those who come after us will not prove our equals?' (*An.* 9.23). As we saw, Mencius uses the image of the child-in-the-well to illustrate his view of human nature. Another widespread metaphor, stretching back as far as *The Book of Odes* and *The Book of Documents*, compares the ruler-subject relationship to that of a parent caring for an infant. But none of these images reveal much about the virtue of youth or the social reality children faced in a society that equated wisdom and insight with progressive old age.

In pre-modern China, the transition from childhood to adulthood took place anywhere between the age of fourteen and nineteen (corresponding in Chinese terms to fifteen and twenty *sui* or years). A 'capping ceremony' marked the coming of age of boys; teenaged girls were hair-pinned. Children were seldom spoken of as children. More prevalent is the image of the precocious child who displays adult features and skills that foreshadow a promising personality and future, such as being able to recite huge chunks from the Classics (the young Confucius and Mencius pretend-performed rituals while hanging out in the temple). Private expressions of parental love, emotions provoked by children, or descriptions of children playing, receive short shrift in the writings of the time. A rare example occurs in *The Master Han Fei*, although, ironically, the underlying message is that the sayings of the ancients are as unrepresentative of reality as children's games: 'Children, when they play together, take soft earth as cooked rice, muddy water as soup, and wood shavings as slices of meat. However, at dusk they must go home for dinner because dust rice and mud soup can be played with but not eaten' (*Han Feizi* 11).

This does not mean, of course, that displaying feelings for children was anathema. Nevertheless, the main focus in Chinese sources tends to be on public life and on those aspects of a child's development that foreshadow his or her promise as an adult. The virtues and values appreciated in children were those of an adult. 'Diligence has its merits; there are no gains to be found in play,' concludes *The Three Character Classic*. Youth was a necessary interval during which the character of the child was to be equipped with the qualities needed to be successful in public life as an adult.

Predicting a child's personality and influencing its character development meant much in a society that held public service and moral rectitude in high esteem. Calendars (also known as 'daybooks') specify certain days as auspicious for giving birth. Children born on unlucky days risked being unhealthy or could develop a flawed temperament. A newborn child's cries and any significant physical features in its appearance were regarded as signs of its character. Newborn boys with a 'wolf-like cry' are destined not to turn out well, according to *The Zuo Tradition* (*Zuozhuan*, Lord Xuan 4). Physiognomy – that is, the practice of predicting and interpreting someone's moral character traits and deportment on the basis of one's physical appearance – is attested early on. Education could start in utero. This was known as 'foetal instruction' (*tai jiao*). A mother's diet supposedly affected the unborn child's temperament. Anything she saw, heard or exposed herself to during pregnancy could influence the development of the child. A queen bearing the future heir to the throne should not crave or eat irregular foodstuffs (that is, produce that is out of season or items presented in an irregular order). Mencius's mother, we are told, was meticulous in her prenatal care: she 'taught him in the womb' by sitting exclusively on a straight mat and refusing to eat improperly cut meat. A balanced diet during pregnancy was thought to produce offspring with a sense of proportion and balance. A Han text uncovered in the early 1970s, entitled *Book on the*

Generation of the Foetus (Taichan shu), recommends eating the chrysalises of caterpillars or drinking a concoction that included a dog's penis to give birth to a boy, eating the flesh of a black hen to produce a girl, or feeding the pregnant mother the meat of a mare to ensure the child's vigorous growth. Another metaphor used to describe the immersion of the child in a morally stimulating environment is that one should handle children in the same way as one dyes silk.

Han-period funerary inscriptions refer to infants as people who had 'not yet become human beings', indicating that they had not yet reached the stage in which they deserved to be accorded full mourning rites. The death of a child mattered less than that of an adult. The Qin legal code notes (painfully) that killing a physically handicapped child (described as 'having strange things on its body') would have no repercussions for the perpetrator. The same article continues by stating that abandoning a healthy child (literally, refusing to 'lift it up'), on the grounds that one already has too many children, should be sentenced as a crime of child murder (D56). The death of an infant had a relatively light impact on government policy and possibly even within the family. Han sources indicate that, during times of deprivation and poverty, parents would rather kill their children than pay the obligatory poll tax. This tax demarcated infancy from childhood and would normally be levied when a child reached the age of six. Children became more valued as they grew older. Infants were entered in population registers when 'teething' at seven or eight months, but many never reached that stage. Qin-period population registers initially did not even register children by their age but by their height – a more reliable indicator for judging whether they were ready for military service. Any male taller than a hundred and sixty centimetres, or five foot three inches, could be recruited into the army (in Qin China this corresponded to the age of sixteen or seventeen; equivalent to modern average-height charts for thirteen- and fourteen-year-olds in Europe or the United States).

Within the household and the family, patrilineage governed attitudes towards children, rendering girls as minor offspring. (Later medical texts mention that the sex of the child may be determined by whether coitus takes places on a *yang* or *yin* day in the woman's menstrual cycle.) Authoritarian behaviour from parents was accepted as the norm. Boys could inherit the father's land and follow his occupation, or be trained for a military or official career. For girls, marriage was the only real way up in society. Family strategizing began at infancy. Heads of elite families schemed and scouted around to secure a promising marriage arrangement for their daughters, by marrying her off into a family better than their own. The gruesome custom of binding young girls' feet emerged in the Tang period and took hold from the eleventh century CE onwards. (Bandages were tied around the feet, bending the toes towards the instep so that eventually the arch broke.) Self-inflicted pain during a girl's formative years, it was argued, paved the way to a good marriage and dowry. Foot binding symbolized the submission and restriction of women. Bound feet were also referred to as 'lotus feet' and an erotic fascination grew up around them. It is not until the end of the imperial period and well into the twentieth century that foot binding was abandoned.

The Ritual Records prescribes that a distinction and separation between the sexes should be upheld in both the private and public spheres. It delineates the spheres of men and women as 'outer' and 'inner' worlds respectively and prohibits direct contact or the sharing of space and possessions between male and female: 'Male and female should not sit together, nor share the same rack for clothes, nor use the same towel or comb, nor allow their hands to touch when giving or receiving' (*Liji*, 'Qu li'). The list of dos and don'ts goes on: a wife does not share her husband's bathing house; women live in the interior quarters of the house, while men occupy the exterior parts; women only speak about domestic affairs ('things spoken inside should not go out, words spoken outside should not come in'); women should cover the face when going out; women should keep to the left side of the road while men take the right side (*Liji*, 'Nei ze'); a wife should remain faithful to her husband even after his death. The rationale given for maintaining a distinction between male and female is that it allows fathers and sons to develop intimacy. This in turn promotes harmony within the household and in the world at large. Without a separation between the sexes, moral virtues cannot develop, and people would live just like animals (as one saying held: 'stags and calves mate with the same doe').

In the first extended text written by a woman for women, entitled *Admonitions for Women* (*Nü jie*), Ban Zhao (*c.*48–116 CE) advises that every woman should uphold the four pillars of feminine good conduct: womanly virtue (this includes being chaste and modest); womanly speech (that is, avoiding vulgar language and choosing one's words carefully; knowing when it is appropriate to speak); womanly manners (keeping one's clothes clean and fresh); and womanly work (weaving and sewing, serving food and drink). Ban Zhao came from a learned aristocratic family. Widowed at a very young age, she chose not to remarry. Instead she devoted the rest of her life to scholarship and literary pursuits, which gave her the reputation in later times for being China's most renowned female scholar. Once married, a daughter-in-law became part of the household of the parents-in-law and had to serve the interests of her new family. For newly wedded girls, the home of the in-laws could be a hostile environment. Ban Zhao's instructions are drawn up as a sort of survival kit for the defenceless daughter-in-law.

Throughout the *Admonitions*, which she wrote for her own daughters, Ban Zhao backs up her guidance with allusions to the Confucian Classics. Girls, Ban argues, require education and training to be able to grasp the principles of model female conduct: 'To only teach males and not teach females, is that not ignoring the essential relationship between them?' Humility, compliance, modesty, composed manners, respect and devotion to one's husband and his parents form a dominant theme. Ban Zhao also underlines the need for physical separation to guard against unbridled passion and too much intimacy:

> If the feeling of fondness between a wife and husband is such that they never leave one another, and always follow each other around in their rooms and quarters, then they will lust after one another and take liberties. From such action improper language will arise between the two. Such language will inevitably lead to licentiousness. And from this will be born a heart of disrespect to the husband. This is what results from not knowing how to keep to one's proper place. (*Nü jie* 3)

Several texts, starting with *The Ritual Records*, state that a woman, as she progresses through life, should follow the principle of 'threefold obedience' (*san cong*). At each stage, she is dependent on a male: when unmarried, she follows her father; when married, she follows her husband; after the death of her husband, she follows her son.

Another text that has influenced views of womanly behaviour over the centuries is Liu Xiang's *Biographies of Exemplary Women (Lienü zhuan)*, compiled towards the end of the first century BCE. It comprises 125 life stories of famous and lesser-known women in history, classified according to the virtues they display (or fail to display): maternal rectitude, sage intelligence, benevolent wisdom, steadiness and obedience, chastity and rightness, and skill in argument. While acknowledging the importance of virtues such as purity, chastity and subservience, these tales also praise the intellectual ability of women and their role in the moral and intellectual upbringing of children (remember Mencius's mother). In later times, episodes from the *Biographies* inspired scenes in illustrated books and on scrolls, murals, paintings, lacquerware and screens.

It would be incorrect to suggest that the fate of wives, mothers and daughters in pre-modern China was universally one of oppression or that women were powerless and always abided by social expectations as silent, passive and obedient victims. We must not forget that the texts that create this impression are normative: they prescribe how a woman *should* behave, which is not necessarily the same as how women *did* behave. Some anecdotes and stories suggest that some elite women operated outside the home and garnered praise for being proactive. Women also acted as tutors and counsellors, and as such they often became powerful operators in the background (at the court, for instance, they could hold sway over a child emperor). Some elite women excelled in literature, medicine, or the arts of divination and fortune-telling. Furthermore, texts on female instruction were mostly directed at elite families who lived in quarters sufficiently luxurious to house multiple wives and concubines and maintain a visual separation. A toiling farmer's wife had no choice but to bare her arms and share in the labour on the field during seeding time and harvest. (The nuclear family during Han times consisted on average of five members only.) Nevertheless, the predominant mindset that was promoted was one of female subservience and obedience. Confucian rhetoric on familial relations was firmly male-centred, despite evidence of individual women of talent who ran counter to the prevailing ideology. 'In the ruler's court, there should be no talk of wives and daughters' (*Liji*, 'Qu li').

None the less, philosophically, at least, some presented the feminine as the stronger power. Alongside the image of a newborn child, *The Classic of the Way and Virtue* includes the female in its arsenal of metaphors to illustrate that what is passive, receptive, soft and compliant will ultimately prevail: 'Know the male but preserve the female, and become a riverbed for the world' (*DDJ* 28). For Laozi, the mother represents the root of all things and the force to which everything returns: 'Knowing the mother, return and know her children; knowing the children, return and preserve the mother' (*DDJ* 52). While the mountain peaks are exposed to the battering of the elements, it is the spirit of the valley below – the 'subtle female' – that rests quietly and never dies (*DDJ* 6). Philosophically, the generative energy of the female was given pride of place, yet socially she had to take a back seat.

Filial piety

Chinese literature has rather more to say about the obligations to parents that children should fulfil than what duties are owed by parents and adults to children. The young had to inscribe themselves within a strict family hierarchy, with an obligation to obey and respect parents and the elderly and to venerate the ancestral lineage. Of all virtues that bond the family unit together, filial piety (*xiao*) is by far the most defining one. Filial piety is the obligation to obey and unconditionally support one's parents and the elderly: morally, materially and physically. It is a commitment that applies during all stages of life. In childhood, it means obedience and respect for those who raise you. As an adult, it implies supporting those who have brought you up. In middle or old age, it entails maintaining rituals and making sacrifices to the ancestors: 'While they are living, serve them with ritual propriety; when they are dead, bury them and sacrifice to them according to ritual propriety' (*An.* 2.5). Thus throughout every stage of life a person is either the recipient or source of filial care, or both. Filiality continues to be a value instilled in children and young people across the Chinese world today, despite the steady challenges of individualism and materialism brought on by a rapidly modernizing society. The meaning of filial devotion has adapted itself to changing times in the past, and it continues to do so today – for instance, in measures such as tax incentives for those who care for ageing parents and grandparents, or encouraging children to live within easy distance of elderly parents.

Confucius did not invent filial piety. It is a concept that already crops up in writings that predate him. The term itself is a rather lacklustre translation for Chinese *xiao*, which in origin also denoted a type of food sacrifice to one's ancestors. Obedience and service to the elderly (and, by inference, one's superiors and the Father State) stood central in the Confucian model of family and society. Rebels at home only make for rebels in later life: 'The gentleman devotes his efforts to the roots, for once the roots are established, the Dao will grow therefrom. Being filial and showing fraternal respect is, perhaps, the root of benevolence' (*An.* 1.2). Mencius lists five forms of unfilial behaviour: to be too lazy to tend to your father and mother; to be distracted from looking after your parents because of games ('chess') and alcohol; to chase goods and property and be partial to your wife instead of looking after your parents; to disgrace your parents because of 'desires of the eyes and ears'; and to be a daredevil or quarrelsome and contentious, so as to endanger your father and mother (*Mencius* 4B.30). Filial negligence at its most severe would be not to produce a male heir (*Mencius* 4A.26).

Filial piety, in theory, does not mean obedience must be totally blind (even though, in practice, that has no doubt been the way many heads of family have interpreted it throughout history; raising children incurs costs, but they also offer a form of social security). It is fine to criticize and correct parents, but affection for them should not depend on whether or not they heed your advice: 'In serving your father and mother, you ought to dissuade them from doing wrong in the gentlest of ways. If you see your advice being ignored, you should not become disobedient but remain respectful. You should not complain even if in so doing you wear yourself out' (*An.* 4.18). When a father, enraged by his son's well-meant counsel, beats him 'until the blood flows', the son 'should not presume to be angry and resentful, but be even more respectful and filial' (*Liji*, 'Nei ze'). In practice, filial piety can imply obeying the father against one's own better judgement. But there are ways to diverge quietly from the path laid out by one's elders. Once the immediate memory of them has begun to fade, and the traditional three-year mourning period has run its course, a son may start to shape his own conduct as he wishes rather than in the form dictated by his father, if that is desirable. But not before then! 'When someone's father is still alive, observe his intentions; after his father has passed away, observe his conduct. If for three years he does not alter the ways of his late father, he may be called a filial son' (*An.* 1.11). Confucius holds firm that filial piety involves more than the mechanical process of providing for parents and the elderly. It must come with an emotional intent of respect and reverence. 'Dogs and horses are given much care. If you do not respect your parents, what is the difference?' (*An.* 2.7). Taking care of the shopping for your parents is a noble thing, as long as you do not consider it a chore or do it with the intention of being let off the hook the next time a request is made of you.

Reverent care for those who have nourished you also entails looking after yourself and the body you have inherited from your parents. One way in which the *Analects* describes filial good conduct is 'to give your father and mother no other cause for anxiety other than your illness' (*An.* 2.6). Fasting and abstaining from acquiring material goods can help concentrate the mind or be a sign of respect during mourning. But leaving the body emaciated and ill as a result would be going too far. As one Han text puts it, it should be a son's duty, 'to honour the limbs and body the ancestors have left to him' (*Baihutong*, 'Sang fu'). Stories from medieval times suggest that some took the duty of filial piety to extreme levels, including foregoing food, wealth and luxuries or even an official career in order to take care of one's parents. Suffering hardship in the service of one's parents was held up as a noble ideal.

One saying that encapsulates very graphically how children might pay off the care-debt they have incurred is that they should be 'feeding [their parents] in return', like a young crow that regurgitates food for its mother. Indeed, *The Ritual Records* contains a series of special recipes to nourish the aged. Filial care also extended to issues such as personal hygiene:

> Every five days [sons and their wives] should prepare
> tepid water, and ask [their parents] to take a bath.
> Every three days they should prepare water for them
> to wash their heads. If in the meantime their faces
> appear dirty, they should heat the water in which
> the rice has been cleaned, and ask their parents to
> wash with it. When their feet are dirty, they should
> prepare hot water, and ask them to wash them with it.
> (*Liji*, 'Nei ze')

In short, filial devotion required the young to conceive of their actions and choices as always directed towards the wellbeing of the elderly and the family as a whole. A son was to avoid disgracing his parents and to call nothing that he possessed his own.

A text that has been central in enshrining filial piety within intergenerational relationships in China is *The Classic of Filial Piety* (*Xiaojing*). Compiled or circulating shortly before the Qin dynasty, it uses a fairly common vocabulary and, at less than two thousand characters, the work is relatively brief. *The Classic of Filial Piety* became required reading in schools during parts of the Qin and Han periods. It sets out how one should behave towards one's parents and elders and, by extension, how to conduct oneself in the service of a superior. The text opens with an instruction by Confucius to his disciple Zengzi (Zeng Shen) on the nature of filial piety. Each section then proceeds as a dialogue between them. *The Classic of Filial Piety* has almost nothing to say about female children, though in practice rigid adherence to filial duties also characterized a good wife or daughter-in-law. By contrast, the father figure is held in the highest esteem: 'Of all creatures produced by Heaven and Earth, man is the noblest. In the entire conduct of man, nothing is greater than filial piety. When it comes to filial piety, nothing is more important than showing reverential respect for one's father' (*Xiaojing* 9).

Although filial piety is grounded in familial relationships within the household and the extended family, it also serves as a political virtue. As such, it was interpreted as loyalty to the state and subservient respect for authority:

> Our bodies – every hair and bit of skin – are received by us from our parents. We cannot risk injuring or harming our bodies. This is the beginning of filial piety. Having

established ourselves by practising the Way [of filial conduct], our reputation will spread to future generations and thereby our parents will be glorified. This is the end goal of filial piety. Therefore filial piety starts with the service of parents; it proceeds to the service of the ruler; it is completed by the establishment of our own character. (*Xiaojing* 1)

We serve our father and in the same way we [learn how to] serve our mother. The love towards them is the same. We serve our father and in the same way we [learn how to] serve our ruler. The reverence we show to them is the same. Thus, we show love towards our mother and reverence to the ruler. But to the father we show both love and reverence. Therefore to serve the ruler with filial piety is to show loyalty; to serve those who are senior with reverence is to show obedience. (*Xiaojing* 5)

During the Han, philosophers such as Dong Zhongshu (*c*.179–104 BCE) explained these relationships as part of a cosmology of *yin* and *yang*: the monarch (*yang*) relates to his ministers (*yin*), like father (*yang*) to son (*yin*), and husband (*yang*) to wife (*yin*) (*Chunqiu fanlu* 53.1). But, like anyone else who abandons family allegiances, a ruler who fails to uphold filial care or reciprocate the service and loyalty of his subjects is in trouble. A morality based on the family model is a double-edged sword and could be harsh: excommunicated from the family, one had few other networks to fall back on.

China is by no means unique in using the family model as a political mirror image for the familial state. Native soil and nation are regularly spoken of as a motherland or fatherland, in the past and the present, East and West. Leaders and national anthems alike hail their founders and heroes as 'father' (in some cases 'mother') or 'forefather' of the nation. Even in modern democracies, in which institutions are organized on the basis of profiling and protecting the individual, politicians make a point of projecting family imagery onto the state. (Likewise, in corporations and businesses large and small, hardly a company jamboree goes by without employees being reminded that they are all part of one happy family.)

To respect the elderly was also considered a mark of civilization. It set the Chinese apart from their 'uncivilized' neighbours, and distinguished the educated person from the savage. In a number of texts, barbarians are defined by their lack of respect for the elderly and for praising the young and physically strong instead. Being constantly on the move and not engaged in sedentary agriculture, nomads allegedly failed to create the space and conditions in which proper family units could develop and moral virtues flourish: 'Barbarians do not eat grain, they demean their elders and value the strong; they have a habit of favouring those with strong *qi*' (*Huainanzi* 1.8). By contrast, the Chinese inculcated filial care and deference as an inviolable custom. During the early imperial period, respect for the elderly became enshrined in legal statutes that allowed the aged exemption from taxes or even from prosecution. Failure to register the elderly in the population registers would incur fines. In the state calendar, an annual ceremony celebrated the aged, and septuagenarians were given meat, silk fabric and a walking stick with a handle carved in the shape of a dove – a bird that never chokes on its food.

Filial piety, which tends to be exclusively associated with Confucians, was a virtue so deeply embedded in Chinese society that even the critics of Confucius acknowledged its importance, both positively and negatively. The received version of *The Classic of the Way and Virtue* mentions the term *xiao* twice (*DDJ* 18, 19), while Master Zhuang notes that a child should love its parents as a matter of destiny, as a sentiment 'inseparable from the heart' (*Zhuangzi* 4.2).

Impartial care – why care?

Not everyone saw the family as the cradle of morality or accepted the family head as the most appropriate figure to sanction the conduct of its members. Was it really better to be affectionate to your family first before extending this sentiment to strangers and other creatures, as Mencius had argued (*Mencius* 7A.45)? Legalists, who had little or no confidence in the autonomous power of individuals except those of the ruler and his ministers, pointed out that the interests of the state and those of the family inevitably clashed. Tying people to the family detaches them from the state. Han Fei puts his finger on this with the following anecdote:

> There was a man from Lu who followed his ruler out to war. Three times they went into battle, and three times the man turned his back and ran away. Confucius asked the man why he had run, and he replied: 'I have an elderly father. If I should die, there would be no one to look after him.' Confucius considered the man a very filial person, so he recommended him and got him promoted to office. From this it can be seen that someone who is a filial son

to his father may be a treacherous subject to his ruler.
(*Han Feizi* 49)

The most vociferous critique of Confucius's idea that family
should take priority over others, including the state, came
from Mozi (Master Mo) and his followers. Little is known
about the historical Mozi (Mo Di; *c.*479–381 BCE), except that
he served as an official in the state of Song, living a little
after Confucius (the date given for his birth corresponds to
the year in which Confucius died). There is speculation that
he had an artisan background, possibly working as a carpenter or wheelwright (one story mentions the construction of
a wooden bird or kite). Later sources tend to present Confucius and Mozi in one breath as intellectual opponents, at
times creating the impression that their lives overlapped. But
there are no sound historical grounds for this. In the seventeenth century, the Jesuits Latinized his name as 'Micius'.
There is some evidence that Mozi's followers lived in well-
organized (paramilitary) communes or sects, led by a Grand
Master. But it is hard to corroborate historically to what extent
Mohism was a utopian movement with followers gathered together in egalitarian collectives.

The Master Mo came together over the course of the fourth
and third centuries BCE. (The extant version contains fifty-
three chapters; the original text was longer – possibly as
many as eighteen chapters may have been lost.) Mozi has been
neglected over the centuries. In China, it was not until the
Qing dynasty and in particular the early twentieth century,
when scholarly interests in the philological study of ancient
texts were rekindled, that Mozi regained some attention.

In the West, Mozi has been given serious scholarly attention only in recent decades. The literary quality of the book is certainly no match for the refined prose of some other philosophical texts. *The Master Mo* contains a great deal of repetition and uses a relatively limited and simple vocabulary. Like most texts of the period, the book is layered and would have been compiled over time, making it impossible to identify any single individual as the author of a particular part of it. As a movement, Mohism disappeared from the scene fairly early on, its influence having waned by the second century BCE.

The value of Mohism, however, does not lie in the historical provenance of those who may have compiled the text. Mozi can be said to be the first real debater among the thinkers of his time. Many of his doctrines are direct refutations of the ideas of Confucius. His style is argumentative and he may be the first Chinese philosopher interested in the question of evidence. Each thesis, Mozi claims, needs to be subjected to three tests (called 'three gnomons'): first, one should establish the origins of a thesis (that is, check the hypothesis against the words and deeds of the sages recorded in ancient texts); secondly, one needs to establish a theory's validity through witness accounts ('the eyes and ears of the people'); finally, one needs to establish whether a theory can be applied in practice and whether it benefits the people (*Mozi* 35.3). In addition to chapters that set out the core doctrines of Mohism, *The Master Mo* also contains chapters on how to defend a city, and it devotes considerable space to technical matters (mathematics, optics, physics), language and logic.

In the previous chapter, we saw that Mozi concurred with

Confucius on the issue of loyalty to superiors and moral conduct as a hallmark of those who rule. The Mohists, however, had radically different views as to where a person's first allegiance should lie. Confucius and his followers argued that relationships of kin solidified by a strong bond with one's ancestors should form the basic building block of a moral society. Mozi objected to this and condemned all forms of preferential treatment based on family or lineage:

> In antiquity, the sage kings especially esteemed and exalted those who were worthy, as well as used and employed the able, showing no special consideration for their own fathers or older brothers, no partiality towards the rich and eminent, no favouritism towards the handsome and attractive. The worthy were promoted to high places, enriched and honoured, and made heads of government offices. The unworthy were demoted and rejected, impoverished and debased, and made menials and slaves. All the people, thus motivated by these rewards and fearful of these punishments, led each other into joining the ranks of the worthy. (*Mozi* 9.1)

Societies flourish best, Mozi argues, if we 'exalt the worthy' and show no partiality or favouritism. Therefore one's love and devotion should extend to every member of a community. As an antidote to the Confucian concepts of loyalty to the few and filial piety within the family, Mozi puts forward the notion of 'impartial care' (*jian ai*; translated variously as 'universal love' or 'caring for everyone'). Concern for others should be inclusive: 'If the people in the world do not love each other, the strong will inevitably dominate the weak, the many would inevitably force the few, the rich will inevitably ridicule the poor, the noble will inevitably be arrogant towards people of lower status, and the cunning will inevitably cheat those who are simple of mind' (*Mozi* 15.3). Mutual care, by contrast, ensures that everybody benefits. Those who are childless and without wives will receive support throughout old age; orphans will be looked after as they grow into adults (*Mozi* 16.4). Mozi takes a highly utilitarian stance on what impartial care should comprise: it is not so much about showing compassion or goodwill, but ensuring that people's material concerns are catered for and their sufferings are addressed. It follows, then, that concern for the universal welfare of a population requires a strong state (rather than a family). The state should discourage and prevent preferential treatment on the basis of family connections, close friendships or other partisan alliances. Any partiality must be eliminated; we should extend the feelings we have for our own parents and relatives to society and the world at large.

What Mozi proposes is not radical or unquestioned altruism. Ultimately everyone needs to fare better. One can have perfectly acceptable utilitarian motives in 'caring for all' since benefit is a two-way street: when you benefit others, you will draw benefits from others. Altruism can be a practical form of egoism. The difference with Confucius is that Mozi is not preoccupied with defining what 'being' good means or represents. Instead, the focus is on how to 'do' good. The implications of this percolate into his other core doctrines, such as his plea for thrift. To be able to extend one's care to the greatest possible group of recipients, rulers should show restraint and moderation and lead a frugal life. Any form of wastage, unnecessary spending or extravagant luxuries (his targets are expenditure on music and rituals) is to be avoided. Out with fashion, decoration, aesthetics or any appreciation of things beyond their immediate utility: 'What is the purpose of clothes? To keep out the cold of winter and the heat of summer. The principle behind making clothes is to provide warmth in winter and coolness in summer. Whatever does not contribute to these objectives should be eliminated' (*Mozi* 20.1). Theoretically, the political consequences of Mozi's philosophy are twofold. First, it liberates people from the encumbrance of the family (and nepotism bred in the shadows of hereditary office-holding and kinship networks) in order to create a pure meritocracy and advance social mobility. Secondly, by 'conforming upwards' the individual will serve a strong and centralized state, and be inclined to show allegiance to a ruler who shows concern for all. Mozi believed in piety; he just did not want it to be filial.

But why care at all? Confucius and Mozi had different views on how a sense of care and concern should be channelled, and to whom and in what order it should be directed. But they both grounded their philosophy in the belief that humans are social beings and that the most fulfilling way to live life is in community with others. Theirs is an ethics in which the individual develops and flourishes in the context of the collective. Not so, others objected. Individuals thrive best at the expense of the collective. One group who took this idea of self, non-participation and non-action to the extreme were the so-called Yangists.

The Yangists gathered around the figure of Yang Zhu, who

was active in the fourth century BCE. Although very influential in his time, no writings by Yang Zhu survive. His ideas are preserved in dialogues and passages recorded in other texts, usually via the voice of his opponents. Yang Zhu advocated total withdrawal from society. For him, neither the effort to conform to society nor attempts to reform it are worthy of pursuit. He offers, to quote the American sinologist David Nivison, a 'drop-out philosophy'. Mencius saw the ideas offered by Mozi and Yang Zhu as the clearest threat to the Confucian heritage he represented and, though they stood at opposite ends of the philosophical spectrum, he aggressively criticized both: 'Master Yang chose selfishness. If by pulling out a single hair from his own body he could have benefited the world, he would not have done it. Mozi chose impartial care. If by shaving himself clean from head to heel, he could have benefited the world, he would have done it' (*Mencius* 7A.26). While the adherents of Mozi are prepared to go to extremes to share their compassion with others, Yang Zhu condemns even the thought of it. If you are prepared to sacrifice a single hair, what will be next: a hand in return for a meal, a night's rest in return for your job?

Yang Zhu has been portrayed as a hedonistic recluse or even a radical egoist. In essence, however, his doctrine is about self-preservation. In his view, it is perfectly sensible to resist the expectation that one should take up public office, with no need to offer any moral justification by way of explanation. A total withdrawal from society need not be seen as a protest in which you opt out on moral grounds (as in, I disagree with my boss so I quit working altogether). Staying out is a deliberate act, it is a utilitarian choice. Yang Zhu argues that it is the best way to shield oneself from those elements that prevent you from living out your natural term and making the most of the years Heaven has allotted to you. To protect the body and its physical health from the false temptations of the world requires relying exclusively on oneself (not the family, nor the unalloyed love of others). Thus the Yangists unapologetically put the well-being of oneself first. A chapter entitled 'Yang Zhu' in a later Daoist work, *The Master Lie* (*Liezi*), encapsulates what may have motivated Yangist hedonism:

A hundred years represents the timespan of the longest life, but not one in a thousand among us will actually live that long. Suppose there is someone who lives out his term, nearly half of it is taken up by infancy and old age. Nights lost in sleep and days wasted even when you are awake take up nearly half of the remaining time. Pain and sickness, grief and toil, ruin and loss, fear and anxiety, take up nearly half of what remains. So in the ten or so years one is left with, if we calculate just how long we are satisfied and content, without the least care, it does not amount to as much as an hour. Then what is life for? How can we be happy? Only with fine clothes, and good food, music and sex. But we can't always have enough good clothes and food to satisfy us, and we can't always play around with beautiful women or listen to music. Then again, there are punishments and rewards that prohibit and encourage us; there is the hope for reputation that drives us forward and the fear of law that pushes us back. Energetically we strive for an hour's empty praise, and plot for glory that will last beyond our death. Even

when we are on our own we go along with what we see
other people do, and hear others say. We feel sorry about
the rights or wrongs of our own thoughts. To no avail
we lose the utmost joy of the prime of our life because
we cannot give ourselves as much as an hour. How are
we different from prisoners held down by chains and
shackles? (*Liezi* 7)

The Yangist message is a version of *carpe diem* ('seize the
day') tempered with a wish to make the most of one's natural
life. Life is too short to be caught up in social commitments that
can jeopardize your health and personal well-being. The Yangists therefore turn self-interest into a positive value: live and let
live. Their motivation is survival and self-preservation. If everybody is given the opportunity to satisfy their natural desire for
health, long life and freedom from anxiety, the sum total will
still be more than a world made up of pure egoists, since no one
will feel the need to intrude upon one another's space.

Perched somewhere in between the ethical and social
commitment espoused by Confucians and Mohists, and the
radical eremitism advocated by the Yangists, sits Zhuangzi,
offering a third way to preserve life by telling us to 'be useless'. Zhuangzi commends the 'use of being useless' not out
of nihilist intent (while at it, life is there to be lived). On the
contrary, the idea is that appearing useless, inept, worthless
or incapable can be a saving grace in a social context (like dragging your tail through the mud when offered a career opportunity). 'Everybody knows the uses of being useful, but no
one knows the uses of uselessness' (*Zhuangzi* 4.9). A number
of parables in *The Master Zhuang* illustrate this point using

trees as a metaphor. The trees that grow largest are those that fail to attract the attention of people looking for timber:

> There is a place in Song, called Jingzhi, where catalpas, cypresses and mulberry trees thrive. But a tree an arm-length or two round will be chopped down by people looking for a post to tether their monkeys. A tree of three or four spans is chopped down by someone looking for a lofty ridgepole. Those that are seven or eight spans will be chopped down by the family of a noble or rich merchant looking for coffin planks. So they do not last out the years Heaven allotted to them but die under the axe in mid-journey. That is the trouble with having worth. (*Zhuangzi* 4.6)

Zhuangzi is highly sceptical of the value accorded to social worth. He refutes the pursuit of happiness and moral perfection in the terms laid out by Confucius and his followers: education, social commitment, moral self-cultivation and the relentless quest for self-improvement. 'When people are pressed too far, they will inevitably respond with poor judgement, not even knowing what is happening to them' (*Zhuangzi* 4.2). The 'genuine person' (Zhuangzi's alternative for the Confucian *junzi* or gentleman) does not identify with these norms. He appears talentless and refuses to nourish the sprouts as a way of self-preservation. After all, ethical norms are merely a social invention. The Confucian zest to transform human beings (whatever their inborn nature) into morally conditioned persons is based on accepting the Dao as the way of humans. But Zhuangzi takes the Dao to be embracing much more and operating beyond human control. He sees the individual and the state as neither moral nor amoral. So while we travel through life in a human world, Zhuangzi suggests alternative mechanisms to outlive and withstand its complex challenges and dangers. In the war-ridden world he found himself in, it was better not to be called upon. Rather than entrusting one's abilities to the service of the human collective, it is better to 'make a cripple of the virtues within you' (*Zhuangzi* 4.7).

Indeed, as much as those who thrust themselves into their official duties warranted praise and adoration, choosing to forego the call to serve is an equally recurring theme in ancient China. As a motif, it is regularly highlighted in biography or alluded to in poetry and prose. Many appear to have taken the strategy to heart by apologizing for not appearing at the ruler's court on grounds of ill-health (classical Chinese boasts a long list of expressions of this kind). Feigning illness or madness provided an expedient way of evading political danger. Why appear at court only to meet the sword? Several figures are on record for using an array of tricks to appear mad in order to get off the hook: they untie and dishevel their hair, walk barefoot or run around naked, cover their face with mud or even ulcerate their skin and flesh with lacquer! Ancient China's most renowned madman was Jieyu ('Carriage Groom'), the Madman of Chu. His most notorious act was to walk past Confucius while humming an air in which he condemned all people in office: 'Phoenix, O Phoenix! How your virtue has waned! What is past is beyond help, but you can still give chase to what is to come! Give it up! Give it up! Perilous is the fate of those who seek office today' (*An.* 18.5). Before Confucius had a chance to reply, the Madman hurried off. For once, the Master did not have the chance to impress.

Harmonious society

During the early 2000s, when China's leadership took stock of how society had changed in the decades since Deng Xiaoping's economic reforms instigated in the 1970s (the so-called policy of 'reform and opening up'), the ideal of the '(socialist) harmonious society' (*hexie shehui*) crept into mainland Chinese political rhetoric. Hu Jintao (b. 1942) made it into an official government maxim for the country's future socioeconomic development at the Communist's Party's Central Committee in 2004. The choice of the classical term 'harmony' in the party's script covered a range of ambitions: tackling corruption and unbridled self-interest; addressing inequality so that all segments in society would share in the nation's newfound affluence; sustainable development; and care for the environment (the 'harmonious coexistence of man and nature'). China's rulers, present and past, have been in the habit of drawing selectively on terms or concepts championed by its ancient philosophers. Quoting verse from past literary tradition for political ends has been common practice. When borrowed as a mouthpiece or slogan for official policy, classical vocabulary is often used with little or no attention to the original context in which it appeared. Quotations are reinterpreted to suit a particular purpose. The 'true meaning' of the Confucian Classics, after all, has been negotiated by countless generations of commentators, so why not continue in the same vein.

'Harmony' (*he*) has trumped successive buzzwords in Chinese political philosophy throughout the ages. It is hard indeed to doubt its central stature in Chinese thought: Confucians want humans to live in harmony with each other; Legalists want people to echo the will of the monarch; Daoists want to live in harmony with nature. Furthermore, a theme that permeates all philosophical traditions is that persons of authority should 'keep to the centre' (*zhong*) – that is, cultivate a personality capable of making balanced judgements and keeping emotions in check. When not used literally, the ideal of harmony clones itself into concepts closely related to it: unity, cooperation, consensus, peaceful coexistence, solidarity, order and even the rule of law. As we will see in Chapter 9, even ancient China's culinary vocabulary rang of harmony.

Throughout Chinese history there have been several visions of what the harmonious society should entail. These range from communities that are egalitarian (as envisaged, for instance, by the Mohists, the Taiping rebels in the nineteenth century or the communist revolutionaries in the twentieth), to views of a strictly hierarchical world in which everyone knows their place and undertakes duties in the service of others. These archetypes of a harmonious world were often projected back to a golden age from which humanity was said to have deviated. It followed that 'reforming' or 'changing' the present could be construed as restoring an originally harmonious order that the sages in antiquity had created (revolution as turning back to what had come before). The late-nineteenth century reformer Kang Youwei (1858–1927), dubbed the 'Martin Luther of the Confucian religion' by his disciple Liang Qichao (1873–1929), branded his own utopian vision of an egalitarian society as a 'Great Union' or 'Great Community' (*Da tong*). The term derives from a passage in *The Ritual Records* where it is presented through the voice of Confucius:

> When the great Dao was still being practised, everything under Heaven was owned in common. People were chosen on the basis of their worthiness and ability. Their words were sincere and they cultivated harmony. Therefore the people did not only treat their closest relatives as relatives, they did not only treat their own children as children. They cared for the elderly until the end. There was employment for the strong and the young were given the opportunity to grow up. Provisions were put in place for widows, orphans, those who were childless, and those who were disabled and diseased. Men had their work and women had their homes. They accumulated provisions as they did not like anything to be thrown away on the ground, but they did not wish to hoard goods for themselves. They did hard physical labour because they disliked the idea that goods other than those that resulted from their own efforts would be used for their personal advantage. For this reason selfish schemes were suppressed and did not arise. Robbers, thieves and rebels did not show themselves. The outside doors were left open and not shut. This was called the Great Community. (*Liji*, 'Li yun')

Who would not wish to be part of a society so blissful that it would even make the Daoist feel content? But these utopian visions of the perfect society need to be seen in their historical context. People in ancient China lived in the knowledge that the state, whether feudal or imperial, could demand a significant part of their time as an adult for forced labour or military service. In regular rotations (still as frequent as once every five months in Han times) one could be called upon to assist in construction works, haul government-owned goods or grain, build roads or repair the state's granaries. Natural disasters or bad harvests called for emergency duties (such as damming a flood, or fighting a locust plague). This often meant serving far away from home and family. In short, the default fate of most ordinary (and many not so ordinary) people in ancient China was not one of protracted domestic bliss, but, rather, one of poverty and hard labour while suffering the prospect of crushing violence and political crisis. China's philosophers would have looked pretty purposeless and ineffectual in their drive to preach harmony and virtue theory, had it not been for the unceasing military and political chaos and disorder that marked society in their time.

In reality, Chinese thinkers conceived of harmony and social order and cohesion in different shades and gradations. For Confucius, harmony also included the possibility of loyal opposition. Seeking consent does not mean that one should always assent. Only small-minded persons say 'yes' even when they do not get on with the other party (*An.* 13.23). Likewise, simply enforcing order does not equate to harmony. It requires rituals and conventions to reach that point (*An.* 1.12).

Mencius proposed a physical model of the harmonious society. He envisaged this as a network of collectively cooperating farming households, which he calls 'well-field' communities. He takes his inspiration from the Chinese character for a 'well' (*jing*) which, pictographically, is shaped like a grid with eight open-sided squares that surround a ninth in the centre (see

Figure 4.1). The idea is that eight individual families work their own plot while their overlord receives the income from the ninth plot that is jointly tilled by all eight families: feudally perfect as a concept. The Mencian utopia (which its author claims flourished in the past) is a society in which households not only look after themselves but contribute a share to the common good (in Mencius's time, the landlord who granted use of the land). There is no convincing historical evidence suggesting that 'well-field' communities ever existed on any significant scale. But the 'well-field' became yet another image symbolizing harmony, cooperation and solidarity.

Mencius's 'well-field' utopia is one of the oldest examples of social engineering based on the belief that human psychology and behaviour is influenced by the physical landscape and spatial layout of the living and working environment. Implied here is the assumption that by assigning household units to live in a space organized in a grid, social order will emerge and, as a consequence, a unity of mind will develop: 'When those in the same village holding land in the same well-field befriend one another in their going out and their coming in, assist one another in their protection and defence, and sustain one another through illness and distress, the hundred surnames [i.e. the people] will live together in affection and harmony' (*Mencius* 3A.3). As a ruler, it makes sense to have population groups registered for the purpose of taxation and general administration. The state of Qin, for instance, on the advice of Lord Shang, used a grid of pathways to divide land into rectangular blocks. However, other motives could impel rulers to assign people belonging to the same class or profession to designated residential wards or

Figure 4.1
Chinese character
for a well (*jing*).

districts: vigilance and control, encouraging specialization and skill in the professions, or safety.

Communal living and working is a model that has been trialled at other junctures in Chinese history. A widely known experiment in recent times was the collectivization of agriculture through the model of the people's commune devised by the Chinese communists in the 1950s (but phased out since 1978). The ambition then was to optimize agricultural production and promote self-reliance by pooling land and organizing the labour force in teams, brigades and communes. Such cooperatives orchestrated not only people's economic subsistence but many other aspects of private and public life, such as schools, social services and hospitals. Everything was to be organized for the benefit of the collective and the purpose of redistributing wealth on a more equal basis.

Had Xunzi been able to time-travel, he would have objected to such radical egalitarianism. It was Xunzi who articulated most clearly that a classless society subverts social order and prosperity. If all social classes were ranked equally and everyone was of like status, no one would be willing to serve anyone else (*Xunzi* 9.3).

It is of the inborn nature of human beings that it is impossible for them not to form societies. If they form a society in which there are no class divisions, strife will develop. If there is strife, then there will be social disorder; if there is social disorder, there will be hardship for all. Hence, a situation in which there are no class divisions is the greatest affliction mankind can have. A situation in which there are class divisions is the most basic benefit under Heaven. (*Xunzi* 10.4)

Xunzi's ideal centred on the 'kingly state': a strictly hierarchical society, overseen by an elite of well-educated and learned individuals, who modelled themselves on the rituals and duties of the former kings and ancient sages. Since he was not confident that humans by nature would wish to do anything apart from fulfilling their own selfish desires, Xunzi wanted the state to be enriched and strengthened so that strong political and social structures were in place to help transform self-interested individuals into willing and useful members of the collective. Governing, then, is the art of tearing down the barriers that prevent the moral transformation of the people. And since the values and standards of the ancient kings and sages act as a yardstick that is universal, absolute, unquestioned and unchanging, their Way can be instructed to everyone, provided there are strong teachers who impose a rigid schedule of learning. Still, educating people into their role is a long and hard grind, an acquired skill people do not take to naturally. Xunzi describes it as a step-by-step process in which one 'genuinely accumulates and earnestly practises for a long time'. A thoroughbred racehorse cannot cover ten paces in a single stride (*Xunzi* 1.6, 1.8).

Xunzi insists, however, that a vertical hierarchy and social class distinctions should not preclude social mobility on the basis of merit: if those of good pedigree are ineffectual, they should rightfully lose their rank and be replaced by talented commoners (*Xunzi* 9.1). Like Confucius, Xunzi allows for the possibility that the people can unseat incompetent superiors: 'The ruler is the boat; his subjects the water. It is the water that sustains the boat, and it is the water that capsizes it' (*Xunzi* 9.4). But not everyone is capable of rising to the top. Society requires a charismatic leader supported by talented ministers who are committed to upholding agreed standards without being partisan or partial. Hence his conclusion: elitism is a necessary condition for social harmony. The corollary is that those who have acquired the expertise to govern should make decisions on behalf of their subjects. Xunzi's ruler is stern. Punishments remain a vital instrument to him. 'If a ruler is too friendly and conciliatory, too harmonious and available ... every sort of speculative persuasion will swarm about him' (*Xunzi* 9.2).

To conclude this chapter, it seems fitting to turn to *The Great Learning* (*Daxue*). No essay in pre-modern China has been more influential in articulating the relationship between the individual, the family and the governance of the state. *The Great Learning* is preserved as a chapter in *The Ritual Records*, possibly dating back to the third century BCE, and later attributed to Confucius's disciple Zengzi. It became famous in the edited arrangement by the neo-Confucian scholar-philosopher Zhu Xi (1130–1200 CE). (Apart from Confucius, no Chinese thinker has been accorded a stature similar to that of Master Zhu.) Zhu Xi and his followers shifted the emphasis away from the Five Classics to a set of texts that came to be categorized as the Four Books (*Si shu*): *The Analects*, *The Great Learning*, *The Doctrine of the Mean* (*Zhongyong*; also a chapter in *The Ritual Records*), and the *Mencius*. The Four Books were presented as part of the same textual lineage. The claim was that a direct link could be traced between their purported authors (from Confucius, to his disciple Zengzi, to the latter's student Zisi, who, in turn, taught Mencius). Along with Zhu Xi's commentaries, the Four Books came to be regarded as distilling the essence of Confucianism. From the fourteenth century CE through to the end of the Qing dynasty, these texts constituted the core curriculum for any aspiring official taking the civil service examinations.

The Great Learning is a short text (less than eighteen hundred characters in length) that has been memorized by generations of students and young (male) children in educated families (in the same way as *The Three Character Classic*). It describes the successive stages through which social order is established: one starts by cultivating the individual self, then extends this to the family, and finally to the state and the world at large ('All under Heaven').

> The Way of Great Learning lies in illuminating bright virtue, in having close relationships with people, and in coming to rest in the highest form of goodness. Only when you know the point of rest will you possess certainty. Only after you possess certainty will you be able to become tranquil. Only after you become tranquil will you be able to be at peace. Only after you are at peace will you be able to deliberate. Only after you deliberate will you be able to attain [your

goal]. Things have their roots and branches, situations have their endings and beginnings. If you know what comes first and what comes after, you will come near to the Dao.

Those in ancient times who wished to illuminate bright virtue throughout the world first ordered their states. Wishing to order their states, they first regulated their families. Wishing to regulate their families, they first cultivated their persons. Wishing to cultivate their persons, they first rectified their hearts. Wishing to rectify their hearts, they first perfected the sincerity of their intentions. Wishing to perfect the sincerity of their intentions, they first brought about knowledge. Bringing about knowledge lies in investigating things. Once things have been investigated, knowledge is brought about. Only after knowledge is brought about will your intentions be sincere. Only after your intentions are sincere will your heart be rectified. Only after your heart is rectified can you cultivate your own person. Only after your own person is cultivated will your family be regulated. Only after your family is regulated will the state be ordered. Only after the state is ordered will the world be at peace.

The point *The Great Learning* makes is that in order to look outward, you need to be prepared to look inward and focus on the inner self: being true to the self leads to good inter-personal relationships within the family and, via the family, with the state. Mencius refers to a similar idea in a popular saying: 'World, state, family.' As he comments: 'The foundation of the world lies with the state; the foundation of the state lies with the family; the foundation of the family lies with the self' (*Mencius* 4A.5). The relationship of the individual to the state flows in both directions: from state, to family, to self; from self, to family, to state. (Read the passage above as you would dismantle and reassemble a Russian doll.) But the crux is that a moral person can only exist within the context of the family and state.

The Great Learning also posits an obligation to investigate and apprehend the principles behind things. The meaning of the phrase 'investigating things' (*ge wu*) has been debated at length among neo-Confucians. Some have stretched the phrase to mean the observation of nature. However, there is no hint here at experimental or scientific learning. What appears to be the message is that self-cultivation necessitates probing the world around you and investigating what lies beyond one's own person. Only when you pause to understand why things are as they are will you be able to react to them appropriately. For Zhu Xi that meant constant study to understand what he called the 'principle' (*li*) that makes things cohere together. Thus the text works as an aide-mémoire for the Mencian view of human potential and teaches the student how to put innate moral knowledge into practice.

The theme that binds the above texts together (not least those in the Confucian tradition) seems clear: in order to stand out, you need to fit in. Fitting in among the collective, however, does not equate to bland conformity, vapid or blind obedience to authority or the erasure of any remaining sense of selfhood and autonomy (although it can be construed as such and often has been). Conformity is seen as a necessary precondition to make your mark in the community, an integral part of what it means to be an authoritative individual. The Confucian gentleman is in a position to lead because he has absorbed the virtues and mastered the roles and rituals pertaining to his position in society and his social network. He becomes a person because of others, rather than despite them. Like an artist whose originality can only be judged when his art is compared with a collective body of work by other artists, the Confucian gentleman becomes part of the vanguard of society because he has managed to 'conform upwards' and navigate around existing structures. To him (and, exceptionally, her) the question is not so much 'Should I be in or out?', but rather 'How can I stand out while fitting in and, by doing so, ensure that I remain in harmony with my surroundings?'

The family model provides the catalyst here. Built around uncompromising hierarchies and strictly enforced customs and obligations, the household is the laboratory in which role consciousness is taught and learned. Being a father to children might make it easier to be a father to the people. Being filial to your elders can shape your expectations for loyalty from others. Knowing your place in society has its returns, Confucians claimed. Without knowing your station and that of others, you won't be able to travel from one to the other. But what are those rituals, codes, rules and regulations that inform human conduct? How do they work, who imposes them and why respect them? That is the subject of the next chapter.

CHAPTER 5

Behaving Ritually

> Duke Ling of Wei asked Confucius about military
> formations. Confucius replied: 'I have, indeed, heard
> something about the use of sacrificial vessels, but I
> have never studied military matters.' The following day,
> he left the state. (*An.* 15.1)

Rituals, not soldiers, are Confucius's favourite topic of con-versation as he journeys from court to court. In the tussle of ideas in Warring States China, Confucius and his followers placed no trust in a world that subsists by the grace of the battle axe. Instead, they argued that human relationships thrive better when human conduct is regimented and shielded by a phalanx of rituals, ceremonies, courtesies and conventions. As usual, Confucius claimed this was nothing new ('I trans-mit rather than create') – such rituals had already flourished in the golden age of Zhou. But his mission was to revive and develop them, adapting them to the needs of his time. This would help bring order and cohesion to society in an age of chaos and disorder. Unsurprisingly, we are told that the Mas-ter's own exemplary conduct rubbed off on others like a sweet perfume. One story tells that after he had been holding office for three years in his native state of Lu, men walked on the right side of the road and women walked on the left, and nobody would pick up things others had lost (*Lüshi chunqiu* 16/5.3).

Rituals abounded in ancient China, but why should the young respond to a question by an elder only after admitting ignorance or declining ('I'm not the right person to answer you, but ...', 'It's an honour to be asked, but ...'); why must one not laugh when visiting a household in mourning or when one's parents are ill; why should it be inappropriate to turn one's back to someone after speaking? What is wrong in turning down a gift from someone senior, even if it is quite trifling? Why should we act ritually at all?

For Confucius, the most valuable outcome of upholding rituals is that they bring about harmony (*An.* 1.12). His adherents too, most notably Xunzi, envisaged order as the most coveted objective (and side-effect) to be gained from channelling human conduct according to a set of firm conventions. Rites are essential not only to temper the ways in which people behave in daily domestic life, but also to bolster the authority of the state and its rulers. If the model kings of old had zealously obeyed the diktats of ritual and ceremony, so no respected ruler thereafter could consider governing his people, or securing the approval of the spirit world and the cosmos at large, without formal ritual procedures. Credible rulers require a measure of manufactured dignity that is upheld via symbols, language and custom (prime ministers and presidents need the national flag more than the flag needs them). Ritual softens the edges: 'it does to government what having a bath does to heat' (*Zuozhuan*, Lord Xiang 31). When the peasant founders of the Han dynasty secured the throne in 206 BCE after the short-lived reign of the First Emperor of

Qin and his indolent heir, academicians at court were quick to advise the new emperor, Gaozu (r. 202–195 BCE): the new ruling house was to draw up a new code of formal procedures and guidelines for behaviour at court. As one scholar, Lu Jia (c.228–c.140 BCE), notoriously advised: 'You can conquer the world on horseback, but you cannot rule it on horseback!' (*Hanshu* 43). To perform a role or task effectively and in a way that reflects its status, it is essential to be equipped with the manners and conventions that affirm the standing of that role.

But how do you sensitize people to behave according to a set of conventions, and ensure that those rules of decorum and polite respect gain public (or tacit) approval across the whole community? If civilized society exists on the basis that its members conduct themselves 'appropriately', who decides what is 'appropriate' behaviour? What if multiple behaviours are deemed acceptable, and who stewards and patrols the norms? Most importantly, is it possible to enforce normative behaviour without the sanction of the law?

Ritual

Anthropologists, sociologists and scholars of religion have produced a vast body of literature trying to define and theorize about ritual. Some see ritual as a code of behaviour that is distinct from day-to-day social conduct: a church service; a state opening of parliament; stage-managed coronations and inaugurations; a healing ritual; or a Maori war dance performed on the pitch before the start of a rugby game. Others claim that ritual (like play) is a spontaneous part of human expression and communication – dressing up to seduce a potential partner, for example, or wailing in public at the loss of a loved one. Adam Seligman and Michael Puett, and fellow authors, propose we should think of rituals as creating a subjunctive realm: rituals help us to live in an 'as if' world. This 'could be' universe is moral, ordered and coherent even if that does not correspond to reality. Ritual actions allow us to temporarily step away from our individual feelings and experiences and into a social space shared with others. There we enact our roles and imagine how the world should be. By behaving ritually, our world is illusory to the extent that it operates according to created conventions – thus, there is no natural basis, say, for placing one's hand on one's heart or on a copy of the Bible during a pledge of allegiance or a swearing-in ceremony. The ritual world is entirely rule-governed and it can stand in tension to lived experience; for example, an on-camera handshake between two former enemies across the pages of a peace treaty about to be signed can pave over the aftermath of any rancorous feelings that remain. Yet it is precisely our willingness to 'perform ourselves' in this shared space that makes proper social interaction possible.

So ritual *is* what it *does*. Rituals create their own meaning through the action itself. They include an element of performance and repetition, they tend to be scripted and, broadly, their aim is to impose order on the world. Ritual language tends to be more formal than natural speech. As artificial conventions, rituals can help us to articulate the relationships between ourselves and between us and the (non-human) world beyond (nature, the gods and spirits, the ancestors). Within a community, rituals provide a flowchart or template that allows people to live in the plural without harming or offending each other; they order and control human behaviour as grammar organizes language.

Rituals also help us to express our state of mind outwardly: a clenched fist can signal resistance, refusal or protest; holding up one's hands can signify yielding or the admission of guilt; white clothes (in Chinese society) signify mourning; to commemorate significant people or events, a flag is flown; to mourn the death of a public figure, it flies at half-mast. Some physical gestures show approval (the proverbial thumbs-up), others indicate disapproval (kneeling or turning one's back when a national anthem is played, or remaining seated while others stand and applaud). We can be ritualized by putting on special clothing (uniforms displaying rank and seniority; graduation gowns indicating the status of the degree obtained), or by marking ourselves with specific signs (a particular hairstyle or tattoo). Rituals can work in two directions: in addition to signalling to others, switching into the ritual mode can be a way of cultivating oneself – for example, by reciting texts, chanting hymns or through guided meditation.

For ritual action to work there needs to be a minimum of genuine intent, otherwise it risks being reduced to a dry and meaningless staging of formalities. Yet that does not mean that ritualized behaviour necessarily makes rational sense. For example, dining partners or fellow graduands may not understand a word of the Latin grace or formula that opens proceedings, yet sitting through those few seconds of incomprehensible jargon creates a connection. There emerges an imagined companionship that prepares you for what will follow next: checking the menu for the hors d'oeuvre or receiving your degree certificate.

Rituals can also fail. Chinese texts often remind the user or reader of the adverse consequences when rituals do not achieve the desired outcome: when they are inappropriately timed or not performed properly; when the wrong text or script is used or when competing interpretations exist; when a community lacks the resources or experts to conduct them, or, conversely, because there are too many self-professed experts who each claim to know how it should be done. Rituals can fail in their primary purpose (for example, when a drought continues despite your rain dance) yet still have a secondary effect (the community got together and everyone contributed something to the ceremony). And there will always be some who simply go through the motions and perform rituals without genuinely expressing or absorbing the values and virtues such conventions are attempting to instil.

'Ritual' translates Chinese *li*, but it is only one of many possible translations that each in their own way reflect one aspect of its meaning: 'decorum', 'proper or polite behaviour', 'rules', 'customs', 'etiquette', 'rites', 'religious worship', 'good manners', 'doing what is proper'. Originally, *li* referred more narrowly to ceremonial activities held at the Zhou court: sacrifices, mourning rituals, protocols for receiving and extending gifts, rules that governed interstate relations, rules for hosting guests or staging marriages, directions on how to have an audience with a superior, and so on. Etymologically, the Chinese character for *li* represents a ritual vessel in which an offering is made to the spirits (see Figure 5.1). It is hard to reconstruct the Zhou ritual world – its inscribed bronze vessels and bells bear the only direct testimony to it. Systematic accounts of the rituals of the ancients were written down

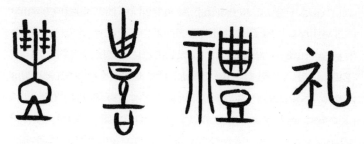

Figure 5.1
Variants of the Chinese Character for *li* 'ritual'.

later. The most significant corpus of texts on ritual, the so-called Three Ritual Classics (*San li*), came together during the Han period. *The Book of Etiquette and Rites* (*Yili*), which may contain material going back to the fifth and fourth centuries BCE, includes chapters on capping and nuptial rites, drinking and banqueting, archery meetings and mourning attire. *The Ritual Records* (*Liji*) were redacted around 100 BCE and possibly later. *The Rites of Zhou* (*Zhouli*) paint an idealized Han picture of the ancient royal state of Zhou and its institutions. The sheer volume of textual materials that reassemble or recreate these rituals reflects their enormous importance in Chinese society in the age before, during and after the time of Confucius.

When Confucius speaks about the rituals of the ancients, he has in mind the ceremonial decorum that dominated court life during the early Zhou period. He comments on the shape and colours of robes and caps, shows his fascination with the nitty-gritty of ritual implements and gestures, and condemns those who take part in rituals above their own standing. However, over time rituals came to be seen as tools for upholding social and political hierarchies; they were understood as norms. As noted by one sixth-century BCE minister in the state of Jin: 'If you complete matters of government according to ritual, the people will be calm' (*Zuozhuan*, Lord Cheng 12). By the time of Confucius, the meaning of *li* had also gained a more pronounced ethical dimension, indicating customary rules that guide interpersonal relationships, not merely formal rules of etiquette, instruction and taboo. To observe 'ritual propriety' (a much-used translation for *li*) entails a mental attitude, an inward sense of appropriate conduct. Confucius argues that humaneness consists of 'overcoming oneself and abiding by the observance of ritual propriety' (*ke ji fu li*) (*An.* 12.1). The morally accomplished person is someone who can discipline his personal self (his private likes and dislikes) and opt to behave 'ritually' – that is, according to a set of conventions or norms that conform with his role in society, as a father, son, brother, husband, teacher, disciple, ruler, minister. Stepping outside your private self into this world of externally agreed norms also means being prepared to yield to others (*An.* 4.13).

So, observing ritual propriety has both a psychological and a socio-political dimension. Confucius advises that it should be part of everything we do: 'Do not look at anything that violates ritual propriety; do not listen to anything that violates ritual propriety; do not speak about anything that violates ritual propriety; do not do anything that violates ritual propriety' (*An.* 12.1). The *Analects* contains a number of passages that help us imagine how Confucius exhibited his own understanding of ritual propriety in daily life. He knows how to dress for the occasion, how to bow or when to pace his steps. He only sits on a mat that is properly straightened (*An.* 10.12), and has good table manners: he never eats to the full, he drinks but never gets drunk (*An.* 10.8). The Master never converses during meals or talks in bed (*An.* 10.10). Even when he is on his own, he is decorous. When sleeping, he does not adopt the posture of a corpse (*An.* 10.24). Confucius makes no strict separation between rituals associated with religious life (the preserve of sacred or higher powers) and those that are part of normal human activity (the so-called profane world). Ritual propriety is to be observed in the face of the spirit world and the ancestors; yet it is equally important to have good table manners and use respectful language during day-to-day life.

But why bother with conventions; how to beat the potential tedium of it all; how to appreciate what ritual does? Confucians argue that certain aspects of life benefit from being choreographed. It is tempting to view this as meaningless formalism, but that misses the point. 'Rituals performed without respect, mourning without grief, I cannot bear to see it,' Confucius exclaims (*An.* 3.26). Human psychology, not least in our emotional dispositions, functions better with a guide or road map. This is especially relevant at points in life that are particularly significant (the birth of a child, the coming of age of a teenager, family reunions), or during episodes that prove taxing or stressful (the death of a close relative or friend, separation). Rituals offer certainty in periods of uncertainty. In times of rupture, shock and emotional crisis, it helps to be able to rely on form and formality: being told how to walk and talk, how to dress, what to eat or not to eat, what prayer or song to recite and when, how or whom to condole. Such formal pointers offer comfort and help us stay on our feet, both physically and mentally.

Rituals work like a plumb line that enables people 'to keep to the middle [*zhong*]' (*Liji*, 'Zhongni yan ju'). They give form to or place limits on otherwise unrestrained emotional responses that might upset someone and those sharing the same space and community. If inborn feelings are a field, rituals are the plough that cultivates it (*Liji*, 'Li yun'). Rituals are like the dikes and embankments that channel waters into the right direction and stop them from overflowing (*Liji*, 'Jing jie', 'Fang ji'). They dam up our individual urges by clarifying or reiterating our separate roles in society, and teach us how to respond in a measured way to external events. Wearing a black armband can give vent to disagreement or protest without the need for a mass rally that could spiral out of control. Observing a minute's silence or flying the flag at half-mast are rituals that seize our emotions in the grip of the moment and serve as a substitute for having to shut down all economic and other activity for the day. Ritual helps us separate things out and think in terms of ordered and distinct sequences.

For Confucians, ritual combines both thought and action; it is not simply a set of conventions to achieve a goal but an inseparable part of human behaviour. As Xunzi puts it: 'Rites reach their highest perfection when both emotion and form are fully realized' (*Xunzi* 19.2c). Hence, Confucians believe that ritualized behaviour comes with a moral payback: it makes us get on with each other and, through it, become better persons. Although ritual can be about the great ceremonial occasion to impress the ancestors or parade the troops in front of the ruler, in reality it is about appropriate manners and acquired elegance in daily life: 'Ritual provides the footing people tread on. When people lose this footing, they stumble and fall, sink and drown. When observance of small matters is neglected, the disorder that results is great. Such is ritual' (*Xunzi* 27.40).

For Mencius, the shoots of such a sense of propriety are growing within us and can be nurtured as part of a person's character formation. Yet Mencius is keen to comment that ritual conventions should not be upheld at all cost, thereby making them meaningless. For instance, the rules of propriety may well dictate that men and women should not touch each other, but that does not mean you should refuse to pull your drowning sister-in-law from the water using your hands (*Mencius* 4A.17). There are times, Mencius seems to concede, that we need to weigh up and assess the circumstances. That may involve having to temporarily suspend certain rules of etiquette. Although propriety should normally take precedence over primal instincts such as eating and sex, in certain pressing circumstances this is not always possible – for instance, when you are starving or under pressure to procreate and produce a male heir (*Mencius* 6B.1). Equally disingenuous would be to merely go through the motions of social convention without sincere intentions: 'To feed someone but not to love him is to treat him like a pig. To love him but not to respect him is to make an animal of him. Honour and respect are what precede any presentation of gifts' (*Mencius* 7A.37).

Xunzi takes a more extreme position and turns ritual into a strict rule-book for a functional society: *li* provides the essential software to transform our hard-wired impulses into behaviours necessary for living harmoniously. Xunzi's chapter 'Discourse on Ritual' ('Li lun') starts with the claim that the ancient kings and sages invented rituals to control human desire:

> How did ritual arise? I say that people are born with desires which, if not satisfied, cannot but lead people to seek to satisfy them. If in seeking to satisfy their desires people observe no measure, and apportion things without limits, it would be impossible for them not to fight over the means to satisfy their desires. Such contention leads to disorder. Disorder leads to poverty. (*Xunzi* 19.1a)

In Xunzi's understanding, rituals are our second nature: they are the taught component that shapes our personality. Human nature requires pruning to be socially functional: 'Rituals trim what is too long, stretch out what is too short, eliminate excess, and remedy deficiency' (*Xunzi* 19.5b). Here he re-iterates Confucius's idea that rituals assist in two ways: they offer a minimal standard where such standards are lacking and they prevent excess. Without being mediated by a sense of propriety, potential positives in someone's behaviour can appear off-putting: having to show respect to someone can wear you down; being careful can turn into anxiety; courage can appear as rowdiness; and candour can seem like rudeness (*An.* 8.2).

Like no other thinker before him, Xunzi politicizes the need for rituals. They are indispensable to the foundation of the state and the fountain of all authority: 'Rites are the highest expression of order and discrimination, the root of the strength of the state, the Way by which the majestic sway of authority is created, and the focus of merit and fame' (*Xunzi* 15.4). Neglecting the rites, then, is depriving society of its main engine for order: 'a nation without ritual will not be tranquil' (*Xunzi* 2.2). Xunzi goes a step further. He believes that ritual as a governing principle even transcends the human order: *li* is a cosmic force, a principle that orders Heaven and Earth, the planets, the seasons and the whole natural world: 'Ritual has three roots: Heaven and Earth are the root of life; the ancestors are the root of one's kin; ruler and teacher are the root of order … If just one of these three were missing, there would be no peace and security for man' (*Xunzi* 19.2a). For Xunzi, ritual is as indispensable in the service of Heaven and Earth and one's forebears as it is necessary to order human society in the here and now. Having turned ritual into a universal principle for order, and the rituals of the ancient kings into the absolute standard to be upheld, Xunzi's notion of ritual sails closely to what Legalists held to be the purpose of the law. There is a difference, however: people can be compelled to follow the law when presented with the prospect of penalties, fines and punishments. By contrast, good manners and a sense of propriety need to develop from within. It cannot be forced upon people. A Confucian challenge to those who believe one can legislate for respect would be to argue that such attitudes can only be acquired through example, habit and constant practice and repetition.

Music

Chinese thinkers often speak of ritual and music in the same breath. Tradition mentions a sixth 'Confucian' classic, *The*

Classic of Music (*Yue jing*). Lost by Han times, it remains a topic of scholarly debate as to what form it might have taken. The significance of music itself, however, was widely acknowledged. Music formed a core component of Confucian moral education. In the latter part of his life, when his career as an adviser had all but dwindled away, Confucius became a student of music. The *Analects* contains several scenes where the plot revolves around the Master's understanding of music. Music affects him deeply: 'When the Master was in the state of Qi, he heard the Shao music, and for three months he did not notice the taste of the meat he ate. He said: "I never imagined that music could reach such heights"' (*An.* 7.14). He enjoys singing in harmony: 'When the Master was in the company of others who were singing and they sang well, he always asked them to sing the piece again before joining in the harmony' (*An.* 7.32). Music unlocks a sense of joy in Confucius. Yet he also stipulates that at times of crisis (during mourning, or when a natural disaster has struck) the gentleman must refrain from finding joy in music and good food, or from seeking comfort in his own lodgings (*An.* 17.21). Just as ritual is not simply about gifts of jade and silk, Confucius insists that music is about more than simply bells and drums (*An.* 17.11). Unless those who perform music or observe ritual propriety harbour within themselves a sense of humaneness, neither ritual nor music is useful or appropriate (*An.* 3.3).

What, then, makes music such a potent force in the Confucian view of the world? As explained in Chapter 2, Chinese philosophers like to think in pairs – that is, they relate concepts to each other in terms of dyadic opposites. Alongside *yin* and *yang*, 'inner' (*nei*) and 'outer' (*wai*) is another much-used set. In the household, women represent the inner sphere, whereas men represent its outer dimension. In geography, the central states are the civilized inner heartland of the world, whereas lands on the periphery are the barbarian outer sphere of 'All under Heaven'. Ritual and music had a similar relationship. Thus the analogy runs: rituals separate things from each other (for example, male from female, bad luck from good luck, humans from animals), whereas music brings people together. Music unites people in the way in which it brings out passions that are common to all (feelings of joy and anger); ritual serves to separate people and grade the differences among them (teacher and pupil, master and subject). Rituals organize our external responses to a situation – for example, when we celebrate or commemorate; music offers a conduit for the emotions that spring from our inner self – for instance, a song can trigger memories that make you despondent or cheerful. In the words of Xunzi, 'Music unites that which is the same; ritual distinguishes that which is different' (*Xunzi* 20.1).

The crux here is that, for Confucians, music is a moral force. To express oneself through music is a way of cultivating and transforming oneself. Music is neither an entirely casual nor a fully calculated assembly of sounds. Its greatest quality lies in the fact that its default order is one of harmony: 'This much can be known about music. It begins with playing in unison. When it gets into full swing, it is harmonious, clear and unbroken. In this way it reaches the conclusion' (*An.* 3.23). Music is best enjoyed in the company of others (*Mencius* 1B.1). Rhythm and melody offer a subtle gateway into human sentiment.

They affect or connect people when verbal communication falls short (you do not need to speak French to dance with a Frenchman). Music mirrors one's frame of mind; it reflects the intentions of those who compose it, perform it, listen to it, or exchange it. As soon as we discover a shared love for the same piece of music with a stranger, there is a connection (I like Bach, you like Bach, therefore I like you; I hate funk, you hate funk – let us get together). Music literally sets people on the same wavelength with each other; it creates a resonance between them. In Han times, a charming term slipped into the Chinese language that referred to intimate pals and friends as 'knowers of sounds'. A 'tone-wise companion' (in a translation by Kenneth DeWoskin) is someone with whom one shares a deep connection. In classical Chinese poetry, a close friend or lover may be addressed as 'someone who understands the sounds'.

For Confucian thinkers, harmony as an aesthetic quality becomes political in the idea that the right music brings people together. Competent rulers and statesmen are those who are able to understand music. They know to commission the appropriate instruments, scores, choreography and performers for the occasion. Music had a central role in court ritual. In the courts of Warring States China, the figure of the blind musician often pops up as a wise adviser to the ruler; being blind, his ears are highly attuned to rumour, so he can catch the mood and 'sound out' what is happening in the world. A Zhou hymn in *The Book of Odes* narrates how the blind music master's enchanting performance convinces the ancestors 'to listen' (*Shijing*, 'You gu'; Mao 280). Confucius treats the blind musician with the utmost respect (*An.* 15.42), while *The*

Ritual Records note that being guided by a blind musician is the hallmark of ritual propriety (*Liji*, 'Li qi').

Xunzi devotes an entire chapter to music. His 'Discourse on Music' ('Yue lun') starts off with the statement that 'music is joy', a pun on the double meaning of the Chinese character for music which, pronounced differently, means 'enjoyment', 'to be cheerful about something'. Humans are by nature responsive to sound and movement. Song and dance are expressions of our emotional state, and these cannot be suppressed, Xunzi argues. However, in order to give proper form to our emotions, music requires direction. Someone needs to control and 'conduct' our inborn passions (as in the Latin *conducere*, 'to bring together'). Like rituals, music fine-tunes our instinctive impulses so that we can function in concert: each note takes its place in a sequence to become a melody; each dancer coordinates his or her movements according to a set rhythm and metre, thereby forging a perfect alignment with the music: 'the strength of the bone and flesh has been so thoroughly trained that every movement is in such agreement with the rhythm of the drums, bells and ensemble that there is never an awkward or wayward motion' (*Xunzi* 20.4). Sound may well start off as an individual expression of one's innermost emotions, but it is not music until it blends into an ensemble. Again, Xunzi affirms, music is about order, about restraining the free flow of instinctive emotions: 'Musical performances are the greatest creator of uniformity in the world, the guiding line of the mean and of harmony; and a necessary and inescapable expression of man's emotional nature' (*Xunzi* 20.1). Thus, when performed correctly, music gets people to act in unison. A military band can prompt a

regiment of soldiers to march up and down in perfect syn-
chrony; a club song or national anthem can silence an otherwise rowdy crowd for a short while and inspire people to
sing along. For a brief moment, the stirring chorus of well-
intentioned belting voices unite the hooligan and the priest
in support of their team.

By Xunzi's time, the cosmos had confidently slipped into
Chinese music theory: music was not a technological invention created out of nothing by legendary first musicians or
sages. Even though the majestic Zhou-period bronze bell sets
recovered by archaeologists indicate that the early Chinese
had a highly advanced understanding of acoustics, patterns
such as tone, rhythm and melody were said by contemporary
thinkers to be embedded in nature. Music and dance were
thought to originate in the natural world: in the sounds and
motions of the birds and beasts. (Bronze inscriptions and
poems in *The Book of Odes* use identical expressions to describe the sound of bells and birdsong.) Pitch standards and
the sound of wind instruments were believed to derive from
the call of the phoenix, while drums and dance mimicked
animal movements.

The idea that the natural world responds to the civilizing
influence of music is a common theme in ancient China. By
mastering music, the sages could transform the natural world:
'Feathered and winged animals will be active; horns and ant-
lers will grow; torpid insects will come to the light and be
revived; birds will brood and incubate [their eggs]; the hairy
animals will mate and nourish [their young]; mammals will
have no stillbirths and oviparous species no broken eggs. All
this can be attributed to the way of music' (*Liji*, 'Yue ji'). The

skilful musician, then, is able to discover and observe the patterning of sound and movement in nature and make it explicit to humankind.

At the heart of the early Chinese philosophy of music was the assumption that there exists a fundamental homology between musical aestheticism, natural processes and, ultimately, cosmic harmony: what sounds good, works well and feels right. Since the pipes and strings of the cosmos are inherently harmonious, human beings, through the performance of music and rituals, can align themselves with the rhythms of the universe. Music thus becomes a cosmic force: perform it well and you can advance 'the harmony between Heaven and Earth, and the balanced fusion of *yin* and *yang*' (*Lüshi chunqiu* 5/2.3). To resonate with and attune yourself to others, therefore, is but a first step. Ultimately, the ambition should be to play 'Heavenly Music' (*Zhuangzi* 14.3) and experience a sense of harmony with the entire cosmos. The world responds to the smallest alteration in pitch or timbre. Every spoken nuance or subtle change in one's voice, or the plucking of a string, has an impact upon the cosmic balance. Percussion prompts repercussion, both positively and negatively.

When aesthetics and morality coincide, music itself is not value-free. Confucians are interested both in those who perform music and those who listen to it. If music expresses the moral character of an individual or group, the implication is that an inattentive touch of the zither, or a mishit chime, reflect a careless character at work. Bad vibes create people that misbehave. Good music reflects well-balanced individuals and harmonious communities. Societies in decline are cacophonous. Unruly musical airs are like a bad air or wind;

they unsettle our bodily senses and psychological equilibrium. The Confucian gentleman therefore should not expose himself to depraved tunes and lyrics, or be seduced by the sight and sounds of daring female dancers. Confucius and Xunzi warn of the corrupting songs of Zheng and Wei and lament those who lack an appreciation of the music and rituals of Zhou. Such unwelcome exposure dislodges the *qi* in the body: 'As a general rule, when lewd music rouses, it is a rebellious spirit [*qi*] that is the response, and where that spirit achieves representation, disorder is born. When correct music stirs men, it is an obedient spirit that is the response, which, when completely represented, gives birth to order' (*Xunzi* 20.3). (Bards of the modern age who have found themselves banned from plying their art in China, Singapore and elsewhere should consider reading, or blaming, Xunzi.) In short, music echoes mores. Folk songs, for instance, are an excellent barometer for gauging the mood and customs of those who produce them. In Chinese literature, a genre of the ballad, the so-called *yuefu* ('music bureau song'), takes its name from a government office set up by the Han Emperor Wu to collect songs of the oral tradition from around the empire for use during rituals at the imperial court.

Like filial piety, refined music, as exemplified by the hymns and poems of *The Book of Odes*, thus represented civilization and high culture. The poem itself, notes the 'Great Preface' to *The Book of Odes*, is the place where 'that which is fixed in the mind' is destined to be – an expression of emotions through words. Poetry in ancient China was sung; it was chanted and accompanied by musical instruments. Poetry and music were therefore often mentioned together as a means of transforming those who had yet to submit to the enlightening munificence of Zhou civilization. A much-used expression was that music 'alters the winds [i.e. habits] and changes customs': in order to turn people into civilized subjects, the Son of Heaven needed to make them appreciate his music, adopt his rituals and embrace his customs.

Coda: like ritual, music too is a means of ordering the mind and the world. Inherent to the structure of music are the gradations and hierarchies that should be present in society. Musical education is about triggering within us a receptivity to these patterns and protocols of order. As the 'Treatise on Music' ('Yue ji'; preserved in *The Ritual Records*) states, each note in the pentatonic scale has its correlate in society: ruler, minister, the people, affairs and 'things'. (As in modern jazz, the five-tone scale was the predominant musical form in ancient China.) Song and dance 'move' us, physically and psychologically. Music creates an unspoken bond that no other medium can achieve. It does so in a way that transcends mere aesthetic appeal. It is ritual lived through sound: 'Music is what sages delight in, and it can be used to make the hearts of the people good. Its effect on people is deep; it can change habits and alter customs. Thus the former kings made manifest their teachings through it' (*Liji*, 'Yue ji').

Dissonance

When writing about music, Xunzi comes across as somewhat irritated. As a staunch defender of Confucius and the ancients, the moral value of music to him is unquestionable and almost self-evident. 'Yet, Mozi condemns it!' is the phrase he inserts disparagingly throughout his essay, the 'Discourse on Music'. What did the Mohists have against music? Mozi and his followers had attacked Confucius's adulation of the family model; they questioned the obligations of filial piety on the basis that loyalty and affection for others should be impartial. Another major source of Mohist criticism was their view on ritual and music.

Mozi does not question the value of respectful manners, or the fact that behaviour should conform to status and rank. The worthy deserve the trappings and rewards of their office as long as these are commensurate. The Mohists also acknowledge the positive power of deference and respect for social hierarchy, as well as the need to demonstrate gratitude towards Heaven and the spirits through sacrifices. However, unlike Confucius, the Mohists see no link between the performance of rituals and the moral cultivation of the self: rituals are a necessary means of thanking the spirits or respecting Heaven, but nothing more. Mozi takes a utilitarian view: sacrifices keep Heaven and the spirits happy and give those who perform them a sense of comfort. Even if one does not believe in ghosts and spirits, taking part in ceremonies still brings people together and encourages them to befriend their neighbours (*Mozi* 31.20). (Christmas or Thanksgiving can be a get-together without Christ or God, and no less important as a family ritual.) But since rituals do not directly benefit individuals, lavish spending on them is morally unjustified as it drains people's resources.

The same applies to music, for which he sees no use at all. Mozi does not refute that music pleases the ears, just as beautiful colours, tasty food and comfortable housing are certain to gratify our other senses. But he condemns it as a waste of resources and energy: people see no return for the levies the state imposes for making musical instruments and bronze bells. Unlike collecting water or digging the soil, strumming a lute does not feed the people; it only serves to entertain the wealthy and distracts from agriculture and weaving. Rather than listening to musical performances, a ruler's time would be better spent lending an ear to governmental affairs (*Mozi* 32.7). Mohist aversion to music is uncomplicated; their criticisms do not address in any detail the moral weightiness Confucians associate with music, but simply focus on the economics of it: it is a non-essential luxury, ineffective as a means of promoting social harmony.

The Mohists strike the same tone in their heated condemnation of funerary rituals. Mozi castigates self-proclaimed Confucian ritual experts as opportunistic beggars: they dash from funeral to funeral with their extended family to stuff themselves with food and drink, 'hoard food like hamsters, stare like goats and rise up like castrated pigs'. Under the pretext of having to conduct elaborate funerals, they live off the people (*Mozi* 39.3).

Why pick on funerals? Among the long list of rituals laid down in the canon, none received more attention than funerary rituals. Ancestor worship (which will be covered in the next chapter) was fundamental to Chinese society. Its status remained largely unchallenged until the emergence of religious Daoism and Buddhism in early medieval times. As an extension of filial duty beyond this life, mourning rites took centre stage. The ritual canon prescribed a mourning period that could last up to three years, in return for the three years of nursing that infants receive from their parents before being weaned (*An.* 17.21). On the matter of burial rites, Xunzi is un-apologetic in his plea that no expense should be spared: 'One treats the dead like the living and one treats their absence just as one treated them when they were still present' (*Xunzi* 19.7a). This means costly inner and outer coffins, a gener-ous batch of grave goods to accompany the dead in the grave, tombs that imitate the houses of the living, and elaborate sac-rifices and banquets in honour of the departed. If even birds and beasts mourn the loss of a mate, how much more should humans dedicate themselves to a lengthy sending-off period for their loved ones: 'the greater the wound, the longer it stays, the more pain it gives, the more slowly it heals' (*Xunzi* 19.9a–b).

Underneath the Confucian commitment to honour the departed in a fitting manner rests the assumption that feel-ings of grief and respect require an outward show and mater-ial expression. During the brief window of time when the recently departed can still be treated with generosity, decorum is essential: 'If the corpse is not adorned, it becomes hideous, and if it is hideous, no grief is felt' (*Xunzi* 19.5a). Beyond the mourning period, the dead would be remembered through cycles of commemorative rituals. However, all this came at a cost, and ritual expenditure became an issue of debate, even among the most devoted advocates of ancestral worship. How to square the material demands of 'behaving ritually' to honour the dead against the finite resources of the living: can one be filial for less; and what if one does not have sufficient means to keep up with the demands posed by such practices? The most contentious issue in discussions of ritual in an-cient China is between form and feeling. At what point does material expenditure on one's moral obligations become immoral; when do moral obligations descend into an empty display of saccharine formalities?

Confucius himself is caught up in this moral conflict. He decides to bury his dog using his own mat, since he does not have the canopy prescribed for such burials (*Liji*, 'Tang gong'). Is it better not to wear mourning garments at all, one might ask, rather than wear the wrong ones? The ritual canon offers creative solutions. Unable to find guidance on what garments they should wear to grieve over the passing of Confucius himself (there can be no more unprecedented case!), his disciples decide to mourn the Master in the style one mourns a father but without putting on mourning clothing (*Liji*, 'Tan gong'). While the need for ritual is unquestioned, a string of comments runs through the canon suggesting that rituals can be adapted to the context and resources of place and time. When living in the mountains, do not look for fish or turtles to offer up in sacrifice; use native deer and pigs instead (*Liji*, 'Li qi'). Like the various formats in which the Christian mass is conducted in the West, Chinese rituals were fluidly stagnant (and this can be said of most forms of ritual activity). Confucius certainly understood the dangers of dysfunctional ceremonies: 'When observing the rituals, it is better to be frugal than extravagant; in mourning, it is better to express real grief than worry about formalities' (*An.* 3.4). Yet his comments probably also reflect a reality of his time. Among elites, expenditure on funerals and other rituals could descend into fierce one-upmanship.

For Mozi, a *sequitur* of not putting one's own ancestors above those of others ('impartial care') dictated that funerary expenditure must be modest. Why stop normal activities for up to three years to mourn your kin when you should be working the fields or weaving or producing offspring? The Mohists invoked the same wise sages of antiquity to criticize ostentatious tombs and promote frugal burial practices. Their rules stipulated that 'a plain wooden coffin three inches thick is sufficient to house the body as it decays. There should be three layers of funeral garments, enough to cover the unpleasantness. In carrying out the burial, the pit should not be so deep as to hit the water level but it should not be as shallow to allow the stench to leak through. The burial mound should be no higher than three feet' (*Mozi* 25.10).

When rituals become an economic burden and no longer a way of benefiting people and enhancing social coexistence, as Confucius (following the ancients) had intended, they risk becoming empty and meaningless. All people are left with is trying to outdo and outsmart each other just for form's sake (my father's gravestone is taller than yours, therefore I am more filial). The incisive Mohist criticism of ritual expenditure (and the staunch counter-defence of ritual mounted by Xunzi contra Mozi) indicates that, among some followers of Confucius, attention to form and material expression was overshadowing the purpose of ceremony. The issue sparked debate far beyond Confucius and Mozi. One perceptively practical observation was that elegant stelae or lavish graves would only invite tomb robbers: 'If one uses the heart of the living to anticipate the needs of the dead, then no tomb will be left undisturbed and none will remain unopened' (*Lüshi chunqiu* 10/2.2).

*

To no great surprise, Lord Shang, the father of Legalist thought, counts music and rituals among the evils that distract individuals from fighting and farming (*Shangjun shu* 1.2, 2.6). The Daoist authors behind *The Master Zhuang* derided the usefulness of ritual and music on other grounds. They argued that artificial codes detract from a genuine life in accordance with the rhythms of Heaven and the cosmos. To the Daoist, the invitation to live in an 'as if' world governed by man-made rules and conventions must have appeared about as plausible as asking a fish for a stroll on the beach. In one encounter, Zhuangzi has two fellows chanting a ditty in the presence of the dead corpse of their friend. Unlike Confucius, who is stuck within this world, Zhuangzi's protagonists wander beyond its boundaries. They make no distinction between life and death, so they are not troubled by the conventions of mourning rituals. They improvise a tune that works for them and let this be their ritual (*Zhuangzi* 6.6). Zhuangzi criticizes ritual specialists and their trivial techniques and taboos. His own sage (whom he calls 'spirit-man') cultivates essential energies within himself, so that spirit forces will come and dwell inside him. Instead of trying to reach the spirits by artificial rituals and sacrifices, spirit-man cultivates himself. He does not depend on things, let alone faux rules and hierarchies. What Heaven does to him, he does. That way 'spirit-man' is 'spirit-like' while remaining human.

Whereas Confucians accept that a degree of artificiality is necessary to get on in life, Zhuangzi sees ritual behaviour as partly disingenuous, partly inefficient. Like the arbitrariness of language (a form of ritual in itself), rituals serve no purpose. 'Rites,' says an old and dishevelled fisherman to

Confucius, 'are devised by the common people in this world; one's true nature is what is received from Heaven – it is of itself so and cannot be changed' (*Zhuangzi* 31.1). For the person sailing through life on the breeze of Heaven, human customs and convention are all but a distraction.

In a commentary on the tradition of Laozi preserved in *The Master Han Fei*, we find what looks almost like a fusion of Confucian and Daoist attitudes towards ritual. The anonymous author behind the text reiterates that 'ritual gives expression to the emotions' and that external embellishments (such as bowing, curtseying, respectful language) communicate our internal disposition. But the text then goes on to argue that, on balance, inner substance is more important than outward appearance, and that ordinary people can sometimes be lax in their commitment to observing ritual propriety (they respect others mostly for the response they will get in return). By contrast, the gentleman 'practises ritual for his own sake'. He cultivates a superior form of propriety which makes him 'spirit-like'. It takes a sage to recognize that there is only so much inner satisfaction to be gained from following rules of propriety for the sake of being approved by others. The true gentleman 'holds on to the inner emotions, and disregards outer expression; he cherishes inner substance and spurns outer adornment' (*Han Feizi* 20). Beware of those who appear boorish, scruffily dressed and gauche. They could be sages!

Law

The 'Treatise on Music' notes that the ancient kings 'used ritual to guide the people's intentions and music to harmonize their voices' but then goes on to mention 'administrative rules to unify conduct and punishments to prevent evil behaviour'. Confucian texts at times seem to give a rose-tinted view of the world, in which ritual norms suffice to guide human behaviour. Yet, no matter how prevalent the influence of ritual and social convention, not everyone wishes or is able to absorb the rules of courtesy and keep up appearances. When etiquette falls short, and when the canon of the ancients seems distant or offers no answers, another kind of authority may be warranted, in the form of legal rules and regulations. Like rituals, laws are a code used to bridge the divide between what is and what should be (recall that for the Legalists laws/*fa* provided the one and only standard). But Chinese thinkers were conscious that laws operate differently from custom and convention. They also acknowledged that there exists an unescapable tension between ritual norms and the rule of law.

Here lies the point of friction: as a code issued by a supreme authority, such as a court or government, the law can challenge the power structure and conventions of the family and vice versa. What is in the interest of the state is not always in the interest of the clan or lineage. This uneasy marriage or dynamic tension between state and family is embedded in the modern Mandarin word for 'state, nation, country', which reads as the binomial *guojia*, 'state-plus-household'. In other words, while a ritual and legal order can overlap in regulating some activities in daily life – for littering in public you can be told off by a friend, or fined by the police, or both – in other domains they stand in opposition. The conflict is set out in the *Analects*:

The Duke of She, in conversation with Confucius, said: 'Among the people in my village there is someone we call "Upright Gong". When his father stole a sheep, he reported him to the authorities.' Confucius replied: 'In my village, those we consider "upright" are different from this: a father covers up for his sons, and a son covers up for his father. "Being upright" can be found in this.' (*An.* 13.18)

Other versions of this exchange appear elsewhere. In one, the son begs the authorities to be allowed to take his father's place and be executed, but he gets pardoned for being honest and filial; there, Confucius condemns it as false honesty on the basis that the son gains his moral reputation at the expense of the father (*Lüshi chunqiu* 11/4.3). In *The Master Han Fei*, the magistrate has Upright Gong executed: good subjects of the state are bad sons to their father. The warning is that Confucian virtues may undermine the authority of the law (*Han Feizi* 49). Yet another author comments that, to be honest and testify against one's father, is not necessarily honourable (*Huainanzi* 13.11). Even if a son feels that it is in the public interest to report his father's crime, that does not give him the right to turn his father in (ritually speaking, this amounts to bad filial manners). The point of the story is to highlight that private loyalty to kin can supersede loyalty to public justice. It is easy to see how such an argument can be used to condone corruption and nepotism. But Confucians were confident that a moral person would naturally know or have learned to avoid such a trap.

Ritual differs from the law both in its reach and its enforceability: laws are prescribed to be followed universally and without personal interpretation or modification; customs such as propriety are a norm you make your own. The law allows for enforcement by officials who can mete out punishments that are specified within the code; ritual conventions need to be learned before they can be obeyed – they are imparted by example and sanctioned by the community that shares them. Laws tackle disagreements and antagonism head on (or at least aspire to do so); rituals help to circumnavigate conflict and find a compromise or common ground. Laws operate on the basis of a culture that recognizes the importance of guilt; ritual norms operate on the basis of shame. When trying to encourage proper behaviour, Confucius suggests that fostering a sense of shame trumps attempting to define guilt: 'If you guide people with administrative injunctions and keep them in line with punishments, they will want to evade [punishment] but will be without a sense of shame. If you guide people with virtue and keep them in line by means of ritual propriety, they will develop a sense of shame and, in addition, they will correct themselves' (*An.* 2.3). Mencius concurs that shame is essential as a catalyst for proper social conduct: 'A person must not be without shame. Shamelessness is the shame of being without shame' (*Mencius* 7A.6).

Confucius is confident that ritual norms are more effective than coercion by immutable laws, rules and regulations. Telling potential criminals that harming another person will result in having their hands chopped off and face branded merely creates a negative motivation not to steal or attack someone. Much better is to foster in people an innate sense of respect for others. In this case, one might try to persuade the potential offender by reminding him that the physical body is inherited from one's parents and that violating his own body (maimed with visible scars from the punishment) and that of others shows a fundamental disrespect for one's fore-bears and a lack of filial piety. Confucian arbitration ideally avoids the courts. To invite judgement of your actions by an external third party (a magistrate) is an admission that you have failed in your role as a father, teacher or senior figure. Laws and courts are most efficient when there is no per-ceived use for them: 'In hearing litigation, I [Confucius] am the same as anyone else. But what we must aim for is to get the parties not to resort to litigation in the first place!' (*An.* 12.13). When it comes to implementing normative conduct, early Chinese legal thought is at variance with itself not so much on the question of what the proper norms should be, but rather how best to enforce them: through the author-ity of the magistrate or official, via the agency of the family, or both.

Despite allusions to the origins of penal law in the mytholo-gical past of the legendary Yellow Emperor, China (unlike, for instance, ancient Greece or Israel) had no God, gods or transcendent universal power assuming the role of divine lawgiver. The Son of Heaven, through his officials, was the supreme authority and lawgiver. The law was man-made, so adopting ancient laws as universal without change would be folly. To be functional, laws (more so than rituals) need to be adapted to circumstances, like medicine that needs to be prescribed according to the illness it is meant to treat (*Lüshi chunqiu* 15/8.2).

The earliest Chinese legal texts appear in the form of covenants and inscriptions on bronze vessels of the Zhou period. Little has survived, however. These early law codes had a religious dimension, as they were addressed to and/or formulated in the presence of the spirit world. Thus, despite its development into a normative system of its own, Chinese law can be seen to have originated in a ritual context. Bronze vessels were used in sacrificial cults. By casting legal codes (or legal cases) onto the vessels, the ancestors and spirits were invited to keep a watchful eye over proceedings. Participants in a covenant swore an oath in the eyes of the spirits by smearing their lips with sacrificial blood and burying a text or formula in a pit together with the animal victim. *The Master Mo* tells the story of a dead sacrificial goat that rose up and then butted and broke the legs of the guilty party in front of the altars of state (*Mozi* 31.8).

Archaeological discoveries reveal that, by the late fourth century BCE, officials took legal material written on bamboo or wood with them to the grave (together with other writings, such as calendars or medical and divination texts). The two most extensive caches of legal texts from early China recovered to date were found in the tombs of such local officials and legal scribes. These are the manuscripts of Shuihudi (Yunmeng county, Hubei province), dating to 217 BCE, and those of Zhangjiashan (Jiangling county, Hubei province), dating to 186 BCE. Were these tomb occupants meant to carry on administering the laws into the afterlife? Were these buried texts intended as a status item for the deceased? Did they grant power to control the souls of the departed or any other ghosts and spirits lurking around post-mortem? There are no certain answers to these questions. But evidence suggests that the spirit world never extracted itself entirely from legal culture and that the law could be used on ghosts and demons. Ritual and religious texts of the time contain administrative and legal language (spirits can be addressed as 'My Lord', or urged on to obey or desist 'as stipulated in statutes and ordinances'). This would remain a common feature in the liturgy of Chinese popular religion.

Li Kui (fifth century BCE), a statesman from the state of Wei, is credited with crafting a law code that would ultimately inspire the early imperial law codes of the Qin and Han. The Han carried forward the laws and procedures of the Qin with only minor revisions and changes in terminology. The Tang code, issued in 725 CE and used until the fourteenth century, drew substantially on Han penal law and its natural philosophy of punishment. (The Tang code, in turn, survives in parts in the Ming and Qing codes, and has influenced legal culture across pre-modern East Asia.) New dynasties tended to publish new legal codes (and rituals) but, in reality, what tended to change was personnel rather than the main principles of government. So the preface to the Tang code still alludes to *The Book of Documents* when setting out its philosophy of punishment: 'Punishments are used to stop punishments; killing is used to stop killing' (*Shangshu*, 'Da Yu mo'). The continuities between these legal codes and their use in communities separated by many centuries are remarkable. But equally timeless, of course, are many of the crimes.

If rituals aimed to firm up the structure of the family, the law projected the authority of the state into the household and was devised to control those who acted as operatives of the state. Its priority was to assist the ruler in managing his officials and, through them, the people. Overseeing the bureaucrats who act as intermediaries between local and central government has been the constant priority of the Chinese state, from its first emperors to its leaders today. Early China's legal codes, therefore, were not so much concerned with theories of justice or the protection of rights, freedoms and privileges of the individual or distinct social groups (so-called civil law). First and foremost, the law served the interests of those who ruled, not those who were ruled. It managed the flow of information and personnel in its service. As in many other traditional societies, administrative and judicial authority were not clearly delineated in ancient China: the local official doubled up as magistrate who, like a father who runs his family, meted out sanctions. Each administrator was responsible for implementing the law in the domain under his jurisdiction. The law addressed wrongs rather than rights; the bulk of China's legal texts dealt with administrative regulations and penal (criminal) law. Laws were formulated into 'statutes' (*lü*) and 'ordinances' (*ling*). (The modern Chinese word for law – *falü* – may be read as 'standard-and-regulation'.)

There was hardly any aspect of life that did not find a place in the legal codes dispatched to officials across the realm. For both the governors and those they governed, life must have felt like an uneasy passage through a maze of regulations, with ponderous inventories of fines and punishments lying in wait behind every corner. In both pre-imperial and early imperial times, the Chinese state licensed its officials to micromanage human activity under their jurisdiction and sent them forth like an army of prying ants. No aspect of civil life was left untouched: love and marriage, food rations for the elderly, salaries and stipends, property, inheritance, tax, trade, agriculture, livestock and parks, transport, manufacturing, the private possession of books, quality control of goods, the quantity of seeds loaned for sowing, among many others. The list of crimes appears equally endless: being in receipt of ill-gotten gains, robbery, kidnapping, absconding, homicide, conspiracy to kill, grievous bodily harm, injury to government livestock, extortion, false testimony, adultery and illicit intercourse (either by consent or by force), damage to government tools, shifting border marks between fields, illicit mining or salt production, melting down bronze coins or illegally casting cash, incest, rape, forging seals or documents, beating or cursing officials, arson, serving spoiled meat, causing miscarriage through fighting, burying a suicide victim without reporting it, receiving stolen goods, using incorrect weights and measures, even cheating at chess. Showing a lack of filial piety was one of the most heinous crimes. Han law also included regulations for training scribes and for testing student diviners and aspiring invocators (their job was to lead various types of ceremonies; in order to qualify, one had to be able to chant a minimum of seven thousand words from memory).

The local official acting as the arm and eye of the central authorities (and ultimately, the Son of Heaven) would bear the brunt of the law as much as those he had to control. Officials were subject to strict expectations. Judging by the volume of rules governing their behaviour, corruption must have been endemic (a charge that has not gone away in modern China): taking bribes, siphoning off state funds or pilfering state-owned property, covering up crime, false bookkeeping, and so on. Some laws read like a syllabus for accountants: 'When drafting accounts, items that are not of the same norm should not be listed in the same way' (A53). Others read like a manual of joinery repair: 'For one [instance of] lubrication when repairing one cart, use one ounce of glue and ten grams of grease ...' (A76). Failure to enforce the statutes, report upwards to higher authorities, or deliver what was required would result in sanctions. Not reporting a theft or loss of government stocks was as unpardonable as stealing the items. Qin law berated officials for the number of rat holes in the granaries under their supervision ('Three mouse holes are equivalent to one rat hole'), or the holes bored by insects in government-owned leather and hides hanging in storage (D130, B18). In Qin law, fines had to be paid in suits of armour and shields (or in laces used to tie pieces of scale armour together); by Han times they were calculated in gold and cash.

Collective responsibility within households runs like a red thread through the laws of the Qin and the Han. Relatives and neighbours could be implicated. Entire families could be made liable for the crimes committed by one of their members. They would be at the receiving end of collective punishments, which could include the execution of an entire extended family or lineage – one punishment was known as 'having three sets of one's relatives exterminated'. Failure to report a crime was as serious as committing an offence. The law enshrined mutual surveillance: in principle, everyone was expected to act as the eye (for which read 'spy') of the law and, as such, the state. The obligation to denounce others as well as oneself, verbally or in writing, was central to legal procedure, although intentionally denouncing someone on false grounds was a crime and resulted in the punishment reverting to the accuser. Denunciation became another element in Chinese legal thinking to have survived into modern times.

Sanctions for failing to comply with the law ranged from minor financial penalties to brute physical torture and death. For the most severe crimes, the purpose was to defame and stigmatize the offender for life. Forced labour, which could run up to five years, was the punishment most advantageous to the state. Convicts provided a pool of disposable labour that was continuously replenished. The early Chinese empire saw convicts, and indeed migrants, as of economic benefit rather than a burden to the state. They were deported to work on grand projects, from repairing dikes, digging canals and building roads and defensive walls to erecting tombs, temples and palaces. You could be convicted to serve as a 'wall-builder' or a 'watchman', or, in the case of women, a 'white-rice sorter'. Forced service in border garrisons provided another option. Starved and worn down by heavy shackles and collars, many did not survive the floggings and malnutrition they had to endure. Banishment, which had also been a way of moving people after the conquest of a city, was a less severe form of punishment. Those with means could redeem it with cash. As a general principle, repeat offenders and those accused of several crimes would be given a sentence corresponding to their heaviest crime. Distinctions were also made between crimes committed with intent, by mistake or by accident.

Mutilation as a form of physical punishment awaited many who had transgressed. Legalist thinkers such as Lord Shang had already put a positive slant on the use of torture: 'the prohibitions of the former kings, such as carrying out executions, cutting off feet or branding the face, were imposed not because they sought to harm the people but only to prohibit depravity and to stop transgressions' (*Shangjun shu* 17.3). In order to work as an effective deterrent, Lord Shang intimates, punishments needed to be harsh, visible and preferably public. Mitigating circumstances were to be dismissed: once you go astray and deviate from the straight and narrow, previous good behaviour no longer counts.

Capital punishment was administered through beheading or, in some cases, by slicing the criminal in two at the waist. Executions could happen in public. If the crime warranted it, the head and disfigured body were displayed at the market for all to see. Methods at hand for disfigurement and mutilation of the body included: being torn apart by chariots; shaving off the hair, beard, eyebrows and moustache for men (a way to symbolically suspend their manhood); tattooing the face on the cheeks or forehead; and cutting off the nose or feet. The law specified the numbers of strokes to be administered in a beating; fleeing from duty or absconding from your registered domicile could cost you fifty strokes of the cane even as an official. Castration was one of the heaviest punishments (for rape, illicit sexual conduct and other crimes); it involved severing both the penis and the testicles. One of the legal terms for it translates literally as 'rottenness', an allusion to the idea that the convict would rot away like a dead tree and no longer produce new life (that is, offspring).

The integrity of the body was important. The body, according to Zengzi, 'is the material form given to you by father and mother; how dare you be disrespectful of it!' (*Lüshi chunqiu* 14/1.3). This is reflected in the degree of attention the legal codes devote to physical injury. The codes are at pains to define the nature of wounds and injuries: how to punish someone for tearing an ear or breaking a joint; what to do when during a fight someone pulls out eyebrows, hair or an entire beard; how to punish when someone bites off a nose, ear, finger or lip, or leaves a bite-mark in someone's cheek. If in any doubt about whether the implement that caused the injury should be referred to as a stick, the Qin code clarifies: 'A stick is a piece made of wood that can be used to strike!' (D76). Such commentary may look pointless but, in the context of legal terminology, it is not. Like ritual, the law creates a language of its own. Laws create an 'as is' world accessible only to those who master the jargon – lawyers' bread and butter. Clarity about terminology appears important in the legal codes of early China. Technical terms for procedures of reporting, investigation and punishment are specified; legal commentary is given for terms that could appear self-evident or arbitrary outside the framework of the law – hence a 'stick' can't be a 'quarterstaff' or any old piece of wood or bamboo. 'Serious' wounds and accidents must be distinguished from 'small' ones: 'A serious wound is when a limb has perhaps not been completely severed, [but the injury] goes so far that the leader or chief has to order two men to support the person out – that is a serious wound' (D188).

Like ritual, the law had a cosmic dimension, keeping humans in harmony with Heaven and the surrounding world. The assumption was that crime was a transgression of a natural state of harmony. Those who transgressed therefore had to repay or compensate for the fissures and cracks they had caused.

Punishment restored this imbalance. Just as *yin* needs to be counterbalanced by *yang*, so no crime could be left unpunished. However, to ensure cosmic balance, procedures had to be correct and properly timed. 'When punishments are not on target,' warned the philosopher Dong Zhongshu, 'this will produce noxious *qi*' (*Hanshu* 56). The result of such bad air in the sky would be a cosmos that is out of kilter, causing natural disasters and abnormalities. (The Chinese character for 'centred, balanced', *zhong*, is a pictograph of an arrow hitting a target.) Executions took place in the dark and cold months of autumn or winter, and not during the seasons of growth. Executioners had to complete all the beheadings before the months of death and decay ended. Inspectors toured the prisons during the same *yin* period of the year. With the arrival of autumn, punishment must be carried out in an orderly way and decisively: 'Resolving civil and criminal cases must be correct and just. Punish those who committed crimes. Be stern in deciding the penalty. Now that Heaven and Earth have begun to be severe, it is not permitted to be tolerant' (*Lüshi chunqiu* 7/1.3). For those charged with administering the harshest punishments in the land, the frosty season signalled the beginning of activity. For the convicts awaiting their lot, it augured the end.

Not everyone was equal in the eyes of the law. It would be an exaggeration to categorize traditional Chinese law as a footnote to Confucian household ethics, yet it certainly embraced the notion of differential hierarchies and graded responsibilities and liabilities as a matter of course. To some extent, custom supplanted private law and the state legislated mostly on matters of public interest. The law differentiated between people based on their status. One could redeem punishments by different means depending on one's rank, title and status. Such trade-offs could be significant for those who had the means to offer valuables or cash for crime (conversely, the government sometimes sold ranks to fill the coffers). Redeeming punishment could amount to the equivalent of what would be called a salary exchange scheme today. Action against high-ranking officials required permission from the capital and, in some cases, the throne. Rulers could grant amnesties on the occasion of an event that merited celebration. Amnesties enticed absconders and unregistered persons back into the fold; they could then be reinstated as regularized taxpayers. The legal equivalent of knowing one's role and place in society was the obligation to be registered. As in China today, there were serious repercussions for flouting the registers. If and when people had to be settled or moved, this could only happen on the state's terms.

Just as obedience to the father was enshrined in ritual codes, so the Qin and Han legal code affirmed the authority of the father figure within the household. Orderly families – remember *The Great Learning* – produce an orderly state. A father could officially denounce a son and ask for him to be killed on the grounds of unfilial behaviour. In one Qin case, a father asked that his son be banished and escorted to the deep south for life. A husband committed no crime by beating or caning his wife, nor fathers their children, as long as they did not die from their injuries within twenty days. Children were executed for killing their father or mother, but, on the other hand, could not officially testify against parents for being abused. Punishments for stealing depended on who stole what from whom. When the head of a household was sentenced for a crime and sent off to do penal labour, the government could enslave his wife and children. Many punishments depended on the proximity of kinship between the offender and the victim. For instance, incest with a distant relative was punished less severely than incest between siblings of the same mother, which warranted execution.

Legal statutes, many scarcely changing over time, tell us little about how the law was put into practice. But we are fortunate to have retrospective accounts of legal cases and judicial interpretations of the law. The Shuihudi texts include a forensic investigation of a suicide by hanging, a dispute over the ownership of a cow, an examination to establish a case of leprosy, and a villager denouncing a man and a woman for fornication ('I have arrested and fettered them and I have come to bring them in'). *The Book of Submitted Doubtful Cases* (*Zouyan shu*) recovered at Zhangjiashan offers another sample of Qin- and early Han-period case law. Scholars debate whether its twenty-two cases were meant to teach officials about legal procedure or whether it is to be read as a compilation of court-crime literature *avant la lettre*. Either way, they illustrate the complexities of judicial inquiry and show that, in the case of doubtful investigations or wrongful sentencing, cases could be appealed and redirected from the local magistrate to be reinvestigated or trialled by higher authorities. Central government exercised regular controls over local magistrates. The *Doubtful Cases* present intrigue and subject matter that would be fodder for any crime writer: eloping lovers, conscripts and slaves who abscond or escape, murder, grain robbery, bribery and cheating, fraudulent officials who mess with accounts, and even the case of a fellow who counterfeits a passport for his horse (needed to pass through checkpoints). It also includes a remarkable case of illicit sex: a newly widowed woman has intercourse in the room behind the coffin of her dead husband while her mother-in-law is in the house to mourn her son. Charged initially for filial impiety towards the mother-in-law, the woman sees her sentence overturned on the grounds that she was not caught in the act and that the crime of contempt for a dead husband was lighter than contempt for a living husband.

The moral conflict between a sense of shame on the one hand and guilt on the other was the natural outcome of the coexistence of a deeply embedded Confucian set of values and a legal system vital for running the administration of a vast empire. The effectiveness of a culture of punishment also touched the conscience of some of China's rulers, most notably Han Emperor Wendi, known for being parsimonious, modest and for having reformed penal law (in 167 BCE), ridding it of some of the most brutal and mutilating punishments. Sima Qian recounts how, when the emperor once discovered that some of his officials were taking bribes, he refused to haul them before the judges. Instead, he would open his own private coffers and shower them with further gifts of gold and cash to make sure they felt ashamed about their behaviour. The emperor's concern, the story goes, was to 'transform the people by means of virtue. Thus all within the four seas enjoyed wealth and plenty and devoted itself to the observance of propriety and duty' (*Shiji* 10). It sounds like fiction, as indeed many at the time would doubtlessly have argued. Harshness and ruthlessness were more likely to be associated with those responsible for administrating the law. The biography of one famous Han official recounts how, as a child, he managed to beat a confession out of a rat who had stolen a piece of meat, and write out its testimony before executing the poor rodent! The good official had to be both morally sound and legally clean. Recommendation for entry into the higher civil service in Han came with the proviso that one had to be both 'filial and incorruptible'.

On balance, then, no matter how sophisticated laws were or how rigorously they were implemented, few Chinese thinkers believed that they could ever compensate for what good customs and habits were able to bring about. Behaving legally only touches the surface of what the good society should be. To reach beyond it warrants ritual behaviour in accordance with inculcated moral standards. The law aims to prevent wrongdoing and thereby works negatively. By contrast, education, etiquette and convention work positively to encourage good behaviour. Not harming your neighbour is not the same as treating him nicely. Laws can be used to execute those who are unfilial and dishonest, but they are unable to turn people into a Confucius or his disciple Zengzi, that paragon of filial piety. Without laws good government cannot be created, but without a sense of rightness and propriety those in charge cannot implement the laws convincingly. States survive, concludes *The Master Huainan*, not because they have laws, but because they have sages, ritual experts and other worthies:

> The reason why we respect sages is not because they issue punishments in accordance with the nature of the crime, but because they know from where disorder arises. If you do not cultivate [the people's] customs and habits yet give them free rein to fall into excess and depravity, and you then pursue them with punishments and restrain them with laws, though you maim and plunder [everyone] in the world, you will not be able to stop them. (*Huainanzi* 20.20)

But laws, sages and ritual experts can only do that much. They can be powerful and persuasive, but they are no match for the two other forces of authority that keep a watchful eye over human conduct and society: ancestors and spirits.

CHAPTER 6

Spirits and Ancestors

Imagine your great-grandfather. You may have a vague and indirect knowledge of him. Your parents and grandparents were in awe of him, they busied themselves with helping him feel comfortable in old age, and the entire family meekly went along with his every whim. At family reunions, older relatives shared stories of how everyone avoided upsetting Great-Grandad, and ran around to make sure he had warm clothes and proper meals. Such respect and care, your father told you, was what he deserved: for most of his adult life, Great-Grandad had worked tirelessly to feed his family, pay for their education and help out relatives. You can still visualize the small altar table that stood in the corner of the kitchen. It had the scent of rosewood. This is the spot where your parents and visiting uncles and aunts would burn incense sticks in front of a wooden tablet. The tablet had your great-grandad's names on it, a traditional Chinese date of birth that you could not decipher, and the name of the county his family came from. There was a dot of red ink on the tablet that stared at you (or were you staring at it?).

Then remember how, as a child, on the day the family graves were swept in early April, you used to peer out of the corner of your eyes at your parents, uncles and aunts. You copied their every move so you could get that prayer greet-ing in front of the gravestone just right: bend the upper body forwards slightly, droop the head a little, clasp both hands together to hold the incense sticks, and gently move them … up and down, to and fro, and slightly forwards. Sometimes in your sleep you can still smell the clouds of incense that turned the uphill graveyard into a misty and mysterious won-derland. You see people burning stacks of fake paper money, and paper clothes, and a miniature paper car, and a paper lighter (Great-Grandad had been a chain smoker all his life). With the rolling eyes of a newborn calf you used to stare at the red trays laid out in front and on top of the gravestones. They were full of fruit, cakes and drinks (some even had cans of beer, or a pork trotter). One year you took a bite from a cake, but it had no flavour. You wondered: what would happen if I pinched one of those oranges? Would I wake up the dead? Will they be angry and make me ill for stealing their fare? You recall the almanac hanging against the door at home: 'When you fall ill on a *bing* or *ding* day, it is your late grandfather who is haunting you.'

Great-Grandad continues to watch over your shoulder, every step of the way as you grow up, study, work and go about your daily business. When you have been rude to your par-ents, he makes you wake up with a headache. When you are surfing the web and land on a page you should never have searched for, the old man magically interrupts your wi-fi connection. When you do not feel like helping your ageing mother with the shopping, he sends down snails and whitefly to nibble away at those blue-green cabbages you are trying to grow in the garden. To get married, you ask for his blessing through the ancestral tablet on the house altar. When you slacken in your studies, fail to pass an exam or gain a promotion, the old man stealthily taps you on the shoulder: 'The clan is watching you – make us proud!' That diploma is not just yours; it belongs to the family, an honour to those who have gone before you. So you study harder, and harder, day and night. Your tutor worries: 'It's only a degree – yes?'

Sometimes it is as if you hear and sense Great-Grandad around you. You try to visualize his presence in your room. To keep him happy, you put offerings in front of his tablet. At mealtimes, you set aside a spoonful of rice or congee at the altar table. He gets the best part of the stew. The ghosts of those who have departed should never go hungry. When offering sacrifices to the spirits, Confucius once said, take it seriously and behave yourself 'as if the spirits are present' (*An*. 3.12). So you keep Great-Grandad happy, even if it means getting his spirit drunk now and then with an offering of fine ale, brandy or rice wine. That way he keeps his distance and you won't incur his wrath. For if that were to happen, there would be no one to save you. You exercise and stay healthy, and look after that body your parents gave you. One day, when your time has come to be turned into an altar tablet, you will expect your children, grand- and great-grandchildren to respect and remember you the same way you looked after the spirit of Great-Grandad. And, if needed, you will remind them of their duties in your own way, like spirits always do.

Ancestors

Confucius never asked the one burning question that has consumed theologians and philosophers in other traditions elsewhere, namely whether or not spirits exist. For Confucius, the good life was to be found amid an orderly society here and now, rather than in a life hereafter: 'The Master did not speak about strange events, the use of force, disorder or spirits' (*An.* 7.21). Instead of theorizing about spirits, Confucius advises that it is more important to get on with them and not be distracted by questions to which there is no real answer. (Here, Confucius is the anti-theologian: there is no logic/ *logos* to God/*theos*.) When one of his disciples, Zilu, pushes him on the issue, he replies: 'If you are not yet able to serve people, how would you be able to serve ghosts and spirits?' Next Zilu asks him about death. 'You do not yet understand life,' Confucius replies, 'so how could you possibly understand death?' (*An.* 11.12). Confucius sees no need for a theoretical proof of a higher spirit power. But he acknowledges that humans have to appease whatever spirit powers might be out there in order to keep them at bay so that they do not cause any harm (*An.* 6.22). This so-called humanism in Confucius found favour with philosophers of the European Enlightenment such as Voltaire and Leibniz: they saw in China an example of a civil society able to function on the basis of moral reason only and without an interfering God. The German sociologist Max Weber (1864–1920) was confident that 'the Confucian ... desired neither to be saved from evil nor from a fall of man, which he knew not. He desired to be saved from nothing except perhaps the undignified barbarism of social rudeness. Only the infraction of piety, the one basic social duty, could constitute "sin" for the Confucian.'

What they did not appreciate was that, despite Confucius's studied evasion in a few passages in the *Analects*, ancient China was full of spirits. Not everyone was as reticent as Confucius in trying to understand how the spirit world works. Mozi's position on ghosts and spirits, for instance, is less wavering. He thinks spirits are intelligent, can bring good or bad luck, bless those who do good and inflict misfortune on those who behave badly. The Mohist attitude towards the spirit world is purely pragmatic: sacrifices do not transform Heaven, but since spirits act in an entirely predictable way, you get out of them what you put in. That means offering sacrifices in the style of *do ut des* ('I give so that you will give something back'). Since neither Heaven nor the spirits can be capricious, they will act according to a clear moral calculus. *The Master Mo* devotes an entire chapter (*Mozi* 31) to the question of whether spirits exist and whether they are capable of punishing the worthy and rewarding the wicked. Mozi offers three proofs: spirits exist because there have been reports and eyewitness accounts of them throughout the ages and in different places; because the sages of antiquity believed in their existence; and because spirits are necessary for a morally functioning society – people will behave better when they know the spirits are watching them. However, Mozi allows room for doubt when he admits that even if spirits did not exist, there are still social benefits to getting people together for sacrifices (*Mozi* 31.19). The Mohists saw ghosts and spirits as intermediaries and all-seeing informants of Heaven. 'Why bother with rituals otherwise,' was the challenge they threw at Confucian ritual specialists: 'To claim that there are no ghosts and yet studying sacrificial rituals is like learning the rites of hospitality while there are no guests or making fishing nets when there are no fish' (*Mozi* 48.9).

Confucius and his followers, however, cannot be classed as agnostics or atheists, and they certainly had a sense of religiosity. In the 1970s, the philosopher Herbert Fingarette wrote a book, *Confucius: The Secular as Sacred*, in which he suggested that, for Confucius, the performance of the rites itself represented the spiritual or 'holy' moment. At the heart of their thinking were the ancestral spirits. Maintaining a bond with ancestors was seen as a form of filial piety that extended beyond death. Unlike in the Abrahamic religions, the dead in ancient China are not distant or supramundane entities, cut off from the world of the living and unresponsive to the actions of their descendants. Few Chinese spirits have a life of their own. Ancestral spirits remain linked to the living through an umbilical cord that extends beyond death. The writer and philosopher Lin Yutang (1895–1976) once wrote perceptively: 'What strikes me most is that the Greeks made their gods like men, while the Christians desired to make men like gods. That Olympian company is certainly a jovial, amorous, loving, lying, quarrelling and vow-breaking petulant lot.' Chinese ancestral spirits do not live on faraway mountain peaks, cavorting with each other while enjoying fine nectar and ambrosia. Their welfare in the afterlife is insecure. In much of Chinese religion, the family forms something of an 'indefinitely perpetuated corporation', as the historian Charles O. Hucker put it. Ancestors need to be nurtured and maintained by the living who offer them prayer, sacrifices and remembrance. As Xunzi noted, 'Ritual means "to nourish"' (*Xunzi* 19.1b), while another text defines sacrifice itself as 'the Way of feeding and nurturing [the dead]' (*Da Dai Liji*, 'Sheng de').

The cult of the dead was the focal point of much of Chinese religious practice, and remains part of the religious fabric in Chinese communities today. To mourn and remember ancestors was an orchestrated proceeding. Both the duration of mourning and the mourning attire were dictated by one's relationship to the deceased (the ritual canon prescribes five degrees of mourning). Even the wail was based on one's place in the kinship network: a close relative had to 'cry as if you can't recover'; a more distant mourner could 'quaver three times and then fade'.

The Ritual Records prescribe that mourners have to subject themselves to staged periods of fasting. According to one description, the fast consisted of a three-day period of total abstention that would be gradually alleviated by the intake of gruel, following which the mourner reverted to solid foods. The chief mourner lived for a time on coarse rice and water. Fruit and vegetables could only be eaten a year into the mourning period, while the intake of meat was deferred by another year (*Liji*, 'Sang da ji'). Thus the grieving descendants went through a cycle that allowed them to return to a full diet in steps, via a vegetarian stage. As they gradually distanced themselves from the deceased, they re-entered the world of the living and all its colours, flavours and sensations.

Distress and pain had to show physically, especially if you were a close relative of the deceased: 'When there was internal sorrow and grief, this would produce a change in [a grieving son's] outward appearance. As severe hurt and pain would take hold of his heart, his mouth could not relish any sweet flavours, nor could his body find ease in anything comfortable' (*Liji*, 'Wen sang'). There were some exemptions from this strict regime. The ill and infirm were allowed to eat meat and drink wine during mourning. Age also provided grounds for being excused from some observances. The ritual canon even includes rules on bodily hygiene to treat exhaustion or prevent illness during a fast: ulcers on the body and wounds on the head should be cleansed and washed; emaciating oneself to the point of illness should be prevented. It is unlikely that the guidelines would have been adopted in full. More likely, they were followed in the manner of the instructions on a seed packet or a recipe: you follow some and adapt the rest according to personal circumstances.

What happened to the dead in the afterlife? The realm of the dead – known, among other names, as the Yellow Springs – as well as the tomb, were associated with shadowy darkness and dimness. According to the directional symbolism of the Five Phases (where cold and dark belong to the water phase – see Chapter 2), the dead were to be buried to the north. Turtles, associated with the north as well as the idea of longevity, are common emblems in Chinese cemeteries in the form of pedestals for stone stelae or columns or tombs in the shape of a turtle's back. Dying was often described as drifting or sinking into a mysterious, permanent darkness. Some literati and ritual specialists argued that humans possessed a dual soul: an ephemeral *hun* soul (associated with *yang*) that returns to Heaven after death; and an earthly *po* soul (associated with *yin*) that remains in the grave. These souls had to be offered sustenance to tempt them back lest they became hungry and angry: 'If a ghost has a place to return home to, it will not turn into an avenging spirit' (*Zuozhuan*, Lord Zhao 7). *The Book of Etiquette and Rites* describes a ritual in which a spirit medium puts on the clothes of the deceased, climbs onto the roof of the dead person's house and then summons back the [*hun*] soul as if wanting to resuscitate the corpse by reuniting the soul with the body before it wanders off again. Two poems associated with the poet Qu Yuan (fourth century BCE) and his disciple, preserved in *The Songs of the South* (*Chuci*), describe this soul-summoning process. In one poem, the soul is warned of the terrifying dangers it will encounter once it leaves the body and flees to the Earth's far corners. 'Oh, soul, come back! Why should you travel so far away?' the incantation pleads. Next, an attempt is made to lure the soul back by means of delicious sacrificial foods (the way to a dead man's spirit runs through the stomach):

> The entire household has come to honour you;
>> all kinds of good food are ready:
> Rice, broom-corn, early wheat, mixed with yellow
>> millet;
> Bitter, salt, sour, hot and sweet: there are dishes
>> of all flavours:
> Ribs of the fattened ox, tender and succulent;
> Sour and bitter blended in the soup of Wu;
> Stewed turtle and roast kid; served up with yam
>> sauce;
> Geese cooked in sour sauce, casseroled duck, fried
>> flesh of the great crane … (*Chuci*, 'Zhao hun')

How can the dead not wish to come back again at the sight of such culinary delights? In reality, however, only elites and philosophers theorized about the fate of the soul. The idea that humans possessed an intellectual soul that would fly off to paradise and an animal soul responsible for the physical functioning of the body (and content to remain there if encouraged to do so) was no more than just a theory. In practice, evidence points to varied perceptions of the soul and its post-mortem journey. In folk religion, both souls could be summoned to the netherworld and located in the grave. Likewise, legendary mountains, such as Mounts Haoli and Liangfu, and Mount Buzhou in the northwest of the universe, provided repose for the souls. Some of these ancient mortuary observances survive in Daoist and other rituals today, where the departed soul is guided from the tomb to the wider spirit world with the assistance of priests or shamanic escorts, or grave-securing writs and petitions are sent up to otherworldly bureaucrats who keep registers of the dead. The Chinese conceived of death as a journey that required rituals, prayer and sacrifices at each stage travelled by the ancestral spirits. One of the most famous pieces of Han art – discovered at Mawangdui (Hunan) and dating to *c.*168 BCE – is a coffin banner depicting the soul being escorted through the hereafter.

As Mencius suggested, being filial in life is one thing, but it is much harder to maintain this bond and invest it across the generations, both emotionally and in material ways: 'Caring for one's parents while they are alive cannot be considered a great thing. It is only through performing the rituals that honour them appropriately in death that one does the great thing' (*Mencius* 4B.13). Securing the welfare and blessings of one's ancestors and progenitors required constant effort. The posthumous titles of Han emperors all carried the prefix 'Filial' (*xiao*) as they continued to offer sacrifice to their lineage, the Liu family.

Once the mourning period had concluded, descendants reverted to a cycle of seasons and years for commemorating the dead. Xunzi states that mourning should be sequenced so that both the dead and the mourner undergo a process of gradual separation: 'with each change, the corpse is adorned; with each move it is taken farther away, and with the passage of time the ordinary course of life is resumed' (*Xunzi* 19.5a). Death rituals worked like a pulley that hauled the living temporarily out of the rhythm of ordinary life to then drop them gradually back in again. The dead, too, were ranked in gradations of time. The offering of sacrifices at altars and the internment of grave goods (also known as 'bright vessels') inside the tomb served to shine a momentary light on the dead as they started their journey into the afterlife and distanced themselves from their living descendants. Like shadows on a wall that become smaller and dimmer as the spotlight pulls away from them, the dead became more distant. The sinologist K. E. Brashier has coined the term 'structured amnesia' to describe what happens during the process of remembrance. Beyond a certain number of generations and degree of proximity, ancestors were allowed to fade away. Rituals could be suspended or conducted less frequently. The spirits themselves, represented by tablets lined up in a fixed order in the family shrine or temple, had a ritually imposed expiration date. Especially for ancestors of those in positions of power (such as emperors), ancestral worship was as much about selectively forgetting than remembering or reviving memory. In the Han period, for example, only the four most recent generations of imperial ancestors, plus the founder, received offerings at their shrines.

The point is that ancestral worship is not simply about the dead. It also underpins the social map of the living, the relationships between them and the claims they make upon each other. While wives, sons, grandsons and great-grandsons all take charge of their own assigned part in the rituals for a deceased father, relationships are (re)affirmed between them and in the eyes of the outside world. Ancestral worship extended beyond the generations to include the entire lineage or clan. The dignity of descendants was measured by the care they invested in the service of the deceased. Kinship in life meant sustained affinity beyond the threshold of death. As remains the case today, there was a politics to remembrance, not least when it concerned the privilege of being remembered on a permanent basis. Being able to claim that one was linked to a common ancestor facilitated a bond of kinship between families. The further back one can trace a shared ancestry, the larger one's family becomes.

By the second half of the Han dynasty, elites started to share their ancestral stock and its achievements with the public through elegant inscriptions on stone stelae, which would be placed above ground, complete with the names of those who sponsored the stela, for all to see. It was yet another way to claim social immortality. Many of these stelae stood for centuries; some still stand today. And even when left to crumble in the ruins of an overgrown graveyard, there was a good chance that a distant relative or local antiquarian would make a copy of the inscription to be filed for posterity.

Searching for spirit

Among the methods that people use to enable them to relate to the spirit world, the offering of sacrifices was the corner-stone of religious activity in ancient China at all levels of so-ciety: from the state to the region and local community, from the Son of Heaven down to ordinary households. Much has been written about the question why people should offer up food and material tokens to invisible powers. Sacrifice has been explained as an integral part of gift culture: my offerings give me controlling powers over the recipient(s). Scholars have emphasized the importance of communion in forging a bond between humans and the spirit world: by sharing food with the spirits (and participating in the banquet that follows the sacri-fice), one can appease or invite the spirits. Two French schol-ars, Henri Hubert (1872–1927) and Marcel Mauss (1872–1950), wrote an influential essay in 1899 in which they proposed that the purpose and effect of consuming or destroying an of-fering is to establish communication between two separate worlds that otherwise have no immediate points of contact: the sacred and the profane. None of these theories were de-veloped with China in mind (drawing mostly on Graeco-Roman antiquity, the Bible and the Vedic tradition), yet they all revolve around one fundamental question that crops up in most of the world's religions: is there a continuity between the human and spirit world – are both worlds entirely separ-ate from each other, or can we be separate while being in touch at the same time? A working definition of sacrifice might describe it as communicating with otherworldly powers through the mediation of a victim or an offering, thereby transforming both those who sacrifice and the spirits who receive the sacrifice. But so much for theory; how are we to imagine a sacrificial culture?

Like festivals and ceremonies of all kinds, the obligation to offer sacrifices demanded rituals that regularly punctuated the calendar of economic and agrarian life. At state level, a ritual year would start in the first month of spring. This is the time when the Son of Heaven held prayers for a bountiful harvest. Accompanied by his chief officials, he would place his hands on a plough on a piece of land set aside as a 'sacred field' – like a politician who turns the first sod at a building site, cuts a ribbon or fires the starting shot at a race. Guidelines would be drawn up that stipulated what should be offered and when. For instance, female animals were not to be used as victims because they were central to the growth of the flocks. The use of live animals could be vetoed in favour of offering precious items such as jade, animal skins or silk.

In late spring, the women would tend to the production of silk used for ceremonial robes. Calves marked for sacrifice were selected and their numbers written down. In early summer, a tax rate on grains and silk needed for ritual purposes would be set. The historian Ban Gu (first century CE) estimated that, in the fourth century BCE, in an average family of five, the equivalent of over half the annual food budget for one family member was set aside for sacrificial obligations throughout the year. To supply exquisite textiles, *The Ritual Records* state, the ancients had designated that mulberry orchards and silkworm houses be built near the river, where the women would wash the silkworm eggs and pick and dry mulberry leaves to feed the silkworms (*Liji*, 'Ji yi'). A flurry of activity followed by midsummer: musical instruments used in ceremonies were tuned and repaired; prayers were directed to mountains, streams and springs; the ruler held the annual sacrifice to ensure a good rainfall and a bountiful harvest. In late summer, the court would levy hay and fodder in all districts to feed the animal victims needed in state and ancestral sacrifices. Silks dyed and decorated for ceremonial robes and flags were inspected.

Well into autumn, the time had come for the annual inspection of the sacrificial animals. Official slaughterers and priests did the rounds to check whether the animals were whole and complete. They measured their height and size, assessed their condition as fat or thin, and examined the fodder. They also inspected the coloration of their coats (a speckled pelt might put off the spirits, for instance), and kept an eye on the horns of the oxen: short and pristine horns, described as 'cocoon-like and chestnut-shaped', were valued most. Sick or injured animals were not to be used. Then the granaries were repaired. Grains for the spirits harvested from the sacred fields were stored in the state's 'spirit granaries'. Like a well-organized farmer, the good ruler had to stock up on sacrificial supplies when he could, so that he would never run out.

In winter, wood was collected, as fuel for sacrifices and raw material for ritual implements (baskets and trays). Certain woods (mulberry, cypress, peach) were believed to be especially potent for ritual purposes. Wood was also needed for the coffins of those who could afford a proper burial. At state level, the sacrificial economy was well run. Religion, in most times and places, is intimately linked to the material world. Fields and parks would be fenced off for supplies, and the law punished unauthorized sacrifices or the theft or illicit trade in sacrificial offerings. One entry in the Qin legal code runs: 'When an official sacrifice is not yet over, stealing the preparations warrants a fine ... having the beard shaved off and being made a bond servant' (D21).

An army of officials beavered away, each a small cog in the giant machine that sustained this ritual economy. They arranged for goods to be supplied for designated sacrifices and other ceremonies that involved the presentation of offerings, such as the hosting of guests and visitors, banquets and funerals. *The Rites of Zhou* list officials charged with supplying fragrant reeds and grasses used to wrap up offerings and strain sacrificial ale, along with meat keepers, wine supervisors and wine makers. 'Ice men' supplied ice for preserving food offerings. Breeders, oxherds, fatteners and animal keepers raised sacrificial beasts, and made sure that the correct types of animal were available for different ceremonies. Foragers supplied firewood, rice paddy supervisors arranged provisions for rain prayers, and mountain and forest supervisors oversaw the preparation of sacrifices to mountains and rivers. Clamshell keepers supplied pulverized shells used to whiten sacrificial vessels and utensils. The list goes on.

The dead in ancient China were an industry. Demand for grave goods (such as miniature pottery figurines) among elites sparked bustling manufacturing activity in workshops and markets near cities, major burial grounds, cemeteries and other cultic sites. Several workshops and factories sprung up in the capital area of Qin, mass-producing luxury items and funerary articles destined for the imperial tombs. The remains of a tomb figurine workshop and its kilns, capable of firing over eight thousand figurines at a time, have been excavated in what was the market area in the north-western corner of the Han capital Chang'an. Great precision was demanded of the craftsmen who produced sacrificial vessels and implements. Strict measurements applied and objects were subject to quality control; some had the name of their manufacturer engraved on them as a trademark. Ideally, ritual implements had a finite lifespan and would not be recycled; ragged or damaged implements would undermine the sense of occasion. Worn or torn ceremonial robes had to be burnt; worn-out sacrificial vessels had to be buried, as did any used turtle shells and yarrow stalks used in divination. At the end of a sacrifice, no material traces should remain visible so that nobody could treat any items with irreverence (*Liji*, 'Qu li').

The market for religious expertise could be a drain on the household economy. This was not just a question of expense. Some complained that the call to become a so-called ritual or religious expert pulled people away from normal economic activity. The Eastern Han thinker Wang Fu (90–165 CE) singles out the particularly adverse influence of these professions on women. In his *Comments of a Recluse*, Wang complained that the lure of quick profits to be made by selling religious services drew women away from their primary occupation: 'They embark on the study of shamanic incantations, drumming and dancing to serve the spirits, thereby deceiving the weak and deluding the common people. With wives and daughters so weak and feeble, disease descends upon the households, and, full of worry and confusion, they easily fall victim to fear, even to the point that some are forced to flee from their seasonal labour and abandon their legitimate homes' (*Qianfulun*, 'Fu chi'). When ritual obligation reduced the labour force (remember Mozi), searching questions arose over the purported benefits of organized devotion to the spirits. As one Han critic remarked, 'funerals and sacrifices that know no measure are a plague that harms the living' (*Yantie lun*, 'San bu zu').

This tension between, on the one hand, needing to be seen as generous when entreating spirits and ancestors and, on the other, avoiding excess expenditure, preoccupied the minds of many thinkers in early China. How much does it take to buy salvation? In return for being fed by the living and having their longevity extended in this way, the ancestors would normally send down blessings. However, the relationship was not always reciprocal. Sometimes ancestors needed to be persuaded to assist or protect the living (for instance, when natural disaster struck, or when someone needed to be avenged). And they could be difficult to please. Disgruntled ancestors had multiple ways of communicating their discontent to supplicants: they could cause illness, appear in dreams or cause freaks in nature. The relationship between the offering and the expected return was shrouded in uncertainty, despite the copious detail and rules the ritual codes provided on the matter. What does it take to prevent the ghosts from going hungry? Should we expect a bumper harvest in return for a pig's ear and a tiny cup of wine? Like the living, the spirits could be whimsical; they were unlikely to be tricked into action if those who made offerings simply conceived of this as an economic exchange.

Indeed, what counted more than the actual offering was the moral integrity of the celebrants. It is the thought that counts – not simply the process of organizing a sacrifice, but, more importantly, what the mind invests in it during the procedure. 'It is not the millet and grain that produce the penetrating fragrance; only bright virtue produces such a fragrance,' one saying went (*Shangshu*, 'Jun chen'). So the ruler of a flourishing state possesses such virtue that it will waft up a pleasant fragrance to the spirit world. Conversely, a state about to perish has a government that is 'putrid and rotten'. Its offerings will fail to reach the spirits; and even if they do, the spirits might even choose to vomit them back up. Likewise, presenting a batch of stolen grain to the ancestors, or requesting their blessing for a prosperous year during the New Year sacrifices, is a wasted effort if you have overindulged or squandered resources for the rest of the year. To connect with the spirits, one needs to have the right frame of mind or allow the performance of the ritual to help one get to that point.

A sacrificial ritual was a multimedia event aimed at making absent spirits temporarily present again through a combination of music, liturgy, dance and offerings. The sacrificial space, hall or altar became a symbolical and psychic arena. This is where the spirits had to be lured in the hope that they would partake of the offerings presented, whether flesh, blood, vegetable, raw or cooked. Once the search for the spirits was on, announcements were made to them several times, each time in a different place or direction. Procedures could be repeated outside the gate of the temple. All along, the participants wonder, 'Are they there? Are they over here?' (*Liji*, 'Li qi'). A living descendant of the deceased acted as a proxy of the ancestral spirits. He was known as the 'corpse', 'ancestral im-personator' or 'representative of the dead'. The 'corpse' phys-ically impersonates the spirit addressed (you could stand in for Great-Grandad and smoke a cigarette on his behalf!). He tastes and drinks from the offerings, he moves and speaks on his behalf, and he toasts the living clan members during the banquet that follows the sacrifice. After the imperson-ator has symbolically tasted the offerings, the leftovers are consumed by the ritual participants in a cascading order ac-cording to status.

There were many types of sacrifice and the selection of offerings could be based on various principles. For instance, dogs were used for sacrifices to the road before one set off on a journey because of their close link with the threshold of the domestic sphere. Generally spirits appreciated blood- and *qi*-rich organs such as the lungs, liver and heart. Sometimes the logic of *yin* and *yang* and the Five Phases came into play. Thus dog meat was to be consumed at times corresponding to the metal phase and the lungs of sacrificial animals were to be of-fered during the summer months, when the cosmic vapours were at their height. The classical Chinese language contains an extensive vocabulary for sacrificial slaughter (burning, drowning, splitting, cleaving, driving over in a cart). Special terms were used to describe the colour of sacrificial animals, the number and size of sets of offerings, or the instruments and implements used. Ritual music, liturgy and coordinated stage management all conspired to produce a language that was coded to connect the ritual officiant and his acolytes with the invisible world of the spirits.

Chinese spirits eat vapour. While we humans dwell in a

world of tangible flavour, spirits, like sages, exist at a higher level. They distil the vital energies or *qi* hidden within the offerings – that is, what evaporates from the food and ale. The recently departed may still appreciate the flavour conveyed by a particular food offering (if roast chicken was Great-Grandad's favourite dish, one might try to reach him by offering this). However, distant ancestors and remote spirits prefer ethereal ingredients above physical foodstuffs. They operate in a world beyond taste, sound and colour; and the living no longer possess a sensory memory of them. Therefore the most effective offerings for reaching the far-off spirits are those that are bland, tasteless or insipid, such as raw and uncooked meats, or water. Alcohol was generally valued as a potent means of penetrating the spirit world. However, 'getting the spirits drunk', to paraphrase a hymn in *The Book of Odes* (*Shijing*, Mao 209), could be a risky business for participants. Consider the drunk and debauched last Shang kings, we are told in the 'Pronouncement on Alcohol' (one of twelve Zhou royal speeches preserved in *The Book of Documents*). They failed to distinguish between ritual drinking and an intoxicating drinking spree. Heaven will invariably punish those who indulge in alcohol, the text continues. Virtue lies with sobriety and one should only drink if and when presenting a sacrifice. Here we may have the first narrative in Chinese history that separates secular alcohol consumption from the sacrificial use of alcohol, condemning the former. Just as drinking the blood of Christ is best limited to one sip from the chalice, the ancient Chinese understood the tension between ritual reverence and drinking for pleasure.

*

If religion is to be defined as the art of managing uncertainty, the Chinese ancestral cult and the practice of sacrifice are prime examples of how we can hedge ourselves against disappointment over unsatisfactory answers to the God question, without diminishing the value of religious experience. They illustrate how, through performing rituals, people can find solace and stability in a world of unknowns. By refraining from wrestling with ontological questions such as whether or not the gods exist, whether the soul survives or whether the afterlife is something to dread or look forward to, the Chinese turned uncertainty into a form of psychological reassurance. 'If the dead are conscious, they will or won't do such-and-such' is a formula that crops up repeatedly in ritual texts. It is a scenario the living should be prepared for in case they need to appease or respond to signals from the invisible world. Yet rather than offering dogmatic certainty, Chinese religious practice was about how to handle the 'if' of it all. The assumption was that spirits would appear in the world of the living when something had gone awry. Just as members in the harmonious society of the living all know their place, the ghosts of the dead, ideally, should stick to their realm, remain strictly separated from the living and leave them alone. Once the tomb is sealed, they should remain hidden. Yet when cracks appear in the moral bearings of society, ancestral spirits will intervene in human affairs, and they will send out signals. This is why the desire to respect those who have gone before keeps the living on their toes: did we get it right, did we do enough, are we sufficiently filial to those who have left us? Confucius was moved to tears when the grave of his own parents collapsed under a heavy rainstorm (*Liji*, 'Tan gong').

The combination of comfort in the knowledge that the ancestors remain part of the family, combined with anxiety over whether we treat them properly, is what makes their watchful gaze so powerful.

A side-effect of being able to turn to ancestors (that is, spirits of one's own lineage) and of accepting uncertainty about the workings of invisible powers as the norm, was the acknowledgement that no single faith or form of ritual worship has all the answers. In the lived religion of ancient China, even when organized through institutions or patronized by the state, a sense of pragmatism tends to overshadow doctrine. There are multiple ways of finding enlightenment and more than one recipe for personal salvation. The ancestral cult, one could argue, relieves people from the need for a god that is sole and supreme. The spirit of Great-Grandad may well be watching you but he does not expect unquestioned loyalty from those not of the same lineage: 'Spirits do not appreciate offerings from someone who does not belong to their kind; people do not sacrifice to those who do not belong to one's clan' (*Zuozhuan*, Lord Xi 10). In the words attributed to Confucius, 'To offer sacrifices to an ancestral spirit that is not your own is obsequious' (*An.* 2.24).

This emphasis on lineage may also have contributed to the fact that religious traditions in China have generally enjoyed more leeway so that they can exist comfortably alongside each other or, at least, have not had to put down roots at the expense or exclusion of one another. To be sure, China has had its fair share of rebellions and moments of crisis sparked by differences in religious conviction or practice. Yet, throughout its history it has witnessed relatively few protracted wars on the basis of religion, and no major international conflicts. China has remained largely spared from episodes equivalent to the Crusades in medieval Europe or the violent sectarianism that grew out of the Reformation. Perhaps it is easier to fall out over one almighty divine creator than to disown your own ancestors.

Spirits for the ruler, spirits of the people

Rulers need rituals and cults to legitimize their sovereignty. As the emblematic link between the human and the spirit world, the Son of Heaven needed regular assurance and support from the spirits to maintain his standing as the sole and supreme monarch. Besides worshipping his own ancestors, a monarch claiming authority over 'All under Heaven' had to preside over the worship of deities, in the form of official state cults, that transcended his ancestral spirits – namely, forces of nature and cosmic powers. The Zhou kings had worshipped Heaven (*Tian*) as the highest power, one that bestowed the mandate to rule upon those who were worthy. During the centuries before China's unification into empire, the regional states also venerated deities linked to their lands. These territorial, pre-imperial Qin deities (also known as *di*) – each governing one direction (east, west, north, south, centre) and therefore, together, the entire world – continued to be the main recipients of state veneration during the Han period until the late first century BCE. The Five Powers, as they were called, were also known as colour deities as each direction was associated with a colour (green for east, white for west, black for north, red for south and yellow for the centre). Emperor Han Wudi introduced state cults for Grand

Unity (*Taiyi*) and Empress Earth (*Houtu*) – a sky god and earth deity respectively. By the late first century BCE, the Five Powers (regional in origin) were superseded by the cult of Heaven, a universal power, with sacrifices conducted annually on a circular platform in the suburbs of the capital. Until the end of the Qing dynasty, Chinese emperors made the sacrifices to Heaven their first priority. The Temple of Heaven complex in Beijing today is the most prominent architectural vestige of this tradition.

Mount Tai in Shandong province, one of ancient China's most holy mountain sites, was the setting for a spectacular ritual ascent and imperial sacrifice. Throughout the centuries emperors, especially when confident of their authority, travelled to this site, at enormous logistical expense and accompanied by a long cortège of officials. The Son of Heaven would first make offerings at the foot of the mountain and then climb or be carried to the summit. There, in total solitude and face to face with Heaven, he would pledge his respect and leave a written message by way of report to the high powers in the sky. The First Emperor conducted the sacrifice in 219 BCE, and so did Han Wudi (twice) a century later. Mountain peaks were shrouded in symbolism. They were the physical point most closely located to Heaven and the edge of the universe where the visible world touched the realm of the invisible. Mountains were the dwelling place of immortals and worshipped as spirits themselves. They embodied the idea of permanence; texts carved and coloured in rocks were indelible messages intended for the eyes of the spirits and for posterity.

Beyond the confines of official state religion, religious

life among the lower strata of society operated with less pomp and circumstance (note that more than 90 per cent of people in the early empires lived in nuclear households away from the cosseted world of educated elite families). Yet in their religious practices, the lower and the lettered classes shared many common elements (for instance, various types of prayer and divination). Elites in turn were not always wedded to the high culture of the ritual classics and dabbled in fortune-telling, exorcisms, healing and other everyday cultic activity that took place in local communities. Educated local officeholders, administrators and landed gentry often patronized religious specialists (priests and spirit mediums) who served the spiritual welfare of their communities. While literati and court officials occasionally fired off derisory comments about these unofficial or local observances, the battle between 'folk' and 'official' religion in ancient China was not hung up on doctrine. More often it centred on control of the population, the use of resources or the prevention of sectarian activity – in short, the politics behind religion.

Many elements of early Chinese religious practice are timeless and survive up until today as a mixture of cosmology and anthropomorphized views of the spirit world. An agent or go-between in the form of a priest or ritual specialist was commonplace, while the main methods for securing the blessing of the spirits or to ward off harm included ritualized prayers, petitioning spirits by means of sacrifice, and requesting recompense. Alongside ancestral deities, people addressed nature spirits and guardian deities beyond the household. Almanacs (known as 'daybooks'), prayer records and funerary documents show a belief in the possibility of personal salvation through direct or mediated contact with the spirit world. Like astrology calendars today, the appeal of standard formulaic texts of this kind was that they enabled the user to determine auspicious and unlucky days by simply consulting them as a manual and then accepting guidance without having to wait for the opinion of an initiated religious specialist.

Daybooks operated on the principle that the spirit world was largely predictable ('If you turn the soil on day X, you will have a good crop; but if you do so on day Y, nothing will grow'). They contained little theoretical speculation and simply told the user what to do. For instance, one of two almanacs recovered at Shuihudi from the same site that produced the legal documents discussed in the previous chapter contains a manual on how to protect against intrusion by demons. It teaches the user how to recognize certain apparitions as genuinely demonic and how to respond. Here we find a world far removed from the elegant rituals of the Confucian canon, as this example illustrates: 'You cannot pass through the dwelling places of the great spirits. They like to injure people. Make pellets from dog shit and carry them with you when you pass through. Throw them at the spirit whenever it appears, and it will not injure people!' It is clear that, alongside the world of the Confucian Classics and the masters of philosophy, ancient China boasted a vibrant tradition of occult thought and magico-religious beliefs. This was the domain of experts interested not simply in probing the workings of nature but also in investigating and manipulating the spirit forces it harboured.

People consulted and propitiated spirits for all sorts of

purposes: to cure illness and ailments, to help with match-making, to ensure a good harvest, fair weather, the fertility of livestock or a smooth transition into the afterlife, to ease childbirth and help construction work, to establish when best to travel, plough the fields or wash one's hair. Spirits hid everywhere: in the stove and in the well, in granaries and walls, in rivers and lakes, mountains and trees, in the stars and other heavenly bodies. At times, the spirit world itself took on bureaucratic attributes, with gods behaving as officials. This would become a lasting feature of Chinese folk religion. Chinese bureaucracy seeped into the religious imagination. For instance, a Controller of Fate was thought to supervise the registers of the dead and could be beseeched with a request to prolong one's allotted lifespan. Real-world administrative documents were adopted into a religious setting. Courteous formulas modelled on official language were used in prayers and incantations. Interactions with the spirit world mimicked administrative and judicial procedures, and people's relationship with the spirit world mirrored the relationship that existed between subjects and their superiors in real life. Several types of administrative-style documents have been found in tombs, mostly of the Eastern Han period. These include land contracts to secure a burial plot, documents that make a formal announcement to the earth to safeguard the deceased's continued status and wealth in the afterlife, and inventories of funerary goods. Writs to secure the grave were placed in tombs to request protection of the living from the netherworld administration and absolve the deceased from any wrongdoing in life. Some seem to have conceived of their relationship with the spirit world as a contractual obligation in which humans owe a sacrificial debt to the spirits in return for the favours performed by the spirits on their behalf. Archaeologists have recovered a written contract made with the spirit world produced in duplicates to be stored by both the human and spirit parties (the so-called Xuning prayer of 79 CE, named after the deceased woman on whose behalf it was offered up). While there is insufficient evidence to show that people in ancient China saw their dealings with the spirit world as a type of commercial transaction, it is clear that bureaucratic pragmatism existed alongside feelings of piety.

Our overall picture of the pantheon of spirits that received worship in everyday religion changes with every archaeological discovery of new texts and artefacts. Several names emerge for a supreme deity: Thearch, Thearch on High, Heavenly Thearch, Sire of Heaven, Yellow Spirit, Spirit of Heaven. By Han times, an astral deity appears who resides in the Northern Dipper, from where he oversees, among others, the ghosts of stillborns and those who died by suicide. The supreme deity generally acts as a judge of human affairs and takes on the role of a supreme monarch at the head of a retinue of subservient spirits. These assistants included the Envoy of the Lord of Heaven and the Controller of Fate. Several spirits were associated with the heavens, so continued efforts were made to advance calendrical and astronomical knowledge to help predict the movements of those astral deities. Among them was the polar spirit Grand One. Other nature spirits included River Elder, Sire Wind, Master Rain and Lord Thunder. Divine Farmer and Lord Millet oversaw agriculture, and Field Ancestor, who appears in *The Book of Odes*, had the power to scorch the fields or send down rain. First Sericulturalist was the patron deity of silk farming. Replicating official hierarchies in the human world, several mountains and mountain ranges were given bureaucratic rank. Mountain spirits controlled natural phenomena such as clouds and rainmaking.

Spirits also lived in the household. Sacrifices were offered to the gates, the path, well, doorway, stove, broom, dust basket, pestle and mortar – among which a set of five household deities was earmarked for worship as the Five Sacrifices. The worship of animal spirits (zoolatry) is not widely documented. Yet deceased animals could turn into vengeful demons or misbehave in response to human wrongdoing. *The Rites of Zhou* even mentions an official charged with destroying the nests of ill-omened birds. An important spirit was the deity of the soil. In Zhou times, the altars to the soil (*she*), together with the altars to the spirit of the grain (*ji*), were the place where blood sacrifices were pledged, primarily to legitimize political authority through entitlement to land. By Han times, altars to the soil deity start appearing at all levels, from the extended household to the hamlet. They became a focal site where a family or local community offered sacrifices. The soil deity could share its altar with other deities and, over time, he became a spirit-bureaucrat (Lord Earth Altar), as did many other spirits. Village drinking gatherings and sacrificial banquets for the deity of the soil became part of local community worship.

Worshippers used various techniques to tap, exploit or appease divine powers. Divination using turtle shells and milfoil stalks continued to be practised alongside astrology. Other techniques included performing incantations and adopting protective body postures as well as the use of charms, curses and talismanic items (objects believed to have magic powers). One of these ritual dances was a series of steps known as the Pace of Yu (the legendary deity who saved China from the Yellow River floods). Spells uttered by a medium or priest were thought to hold magical powers that derived from the *qi* or vaporous breath they emitted. Spitting and spouting and the use of breath magic to ward off demons were associated with the southern regions, an area with a sweltering climate conducive to shamanic activity. To exorcise baleful spirits or demons, common techniques included beating or stabbing at them. Exorcisms could be accompanied by drumming and cursing, unravelling one's hair, digging up the soil to get at the demon or using ashes. Another trick was to imitate the demon's actions (a form of sympathetic magic), or shoot in the direction of the demonic influence with arrows made of wood that had protective powers, such as mulberry, jujube or peach. The use of faeces and figurines is well documented, as is the use of natural objects that are white in colour, such as stones or sand.

The intriguing make-believe world of ghosts, demons, astral and nature spirits outlined above did not figure prominently in the works of the philosophers. As Confucius had said, do not try to explain it all – just deal with it. Yet this realm of spectres, demons and capricious ancestral spirits, whether pleasant or unpleasant, loomed large in everyday life in ancient China. The ghost story would become a major genre in Chinese literature and it remains popular today, in novels and on screen. With the exception of certain Mohists, the masters of philosophy had generally been sceptical of those who believed they could predict, calculate or manipulate the workings of Heaven and nature. Most not-able among them was Xunzi. In his 'Discussion of Heaven', a chapter in *The Master Xun*, he takes issue with the belief that freaks in nature should be regarded as omens from Heaven. Xunzi's Heaven has no ethical impulse and is not subject to the will of humans. Heaven generates resources and products at the disposal of humans, but it is up to humans to figure out what to do with them. For Xunzi, nature (Heaven and Earth) and humans have separate roles and no sage or tyrant will throw Heaven off its fixed course: 'Heaven does not sus-pend winter because men dislike cold weather. Earth does not reduce its broad expanse because men dislike long dis-tances' (*Xunzi* 17.5). When something appears as strange or portentous, it does so because we have not understood that this is just a normal part of nature: 'We may marvel at it, but we should not fear it' (*Xunzi* 17.7). It will rain (or remain dry) regardless of whether you perform a rain dance or not.

However, this largely philosophical stance – one that denies a causal link between human affairs and the workings of Heaven – amounted to little more than a shout in the desert. As the next chapter will show, the incontrovertibly dominant sentiment in ancient China was that the human and natural worlds were deeply implicated in each other's affairs. Nature reflected human actions and human actions impacted upon nature even if, for some, Heaven's reactions appeared un-predictable or incomprehensible. Returning to religious life, then, accepting this interrelatedness became the norm rather than the exception. The aim was not so much to seek proof for the invisible spirit powers that lie beyond normal human perception but, rather, to decide when it was appropriate or necessary to interpret signs from the spirit world as significant and follow up on them. Excessive, unorthodox or esoteric cults were rarely condemned on ideological or theological grounds. This becomes clear in the writings of critics such as Wang Chong (c.27– c.100 CE), Wang Fu and Ying Shao (c.140–204 CE), who all lived in the latter half of the Han period. As keen observers of the religious creeds and customs of their own time, they could also reflect retrospectively on records and stories of how people had handled the supramundane since the days of Confucius and before. On the one hand, they dismiss many practices as superstitious or even vulgar. Yet, at the same time, they accept the very existence of the spirit world or, at best, leave it unquestioned. The critics of organized religion did not target the spirits so much as the social consequences of the efforts invested in worshipping them. To quote from one of many rants by Wang Chong in his *Discourses in the Balance*: 'People produce dummies to serve the dead in their coffins and they stuff the latter with edibles to please the spirits. These practices have now become so persistent and widespread that some will ruin their families and deplete their resources to fill the coffins of the dead' (*Lunheng* 67).

Death and immortality

There are many ways 'to die but not perish' (*DDJ* 33). The Han philosopher Xu Gan (171–218 CE) claimed one could achieve immortality within one's lifetime by acting humanely (*Zhong lun* 14). Yet, to be physically dead but socially alive as an ancestor (in name or reputation) is a form of longevity that lasts only as long as living descendants choose to remember and honour you. For some rulers and elites in ancient China, social immortality was not enough. In sources from the Warring States period, a female goddess emerges with the power to grant everlasting life. She became known as the Queen Mother of the West (see Figure 6.1). 'No one knows her beginning, no one knows her end,' *The Master Zhuang* notes (*Zhuangzi* 6.3). Legend held that the Queen Mother resided in the Kunlun Mountains on the western edge of the world, where she supervised the operations of the cosmos. Those privileged to meet her could be granted everlasting life, and such wishful spirit journeys and encounters are described in the literature of the time. In murals in Han-period tombs, she appears seated sometimes on a dragon or a tiger, sometimes on top of a cosmic tree or pillar, wearing a crown and surrounded by a group of emblematic animals: a hare pounding the herbs of immortality in a mortar; a toad in the moon; a three-legged bird in the sun; and a nine-tailed fox (nine being an auspicious number). Reference is made to the spontaneous outbreak of a cult and processions in her honour in 3 BCE in response to a drought, but the Queen Mother's main manifestation is as an icon in funerary art. There, she is sometimes accompanied by the reptile-bodied Fu Xi and Nü Gua, a divine couple who, in a mythological past, ordered the universe and brought the world back from chaos.

The eastern edge of the Chinese world, too, became associated with a paradise of immortals. Somewhere in the seas off the coast of the Shandong peninsula arose Penglai, the Islands of the East. Climb to the top of Mount Tai and, on a very rare day when the skies are clear, imagine the winged creatures frolicking in the cloud formations over the coastline

Figure 6.1
The Queen Mother
of the West.
Line drawing; Yinan
tomb, Shandong;
Eastern Han.

three hundred kilometres to the east; or, follow the First Emperor and travel to Zhifu island near Yantai to solicit an invitation from the immortals. Immortals have wings, partake of jujube and jade dust; they suck wind and eat dew rather than grains, tend to fungi and peaches of immortality, and embark on cosmic journeys, pulled through space by dragons and phoenixes. The First Emperor constructed towers and elevated walkways between his palaces to be closer to them. Once he ordered an expeditionary fleet and a troupe of several thousand virgin boys and girls to set sail in search of the elixir of immortality; the children drowned, and the emperor died before he reached the age of fifty.

The First Emperor had been patronizing experts to teach him alchemy and the arts of immortality. Ironically, it was the toxic effects of ingesting cinnabar pills (a type of mercury) that probably poisoned him. Alongside alchemical concoctions, other methods held the promise of eternal life, such as wearing or ingesting jade. Some Han royals had their corpses wrapped in suits made of hundreds of squares of jade stitched together with gold thread (see Figure 6.2). Cavities in the body (the so-called 'nine apertures': ears, eyes, mouth, nostrils, genitals and anus) were plugged using jade stoppers in the belief that this would prevent the life force or *qi* from escaping. Only those who had no trouble keeping food in the mouths of the living could afford jade in the mouths of the dead. While there is some evidence of embalming corpses in Central Asia, there is no significant tradition of embalming in China, and only a few mummified corpses have been recovered there; the party faithful embalmed Mao Zedong's body, but not at his own request.

Incense burners designed to look like misty mountains may have been used by some to induce hallucinogenic trances that could temporarily carry one off to the realm of the immortals (or simply get high!). Others tried macrobiotics and various dietary regimes, along with yoga and sexual exercises, to ensure a long life. Han medical texts, going by such titles as 'Methods for nurturing life' or 'Methods to abstain from grain and eat *qi*', provide recipes and exercises for building up one's physical well-being to avoid illness. According to Sima Qian,

Figure 6.2
Jade burial suit of Zhao Mo, King of Nanyue (died 122 BCE).

one retired chancellor during the early Han period 'was so old that he had not a single tooth in his mouth, but lived on milk, using a young woman as his wet nurse. His wives and concubines numbered by the hundreds, but whenever one of them had become pregnant, he never slept with her again. He was over one hundred years old when he died' (*Shiji* 96). Others took a dim view of this culture of physical long-life experimentation (which, no doubt, in some cases led to premature death). Drugs kill in all times and in all places, as the following story insinuates:

> There once was a man who presented some herbs of immortality to the King of Jing. His usher took them to bring them in, when a palace guard asked: 'Are these

edible?' 'Edible indeed,' responded the usher. The guard thereupon snatched the herbs and ate them. The king, greatly enraged by this, sent someone to execute the palace guard. But the palace guard sent him back to plead with the king, saying: 'I asked the usher whether these things were edible and, because he said they were, I ate them. So if anyone is guilty it is not me but him. Furthermore, you have a guest presenting you with [so-called] herbs of immortality and you wish to kill me because I ate them. This *de facto* means that these are herbs of death and that your guest is trying to cheat you. So you would kill an innocent man and, by doing so, make it known that someone is trying to dupe you? It would be better if you released me.' As a result, the king did not execute the man.
(*Han Feizi* 22)

For those putting their trust in chemical, medical or magical ways of achieving everlasting life, the search for immortality invariably ended in disappointment and often illness or even death. However, one dimension to the Chinese quest for long life and transcendence operated at a more detached level. The ideal here was not so much to prolong the physical existence of the body, grow wings or be 'released from the corpse', as one expression went, but to enhance one's capacity to live out a natural lifespan without major obstacles and, therefore, not fear death. Why live for ever if we fail to live out our allotted lifespan in the first place? One argument put forward in various adaptations emphasized self-preservation as a means of keeping one's natural endowments (what we receive from Heaven) intact, medically and otherwise, and optimizing the workings of the senses. Texts of a Daoist signature link sagehood and physical self-cultivation with meditative practices. *Inner Training* (dated, with no certitude, to sometime in the fourth century BCE) is one of the oldest texts to advocate such a regimen of breath control, bodily posture and balanced diet: 'The middle ground between gorging and abstention is called perfection; it provides a place for the vital essence to dwell and for wisdom to develop' (*Nei ye* 14.1). Some scholars see in it one of the earliest Chinese descriptions of mystical experience: the adept becomes one with the universe through channelling and storing up its vital forces, conceived of as refined essential *qi* energies within the body:

> When vital essence is present it spontaneously
>   produces life,
> The outside of you produces a contented glow;
> Internally it is stored like a fount and source.
> Flood-like, it is harmonious and calming,
> And it becomes the wellspring of *qi*.
> As long as the wellspring does not run dry,
> The four limbs are firm.
> As long as the wellspring is not drained,
> The nine bodily orifices will allow clear passage.
> Then, you are able to explore the limits of Heaven
>   and Earth,
> And spread over the four seas. (*Nei ye* 8.4)

The question of what divides life from death preoccupied Daoist thinkers. The topic receives its philosophically most charming treatment in *The Master Zhuang*. We know next to nothing about the personal life of Zhuangzi (Zhuang Zhou; fourth century BCE), the thinker and rhetorical genius who lent his name to a text that turned out to be so provocative in questioning the views of life and death professed by Confucians and other contemporaries. Like most early Chinese texts, *The Master Zhuang* (consisting of thirty-three chapters) is a composite work and the product of several if not many hands. The transmitted version of the text came together around 300 BCE. Traditionally it is divided into seven 'Inner Chapters' (1–7), fifteen 'Outer Chapters' (8–22) and eleven 'Miscellaneous Chapters' (23–33). The first seven chapters are generally considered to best reflect the thoughts of Zhuangzi himself. One of the book's many translators, Victor Mair, describes it as a relaxed work written in a 'rambling' mode, which captures well how the text shifts around between tales, fables, anecdotes, essays and poetic passages.

The authors of *The Master Zhuang* seem puzzled by all those helpless souls who, like New Agers of their time, go to such great lengths to engage in tortuous but ineffective training regimes in a vain pursuit of longevity:

> Blowing and breathing, exhaling and inhaling, expelling the old and taking in the new, bear strides and bird stretches [i.e. gymnastics] – all of this is merely indicative of the desire for longevity. But it is favoured by scholars who channel the vital breath and flex the muscles and joints, men who nourish the physical form so as to emulate the hoary age of Ancestor Peng [a legendary immortal].
> (*Zhuangzi* 15.1)

Zhuangzi's answer to those obsessed with either social or physical longevity is that they would all fare better if they accepted a simple truth: life and death are just part of one and the same process of transformation. In other words, if we are content to live out our natural lifespan, in accordance with the rhythms of the Dao, we will have achieved our own version of immortality. If we accept that every day we die a little, then there is no need to fear death. Dying is nothing more than another stage in the cycle of constant change that drives the cosmos, so we need not be distressed by the thought that each day we live brings us closer to death:

> Master Lie [a Daoist thinker after whom the *Liezi* is named] was travelling and had a meal by the side of the road. There he saw a hundred-year-old skull. He pulled away the weeds and pointed at it, saying: 'It is only you and I who know that you have never died and that you have never lived. Are you truly unhappy? Am I really happy?' (*Zhuangzi* 18.6)

Realizing the relativity of the boundaries between life and death will prevent us from feeling the need to invest all our energy into life as if it is the one and only stage of the journey. It will stop us from needlessly clinging on to artificial techniques or dubious teachings that offer the false prospect of extending our natural lifespan. Dying may well mean an end to our existence as individuals, but our energy never disappears. It merely returns to nature, where it survives, like a drop of rain returning to the ocean. One cannot add to or take away from the Dao:

The Dao has neither end nor beginning,

But things have life and death.

Not being able to rely on their completion,

One moment they are empty, one moment they
    are full,

Without a stable form.

The years cannot be advanced,

Nor can time be arrested.

Decay and growth, fullness and emptiness –

Whatever ends has a beginning. (*Zhuangzi* 17.1)

Note the subtle difference here. The last line does not read: 'Whatever begins will end.' If we fail to keep this broader picture in mind, we are merely living like a frog in a well, under the illusion that the world coincides with the narrow contours of a sky merely visible from our comfortable borehole (*Zhuangzi* 17.4).

As Zhuangzi lay dying, he objected to his disciples' wish to give him a lavish funeral: 'I will have Heaven and Earth as my inner and outer coffins, the sun and the moon for my pair of jade discs [i.e. funerary objects], the stars and the constellations for my pearls, and the myriad creatures as my mortuary gifts. Is there anything missing in the preparations for my funeral? What would you add to these?' Unruffled by the prospect that wild birds would peck away at his dead body as it lay on the ground, Zhuangzi insinuates that in death, all judgement and partiality should be abandoned: 'Above ground, I will be eaten by crows and kites; below I would be eaten by mole crickets and ants. Why show your partiality by snatching me away from one to give me to the other?' (*Zhuangzi*

32.14). Here is a significant departure from the desire to continue social memory beyond the point of death, which also allows Zhuangzi to brand ritual as a cumbersome waste of time and resources. Why bother with it at all? Instead of wishing to preserve an identity after death in the form of an ancestor or a spirit that commands moral powers and passes judgement, Zhuangzi sees dying as a total transformation. *The Master Zhuang* parades characters that appear not in the least bit troubled by physical deformity or by what might happen to their bodies when they are dead: 'If [the force that creates us through transformation] borrows my left arm to transform it into a cock, I will crow to announce dawn ... if it transforms my buttocks into wheels and my spirit into a horse, I will ride it'. The message is not to overvalue life or fear death, even if it might 'turn you into a rat's liver or a fly's leg' (*Zhuangzi* 6.5).

For Zhuangzi, dying must mean ceasing to be human. But the transition from life to death is no different from the change between day and night, waking and sleeping, light and dark. Life and death are nothing but a process of metamorphosis, like that of silkworms transforming into moths. The 'authentic person', Zhuangzi's ideal individual or sage, accepts the correlative nature of life and death and humankind's continuity with nature. Hence he is not dispirited by prospective loss but approaches death with a sense of wonder. When Zhuangzi's wife dies, Master Hui finds him squatting down on the floor, beating a tub and singing. Instead of humming a tune, Master Hui asks, should you not mourn the loss of the person you grew old with and who has raised your children? 'Not so,' Zhuangzi replies; 'when [my wife] died first, how could I, like everyone else, not feel sad? But then I thought about her beginning and realized that originally she was not born. Not only was she unborn, originally she had no form. Not only did she not have form but originally she had no vital energy [*qi*]. Intermingled amidst the blurry mass, a transformation occurred and there was *qi*. This *qi* transformed itself and there was form. This form transformed itself and there was birth. Today there was another transformation and she has died. It is just like the progression of the four seasons, from spring to autumn, from winter to summer' (*Zhuangzi* 18.2).

Zhuangzi's wife lives on, not because she is remembered as a person through ritual within a circle of relatives and friends, but because she is passing through the various stages of change that affect everyone and everything. If I think my life is good, then I must think my death will be good too. In one famous story, Zhuangzi has a conversation with a parched skull lying by the roadside, a scene similar to that of Master Lie above. How did you come to this, he asks, and puts the skull under his head as a pillow. Then the skull talks to Zhuangzi in a dream insisting that there is no greater joy than to be dead and saying that he has no desire to be brought back again: 'When you are dead, there are no rulers above you and no subjects below you, there are no chores associated with the four seasons; instead time passes endlessly as it does for Heaven and Earth. Not even a south-facing king can have more happiness than those in death' (*Zhuangzi* 18.4). So for the 'authentic person', fear of death itself is selfish. It betrays an attachment to your individuality that Zhuangzi considers misguided. When you lose a friend or close relative, you will feel that loss more deeply if you think of this person as *your* friend, and *your* friend only. Thus, for Zhuangzi, the Confucian family model with its ancestral cult makes dying harder to accept as it fosters emotional ties that are exclusive or privilege a limited number of persons. But drumming on a basin with joy at the passing of your relatives can be hard in a world where convention requires us to wail and mourn.

As these stories show, *The Master Zhuang* captures its views of life and death through anecdotes that are full of wit, innuendo, shock and surprise. *The Classic of the Way and Virtue* is more serene in its portrayal of life and death as one singular process of transformation. Yet, in essence, the contours of its philosophy are similar:

> Heaven and Earth are long-lasting and enduring. The reason why Heaven and Earth are long-lasting and enduring is because they do not give themselves life. And so that is why they are able to be long-lived. Therefore sages put themselves last and yet come first; they treat themselves as unimportant and yet are preserved. Is it not because they have no thought of themselves that they are able to perfect themselves? (*DDJ* 7)

Daoist thinkers are emotionally prosaic in the way they confront us with the blunt reality of death and the futility of the human desire to live on for ever or, at least, a bit longer: being content to live out our natural lifespan, and accepting that we just continue transforming, dispels any anxiety about death.

When studying Daoism, it is important to note that, like Confucianism, Daoism is an umbrella term that covers several strands of thought. A significant gulf separates the philosophical Daoism of the authors behind *The Classic of the Way and Virtue* and *The Master Zhuang* from Daoism as a religious movement. The latter developed in early medieval times and, over the centuries, it evolved into an institutionalized religion, with its own clergy, pantheon, scriptures and rituals. Daoism continues to be observed as a living religion today (with modern hermits who dwell on distant mountain peaks). Paradoxically, it upheld the promise of physical immortality as a prospect for salvation for all its adepts. As the sinologist Angus Graham once poignantly wrote: 'It is a fascinating irony of intellectual history that the label "Daoism" came to apply both to a philosophy which demands before anything else reconciliation to the natural cycle of life and death, to the decay of the body and the loss of personal identity, and to magical, religious and proto-scientific measures for reversing the spontaneous course of biological process to fulfil the most unrealistic of our hopes, to live for ever.'

Laozi's biography as it appears in Sima Qian's *Historical Records* (*Shiji* 63) is a hodgepodge of information. It feeds into the philosophical treatise he is associated with (*The Classic of the Way and Virtue*) and provides the basis of some of the hagiographic tradition that evolved around him as a Daoist deity later on. Sima Qian admits freely that he is puzzled about certain biographical details. Laozi would refer to a man named Lao Dan ('Old Dan'), who acted as court archivist for the kings of Zhou. 'Lao', meaning 'old', is unlikely to have been his real surname. By Han times, stories did the round that Laozi had reached the venerable old age of nearly two hundred years. His other two names 'Er' ('Ears') and

'Dan' ('Long Ears') also suggest a connection with the idea of long life and wisdom. Some sages were portrayed with long ears. His last known act was to travel westwards through the mountain passes, leaving his treatise with the 'keeper of the pass', Guan Yin. He then disappears for ever.

A famous biographical episode relating to Laozi (which is repeated in both Daoist and Confucian writings) concerns his alleged meeting with Confucius. Although some scholars have speculated that Laozi may have been a senior contemporary of Confucius, there is nothing demonstrably historical or factual about it. Yet the story became so popular that, by

Figure 6.3
Confucius meets Laozi. Drawing based on ink rubbing, Wuliang family shrine, Shandong; 2nd century CE.

Han times, new versions emerged and the scene was depicted on tomb murals in Shandong province (see Figure 6.3). 'When Confucius met Laozi' also becomes a motif in paintings in later times. In a reversal of what one would expect from their respective philosophies, *The Ritual Records* has Laozi instructing Confucius about nothing less than ... funerary rituals (*Liji*, 'Zengzi wen'). In Sima Qian's versions of the encounter, Confucius is subjected to an outright condemnation of his teachings. Left speechless at the wisdom uttered by Laozi, he concludes: 'When it comes to the dragon, it is beyond my knowledge to understand how it ascends into Heaven on the clouds and the wind. Today, I have met Laozi, and he is like a dragon!' (*Shiji* 63).

Narratives about personalities and cultural heroes shift with the times and getting a message across in the voice of someone construed as your intellectual opponent is a powerful rhetorical tool. We will probably never know whether Confucius ever contemplated sitting still or giving up on his rigid programme of rituals and ancestor veneration, nor will we know with certainty whether the earliest Daoists were simply creative thinkers who dissented from the Master on a philosophical level only. After all, complex rituals and rule-guided behaviour have become a core feature of religious Daoism, although it rejects blood sacrifices. Nevertheless, it is safe to conclude that, on the matter of how to reach the spirits or become spiritual, and how to live a long life, possibly beyond death, two main traditions define ancient China: a tradition of those who tried, and one of those who tried not to try.

After Confucius

The Confucian ideas decanted into this book so far derive from the classical period, when Confucianism appears as a set of predominantly human-centred and this-worldly ethical teachings. To the learned of the time and in the eyes of tradition, the Five 'Confucian' Classics held the key to all aspects of life: cosmology, rituals and customs, human relationships, government, history, harmony. Learning involved taking a teacher and consulting the Classics for guidance. Confucius seems sceptical about getting lost in one's thoughts without a steer from the outside: 'I once spent all day thinking without eating and all night thinking without sleeping, but I found that I gained nothing from it. It would have been better for me to have spent that time learning instead' (*An.* 15.31). For aspiring officials and literati at court, the Classics had acquired a reputation as the canon that provided information on all there was to know. As Sima Qian summarizes:

> *The Book of Changes* describes Heaven and Earth, *yin* and *yang*, the four seasons and the Five Phases; therefore it is the best guide to studying change. *The Ritual Records* thread together human relationships; therefore it is the best guide to studying human conduct. *The Book of Documents* records the affairs of the former kings; therefore it is the best guide to studying government. *The Book of Odes* records mountains and rivers, gorges and valleys, birds and beasts, herbs and trees, males and females; therefore it is the best guide to studying the prevailing atmosphere. *The Book of*

Music is the means whereby one establishes joy, therefore it is the best guide to studying the concept of harmony. *The Spring and Autumn Annals* discuss what is right and what is wrong, therefore it is the best guide to governing people. (*Shiji* 130)

As noted earlier, there clearly was a religious or spiritual dimension to Confucian (or 'classicist') ritual and ancestor worship. Yet, among the early Confucian philosophers, few engaged in metaphysical speculation about the sphere beyond the physical world and the principles that might govern it. In the next chapter, we will learn how philosophers, especially by Han times, sought to explain the workings of nature and its relationship to the human world as part of larger correlative schemes. But before we consider the impact of Confucian thought on Chinese perceptions of nature, it may be appropriate to briefly sketch those intellectual developments that affected Confucian thought over the many centuries following Confucius. While the core values and ideas as they were formulated in the classical period remained the staple of Confucian philosophy, these ideas, and the fate of the texts in which they were formulated, underwent various transformations over the two and a half millennia from the time of Confucius up until the present.

The most influential reincarnation of Confucian thought occurred during the Song period (960–1279 CE), and is known as neo-Confucianism. What was new in neo-Confucianism? A loose term adopted in the West, it covers several strands of Confucianism as they developed from the eleventh century CE onwards, and refers to Confucianism as it expressed itself in the wake of centuries of Buddhist and Daoist speculative thought that started to flourish since the end of the Han dynasty. Its founding thinkers and their intellectual descendants referred to their doctrines collectively as the 'Learning of the Way' (*Dao xue*).

Since the fall of the Han, Buddhism and Daoist cosmology had infiltrated the thinking of elites and intellectuals as well as the religious life of the population at large. Buddhism was a foreign import that had entered China from India during the centuries of political disunion that followed the collapse of the Han dynasty. Daoist speculative philosophy, and Daoist religion, developed both as a reaction to and conversation with Buddhist ideas and institutions. With its theories on being and non-being, emptiness and impermanence, karma and rebirth, and the belief that enlightenment is to be found when individuals extinguish the self and transcend this life (the search for nirvana), Buddhism injected a powerful metaphysical dimension into the classical Chinese imagination. Heavens and hells opened up in multiple layers. Indigenous ghosts and spirits had to share space in a pantheon populated by new deities and demons. Concepts of time were stretched to follow cycles of unimaginable length (known as kalpas or aeons). With the arrival of monks and monastic communities, Confucians grappled with the challenge that self-cultivation and enlightenment could be found in spite of the family – leaving the household was the first step any aspiring Buddhist monk had to take. During the Tang dynasty, the poet and essayist Han Yu (768–824 CE) had already entered a plea for the restoration of Confucianism as the dominant ideology. Most famously, he denounced Buddhism in a sharp essay criticizing the worship of a relic of one of the Buddha's finger bones. 'I submit,' his memorial began, 'that Buddhism is no more than a barbarian teaching.'

Neo-Confucians continued this repudiation of Buddhism, which they held responsible for diluting the true Confucian way. But, in doing so, they absorbed some of these Buddhist and Daoist cosmological ideas and ethical theories. Moreover, in their attempt to draw on the Confucian Classics to tackle questions posed by Buddhists and Daoists, neo-Confucian thinkers formulated their theories in a language that was more abstract and dense than that of those ancient works themselves. The aim was not only to reinvigorate Confucian thinking for the purpose of intellectual debate, but also to scour the ancient texts for ideas that would make Confucianism persuasive as an alternative method for self-help and spiritual guidance to those offered by Buddhism. That meant introducing a metaphysical dimension into Confucian moral virtues and substantiating them as abstract principles that are inherent in the cosmos. It also meant countering the fallacy (in their view) that self-realization can be achieved by detaching oneself from community and society, as was suggested by several Buddhist and Daoist schools of thought.

Some eleventh-century thinkers – such as Zhou Dunyi (1017–73) and Shao Yong (1011–77) – sought to visualize the origins of the world and the workings of the cosmos through diagrams and speculative formulas drawing on *The Book of Changes*. Others – such as the brothers Cheng Yi (1033–1107) and Cheng Hao (1032–85) – argued that the world was made up of energy or *qi*, but that things are formed when this raw and physical 'stuff' is guided by a substance or principle (*li*;

not to be confused with *li* meaning 'ritual'). 'Principle', they argued, describes both what a thing is and what it should be. It remains unchanged and lies behind all truth and values (think of it as form without which no matter can be made manifest). The principle of a horse is that one can or should ride on it, that of human beings that they can (and should) be humane persons. There is a principle of kingship and a person who inhabits the throne. Even when there is no actual instance of someone suitable to take on the role, kingship remains out there as a constant and unchanging principle, to be activated or instantiated at any moment. Ultimately, principle is one: the force that glues everything together can manifest itself in many ways, but it is one and the same thing, stable and good.

This attempt to understand the world in terms of a combination of material forces that are guided by unchanging principles draws Confucian ethics into the realm of metaphysics. It allowed for ideals such as 'humane conduct' or 'ritual propriety' to exist as universal and absolute norms, independent of individual people or actual circumstances. Thus humaneness as a virtue gets a cosmic footing and exists as a principle, even when there are no concrete individuals to put it into practice. This fusion of the age-old humanist virtues of Confucius with metaphysical theory is best illustrated with a quote from Zhang Zai's (1020–77) 'Western Inscription' ('Xi ming'), one the most celebrated pieces of neo-Confucian writing: 'Heaven is my father and Earth is my mother, and even an insignificant creature such as I finds an intimate place in their midst. Therefore that which extends throughout the universe I regard as my body and that which directs the universe I see as my nature. All people are my brothers and sisters, and all things are my companions.' So for the neo-Confucian, the household family has become a cosmic family. The human mind is one with the mind of the universe.

This is not to say, however, that neo-Confucians conceived of the world as a realm that exists merely of principles or ideas in the abstract, in the sense of the shadows in Plato's cave. Without 'stuff' (*qi*), nothing can form to exist; the idea of a dog does not make a dog. Compassion, goodness, a sense of justice, and knowledge or insight are of themselves useless as abstract principles until each is given shape through human action. Furthermore, the *qi* that makes up things can be of different quality. 'Mountain-ness' can show itself in the form of an untidy molehill as well as in the shape of elevated slopes leading to a majestic mountain peak. Your *qi* can be impure, in which case there is no guarantee that you will ever become the good person you should be, except through hard work and a step-by-step programme of self-cultivation.

The grand synthesis of neo-Confucian thought was orchestrated by the Song scholar-philosopher Zhu Xi (twelfth century), previously encountered in Chapter 4. Master Zhu was China's most influential Confucian thinker next to Confucius himself. Zhu Xi anthologized the philosophies of his predecessors in a volume entitled *Reflections on Things at Hand* (*Jinsi lu*, compiled in 1175). The teachings of Zhu Xi and those who preceded him did not give pride of place to the Five Classics. Instead, they argued that the correct transmission of Confucius's thought ran through *The Analects*,

The Great Learning (discussed in Chapter 4), *The Doctrine of the Mean* and the *Mencius*. These were classified as the Four Books, henceforth considered as the foundational texts of Confucianism. Since the focus of these texts was on the cultivation of human morality and human nature, they ranked first in a programme of neo-classicist education, where the ultimate aim was to develop a student's internal sense of morality. Zhu Xi's interpretations of the Four Books thus became the orthodox curriculum for the civil service exams. From 1313 onwards until 1905, every aspiring official in China would be required to study and regurgitate Zhu Xi's version of the Classics, his commentaries and his annotations. In terms of the institutional dissemination of ideas, this is an intellectual legacy no other thinker in China can lay claim to, not even Confucius or Mao Zedong.

Neo-Confucians set themselves the task of finding the enduring 'true' meaning in the texts from antiquity. They took the Confucian ideal of self-cultivation to a new, quasi-religious level. The apprentice in search of moral perfection was to devote unstinting effort to studying the guiding principles that lie behind everything. Yet, this key to 'investigating' and 'knowing' things could not be found so much in the experiential observation of nature (although observation at first hand should not be excluded) as in the words of the sages and worthies themselves – that is, the books of old. Only a lifelong study of the Classics, neo-Confucians believed, would get you there. Many therefore organized themselves in schools and academies inspired by prominent Buddhist temples that had developed into centres of learning. Here they engaged in scholastic debate and wrote commentaries on the true meaning of the Classics. Youngsters had to be educated in the image of the scholar-official who, in addition to fulfilling his duties as an upright administrator, also engaged in contemplative activities through poetry, calligraphy, the arts and the study of literature. In what appears as a turning away from the human body, neo-Confucian ruling elites harboured contempt for physical effort and skill, which they believed to be the domain of the lower classes and reminiscent of a barbarian and militaristic culture.

For Zhu Xi, a sage or morally perfect person lurked inside everyone. Thus broad learning, moral discipline and cultivating the sage within lay at the very heart of his philosophy. The aim was to learn to detect the principle in all things in order to attain a deeper understanding of the world so that one could act upon it. Yet this emphasis on cultivating personal morality over and at the expense of practical learning already had its critics in Zhu Xi's time. How would all this benefit the state and the people? If truth and knowledge are to be found in the books of the ancients, why open the window of your study and look outside? What use is there in being able to recite a passage from Confucius when you need to build a bridge, dam a river or fight a plague of locusts? There is no point populating the Inland Revenue with specialists in Shakespeare who cannot count. This subdued attitude towards practical learning became a main point of criticism directed at Confucian ideology at several junctures in later history, not least when calls to modernize China and dismiss the old imperial order became more insistent in the late nineteenth and early twentieth centuries.

*

With the collapse of the imperial order in 1911, China embarked on a century of social and political transformations spurred on by various models of nationalism and ambitions for modernization. Both Nationalist (Guomindang) and Communist elites squarely laid the blame for China's slow response to a century of humiliation by Western powers at the feet of traditional Chinese culture. Confucianism was seen as a scholastic pastime, an ideology that had left China sclerotic and unable to adapt to the challenges of modernity and (forced) globalization in the wake of the Opium Wars of the mid nineteenth century. Some reformers, such as the late Qing official Zhang Zhidong (1837–1909), remained conservative in their view of what modernization should entail ('Chinese learning for substance; Western learning as practical application'). The writer Lu Xun (1881–1936), China's most accomplished literary figure of his time, condemned the feudal traditionalism that had 'cannibalized' (his words) Chinese society in his famous short story *A Madman's Diary* (*Kuangren riji*, published in 1918). The students, workers, writers and intellectuals who launched the May Fourth Movement in 1919 professed that Confucianism was to blame for China's backwardness in the face of the West and Japan. A 'new culture' was needed, they argued, one in which Confucius (in their words, the old 'Confucian Curiosity Shop') would be smashed and make way for Mr Science and Mr Democracy. The fettering admiration for past traditions that had paralysed China yielded to an ambitious concern with the future. What remained standing of the study of China's old masters of philosophy was largely relegated to university campuses. A short-lived New Life Movement was promoted in the 1930s by Chiang Kai-shek (1887–1975) and the Nationalist Party. Its aim was to revive the virtues of Confucian morality to combat corruption, clean up people's lifestyles and strengthen the nation, but the movement failed to connect with the masses.

When Mao launched his Cultural Revolution in 1967, Confucius and the tradition he stood for were condemned as the anti-proletarian Four Olds (old customs, old culture, old habits, old ideas). With Mao's death in 1976, the momentum of this destructive movement, packaged as class conflict, gave way to a more utilitarian and practical spirit following the economic and political reforms launched by Deng Xiaoping (1904–97). In the 1980s and 1990s, a political discourse on Asian values surfaced in Hong Kong, South Korea, Singapore and Taiwan (the so-called Four Asian Tigers) that sought to promote the benefits of Confucian values for economic modernization and political stability. Its impact on China, which had yet to catch up in economic growth with its neighbours, remained marginal. Throughout the twentieth century, though, prominent philosophers – such as Xiong Shili (1885–1968), Liang Shuming (1893–1988), Mou Zongsan (1909–95) and Tang Junyi (1909–78) – stoutly defended the vital contribution of Confucian ethics, often in dialogue with Buddhist and Western philosophy. These intellectuals became known as the proponents of (contemporary) New Confucianism.

Since the beginning of the twenty-first century, the language of China's leadership has changed. Publicly endorsed catchphrases such as 'the harmonious society' (discussed in Chapter 3) and the selective use of quotes from the *Analects* and other Chinese masters of philosophy in official speeches, commentaries and editorials are symptomatic of the more benign press the Master receives in China today. In the academic world, some philosophers and political scientists now embrace Confucian thought and advocate their interpretation of it as a recipe for tackling social problems or strengthening the fabric of a rapidly modernizing society. Both the Chinese government and its detractors seem to discover in Confucius a symbol of universal values and a brand that can be exported beyond China. Since 2004 a significant part of China's official cultural diplomacy is handled through a worldwide network of institutes named after him – the so-called Confucius Institutes.

The participants in what is now starting to look like a Confucian revival come from all walks of life and cross social strata. While some of it is no more than top-sown political rhetoric, Confucius also seems to have burrowed his way through to grassroots level. Reading classes that focus on the Confucian Classics pop up in state schools and private academies, in temples and companies. There the children of the aspiring new middle classes are taught by activists how to read, memorize and recite large chunks of text. 'National study classes' are held for Communist Party members, and company executives organize sessions on the ancient classics for their employees (at a substantial fee). Confucius is good for business in other ways too. There is a publishing industry that churns out popularized versions of the classics and the ancient masters, including cartoon and manga-type editions. Some writers, media-savvy academics and journalists are making a lucrative living out of the Master through public lectures, television and recordings. The level of vulgarization and oversimplified cultural patriotism displayed by some of these interpreters for the masses has invited criticism from Chinese academics and intellectuals.

Attempts to revive and adapt Confucius to new circumstances are as old as Chinese history itself. It is therefore hard to assess whether today's as yet relatively marginal revival movement is symptomatic of a more substantial reappropriation of Confucius as a voice for a genuinely desired return to Chinese traditional values, or whether it is shared by a wide enough segment of Chinese society to be meaningful. After all, Confucius prided himself on transmitting ideas from the past rather than creating new ones. What is new this time, however, is that the Confucian revival is no longer the exclusive domain of intellectuals, university campuses and philosophers. It extends to ordinary people, workers, peasants and activists, many of whom now see the countryside as the laboratory of Chinese civilization and hence a cradle of Confucian values. It is also seen in a resurgence of rituals and religious ceremonies, including mass celebrations in large sports stadia, patronized by local politicians, in places such as Confucius's hometown of Qufu or at established Confucius temples. But these are not limited just to state ceremonies on a large scale; they also take place more discreetly in local communities. Anthropologists Sébastien Billioud and Joël Thoraval have followed the movement through a decade of extensive fieldwork and describe it as an encounter between the sage and the people.

What the neo-Confucian movement, New Confucianism and the emergence of a revived interest in Confucius today have in common is that, in one way or another, consciously or subconsciously, intellectually or emotively, they announce themselves as a 'restoration' – that is, as a search for a return to 'core' or indigenous values sourced in the texts of the ancients (even when people at times failed to identify or be explicit about the source, or failed to acknowledge how much their 'neo'-thinking was influenced by the trends of their time). Whether presented as a reaction to ethics or philosophies imported from the outside (such as Buddhism or Western ideas), or revitalized as a tonic to remedy the ills and excesses caused by sliding moral standards of a particular time and place, much of Chinese thought has evolved and continues to evolve as a (virtual) conversation with Confucius.

There are as many definitions of religion as there are voices wishing to define it. Scholars of China have made such widely opposing claims that Confucianism is entirely profane or pious to the core. If we describe religion, minimally perhaps, as an attempt to link the world of the invisible to what is visible, it is clear that probing the realm of the spirits was very important to the ancient Chinese. As in the world of today, many also 'did' religion without thinking about it. In the ancestral cult, the spirits were conceived within the model of the family lineage, either real or fabricated; state cults aspired to seek the blessings of spirit powers that transcended the confines of the ancestors; and scores of ghosts and spirits, many residing in nature, were approached to secure salvation. There were cults inspired by the traditions laid out in the ritual texts of Confucian scholars and literati; and there were beliefs and practices with no scriptural origins. Despite scholastic debates and doctrinal disagreements, however, attitudes towards the spirit world tended to be eclectic. There are benefits to accepting that what is orthodox is what works for you at any given moment. It allows you to behave like a Confucian in the office, to relax as a Daoist after work, and to wonder about rebirth in front of the Buddha when you are feeling your age.

CHAPTER 7

The World of Nature

The natural world operates according to physical and biological laws. That is a truism. But nature is also a cultural construct. Humans develop their own social perceptions of nature, and such perceptions reflect what humans know about themselves. This applies to all cultures, in all times and places. Many motives can shape our attitude towards nature: we may wish to understand it, name and order it, conquer it and exploit its resources, collect it, protect and preserve it or live in harmony with it. We may hope to reinvent and manipulate it, choose to befriend or fear it as a benign or hostile force, look at it as durable or fragile, romanticize or deprecate it. The ways in which people conceive of the human–nature relationship and translate observations about the natural world into a vocabulary of their own vary, and this too applies across cultures, societies and time.

A common characterization of Chinese thought is that, for the majority of China's philosophers, nature went largely unnoticed as they were more interested in explaining the workings of human society, in particular, statecraft and social relationships. At first sight, Chinese thinkers rarely display an interest in nature beyond its utility as an analogy or metaphor in philosophical or political arguments. Sages, the Han philosopher Dong Zhongshu (second century BCE) remarks, talk about human virtues; they are not interested in explaining the species of birds and beasts (*Chunqiu fanlu* 13.2). Allegedly Dong was so engrossed in his world of books that he could not tell whether he rode a mare or a stallion. Very few Chinese thinkers saw nature as a realm separated from human affairs and therefore knowable through detached observation, description and experiment. As the sinologist Derk Bodde has put it: 'Persons who think of bamboos as "men of moral worth" and of the downward flow of water as an example of the Confucian virtue of propriety (*li*) are unlikely to have much interest either in the growth of bamboo or the movements of water as scientific phenomena. Or even if they have, they are not going to know the methodology necessary to satisfy this interest.' The writer Lin Yutang (1895–1976) quipped that the Chinese did not develop a tradition in the biological sciences as they reduced what is knowable to what is edible: 'the reason why the Chinese failed to develop botany and zoology is that the Chinese scholar cannot stare coldly and unemotionally at a fish without thinking immediately of how it tastes in the mouth and wanting to eat it'. What does it take to get a philosopher to look at bamboo as bamboo?

There is certainly truth in the assertion that in ancient China theoretical interest in the workings of nature was overshadowed by a preoccupation with human ethics and political philosophy. After all, the social chaos and upheaval that prompted China's masters of philosophy to formulate their theories was the outcome of human behaviour. It was the extremes of the human experience in a violent world that inspired them, not the serene mountain peaks and meandering rivulets that grace Chinese landscape paintings. When his stables went up in a blaze, Confucius inquired whether anyone was hurt, but 'he did not inquire after the horses' (*An.* 10.17). Whether we ought to interpret this passage to mean that Confucius had no interest in the fate of animals, or just as a way of saying that he did not care about his own material possessions in times of crisis, it is a fact that the men of his time and later did not produce a body of zoological and botanical literature in which they studied topics such as the growth process of plants or the locomotion of animals. Here China differs from the Greek world, where, as early as Pythagoras in the sixth century BCE, and through to thinkers such as Aristotle, such curiosity in nature did inspire theoretical and analytical writings.

However, to claim that the ancient Chinese did not develop a 'science of nature' on the grounds that their observations rarely take the form of subject-specific or experiment-based treatises or discussions in a language that mirrors that of the Greeks and Romans (or the conventions of natural history in the West) would be a misrepresentation of Chinese achievements in many fields, including medicine, pharmacology and astronomy. It is akin to suggesting that tea can only be appreciated when drunk from a teacup on a saucer and not from a bowl, or that someone is inarticulate because she or he does not speak or write in a language perceived as dominant. It is not prudent either for modern observers to impose their understandings of biology on the epistemology of the ancient Chinese.

Two general principles underpin the Chinese understanding of nature. First, a sense that everything in the world is interconnected, interrelated and interdependent, and that human activity (in the form of society, government, politics) both influences and is influenced by the workings of nature and the cosmos at large. Second, that explaining the natural world, therefore, is about teasing out and clarifying these relationships and connections rather than isolating and analysing its component parts as disconnected building blocks within a separate and purely biophysical world. Instead of defining nature, antithetically, as that part of reality that operates independently of human action, the Chinese integrated it within a human template. The boundaries between the human and non-human, or the political and the physical, were often porous and subject to the all-pervading laws of change and transformation that affect all and everything in the universe (a concept of change already examined in Chapter 2). To be sure, some were sceptical and sought to disconnect the filaments that linked the workings of Heaven (nature) to events on Earth (human society). However, by the time Han philosophers had selectively absorbed and synthesized ideas of philosophers from the age of the Warring States into their own models, those wanting to uncouple the human world from the world of nature were no more than an eddy twisting along the surface of a fast-flowing stream.

Body and body politic

Our first point of contact with the physical world is via our own body, and we tend to speak and inquire about it most when things go wrong with it. Although records are scant, it is clear that already in Shang society attempts were made to understand illness and find ways to handle physical stress or injury. In Shang times, most symptoms of illness were said to derive from the same source, the infamous 'curse of the ancestors'. Deceased ancestors could cause all sorts of discomforts. Oracle bone inscriptions record a royal toothache as well as a swollen abdomen, for instance. In addition to ancestral influences that impacted the health and well-being of the living, other potentially dangerous forces in nature merited placating, such as malign winds or snow.

We have to wait for the Zhou for the development of rudimentary theories about the body and the causes of illness. The earliest medical practitioners were shamans or priests. As the historian of Chinese medicine Paul Unschuld explains, the prevailing view of illness during the Zhou revolved around demonic medicine – that is, the belief that the body could be possessed by demonic influences. To ward off these disease-causing ghostly agents, officiants used a mixture of exorcisms, incantations, maledictions, drugs and other pharmaceutical therapies. Perceptions of illness were intricately linked to contemporary politics; an 'illness of our time' can only be explained in a language of our time. A society under siege meant the body, too, could be under siege. In a world where politics was dominated by anxiety and fears about military violence, illness was explained as a process in which ghostly pathogens 'attacked', 'hit' or 'assaulted' the body. The doctor, in turn, had to 'attack' the disease. One of the earliest Chinese graphs for a healer or physician (*yi*) contains the element for 'shaman', on top of which there is a quiver with an arrow on the left and a lance on the right. In the classical Chinese language, the verb meaning 'to cure' doubles up with the meaning of 'to bring order'. So treating an illness was akin to ordering the state and controlling its rivers. These visible and invisible pathogens were no longer exclusively ancestral spirits. They included malign forces present in nature, in dark corners of human residences, in kitchen stoves and latrines, or any other visible and invisible location.

From the fourth century BCE onwards, Chinese medicine started to develop into a discipline grounded in more complex theories, although demonic illness and magico-religious healing practices never really disappeared. Practical treatments circulated in so-called recipe literature, an example of which are the *Prescriptions Against Fifty-Two Ailments* (*Wushier bingfang*) discovered at Mawangdui in 1973. This manuscript contains a wide range of cures for ailments as varied as wounds and burns, spasms and convulsions, bites, internal swelling, urine retention, and 'male' and 'female' haemorrhoids. Here are a couple of recipes to treat an itchy scab, in a translation by Donald Harper, who has studied this corpus of texts extensively: 'Soak the feces of a black ram in the urine of an infant. Leave for one whole day. Spread [the medicine] on it ... Another: Slit the throat of a red lizard and daub the blood on it.' A mixture of treatments is described in this manuscript. Alongside conventional methods such as ingesting a concoction of ingredients, we find spells and incantations addressed to disease-causing spirits, or the shooting of arrows with magic powers.

During this period between the fourth and first centuries BCE, theories also emerged according to which bodily functions were thought to be governed by a set of (*yin* and *yang*) vessels. These vessels were believed to carry blood and *qi*, and illness became associated with the state of *qi* in certain vessels. Prior to the use of acupuncture in treating vessels, the main therapy was to cauterize them (to correct the flow of *qi*, one applies heat to the vessels; this causes a bump of unbroken skin to rise up, drawing up the *qi*; it can be done by burning dried mugwort powder on the skin – also known as moxibustion). As time went on, pricking with metal needles became the common therapy for vessel treatment, continuing an older practice of using lancing stones.

The ancient Chinese explored other ways to stay healthy. One tradition promoted personal hygiene and improving the body's vitality through diet, exercise and massage, as well as breath cultivation – therapies also used by the hopefuls of immortality encountered in the previous chapter. A well-preserved 'chart for guiding and pulling' from Mawangdui depicts the type of bodily postures and gymnastic stretches that could have been part of a daily exercise routine (see also Figure 7.1). Similar exercises are described in *The Pulling Book* (*Yin shu*) discovered at Zhangjiashan, dating to *c.*186 BCE. Why not start the day with some 'rabbit bolts' or a 'monkey's squat' or learn to do the gibbon walk? You will feel much better. The belief that the body is replete with *qi* vapours survives today and can be seen, for instance, in *qigong* breathing exercises.

In ancient China, sex was regarded as part of maintaining good health. The earliest Chinese writings on sex ('the art of the bedchamber') are not so much about pleasure and eroticism, although some of it is certainly there in descriptions of sexual positions and movements. The main focus instead is on the therapeutic use of sexual intercourse as a way of producing and stimulating the circulation of essential energies

Figure 7.1
Reconstruction of the 'Guiding and Pulling Chart' from Mawangdui Tomb no. 3 in Changsha (c.168 BCE).

to be absorbed, stored and retained within the body (health as pleasure). The use of aphrodisiacs to stimulate passion is well documented. It is the elite male who is generally the targeted beneficiary of sexual exercise. This is how a manuscript entitled *Conjoining Yin and Yang* (*He yin yang*), in Harper's translation, describes it: 'In the evening a man's essence flourishes; in the morning a woman's essence accumulates. By nurturing the woman's essence with my essence, muscles and vessels both move; skin, *qi*, and blood are all activated. Thus you are able to open blockage and penetrate obstruction. The central cavity receives the transmission and is filled.' Untimely sexual intercourse damages the body's *qi*. In sum, multiple views of illness and treatment existed alongside each other in ancient China. Many discomforts and ailments were blamed on external agencies, yet there also developed a strong sense that you should take care of your own health and prevent illness ('treat those who do not yet ail').

Learned physicians based their practice on knowledge contained in texts. Like the philosophers, they offered their services at the courts of the various rulers and elites. *The Inner Canon of the Yellow Emperor* (*Huangdi neijing*) is the oldest surviving Chinese medical classic, consisting of four texts. It came together in the first century BCE from a variety of other sources, and takes the form of dialogues between the Yellow Emperor and a number of legendary ministers. The *Inner Canon* offers a medical theory that is based on the idea of 'systematic correspondence', linking the human body to the cosmos. Your system is in good shape when it corresponds properly with the cosmos. A healthy person is someone able to maintain the natural harmony of the body and its organs.

The body's physiological rhythms are in accordance with the phases of the moon: a full moon fills the body or makes it replete; a waning moon phase makes it weak and susceptible to injury. Winds, conceived of later as more abstract, malign influences, are a primary cause of illness. Environmental influences from the outside, but also present within the body, affect the condition of the organs. Pathogens include heat, wind, humidity, cold, damage through excessive eating and drinking, exhaustion and fatigue. Cold congeals the flow of *qi*, heat stimulates it; so the body's own influences and those it absorbs externally need to be in balance. Theories of *yin* and *yang* and the Five Phases underpin the workings of the body and its organs. There are thus five key organs: heart, spleen, lung, kidneys and liver, corresponding to fire, soil, metal, water and wood respectively. Acupuncture is the main method for adjusting the *qi* within the body's vessels and for curing illness. The aim is to secure and preserve the internal free-flow of blood and *qi* and avoid blockage and stagnation.

Picture a network of channels that run up and down the body, from the chest into the hands, from the hands to the head, from the feet to the chest, and from the head to the feet. The Chinese, early on, correlated the body with earth and the blood vessels with rivers. Blood and *qi* flows through these conduit vessels, and this network of vessels communicates with the organs (known as 'depots' and 'palaces') and with one another. To ascertain its flow, the physician may want to feel the pulse. The first detailed accounts of pulse diagnosis occur in the biography of a Han doctor called Chunyu Yi (215–*c*.150 BCE), which contains twenty-five medical case histories (*Shiji* 105). On the body, holes ('pits') are located at

specific points along the path of the vessels. These are external access points, through which the physician can correct
the internal flow in the vessel by applying pressure (palpat-
ing it with the hands, pressing down towards the bone with
different degrees of pressure) or by using acupuncture to drain
the vessel in the case of surplus *qi*, or to allow more *qi* to
penetrate the body in case of deficiency. The origins of acupuncture remain unclear. There are references to the use of
pointed stones and needles of bamboo or bone that predate
The Inner Canon of the Yellow Emperor, and earlier practices
such as lancing abscesses and bloodletting may have inspired
the use of needling. But for more detailed theories we have
to wait for the first century BCE and the *Inner Canon*, which
mentions over three hundred acupuncture points.

In Chinese medicine, healing means, first and foremost,
attempting to keep the bodily functions in balance and the
body intact. Procedures to open up the body to examine or
affect the morphology of individual organs never featured
much in early Chinese medicine. Given the carnage of warfare and the liberal use of executions in penal law there was
hardly a shortage of corpses, which could have prompted an
interest in anatomical inquiry. Yet there are almost no records
of actual dissections from ancient China, except for one case
in 16 CE when the emperor ordered his personal physician to
dissect the body of a rebel with the help of butchers; he told
them to measure and weigh the organs, and 'use fine bamboos to trace out the course of the vessels, so as to find their
beginnings and ends, claiming that this knowledge could be
used to cure illness' (*Hanshu* 99B).

Rather than drawing on anatomical evidence, the physician's

focus was on understanding the various functions of the bodily organs, how they connected to each other, and how, by analogy, they related to the cosmos as a whole. Knowing the body involved establishing the connection between its visible outward signs (colour and countenance) and invisible inner workings, including feelings and emotions. An example of a classic articulation of body–cosmos correspondence is the following passage associated with Dong Zhongshu. Here the body is pictured as a microcosm:

> Humans have 360 joints, which match the number of Heaven [i.e. they roughly correspond to the number of days in the year]. [They have] form, frame, bone and flesh that match the thickness of Earth. Above they have ears and eyes that, with their keen sense of hearing and seeing, resemble the sun and moon. The body has orifices and pores, veins and arteries, resembling rivers and valleys. The heart has feelings of sorrow, joy, pleasure and anger, which are the same in kind as the spiritual *qi* of Heaven … These examples make it clear that humans are distinct from other living things and that they join with Heaven and Earth. This is why with the human body, the head, tilted and circular, resembles the appearance of Heaven; the hair … resembles the stars and planets; the ears and eyes, side and front, resemble the sun and the moon, the nose and mouth, inhaling and exhaling, resemble the wind and *qi*; the chest and the middle, penetrating and knowing, resemble spirit illumination; the abdomen and bladder, filling and emptying, resemble the numerous things.
> (*Chunqiu fanlu* 56.1)

Not only is the body fashioned in the image of the cosmos but all its functions operate in harmony with the workings of the cosmos. Without the cosmos, there is no body.

The Chinese often described this holistic view of the human body in political terms, modelling the body on images of the state and its economy. The body was said to function like a smoothly operating empire and the state was said to function like a body. *Qi* flows through the vessels like goods being transported along a network of rivers. Some medical terms that describe the network of vessels and organs mirror the language of irrigation and water control: vessel theory speaks of gutters, ditches and underground passages, and of unclogging blockages. Government and statecraft were described with an endlessly creative assortment of medical and physiological analogies. In a world where good government was explained as a process of containing disorder and restoring balance and harmony, rulers were like physicians: 'Governing the body and governing the state are a technique based on the same principles' (*Lüshi chunqiu* 17/1.1).

So the physical body and the body politic receive analogical treatment: ministers serve superiors like the teeth that serve the tongue without ever biting it; the ruler is the head and ministers his arms and legs; failure to extend one's powers compares with blockages in the circulation of the vital energies in the body; talents and ability are like the needles and medicinal drugs of a country; the good physician knows whether a patient's illness is critical or not, just as a good ruler knows what actions make for success or failure; the ruler rids the state of bad elements like a physician who lances a boil; illness is the sickness of the body, disorder is the sickness of the state;

floods, droughts and disasters are like malign vapours that ruin the state; and so on. This use of medical imagery in political rhetoric is of course not exclusive to China ('Disease is not of the body but of the place,' said the Roman philosopher Seneca), but the prevalent tendency to 'think through correspondences' in China makes this political body analogy stand out. Thus the ancient Chinese not only projected physical landscapes onto and into the body, but also imagined the body to function like the social and bureaucratic world, with organs compared to storehouses or with officials patrolling the flow of *qi*.

China's most famous legendary physician is Bian Que (the Chinese Hippocrates), who appears in Han stone reliefs as a winged creature holding a stone needle (see Figure 7.2). Opinion remains much divided, especially among Chinese

Figure 7.2
Bian Que, the legendary inventor of acupuncture.
Ink rubbing fragment of an Eastern Han tomb relief, Shandong.

historians of medicine, as to his historicity. However, while Bian Que's life is shrouded in mystery, China's masters of philosophy and court debaters were keen to parade him in political dialogues. Indeed, the human body and the experts who tended to it offered the perfect vehicle for moral comment and political criticism, as is shown in the following anecdote – one of many stories that feature Bian Que, the doctor-politician:

> The great physician Bian Que visited King Wu of Qin and the king showed him the carbuncle on his face. Bian Que offered to remove it. 'Your majesty's carbuncle is forward of the ear and below the eye,' cried the king's attendants. 'If the physician does not stop soon enough while removing it, he might cause your majesty to lose his hearing or the sight of an eye.' As a result, the king dismissed Bian Que. Bian Que was furious. He threw down his flint lancet and said: 'Your majesty planned this by consulting someone who has knowledge [of medicine], but now he calls it off on the advice of those who know nothing about it! If the government of Qin were run in the same fashion, the country would perish with your first action.' (*Zhanguo ce*, Qin 65).

Fauna and flora

In his much-acclaimed novel *La Tentation de l'Occident* (*The Temptation of the West*), André Malraux presents a fictional correspondence between a young Frenchman travelling through China in the 1920s and his Chinese friend who is visiting Europe at the same time. In one letter, the Chinese correspondent, Ling, writes to his European counterpart about the principles of Chinese art and aesthetics:

> The idea of species is for you [Europeans] quite abstract; it allows you to classify; it is a means toward knowledge. In us [Chinese] it is closely connected with our sensibility ... When I say 'cat' what dominates my mind is not a picture of a cat, but an impression of certain supple, silent *movements* peculiar to cats. You distinguish among species only by their outlines. Such a distinction applies only in death ... The notion of species ... can no more be exactly defined than can style; but style can be achieved, the sense of species, only suggested.

When observing nature, Malraux's imagined 'Western' mind wants to understand it by describing, classifying and differentiating kinds and species by their formal characteristics. The Western mind wants to know about outlines, contours, identity (a quadruped has four legs, the dolphin is a mammal and not a fish, a tomato is a fruit and not a vegetable). By contrast, when looking at animals and plants, the Chinese observer is interested in their movement and changes. The artist's mind is aligned with the natural image to be represented and does not turn it into an object detached from her or his subjectivity. The painted image becomes an extension of the hand and brush. Subject and object merge, painter and cat become one.

When it came to describing non-human animals, biology was never the mainstay for the Chinese masters of philosophy. This does of course not mean that they did not distinguish dogs from dragons; they simply did not theorize at length

Figure 7.3
Illustrations from an early Chinese dictionary. Song-period block print edition of the *Erya yin tu* by Guo Pu, 276–327 CE.

about the differences between the species in physiological terms. As shown in Chapter 2, when correlative thinkers divided animate species into five groups matching the Five Phases (scaly, feathered, naked, hairy and armoured), they focused not so much on an analysis of specific animals but rather on ensuring that they, like all things in the physical world, could be sorted into categories of five. Alternatively, when they sought to explain biology in terms of *yin* and *yang*, their main purpose was to compare and contrast functions in pairs. For instance, birds and mammals fly and run so they belong to active *yang*; hibernating animals belong to passive *yin*. Naturally, direct observation played a significant role ('silkworms eat but do not drink, cicadas drink but do not eat'). Yet more important was the ability to articulate how species correlate and function within the world at large, within space and time ('creatures born during the day resemble their father; those born at night resemble their mother' – *Huainanzi* 4.11).

What makes an animal? Rather than developing detailed theories about the physiology of different beasts or the principles of embryology, Chinese thinkers grappled with the question of how humans could be distinguished from other creatures of 'blood and *qi*'. Using various arguments, they claimed that the difference between humans and animals was one of degree rather than kind, and that it was based on morality as much as biology (some people are more dog than other people are). Let us start with Confucius. Frustrated by criticism of his refusal to turn his back on society, he ponders: 'I cannot run together with the birds and beasts. Am I not a member of this human species? If not them, with whom, then, should I associate myself?' (*An.* 18.6). Confucius dissociates himself from the birds and beasts, but by suggesting that he can only associate with morally superior members of the human species, he implies that the divide between human and bestial conduct does not necessarily correspond to the biological distinction between human and non-human animals. Mencius puts it as follows: 'What distinguishes man from birds and beasts is but small. Ordinary people cast it aside, only the gentleman preserves it' (*Mencius* 4B.19). So there is a distinction between human and non-human animals, but this distinction is flimsy. It takes a moral person to stop humans from behaving like animals. Xunzi continues the argument: 'What makes a man really human is not so much the fact that he is a hairless biped but his ability to draw boundaries' (*Xunzi* 5.4). What sets apart humans from animals are their moral antennae and their capacity to 'make distinctions'. Humans possess (or should possess) a sense of right and wrong: 'Water and fire possess *qi* but do not have life. Plants and trees have life, but have no awareness. Birds and beasts have awareness, but lack a sense of righteousness. Humans possess *qi*, have life and awareness and also a sense of righteousness. That is why they are the noblest creatures in the world' (*Xunzi* 9.16a). As explained in Chapter 5, ritual then becomes the tool of preference for curbing the supposedly animal aspects of human nature.

The ancient Chinese often framed and explained their observations of nature in moral terms. The crow disgorging food to nourish its parents was 'filial', unlike the 'unfilial' cuckoo which has its eggs hatched by other birds; lambs getting on their knees to suckle from the mother know the rites. As the natural world was part of one and the same moral universe, the Chinese perceived a direct relationship between human behaviour and occurrences in the heavens and nature. For instance, their explanation of plagues and attacks by wild animals followed a moral logic: when animals engage in predatory attacks on humans, this is not because they possess an inherently evil character, but because a balance has been disturbed within human society or between humans and nature. So tiger attacks are the result of negligence in government. They are caused by 'low-hearted officials who put all efforts into catching them' (*Hou Hanshu* 41). By contrast, when the sages ruled human society, their good government would spontaneously turn the wilds into a civilized place without danger, 'tigers and leopards could be pulled by the tail, and you could tread on vipers and snakes [without harm]' (*Huainanzi* 8.6). In the face of human virtue, wasps and scorpions will not sting young babies. Virtuous human behaviour can morally transform animals: they will come down from the forests, dance to human music and obey human orders. Several stories portray animals with an innate sense of humaneness and compassion. In one such tale, a servant releases a young fawn because he could not bear the cries of the mother deer who kept following him (*Han Feizi* 7). When human society is harmonious, the natural world will respond in harmony. When a ruler's virtue 'extends to birds and beasts', auspicious creatures such as phoenixes, dragons and unicorns will also appear.

However, intervening in the natural world requires extreme caution. Beware that 'if you overturn birds' nests and smash their eggs, phoenixes will not arrive. If you rip open wild beasts and eat their foetuses, the unicorn will not come. If you dry up the marshes and strand the fish they contain, dragons will not appear' (*Lüshi chunqiu* 13/2.1). Those who chase animals must be moral hunters, who take but do so in a considered manner and without depleting nature's resources. The founding king of the Shang people won praise for inventing the so-called 'three-sided attack', an encircling manoeuvre whereby a fair number of prey were given the chance to escape via an unguarded side. The good ruler never surrounds an entire flock or rounds up a whole herd. *The Ritual Records* stipulates that animals killed out of season should not be sold at market, and that the Son of Heaven should not eat or sacrifice pregnant animals.

Confucius – who else – is sometimes paraded as a protoecologist. Allegedly the Master fished with a line but did not use a net; he used a stringed arrow (to retrieve and pull in his catch and not lose it) but never aimed at roosting birds (*An.* 7.27). He praises one of his disciples for throwing back undersized fish (*Lüshi chunqiu* 18/8.2) and speaks of the unseasonal killing of one single animal or untimely loss of a tree as an act that is 'contrary to filial piety' (*Liji*, 'Ji yi'). Mencius notes that if close-meshed nets are not used in pools and ponds there would be more fish and turtles than anyone could eat (*Mencius* 1A.3). If Confucian moralists had their way, man would be living in an ecological El Dorado. History in China, and elsewhere, has not obliged.

China's sacred animals were creatures able to undergo change and metamorphosis, or hybrids that combined behavioural and physical features that transcended the species. They distinguished themselves from ordinary species in the same way that morally accomplished persons stood out from the crowd: they move from the land into the sea, from the mountains to the plains, from Earth to the heavens, or from remote regions into the Chinese cultural sphere. The dragon incorporates the bodily parts of multiple species: 'If it wishes to ascend, then it rises with the cloudy vapours. If it wants to descend, then it enters into the deep springs. There is no [fixed] day for its transformations and no [fixed] season for its ascending and descending' (*Guanzi* 39). The unicorn has the body of a deer, the tail of an ox and a horn on its cranium. Even the anatomy of the phoenix was associated with Confucian virtues that could, literally, be read off signs displayed on its feathery coat. Born in the deep springs and growing up on the yellow earth, the sacred turtle knows the ways of Heaven and understands the past. Its dome-shaped dorsal shell resembles Heaven while its ventral part is square like the earth – the universe in miniature. The turtle symbolized permanence and longevity. Legend held that turtles with divine powers could be found in the waters of the Yangzi. Locals ate them believing it induced the onset of vital *qi* and helped stave off old age (*Shiji* 128).

The sight of silkworms metamorphosing into spinning cocoons firmed up its status as a special creature. Xunzi even wrote a poem about it which presents the silkworm's biology as a metaphor for the sage's responsiveness to constantly changing circumstances. Like the larva of the silkworm moth which transform itself into a silk cocoon after twenty-two days, the sage 'continuously transforms like a spirit … without growing old'. Just as the silkworm devours mulberry leaves and emits them as silk thread, so the sage turns chaos into order (*Xunzi* 26.4).

Confucius had a dog. Archaeology has shown that dogs

figured prominently in daily life as early as the Shang period and possibly earlier. According to *The Ritual Records*, dogs were for hunting, guarding, and ... eating (*Liji*, 'Shaoyi'). The dog belonged to the so-called 'six domestic animals' (horse, cow, dog, pig, sheep, chicken). Because of their proximity to people, dogs behaving badly (or just strangely) are a popular theme in the folklore of the time: be wary when dogs intrude where they should not, or start to walk upright and behave like humans, seize men, sport with women or tend to the fire. In one curious story (dated to 28 BCE) two men 'lodging in the same room' all of a sudden spot a human-like shape. They start beating at the phantom, which then turns into a dog and runs out (*Hanshu* 27). Chiding comments at the expense of those who spent more on animals than people suggest that some pets lived like kings. Yanzi (Yan Ying; *fl.* 547–489 BCE) persuades his lord not to bury his favourite racing dog with sacrifices. In a remarkable change of mind, the latter has the dog cooked and served up to his ministers instead (*Yanzi chunqiu* 2). How is it possible, Mencius reprimands King Hui of Liang, that 'your majesty's dogs and swine are eating food intended for human beings and your majesty does not know enough to prohibit this?' (*Mencius* 1A.3).

Interpreting technical references to plants and animals in ancient Chinese texts remains a difficult exercise. Natural history was a pastime of several early sinologists in the nineteenth century. They were interested in deciphering language but also in unearthing information about China's natural treasures. Many animal and plant names had regional origins, and there were often several variants referring to the same species. For instance, in the eastern state of Qi, the bat was known as an 'immortal rat' according to one source (immortals were winged and could lift off, like bat-men). Furthermore, Chinese scholars had a tendency to base explanations about nature not on personal and direct observation, but on information they could trace in ancient texts. Thus where one might expect a biologist to explain his findings, derived from direct observation, in the 'I' voice, we are presented instead with a textual scholar attempting to link the appearance of a plant or animal with a record of it somewhere in the classics.

Of all classics, Confucius intimates, *The Book of Odes* contains the richest repository of plant and animal names (*An.* 17.9). But the fact that Confucius recommends a collection of poetry as a resource suggests that he was interested in plants and animals primarily as imagery or literary metaphor. A pepper plant for heat of passion; mandarin ducks for lovers; fish for fertility, abundance and marital bliss; a usurping cuckoo chick filling a magpie's nest; densely growing creepers for complex relationships. The aim of familiarizing oneself with the fauna and flora in the classics is to decode the moral meaning behind the plants and beasts: it is about moral self-cultivation, not the study of nature per se. This does of course not mean that nobody observed and attempted to classify the animals, rocks and plants around them. In addition, for an image to be powerful, it needs to be shared and understood. If you have never seen a plum tree in spring, how would you appreciate an admirer's compliment that you are as radiant as plum blossom?

In its description of how the legendary Yu the Great divided the known lands into nine provinces, *The Tribute of Yu* (*Yu gong*; included as a chapter in *The Book of Documents*) comments on the soil, mountains and rivers in each region, listing herbs, crops and trees for some. Another, more detailed, account of plants and the type of soil in which they grow is preserved in a chapter entitled 'Categories of Land' in *The Master Guan*, the earliest parts of which could date to the third century BCE. The text describes five types of alluvial or irrigated soil and their vegetation. It lists different types of hill land and mountain terrain, the depth of their water tables, and the trees and plants for each soil level: 'The Dao of all plants and soils is that each should have what is special to it. Whether the elevation is high or low, every place has its characteristic plants and soils' (*Guanzi* 58). There is no consensus of opinion about the exact geographical areas to which the text refers. However, it clearly has a practical purpose since it identifies the varying degrees of fertility and productivity of the soil and indicates whether it is best suited for livestock, crops, horticulture or forestry.

In short, most information on plants and animals in ancient China appears as applied science. This is why works dealing with medicine and dietetics offer rich pickings of fauna and flora. For instance, China's purportedly oldest classic on pharmaceutics, *The Divine Husbandman's Classic of Pharmaceutics (Shennong bencao jing)*, dating back to the second and first centuries BCE but known only through a later commentary by the medieval scholar Tao Hongjing (456–536 CE), divides its drugs into categories based on natural objects: jade and other stones, herbs, trees, fruit, vegetables, grains and animals. However, the emphasis is not so much on how animals and plant species function, but how they work for the user. For the poet, the fragrant aroma of the cassia tree could be evoked in verse to beguile the reader; for the physician, cinnamon bark could be pulverized to treat swellings in the groin; for the cook, it could be added to dishes as a tasty condiment.

Ancient China's fields, rivers, lakes and forests comprised a vast natural resource, producing edible crops, supporting livestock and supplying other natural assets. China was covered by deciduous hardwood and broadleaf forests (elm, oak, maple) in the north, semitropical forests in the Yangzi area, and tropical jungles in the south. Environmental historians now believe that the first significant pressures on forests resulting from expanding agriculture became evident around 1000 BCE. This is when a number of animal species, such as the elephant and tiger, start disappearing from the zooarchaeological record for the north China plain, which, by the time of the Han dynasty, had been almost entirely cleared of forests. Among the managed woodlands were forests that contained timber-producing woods, bamboo groves and lacquer trees. The notorious highways built by the First Emperor were flanked by pine trees, while the Wei river valley was home to bamboo plantations. Bamboo was grown for timber in this region; it continues to be used for scaffolding in the building industry in China today. Fruitless trees grown in the early empire included the elm, locust, white poplar and willow. Fruit trees included the date or jujube tree, tangerine, peach, chestnut and plum. Grapes, pomegranates and alfalfa entered China via the trade routes alongside the Taklamakan Desert (a part of the corridor known as the Silk Road).

In ancient China, all non-agricultural natural resources (mountains, marshes, forests, waterways and parks) were considered the private property of the feudal lord, king or emperor. The court managed these resources. A standard way in which a ruler could show charity or largesse was, periodically, to grant access to parks (normally known as 'forbidden parks') and their resources for the common people. It is not the size of a park that matters, Mencius notes, but the fact that people are granted free access to it (*Mencius* 1B.2). But parks also provided a potent symbol of the far-reaching authority of those who ruled. The Shanglin park, which occupied an area of around one hundred square kilometres south and south-west of Han Chang'an, was the most famous example. Built by the First Emperor and given a makeover by Emperor Han Wudi in the late second century BCE, the plants, rocks and animals collected there represented the Son of Heaven's power over all species. They were a reflection in microcosm of the empire and the world at large. By roaming through parklands, watching or hunting exotic beasts in an artificial landscape, the ruler symbolically traversed his realm. He could conquer the world and its flora and fauna all over again. Inside the parks a sense of cosmic and geographic order prevailed. Plants and animals were distributed geographically according to their region of origin.

Officials supervised the forest economy: 'If whoever acts as a ruler is unable to exercise care in controlling his mountain forests, marshes and grasslands, he will be unable to achieve supremacy in the world' (*Guanzi* 80). Ritual calendars suggest one did well to consult them for an auspicious day before felling a tree: unpleasant consequences could result from chopping down the wrong tree on the wrong day. In reality, however, the trend was towards gradual deforestation. In addition to harvesting wood for timber, the large-scale burning of logs in charcoal furnaces and uncontrolled copper-mining contributed to the gradual denuding of landscapes (remember the parable of Mencius's Ox Mountain in Chapter 4). Here is how one official describes the environmental perils of mining (in 44 BCE) with alarmingly accurate foresight: 'People drill several hundred feet into the earth, destroying the essence of the *yin qi*. The soil is plundered until it is empty and is no longer able to hold the *qi* from which clouds are formed. They cut down the trees and forests, and they ignore the prohibitions and the right seasons for cutting. How can we not be sure that disastrous droughts will result from this?' (*Hanshu* 72). One tragic story linked to charcoal production, on the estate of a private iron industrialist (around 190 BCE), is that of a boy kidnapped from a poor family at the age four or five, and sold into slavery. Having stripped the hillside upon which they were working of its vegetation, the entire mountain collapsed one night, burying him and more than a hundred other men and boys alive (*Shiji* 49). The similarities with mining accidents today are eerie.

Of water and jade

China's main rivers and streams flow east. Welling up from springs in the Tibetan Plateau, they carve their way through the landscape like a life-giving force, like *qi* flowing through the vessels of the body. Rivers collect the rains and irrigate the plains, they gather and distribute. Along the way, their waters give life and destroy, they fertilize and flood. Rivers may twist and coil, dry up or breach their course, but everything that flows, ends up in the four seas that form the border of All under

Heaven – 'Within the four seas, all men are brothers', runs one of the lines from the *Analects* most quoted by diplomats and politicians (*An.* 12.5).

When the waters rose too high and inundated the Central Kingdoms, the legendary emperor Yu the Great dug out the earth so they would flow again through their channels to the sea. He tamed the rivers, gave the people dry land and saved humankind from the floods (*Mencius* 3B.9). The Yellow River, China's second-largest river, running over a course of nearly five and a half thousand kilometres, is both the cradle of Chinese civilization and its curse. Cutting through very fine yellow-brown loess soil on its way through China's north-west plateau, the river erodes large volumes of soil and rocks which it deposits as silt in the lowland plains. These deposits push up the riverbed like rising dough, until its banks burst and floods devastate the surrounding area, causing the river's course through the North China plain to change numerous times throughout history.

Those who ruled China were those who could tame its rivers and control its irrigation canals. In 1957 the German-American historian and sociologist Karl A. Wittfogel wrote a seminal work entitled *Oriental Despotism: A Comparative Study of Total Power*, in which he argued that agrarian societies that depend on large-scale irrigation require strong governments to manage and control the labour force. Such societies (which he called 'hydraulic societies') would inevitably require highly centralized, and therefore often oppressive, political regimes. Wittfogel had his critics but, nevertheless, the link he posited between water control and political power is one that reverberates through much of China's history. The good sovereign is one who will 'channel flood waters, improve dams and ditches, clear whirlpools and sandbars, remove mud and other obstacles, open up places blocked by weeds, and make fords and bridges passable' (*Guanzi* 10). China's earliest hydraulic engineers were masters of their trade. The water-diversion works on the Min River at Dujiangyan (Sichuan province) constructed by governor Li Bing in the third century BCE that opened up the irrigation of the Chengdu Plain, are still visible and in use today. But raging waters also brought despair to those who ruled. Nowhere do we find it recorded so movingly than in a desperate plea by Emperor Han Wudi to the river gods when the Yellow River once more broke its banks (in 109 BCE): 'Why are you so cruel? Your surging floods do not cease. You grieve my people!' (*Shiji* 29).

But to control the waters, one has to follow the Way (Dao) of water, Mencius reminds us. You need to lead it to the seas rather than into your neighbour's backyard, where it will do nothing but wreak more havoc and discontent (*Mencius* 6B.11). It is no coincidence that, in a land ravaged by capricious rivers, water held a prominent place in the conceptual armoury of its philosophers. Almost every thinker or poet, at some point, drew on the powerful imagery of water. The sinologist Sarah Allan suggests that water, together with plant life, was a 'root metaphor' for the Chinese. Water and plants provided a concrete model from which abstract ideas (such as time or growth) could be derived. Do philosophers develop abstract ideas first and then look for a suitable image to give them structure ('time passes by like a floating wave'), or is the concrete image itself an inherent part of the abstract idea? What comes first: ideas or words, concepts or images, perceiving flow or defining water? It is a bit of a chicken-and-egg question. Nevertheless, it is clear that when Confucius stood at a riverbank he thought of time as 'water passing by': 'Isn't what passes just like this, never letting up day or night?!' (*An.* 9.17).

Water made people think. Such is the power of the image of watery flow that even *Master Sun's Art of Warfare* uses it to describe military configurations: 'The formation of troops can be compared to water. Just as the flow of water avoids heights and rushes to the lowest point, so on the path to victory you should avoid the enemy's strong points and strike where he is weak' (*Sunzi bing fa* 6). Chinese thinkers found in water the perfect image to illuminate the idea of passive and invisible power. *The Classic of the Way and Virtue* employs the metaphor extensively: 'The rivers and ocean are able to rule over a hundred valley streams because they are able to place themselves in the lower position' (*DDJ* 66). Rivers are receptive and collect the rains that come down from the mountains. Mountains may catch the eye, but their life force drains into the hidden gullies and streams in the valley. Water is soft, yielding, compliant, colourless and tasteless, yet it extends everywhere. Give it time, and it will conquer everything: 'There is nothing more supple and weak in the world than water; yet in attacking what is hard and strong, nothing can surpass it' (*DDJ* 78). The good Daoist goes with the flow, but, by doing so, he carves out a strategy for life that is fluid and adaptable, like water that spontaneously negotiates any blockage or obstacle along its course. Think of the Dao as a water course: 'The highest good is like water; water excels at benefiting the myriad creatures, without contending with them; water resides in the places that people find repellent; and so it comes close to the Dao' (*DDJ* 8).

Zhuangzi literally puts water in the mouth of Confucius – there is no better rhetorical strategy than having your views articulated through the voice of your opponent. In one of many references to water, he suggests that water is to fish what the Dao is to humans:

> 'Fish develop in water,' said Confucius, 'and man develops in the Way [Dao]. Growing in water, fish find adequate nourishment just by passing through their ponds. Developing in the Way, man's life is stabilized without ado. Therefore, it is said, "Fish forget themselves in the rivers and lakes; men forget themselves in the arts of the Way [Dao]."' (*Zhuangzi* 6.6)

As a substance that is constantly present yet always moving and flowing, water offered endless possibilities for Chinese thinkers to evoke the subtlety of the Dao and the reach of soft power. One of the most eloquent summaries of its virtues appears in *The Master Huainan*. This book, from which I have quoted extensively in previous chapters, came together around 139 BCE. It was presented at court by Liu An (?179–122 BCE), the King of Huainan, and a vassal and paternal uncle of Emperor Wu, with the aim of helping the young emperor understand the world – the same emperor who earlier begged the Yellow River to have mercy on his people.

> Of all things under Heaven, none is more pliant
> and supple than water.
> None the less, it is

So great that its limits cannot be reached;

So deep that it cannot be fathomed;

So high that it reaches the infinite;

So distant that it merges into the boundless.

Increasing and decreasing, draining away and
    filling up,

It circulates without restraints into the immeasurable.

When it ascends to the heavens, it becomes the rain
    and the dew.

When it descends to the earth, it becomes moisture
    and dampness. [...]

It circulates everywhere, yet we cannot exhaust it.

It is so subtle that we cannot grasp it in our hands.

Strike it, and it is not wounded.

Pierce it, and it is not injured.

Chop it, and it is not cut apart.

Try to set it alight, and it will not burn.

Seeping, draining, flowing, disappearing,

Mixing and blending, intertwining with things,
    it cannot be differentiated.

It is so sharp it can pierce a hole in metal and
    stone.

It is so strong it can give sustenance to the entire
    world. [...]

Thus of all things that have shapes, none is more
honoured than water. (*Huainanzi* 1.12)

One wonders what the emperor made of his philosophizing courtiers. Likewise, for a farmer who has his crops wiped out by floods, or a general piercing the dikes to flood an enemy's city, the poetic power of water could hardly have seemed relevant.

Some thinkers argued that waters and rivers, like the soil, influenced the character of the living species that lived near them. One passage in *The Master Guan* notes that the sages must understand water since it is a resource that shapes human behaviour: people in Qi (Shandong province) are greedy, rude and violent because its waters are forceful, swift and twisting; those of Jin (a state known for its merchants) are flattering and deceitful, cunning and profit-seeking because the water there is 'bitter, harsh and polluted, choked with silt and wandering in confusion, free of its banks' (*Guanzi* 39). Elsewhere the relationship between water and people is explained in physiological or medical terms: brackish waters make you go bald and develop swellings on the neck; water filled with sediment causes lameness and swollen feet; sweet waters produce handsome and beautiful people; chalky waters cause ulcers and boils; bitter water causes back problems (*Lüshi chunqiu* 3/2.4). In sum, and tellingly relevant to all ages, clean water produces healthy people of good moral character – another reason why those who seek to rule the world should learn to control the waters. The art of government, then, resembles water management: guide the people but do not block their natural flow; dam their ambitions without damming their talent; store up reserves without drying up the source.

Confucius and his followers, too, discover in water a vocabulary that helps them illustrate Confucian virtues. Why is it, one of his disciples asks, that whenever a gentleman sees a big stream, he feels the need to throw a contemplative gaze at it? Confucius's answer is almost predictable: like virtue (*de*), water extends everywhere and gives life to everything in a spontaneous manner; like rightness, water always flows in one clear direction, despite twisting and turning; like morally transformed people, the river purifies and cleans what comes into contact with it; and so on (*Xunzi* 28.5). In a very rare statement on nature in the *Analects*, Confucius singles out water and mountains in an allusion to human psychology: 'The wise enjoy water, those who are humane enjoy mountains; the wise are active, those who are humane remain still; the wise find enjoyment, those who are humane are long-lived' (*An.* 6.23). Here water symbolizes motion and ceaseless activity, mountains stand for stability and endurance. Art historians sometimes link this passage to the aesthetics of landscape, translated as 'mountains and water' in Chinese. It is hard to imagine, though, that Confucius was inspired by a panoramic view here, let alone that he had painting in mind, we simply do not know.

If water furnished the Chinese imagination with the ultimate image for change, flow and compliance, jade evoked pristine beauty, inner power and long life. Jade (either nephrite or jadeite) is a mineral that is rock hard, partly translucent and which exists in a range of colours and shades, white and deep green being the most popular with jewellers. It cannot be cut or shaped with a knife or any other metal tool, but requires an abrasive agent (sand and grit) together with water to polish it. In short, it has to be ground and worked hard.

Elites in ancient China used jade for personal ornament (as pendants, girdle hooks or carved plaques). It had, above all, an important function in ritual. It passed as a gift among dignitaries during diplomatic missions or court visits. Pendants with sonorous pieces of jade were worn according to rank and occasion as prescribed in the ritual codes (their sound allegedly announcing the status of the person wearing them). Auspicious pieces of jade were offered to the spirits, in sacrifices to rivers, the sun and moon, Heaven and Earth, the four directions and the constellations. Jade cups were used to offer libations. Its value was recognized by those in authority. Qin law, for instance, included sanctions for the smuggling or illicit sale of jade.

Jade has the appearance of something ordinary while being extraordinary in its symbolical power. Among all the veined and coloured stones and rocks that make up the Chinese lapidary, none inspire writers and philosophers more than jade does. It is praised for its hardness and unyielding nature; and for its pristine and polished purity that results from the long and assiduous process of working raw jade with liquid abrasives (sand and water). As relatively small objects in which are frozen tremendous amounts of human (vital) energy, jade embodies all elements of sensory and aesthetic perfection. Do not judge it for its size but for its beauty:

> When a piece of jade is moistened, it looks bright. [When struck], its sound is slow and harmonious. How expansive are its aspects! With no interior or exterior, jade does not conceal its flaws or imperfections. Close up, it looks glossy; from a distance, it shines brightly. It reflects like a mirror, revealing the pupil of your eye. Subtly it picks up the tip of a tiny autumn hair [i.e. a minuscule

thing]. It brightly illuminates the dark and obscure.
(*Huainanzi* 16.19)

Jade and pearls are the sages among stones, radiating their
fortifying influence on their natural environment: 'Where jade
is buried in hills, the plants have a special sheen, and where
pearls grow in the deeps, the banks do not become parched'
(*Xunzi* 1.7). When there is jade in the mountains, its vegetation will be lush. To appear genial, like jade, or have a 'jade
countenance' characterized wise and worthy people: people
with an inner brilliance who have the power to influence those
around them. Wise people may look ordinary on the outside but, inside, they are precious like jade (*DDJ* 70). Jade
represents inner substance over outward appearance. As an
idiom, it qualifies all things that are precious or life-giving.
The literature of physical self-cultivation speaks of the 'jade
wellspring' where essential energies of the body are stored,
the 'jade whip' (penis) and 'jade hole' (vagina). Immortals
drank from jade springs. In later Daoist religion, jade maid-
ens escort accomplished adepts to the Queen Mother of the
West (discussed in Chapter 6).

For the philosophers, jade provided a valuable metaphor for
ethical theory. Jade is so much more precious than soapstone,
Confucius tells his disciple Zigong, not because of its rarity
(moral persons should not crave exotic goods anyway), but because 'it is a thing the gentleman compares to inner power'.
Jade is smooth and refined, like the virtue of humaneness; it is
hard and inflexible, like someone who knows right from wrong;
its veins are ordered in regular patterns, like someone who is
knowledgeable; it can be broken but not bent, like someone

who is brave; its cracks and flaws always show, like someone
who is sincere; when struck its sounds reverberate in the distance, like someone with a refined expression (*Xunzi* 30.4).
In short, to be like jade means to be a noble person: beautiful within, and charismatic to others. We should all strive to
become one.

To work jade is a much-used metaphor for education –
that is, the polishing and grinding of human talent and character. An uneducated person is like an uncut and unpolished
piece of jade. Only wisdom and insight can unveil the inner
beauty of jade. Hence it requires a fine craftsman or teacher
to separate the talent of jade from the base nature of ordinary
stones. People in authority must be able to spot those with jade-
like qualities in society and distinguish them from common
pebbles. As the well-known parable 'Mr He's Piece of Jade' tells
us, it is better to have your feet amputated than fail to spot
talent and compromise your own integrity:

Once a man from Chu named Mr He found an unpolished
piece of jade in the hills of Chu. He took it to court and
presented it to King Li. King Li instructed a jeweller to
examine it, and the jeweller reported, 'It is only a stone.'
The king thought that Mr He was trying to deceive him, and
ordered that his left foot be amputated [as punishment].
With time King Li passed away and King Wu came to the
throne. Immediately Mr He once more took his piece of
jade and presented it to King Wu. King Wu ordered his
jeweller to examine it, and again the jeweller reported, 'It
is only a stone.' Again the king thought that Mr He was
trying to deceive him, and ordered that his right foot be

cut off. King Wu died and was succeeded by King Wen. Hugging his piece of jade close to his breast, Mr He then went to the foot of the Chu mountains. There he wept for three days and nights, and when all his tears were finished, he continued by weeping blood. The king, hearing of this, sent someone to question him: 'There are many in the world who have had their feet amputated, so why do you cry about it so desolately?' Mr He replied, 'I do not grieve because my feet have been cut off. I grieve because this precious jewel has been dubbed a mere stone, and because a man of integrity has been called a cheat. That is why I weep.' The king then ordered the jeweller to cut and polish the piece of jade and so a precious jewel emerged. Accordingly it was given the name 'Mr He's Piece of Jade'. (*Han Feizi* 13).

In the Olympics of Chinese metaphor, champions are those who float along the river of life with ease, accompanied by a teacher or loved one and with the looks of a dragon and a character like jade.

Freaks of man, freaks of nature

If you accept that the course of nature and that of human affairs are intimately linked, and that the flow of your life is mirrored in the passage of the clouds, then the appearance of an unusual cloud in the skies is a significant sign. It might be telling you that you have veered off course – a bad cloud hangs over your head. Omens or portents are unusual signs or occurrences in the natural world that are believed to prefigure or predict certain events. Abnormalities or anomalies can be taken as nature's ongoing response to events. To the Chinese, there was a script written in the skies and the natural landscape that, to those able to read it, could throw light on human affairs. Disorder in nature meant malfunctioning in society, or the moral failing of those in power. Strange animal behaviour, abnormally shaped plants and trees, snow in summer, earthquakes, hurricanes and other freaks of nature appeared for a reason. These changes in nature were thought to tally with changes in the socio-political world and vice versa. Heaven, as the supreme power, showed its will through natural disasters and bizarre events: 'When Heaven goes against the seasons it causes calamities; when Earth goes against [the normal nature of] its creatures it causes prodigies; when people go against virtue they cause chaos; when there is chaos then calamities and prodigies are produced' (*Zuozhuan*, Lord Xuan 15). To be able to predict and explain these unusual phenomena had a double function: you could act upon it or explain a portent away so that it lost its significance.

Needless to say, no hard science existed to help people decide what constituted a freak of nature. What is regular or normal in life is often left unsaid or implicitly understood – we tend to spend most of our time debating and clarifying what is 'noteworthy'. A painter, Han Fei remarks, finds drawing dogs and horses harder than ghosts and demons since people see dogs and horses on a daily basis and therefore know what to expect. It is so much easier to improvise with ghosts, as you can present them in any guise you like (*Han Feizi* 11). Omens are not factual. Like nature itself, they are cultural constructs and understood against the background of a shared notion of order and normality. For instance, a flood or drought might be experienced unambiguously as a disaster, but interpreting the shape of a cloud, the veins in a rock or the aerial formation of a flock of geese leaves more room for speculation. Reading and interpreting such signs in nature therefore was a subtle and important political art. Indeed, one could think of omen interpretation as social and political commentary *avant la lettre*.

What happens when we see (or think we see) something unusual in nature? According to one early explanation, it starts with fear: when you are afraid or experiencing anxiety, your *qi* will flare up and you start to see strange things, as if delirious due to fever (*Zuozhuan*, Lord Zhuang 14). These oddities can appear to you at significant moments when you go about your daily business, or they can materialize during an altered state of consciousness, such as a dream. When his magicians told the First Emperor that large fish had blocked access to the isles of immortality, he dreamed of a battle with a sea spirit. His diviner identified this creature as an evil water god that appears in the form of a gigantic fish or dragon, and so the emperor went off to personally shoot a giant fish in order to help unblock access to the (legendary) isles of immortality (*Shiji* 6). The dream interpreter, like the physician, can wield significant power as it is his job to explain dream visions and link them to the fortunes of the dreamer back in the real world. Being able to respond effectively to strange visions was often presented as an indication of future success. Everything revolves around the control of perception. The issue is not whether or not something appears odd or scary to the observer, but rather how he or she responds to it. Take Sun Shu-ao (sixth century BCE) as a young child. He meets a two-headed snake while playing, kills and buries it, and then runs crying to his mother, fearing that what he has seen is a sign that he will die early. But his mother comforts him, saying that on the contrary it shows that he is special and that people with 'hidden' (*yin*) virtues will be compensated by Heaven. In the end, the child becomes a successful minister; the way he handled a freakish serpent in childhood was a sign of his talent in later life (*Xin xu* 1).

It takes a sage (not a weatherman or a politician) to be able to peer into what lies behind events and make sense of what appears weird and uncanny. The Confucius figure is often put in this position. When presented with strange creatures or plants, he gives them a name (naming something means explaining it). He identifies monsters and freaks and advises people how to react to them when they appear, as he did in the case of a poor family in the state of Song. They had been a model family for three generations, when, one day, for no apparent reason, they witness a black cow giving birth to a white calf. This is a good omen, thinks Confucius, and he advises them to sacrifice the calf to the spirits. However, as a result the father of the family goes blind. When the cow gives birth to another white calf, Confucius is once again consulted. He sticks to his opinion and again calls for the calf to be killed and offered to the spirits. Next the son, too, loses his eyesight. Bad luck, one would think – that is, until their city falls under siege and all able-bodied men are called to its defence. Saved by blindness, father and son avoid conscription, and regain their eyesight once the siege is over. Confucius was right after all: one should not be perturbed by what might appear strange at first sight (*Liezi* 8).

The list of portents alerting people that boundaries had been overstepped was endless: odd trees growing in the courtyard; plants developing an unusual number of stalks; wild animals playing about in the ancestral temples or palaces; pigs breaking out of the pen and entering residential halls; snakes appearing in the capital; rats dancing at the palace gates or nesting in trees. Diviners also explained physical deformities. People sprouting horns could be a sign of imminent military violence – a rebellion perhaps. Lower limbs growing on the upper part of the body could indicate that low-ranking officials planned to overthrow the ruler at the top. Omens could lead to direct action. For instance, when Emperor Han Xuandi (r. 74–49 BCE) heard of the appearance of spirit birds (birds with auspicious colouring), he issued an edict (in 63 BCE) instructing folk in the metropolitan areas not to remove eggs from nests during the spring and summer, or fire pellets at overflying birds (*Hanshu* 8). Omens were classified and manuals written to teach officials how to interpret them.

Unusual movements in the firmament were equally significant. By the time of the early empires, two theories of the cosmos had gained ground. One, current in the second century BCE, claimed that the heavens, in the shape of a hemispherical canopy or umbrella, rotated about a vertical axis over a flat Earth. The sun, stars and other heavenly bodies moved along the underside of this umbrella (once daily), the highest point of which was the northern pole star. About a century later, a theory prevailed of Heaven as an egg and the Earth as the yolk inside the egg. It was the job of court astronomers to predict the occurrence of significant signs from the heavens. The ability to predict phenomena such as lunar or solar eclipses, or interpret the shape of comets or of haloes around the sun, gave the Son of Heaven power to control and prepare for the consequences of these portents, or to reduce their importance. As the guardian of cosmic harmony, the Son of Heaven had to be seen to understand the structure of the heavens and the subtle and not so subtle patterns in the sky. Equally, it was in his interest to control how these celestial events were interpreted, which is one reason why astronomy, like national weather agencies today, tended to be institutionalized and the preserve of the court.

China had its own share of polymaths and technical masterminds. One such figure was Zhang Heng (78–139 CE), a writer, engineer and inventor as brilliant in mathematics and astronomy (he created an armillary sphere) as he was in poetry and calligraphy. Zhang is known for having made major contributions to cartography, and he is credited with inventing a tool to help predict that other timeless vagary of nature: earthquakes. The surface of Zhang's bronze seismograph was said to be decorated with designs of mountains, turtles, birds and beasts. An earth tremor would register when a bronze ball dropped from a dragon's mouth at the top of the vessel into an object shaped like a toad underneath, the process set off by a pendulum mechanism inside the vessel (see Figure 7.4). Zhang's device has been reconstructed with mixed success. But perhaps more telling is the choice of animals – reptiles and amphibians – on the domed cover and body of the device. Zhang was inspired by the idea that these animals could sense motion and transmit its vibrations, as snakes and toads are known to sense a pending earthquake days in advance.

*

The political significance of natural disasters and crisis management is as pertinent today as it was in the past (a situation not unique to China, of course). The ramifications of
such freaks of nature ripple out into politics, as if Heaven
challenges the harmonious society now and then by driving
a tectonic fissure through it. China's leaders and local officials,
and the People's Liberation Army, need to be seen at the scene
of the disaster, providing relief assistance and moral support. Many viewed the devastating earthquake at the popu-
lous coal-producing city of Tangshan on 28 July 1976 (which
claimed over two hundred and fifty thousand lives) as a portent for the pending death of Mao, who died on 9 September that year. Was it forewarning the end of yet another
dynastic cycle (albeit termed a revolutionary one this time;
Zhou Enlai had died earlier that year)? The great Sichuan
earthquake of 12 May 2008, in which eighty-seven thousand
people were killed or went missing and five million people
were left homeless, showed up both the virtues and short-
comings of those who ruled. It brought government and
voluntary organizations together in an unprecedented and
large-scale response shouldered by many internal stakehold-
ers and supported by external aid. But it also exposed shoddy
building practices, with the collapse of scores of mud-brick
houses and flimsy school buildings being responsible for the
high number of casualties. Some of this was blamed on corrupt local officials and contractors; parents who lost children
were silenced or paid off by local government. Like those
charged with interpreting the freaks of nature at China's imperial court, the authorities spun their own version of cause
and effect. In ancient China, as in most societies today, there

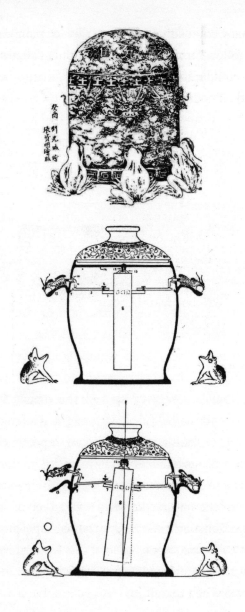

Figure 7.4
Reconstruction of Zhang Heng's seismograph.

were many contending views as to which path was the right one to follow for the governing of human affairs. However, no one could misinterpret the signs in nature when rulers swerved off course:

> According to tradition, in a state that is without the Dao there will be whirlwinds and pestilence; torrential rains will break down the trees. *Yin* and *yang* will emit a wayward atmosphere; summer will be cold and winter warm; things will be ripe in spring and grow in autumn; the sun and moon will have no brightness; stars and constellations will go astray; the people will suffer from many diseases; the state will endure many inauspicious events; humans will not live out their natural span and the five grains will not ripen. (*Han shi waizhuan* 2.30)

Environment

The idea that nature (i.e. Chinese Heaven) speaks and behaves in response to the politics of human behaviour sounds contemporary. Human–nature resonance – holism or the idea that everything is one – is a theme echoed in environmental ethics, where the interconnectedness of human activity and the fate of the natural world is highlighted as a matter of principle. For some time now, sustainable development and care for the environment have been the new Latin for governments of all colours in both East and West. It is perhaps no surprise then that, in recent years, some have turned to China's masters of philosophy to point out that environmental consciousness is deeply rooted in Chinese thought and its past traditions. The argument is that China's philosophical and religious traditions offer a more desirable framework for the relationship between humans and the environment as they insist on the 'Unity between Heaven and Man' (*Tian ren he yi*) and offer an alternative to the domination of nature by humankind. Indeed, they show that man is not omnipotent. Yu the Great 'diverted the Yangzi and cleared the Yellow River in order to bring great benefit to the world, but he could not get the water to flow westward' (*Huainanzi* 9.17).

In a book entitled *Mao's War Against Nature* (2001), the historian and environmentalist Judith Shapiro offered a fascinating and challenging hypothesis, namely that the abuse of people and the abuse of nature are often interrelated. When it comes to benevolent attitudes towards nature, however, environmentalists are perhaps too quick to rush to China's harmony-loving philosophical past to find a nemesis for the story of environmental devastation that took place in China throughout the twentieth century. The ambition of humankind to conquer nature belongs to all times and places, and is certainly not unique to socialist China. It is hard to see how, with power residing in the hands of a monarch, nature would always fare well, as there is always the risk of disproportionate usage. *The Master Huainan* puts it eloquently: 'When the ruler wants a plank, his ministers cut down a tree; when the ruler wants a fish, his ministers dry up a valley' (*Huainanzi* 16.51). On the other hand, were a monarch or one-party state to make sustainable development and environmental protection their top priority, they could, in theory at least, be more efficient at achieving it than drawn-out democratic consensus allows for.

The language of ancient China's philosophers was no less

violent than that of Mao where the conquest of nature was concerned: both trees and political opponents were 'attacked' (classical Chinese uses the same verb). A lack of harmony plays an equally important part in China's story of nature. Dynastic histories report natural disasters in meticulous detail; the interpretation of what constitutes a disaster, then as now, was no doubt prone to political pressure. Not coincidentally, there appears to be a relationship between disaster frequency and political stability. Likewise, large-scale construction projects that have left a lasting imprint on China's landscape are not necessarily a product of modern times. Extending over more than a thousand miles, the series of waterways known as the Grand Canal was no less ambitious in scale in its time, for instance, than the Three Gorges Dam of today. Constructed during the Sui and early Tang periods, the Grand Canal became the economic artery linking the fertile Yellow River floodplain to the agricultural heartlands of the central plain and the southern Jiangnan region.

There can be no doubt that harmony with and respect for the natural world was one of the strands in traditional Chinese philosophy. Yet, to what extent these moralizing theories reflected actual behaviour remains open to debate. Let us not forget that most of our authors prescribe how the world *should* be rather than account for how things are. One could even take the opposite view and argue that the more philosophers emphasize the harmony between man and nature, the more this should be taken as a sign that, in reality, nobody cared. Then again, to denigrate philosophers merely as orators or moralists who profess the opposite of what reality represented might be a step too far. It is quite clear that sustainable usage and human–nature resonance were important themes in Chinese thought. This is evident both in accounts of how nature can be exploited for the benefit of humans, and in those that advocate moderate usage and the proper timing of human activity. In the end, exploitation and conservation are complementary opposites – they are *yin* and *yang*.

Intentional conservation, as a concept, is not exclusively modern or Western. Critical comments on the appropriate use of natural resources appear regularly in Chinese philosophical discourse (as well as in ritual calendars) by the third century BCE. The following example by Xunzi, introduced as 'the regulations of a sage-king', illustrates the general gist of these narratives, which revolve mostly around the timing of human activity:

> In the season when grasses and trees are in the splendour of their flowering and sprouting new leaves, axes and halberds should not be permitted in the mountain forests so as to not end their lives prematurely or to interrupt their maturation. In the season when the giant sea turtles, water lizards, freshwater turtles, loach and eels are depositing their eggs, nets and poisons are not permitted in the marshes so as not to prematurely end their lives or to interrupt their maturation. By ploughing in spring, weeding in summer, harvesting in autumn, and storing up in winter, the four activities are not out of their proper season; thus, the production of the five grains is not interrupted, and the hundred clans [i.e. all people] have more than enough to eat. The ponds, lakes, pools, streams and marshes being strictly

closed during the proper season is the reason that fish and
turtles are in plentiful abundance and the hundred clans
have surplus for other uses. The cutting and pruning, the
growing and planting, not being out of their proper season
is the reason the mountain forests are not denuded and the
hundred clans have more than enough timber. (*Xunzi* 9.16b).

It is likely that some of this guidance was put into practice, as
similar prohibitions appear in the legal codes of the Qin and
Han periods (including a ban on damming rivers and waters
with wood and rocks and catching fish with poisonous bait
or by stunning them). Although the primary purpose of these
rules was to optimize agricultural output and maximize returns
from hunting and foraging, these regulations can nevertheless
be considered early examples of environmental law as they
reveal the intent to conserve. Another goal behind them was
to protect the farming season: once people are tempted by
the natural riches of the forests and rivers, they might abandon the fields, which is where the state needs their labour. So
the underlying motives for conservation are utilitarian: safe-
guarding nature's plenty. The exploitation of natural resources could be curbed by banning entry to certain mountains and
forests. *The Master Guan*, for instance, recommends that hills
rich in ore be declared forbidden territory: 'Anyone moving
the markers indicating that the mountain has been sealed off
should be sentenced to death with no pardon. Those violating these orders by placing their left foot inside the boundary
should have their left foot cut off. If it is the right foot, the
right foot should be cut off' (*Guanzi* 77). Another trick was to
declare an area as holy or sacred and make access to it taboo.

For well-to-do literati or officials, nature offered a place of refuge, where they could find solitude and enjoy reflection. To most ordinary people, however, China's wilds – territory untouched by farming – were not a Daoist dreamland. Nature was linked to the treasury. It was the private property of those in power, land that could be commodified and exploited by the privileged few. It provided goods and wealth, and, as in Europe, entertainment for the powerful and well-off. For the philosophers, hunting was about character building and self-cultivation, not nutrition: 'The worthy man does not avoid hunting, riding fast, using hunting dogs and shooting stringed arrows; but in doing these things, he regularly improves his ability to think, whereas an incompetent ruler regularly becomes more muddled by doing them' (*Lüshi chunqiu* 24/6.2). As in other aspects of life, people of talent hold on to the mean and avoid extremes when engaging with nature, including bird catching: 'If the netter of wildfowl casts his net in a place where there are no birds, he may cast all day long and capture nothing. If he casts his net in a place where birds are too numerous, then he will flush the whole flock. He must cast in an area between where the birds are numerous and where there are none; then he will take wildfowl' (*Zhanguo ce*, Zhou 33).

We end with fish. In the late first century BCE, a grand secretary at the Han court reported that, in the past, in Donglai commandery (an administrative unit located near the coast in Shandong) fish would refuse to show themselves whenever additional duties had been placed on seafood. Its village elders claimed that ever since the emperor had imposed a government monopoly on sea produce, the fish had remained hidden, deep in the sea. Later, however, when permission for free fishing was granted again, the fish resurfaced, ready to be caught (*Hanshu* 24B). The lesson: a good sovereign shares nature's treasure with his people.

It is easy to dismiss such stories as moralizing fiction. However, concealed within them is an acknowledgement that when human actions impact upon the environment, the natural world itself will be the first to let us know. When societies use moralizing and figurative language to describe nature, it is tempting to treat this as fable or allegory, or deny that it conveys valuable information. Yet, while ancient civilizations do not speak the language of modern conservation science, they nevertheless developed sophisticated institutions and procedures to manage the natural resources around them. In the case of China, moralizing jargon, metaphors and analogies simply *were* the language through which Chinese thinkers explained nature. Whether a philosopher looks at bamboo as bamboo, or examines jade as a mere rock, or speaks about natural objects as a symbol for something else, is of secondary importance if one focuses on the actual information that is imparted. Even scientists can take advantage of the fact that 'animals are good to think with', as the French anthropologist Claude Lévi-Strauss once put it.

Science or sentiment

If the above makes you wonder whether no thinker in early China was of an Aristotelian turn of mind and set out to monitor, study and test the workings of nature, then you need to think again. Without observing the flow of water, there can be no water works; without an eye for the seasonal changes in vegetation, no fields would be tilled; without careful scrutiny of the heavens, the Chinese would not have left us with sophisticated writings on astronomy and mathematics. Correlative thinking, exploring the resonances between human and non-human organisms, linking the patterns of nature and the skies to the understanding of what happens on Earth – all these can be said to be proto-scientific attempts at explaining the world.

But it was not until the mid twentieth century that scholars in the West started to think seriously about China's contributions to the development of science, medicine and technology. The Cambridge biochemist, sinologist and historian of science Joseph Needham (1900–1995) galvanized this entire field by asking one searching question: why did China not produce modern science, despite its great advances in applying knowledge of nature to human needs between the first century BCE and the fifteenth century CE – from medicine, biology, engineering and printing to gunpowder, ceramics and hydraulics? To quote Needham himself: 'What were the inhibiting factors in Chinese civilisation which prevented a rise of modern science in Asia analogous to that which took place in Europe from the sixteenth century onwards, and which proved one of the basic factors in the moulding of the modern world order?' For a while the so-called Needham question (or problem or paradox) became one of the most cited intellectual puzzles among China historians. To tackle it, Needham wrote and commissioned a monumental and still ongoing series known as *Science and Civilisation in China*. It has become a classic, not least in China.

The greatest minds stand out because of the questions they pose, rather than the answers they give. There are no easy answers to the Needham question. Needham and his collaborators have hinted that the combination of Confucianism, with its emphasis on social ethics, together with hierarchical and highly centralized bureaucratic institutions, are what impeded the development of science in China. Confucianism exerted a paralysing influence akin to that of medieval theology in pre-Enlightenment Europe. China invented things, but it did not experience an industrial revolution. Its political isolation during the Qing dynasty and lack of internal intellectual and technological competition failed to incite the development of abstract thinking. Others have argued that the Needham question itself is very much a product of the twentieth century, formulated at a time when historians were mostly interested in examining China's failures to modernize at a speed dictated by the West. It is doubtful whether the Needham question will survive into the twenty-second century given the current pace of development in China. That is: *if* China manages to retain and recruit the highly trained new generations of scientists and engineers of the post-Needham era; and *if* it is able to foster institutions and an intellectual sphere in which scientific inquiry can thrive – both remain big ifs in the eyes of some observers.

Had he been around today, critical minds such as that of the Han philosopher Wang Chong (first century CE) would certainly rank among the new cohort of fact-finding intellectuals. Poor, self-taught and a prodigy in his youth (he allegedly memorized in a single reading books he could not afford at the market stalls), Wang has been labelled China's first sceptic or rationalist. His *Discourses in the Balance* (*Lunheng*), preserved in more than eighty chapters, deals with almost any subject he could think of: history, philosophy, politics, literature, folklore and natural science. At first Wang appears as an arch-contrarian who wants to pick an argument with everyone and about everything. So he takes a swipe at Confucius and Han Fei, at the golden age of the ancients, and all those who fear ghosts and demons or believe in immortality. In doing so, and in contrast to his contemporaries, Wang builds up his arguments in a methodological way, and calls for empirical proof to back up assertions. In his unrelenting eagerness to overturn the views of others, though, he does not always appear consistent to the modern reader, and sometimes contradicts himself or argues in circles. Nevertheless, his style was revolutionary for the time.

Wang dismissed the widely held view that events in nature – such as thunder and lightning, or the freakish and weird creatures discussed above – should be taken as warnings from Heaven (nature) in response to human transgression. Most of what happens in nature and the human world Wang attributes to the movement of various forms and flows of *qi*. Nature operates spontaneously and does not need a steer from Heaven. Wang does not accept that Heaven has a will (out goes the moral 'action–reaction' universe) or that what happens to us is predetermined by Heaven or supramundane forces. Nevertheless, he strongly believes that there are various forms of destiny (*ming*) out there and that, however hard you try to influence your individual fortune, or that of the state, the outcome will depend on fate and whether yours is a favourable, adverse or neutral lot. How you fare and how you react to events is fixed by the *qi* you have from birth. A doctor can read your destiny from the structure of your bones. Our lifespan is determined from birth and when we die our 'five organs' simply rot and decay (*Lunheng* 62).

Thus, Heaven, according to Wang at least, takes no action. It has neither mouth nor eyes (*Lunheng* 54). If strange things happen in the world, we should just accept that these are merely the changes and transformations of the fluids and vapours that are inherent in it. Thus one should not fear the sight of a dragon or other freaks of nature. Such transformations will also pass:

> Sometimes, in times of universal peace and when the *qi* is in harmony, a hornless river-deer may turn into a unicorn and a snow-goose into a phoenix. This surely is just the nature of their *qi*; they transform and change with the seasons. Why should there be a species that remains permanent? (*Lunheng* 50)

CHAPTER 8

Work and Wealth

In the eighteenth century, the French court physician and economist François Quesnay (1694–1774) and his followers argued that economic power should derive, first and foremost, from agriculture. The physiocrats, as they were known (from the Greek for 'nature', *phusis*, and 'power', *kratos*), believed that economies must draw on the natural order. They saw land as the primary form of wealth. Societies prosper when goods and produce flow freely and are distributed widely, like the circulation of blood in the body. The state should not intervene or do so only minimally, its task being to limit any impediments to the agricultural base of society. Thus physiocrats opposed mercantilist theories that favoured protectionism through state regulation of trade.

Quesnay was a sinophile; he adored China, as did many others at the court of Versailles at the time. In his *Le Despotisme de la Chine* (1767) he admired the Chinese for making farming the predominant mode of production. China, he alleged, had taught its people the natural law of economy since antiquity. The physiocratic motto, '*Laissez faire et laissez passer*' ('Let be and let pass'), closely echoed the Chinese concept of *wu wei*, 'non-interference' (the 'doing nothing' discussed in Chapter 3). To be sure, accounts of Chinese thought circulating in eighteenth-century Europe were selective, part imagined, part *chinoiserie*. Confucius probably never thought of himself as an economist. Nevertheless, China's masters of philosophy reflected at some length on how to create wealth, and what professions or labour force were most valuable to society. How should a ruler handle people's natural tendency for profit seeking and greed – wherein lie the virtues of altruism and charity? When is a gift no longer a gift but a bribe – how can a person benefit society while also benefiting from it?

Farmers first?

The philosophical origins of liberalism, the free market and free trade are not to be found in ancient China. Yet the fate of agriculture and its relationship with commerce have provided an enduring topic of debate in Chinese political thought. Those who ruled often claimed that the distinction between the productive and non-productive classes in society coincided with that between farmers and merchants, agriculture and trade. Nearly every emperor who ruled China during its first two centuries of empire publicly declared that farming, and the peasant, are 'the root of All under Heaven'. The First Emperor had the principle enshrined in one of his mountain inscriptions: 'The merits of the August Emperor lie in being diligently devoted to basic affairs, promoting agriculture and eradicating the branch occupations, so that the black-haired people [a name for the people of Qin] will be rich' (*Shiji* 6). Another tenet held that the good ruler should keep the professions (the so-called 'four professions': scholars, farmers, artisans and merchants) strictly separated so that they would not interfere with each other's productivity.

This tension between agriculture and commerce would persist throughout Chinese history and still exists today. It can be seen, for example, in the conflicting models of agrarian self-sufficiency (the ability to feed one's own people) versus a surplus-producing economy reliant on trade, commerce and foreign investment; in the fate of rural versus urban economies and their populations; in the issue of rural migration and pressures on China's labour force; or in phenomena such as the outsourcing of food production outside Chinese territory. The slogan that agriculture is the root of Chinese society continues to be sounded today and rural reforms remain a government priority. The so-called Three Rural Issues policy, launched by former president Hu Jintao, aimed to intensify agriculture, improve the plight of farmers and advance the welfare of rural areas.

The enduring image of the servile Chinese peasant, the small family farm and the peasant mode of production can be traced back to feudal times. During the Spring and Autumn period (770–481 BCE), an armed nobility resided in walled capitals and lived off a hinterland of toiling farmers; the countryside where tenant farmers eked out a living (also called 'the wilds') surrounded and supported these city states. As the post-Bronze Age economy grew more complex, some statesmen and philosophers praised farming as the pinnacle of economic endeavour while brushing aside commerce with lofty disdain. The argument was that farmers produce to sustain life, whereas merchants speculate on transactions and seek profit at all cost. Scholars and farmers are the brains and sweat of a morally productive society. Peasants are tied to the land and are easily registered and taxed. By contrast, merchants move around, escape state control, evade tax and do not depend on landownership. Lord Shang and the early Legalists were most radical in this respect. They favoured forced registration of merchants so that they could be taxed out of existence. Lord Shang also opposed the monetary economy: 'When grain is born, gold is dead; when gold is born, grain is dead' (*Shangjun shu* 4.9). The Legalist ruler therefore must do everything possible to promote agriculture and make life miserable for the merchants:

> Do not allow merchants to buy grain nor farmers to sell grain. If farmers cannot sell their grain, then the lazy and inactive ones among them will exert themselves and be energetic. If merchants cannot buy grain, then they have no particular joy over abundant harvests. Having no special joy about bumper harvests, they do not make copious profit in years of famine, and making no copious profit, merchants get to be fearful. Being fearful, they will wish to farm.
> (*Shangjun shu* 2.5)

In reality, however, anti-mercantile language in ancient China often appeared rhetorical rather than grounded in economic reasoning or reality. The masters of philosophy had split views on whether one should promote farming or commerce. Although Confucius does not personally put his hands to the plough, he is quite clear that feeding the people and ensuring material comfort is essential for the state's welfare: it is the task of every ruler or government. Yet the Confucian gentleman also prefers to leave hard physical labour to others: 'A gentleman devotes his mind to the Way and not to securing food. When you till the land, ending up hungry could be a matter of course; when you study, ending up with an offi-cial salary could be a matter of course. The gentleman wor-ries about the Way, not about poverty' (*An.* 15.32). Elsewhere, Confucius insists that agriculture and horticulture are the business of the petty person (*An.* 13.4). So while food pro-duction is deemed essential, the most secure way to a salary and social status is to become an official. The good Confu-cian prefers to orchestrate farm labour rather than have to dig the fields in person.

One group of thinkers, known as the Agriculturalists or School of Tillers, idealized farming to the extreme. Although they have left no significant writings, their ideas appear in debates that survive in other texts. The Tillers were a utopian community of hermits devoted exclusively to agriculture under the patronage of the Divine Farmer (Shennong), the god of agriculture. In Chinese legend, the Divine Farmer is associ-ated with the original stages of civilization, a time when the world had not yet been spoiled by violence and human ac-tivity. He is the legendary inventor of agriculture, having introduced cereal crops and crop fertility to the world. Divine Farmer also identified edible foods for the people by tasting wild plants on their behalf, poisoning himself in a good cause multiple times a day. He lives on in statues and monuments in present-day China. The Tillers envisaged a world of small, self-sufficient communities in which everyone worked the land, and where political institutions, ministers or officials would not be needed. The ruler's only task was to teach agri-culture to the people, monitor land and resources, and ensure that nothing stood in the way of working the fields.

Mencius has no patience for this utopian dream where

Figure 8.1
Divine Farmer (Shennong).
Ink rubbing, Wuliang
family shrine, Shandong;
2nd century CE.

everyone in society lives off the produce from their garden or allotment. In a heated exchange with Xu Xing (*fl. c.*315 BCE), a follower of the Tillers, he slams the ideal of the autarkic (entirely self-sufficient) community, on the grounds that it is an impediment to wealth creation: 'If each person had to make everything he needed for his own use, the world would be full of people chasing after one another on the roads.' Society needs market mechanisms, Mencius argues, since it is in the nature of things to be unequal: 'If fine shoes and poor shoes were priced the same, who would make fine shoes?' This also means rulers should uphold a proper division of labour so that each member of society flourishes to the best of his or her talents: 'Some labour with their minds, others labour with their physical strength. Those who labour with

their minds govern others; those who labour with their physical strength are governed by others' (*Mencius* 3A.4). Thus
farmers may come first as long as the sages do not have to
farm and can apply their talents elsewhere. Xunzi concurs that
a division of labour is necessary. Only when everyone sticks to
their job according to their skills will enough wealth be created to be shared by everyone (*Xunzi* 9.15, 10.7).

But that involves controlling the occupations and movements of people, and ensuring that the peasant does not leave
his fields to become a shopkeeper or trader. In some texts
from the Warring States period, the professions are ranked
in order of importance: artisans and merchants are inferior,
while office-holding scholars are the highest-ranking, followed
by food-producing farmers. Ideologically, at least, merchants
were ranked lowest. However, the fact that it required a theory
to separate the professions and emphasize that peasants
should come first implies that, in all likelihood, many were
multitasking, tempted away from the fields by the prospect
of more lucrative commerce. At any rate, the ideological bias
against merchants did not prevent China from developing into
one of the most mercantile-minded societies in global history.

Han Feizi advises that a good ruler should maintain a
balance between the professions. Since commerce is a faster
way to attaining greater wealth, and therefore the power to
purchase office and influence, government should restrict
the number of traders and talk down their reputation. Then
people will concentrate on 'root tasks' (agriculture and manu-
facture), and the ruler can urge them away from 'branch occupations' (buying and selling) (*Han Feizi* 49). This is a brilliant
move in political spin: since it is hard to knock traders as

a vital component in the economy, the ruler should tarnish their moral reputation but keep them in the job (Han Fei ranks merchants among 'five types of vermin' in society). Today, Han Fei might argue that bankers are needed but that their numbers should be controlled and their profession not glorified, lest more are tempted into their ranks and nobody produces anything any more. The aim is to prevent an escalation of people aspiring to (purchase) office through alternative forms of private wealth. Thus presidents and prime ministers should have a feel for the soil rather than the stock market, not because commerce is unimportant, but because, socially, it is more divisive than farming. Commerce creates greater wealth inequality and draws attention away from farming and the productive industries.

Public perception therefore required the Chinese ruler to support the peasant and avoid being seen to patronize markets or condone the proliferation of merchants. In an annual state ritual, he put his hands to the plough during a ploughing ceremony on designated sacred fields. In Han times, the Eastern and Western Market in the capital Chang'an were located in the north-western part of the city. Public access was restricted to three out of nine city gates to ensure that merchants and their entourage were kept well away from the imperial palaces. Not by accident, the first public anti-mercantile turn in Chinese history recorded in official sources coincided with the establishment of empire, when the Han emperors desperately sought to control the power of merchants and monopolize revenue (from salt and iron, among other things) in the hands of the state. Merchants were forbidden to show off their wealth by wearing silk or travelling on horseback. They (and their descendants) were not permitted to become officials, and they paid much heavier taxes. Given where China finds itself today, it is perhaps ironic that its first laws on trade were meant to discriminate against merchants.

The Chinese peasant was thus more than just an economic pawn in society. He represented a political philosophy and an ideal within human psychology. Unblemished by the lure of commerce, the peasant was pure, honest and simple. He was an uncarved block, totally dedicated to hard labour, and untouched by education and intellectual pursuits that might give him alternative ideas. Working the land shaped human character, in line with the expectations of the ruler. The farmer knows his place; he has simplicity of mind, is psychologically unadventurous and will not question authority: 'When people engage in agriculture, they are simple, and when they are simple, they are at peace in their dwellings and hate going elsewhere' (*Shangjun shu* 6.8). Governing, too, should be like farming, according to a statesman from the sixth century BCE: one should be dedicated to it day and night and know one's boundaries, like a farmer who rarely oversteps

Figure 8.2
Working the fields.
Drawing based on an ink rubbing; Sichuan, Eastern Han.

the ridges between the fields (*Zuozhuan*, Lord Xiang 25). One of the greatest fears of those who ruled China, in both pre-modern and modern times, has been the prospect of a vagrant population of malcontent farmers, abandoning the fields and roaming the countryside and entering the cities to find work or to revolt. The state therefore had good reason to keep farmers in the fields, other than to produce food. Farming allowed governments to organize and control human labour and populations; farming stood for a stable society:

> Of the methods used by the sage-kings of antiquity to guide their people, the first in importance was devotion to farming. People were made to farm not only so that the earth would yield benefits, but also to ennoble their goals. When people farm, they remain simple; being simple they are easy to deploy. [People] being easy to deploy, the borders are secure, and the position of the ruler is honoured. When people farm they are serious and they rarely hold personal moral beliefs. When they seldom hold personal moral beliefs, then the law common to everyone is firmly established and all efforts are united. When the people farm, household income increases, and when income increases, they are reluctant to move away; they will spend their whole life in their home villages and will not consider any other occupations. (*Lüshi chunqiu* 26/3.1)

Wealth and profit

As long as rulers are able to maintain control over those who prove enterprising, and manage to siphon off (or monopolize) a good share of the revenue that such individuals generate, they are not inclined to impose taboos on wealth creation. The philosophers, however, looked at wealth and profit through a more 'ethical' lens. All Chinese thinkers, regardless of their intellectual allegiance, highlighted that wealth has the potential to corrupt. Wealth requires management. Like 'bolts of cloth and silk that have proper measurements, dimensions are set up for them so that there will be no deviations'. Society needs a value system to keep profit-making within proper bounds, so that there is neither want nor excess (*Zuozhuan*, Lord Xiang 28). Yet profit and prosperity encompassed many meanings, ranging from purely material welfare to good health and well-being.

Generally Confucian thinkers do not condemn the accumulation of wealth. Confucianism is a philosophy that is acquisition-oriented: in order to better oneself, one should acquire skills and new means, rather than relinquish one's potential or shed possessions. They acknowledge that seeking material reward is part of human nature, but qualify this with a strong caveat: wealth should never be acquired by immoral means. Confucius expresses this sentiment in several passages in the *Analects*: 'Wealth and position gained through improper means are no more to me than the floating clouds' (*An.* 7.16). In the end, one should judge people not by how much wealth they generate but by how they do it, and what they use it for: 'Wealth and honour is what people want but if they are obtained by deviating from the Way, I will have no part in them' (*An.* 4.5).

When taking on a job, therefore, the moral integrity with which a task is seen through should always be more important than salary (*An.* 15.38). Confucius understands that pursuing wealth can motivate people, yet to him personally it is a distraction: 'If wealth were an acceptable goal I would pursue it, even if that meant serving as an officer holding a whip at the entrance of the marketplace. But if it is not acceptable, I prefer to follow what I love' (*An*.7.12). Ultimately, the pursuit of personal profit can cause much resentment among others (*An*. 4.12). Confucius seems reluctant to speak publicly about profit (*An*. 9.1). It is as if the laws of economics are a necessary irritant to him: they are indispensable to basic welfare but do not always match the standards of moral decency demanded in public life. Within the context of the family and its lineage, values such as reciprocity and charity prevail. Yet this community-based moral economy is constantly challenged by the market economy, where the gift is substituted by a sale or purchase, and reciprocity turns into a competition for profit. Given the choice, the gentleman would rather take time to consider the moral implications of his actions; a petty person, by contrast, understands only profit and personal advantage (*An*. 4.16).

So while the Confucian does not resist money-making, he is looking for a moral justification for doing so. Occupying the moral high ground, however, does not mean neglecting one's own material well-being. Confucius praises his own disciple Zigong for not accepting his lot and trying to better himself by making money (*An*. 11.19). The key lies in sharing and circulating wealth: 'The gentleman helps out the needy; he does not make the rich richer' (*An*. 6.4). Confucius therefore condemns the accumulation of unused wealth. When Zigong asks whether he should store away an exquisite piece of jade or sell it for a good price, Confucius replies: 'Sell it, of course

I would sell it. All I am waiting for is the right price' (*An.* 9.13). Talent and virtue (the jade in all of us) is there to be put to good use when the time is right.

Mozi is mocked in *The Master Zhuang* for turning self-misery into a virtue, 'wearing furs and clothes made of hemp, and putting on wooden clogs and grass sandals' (*Zhuangzi* 33.2). Although some stories suggest that some of Mozi's followers deprived themselves to an extreme degree, there is no suggestion in *The Master Mo* that this should be a preferred course of action. Mozi acknowledges the need for material comfort as long as it is not extravagant. The ancient sage-kings are praised, not because they lived like savages in the woods, but because their functional lodgings could withstand the climate, unadorned and without unnecessary luxuries (*Mozi* 21.7). While the ancients did not starve themselves, they eschewed culinary delicacies or exotic ingredients (*Mozi* 21.3).

The core doctrine of Mozi is that we should judge our actions on the basis of whether they benefit others. Everything we do must generate certain benefit. Unlike Confucius, Mozi is less concerned with the ethics of decency; he takes a utilitarian view. If something is beneficial to society, you should do it. If no tangible advantages follow from your actions, refrain from embarking upon them altogether. This does not entail being averse to material rewards. To enrich the state, one should promote the worthy, 'enrich them, ennoble them, respect them, and praise them' (*Mozi* 8.3). The determining factor, however, is that wealth generation has an altruistic dimension and is not motivated by self-interest. Successful people must be judged by how well they benefit others first. What is good for the family will benefit the state and,

ultimately, the entire world (*Mozi* 13.6). Personal gain resulting from this is acceptable provided it is not the primary motivation. It is the duty of the elite to provide for the welfare of
the masses, not by incessantly creating more wealth, but by
distributing it widely and encouraging thrift.

The pursuit of wealth through means other than farming is
regarded positively by Mencius, as long as it is shared wealth
(*Mencius* 1B.4). The aim should be to provide the people with
a 'constant livelihood' that will give them 'constant minds' –
that is, a steady heart and freedom from anxiety (*Mencius*
3A.3). Again, Mencius does not call into question wealth creation as such but wishes to clarify the intentions behind it.
Once a sense of rightness becomes secondary to the urge for
profit, people will stop at nothing to grab whatever they can
(*Mencius* 1A.1). Mencius is a market optimist. Taxation is not
so much an attack on the nature of commerce or an attempt
to annihilate merchants, but, rather, a way to restore balance
in society (*Mencius* 1B.5).

Mencius also points out that gifts can be part of normal
social protocol, provided that the circumstances merit an exchange of gifts. To accept a gift when the occasion does not
justify it is to give in to bribery, and a gentleman should never
allow himself to be bribed (*Mencius* 2B.3). Mencius argues
that social interchange and friendship should always be
driven by respect, however. Declining a gift can be considered
disrespectful. On what basis, then, can one accept a gift? Here
Mencius defines 'giving' in a way which, in a modern reading, could amount to a bribe: you judge a gift not by its origins but by your association with the person who gives it to
you. If the giver is an esteemed individual, you should accept

a gift without questioning whether that person acquired it by proper means. If you know a gift is tainted, can you make up an excuse to refuse it? Well, Mencius notes, if your relationship with this person follows the Way, and if the gift is offered according to ritual propriety, you may accept it, as indeed Confucius would have done (*Mencius* 5B.4). Impersonal gifts therefore are unworthy gifts. Unlike in a market economy where people enter into a relationship for the sake of a commodity, in the gift economy commodities are exchanged in order to forge or reaffirm social relationships. This can lead to conflicts of interest, as the example given by Mencius suggests. Yet the gift exchange is often considered morally superior as market transactions can threaten or undermine social networks created through the ritual economy. For instance, charging the elderly for their upkeep in old age may appear to make economic sense (they tend to have assets), yet the ethics of filial piety would make this unacceptable as it is the obligation of younger family members to provide for the elderly.

Xunzi, too, condemns personal profit at the expense of rightness and moral duty as 'utterly malicious' (*Xunzi* 2.3). The gentleman should show restraint in the pursuit of profit (*Xunzi* 2.13), and important matters of policy should be guided by the principle that a ruler 'places moral duty first and only then considers profit' (*Xunzi* 11.2c). Yet Xunzi also takes issue with Mohist frugality. Frugality merely leads to poverty. If Mozi had his way, 'all clothing would be coarse and gross and all food would be bad and detestable, with only hardship and grief when music and joy have been condemned' (*Xunzi* 10.8). While one should be moderate in one's consumption and the use of resources, people must be encouraged to make a rich and generous living: poor farmers would otherwise have fields that are unproductive and overgrown with weeds (*Xunzi* 10.2). Therefore, when assigning people a task, they should be paid a living wage. The way to generate surplus is to allow people to do well for themselves and then skim off the extra revenue through levies and taxes applied according to social status, the law and ritual principles.

When China's masters of philosophy discuss profit (Chinese *li*), they make clear that it is a concept far more complex than simple self-interest. Profit or benefit has a dual nature: it can be positive and negative, altruistic and egoistic. Our actions can benefit others (they profit from our efforts), yet, equally, we also benefit from others (we gain advantage from being associated with someone and benefit from the actions of others). Confucians would argue that an awareness of both dimensions of profit is important to avoid profiteering or other abuse. In the first instance, the orientation should be towards others and sharing out the wealth one generates. Good rulership is 'taking "benefiting without deriving benefit" as one's standard' (*Lüshi chunqiu* 20/1.2). But by doing this, you will reap rewards and will be able to cement your own position – a well-fed population is less inclined to question those in authority. To obtain material rewards, altruism must come before self-centredness.

Government, therefore, should always be involved to some extent where the creation and distribution of wealth are concerned, even if that involvement is not overt. The good ruler controls the circumstances in which wealth is generated and ensures that his people are content. As *The Master Guan* suggests, 'he is like a bird hatching an egg: there is neither shape nor sound but the young suddenly appear, quite complete' (*Guanzi* 53). Yet markets and ministers should not meet. The court should never become a venue for merchants and traders, or there will always be a risk that goods and wealth 'flow upwards' in the form of bribes and corruption; or that official titles and rank will 'flow downwards' as favouritism (*Guanzi* 3, 4). Ultimately, shared benefits are better for all: 'If you share your profits with All under Heaven, it will support you; if you monopolize the profits in All under Heaven, it will scheme against you' (*Guanzi* 66).

Unless, of course, you take a Daoist approach to it all. Zhuangzi advises that an obsession with wealth disconnects us from the world, and merely creates another prop to cling on to: 'He who considers wealth to be the right thing will not be able to part with his earnings' (*Zhuangzi* 14.5). The rich 'embitter themselves through frantic work'. By accumulating more wealth than they can possibly use or consume, they think they are doing all this to comfort their own body but, in fact, they alienate it (*Zhuangzi* 18.1). A merchant is no more than a person who has focused his entire will on the expectation of gain. He may look imposing, but people will spot his anxiety (*Zhuangzi* 23.1). The merchant also never gives without attaching strings: 'To give favours to others but to be ever mindful of them is not Heaven's way of conferring. That is why merchants and traders are disregarded by others. Even if, on account of some business, regard is paid to them, the spirit will disregard them' (*Zhuangzi* 32.7). Whatever the philosophical merits of laissez-faire, it is hard to imagine that those entrusted with running an economy would have found much direction in *The Master Zhuang*.

The market

One of the earliest definitions of trade in China occurs in *The Book of Documents*, where the legendary Yu the Great, having controlled the floods and taught people how to hunt, gather and grow food, 'urged them to exchange what they had for what they had not' (*Shangshu*, 'Yi Ji'). The Confucian Classics contain other utopian descriptions of the market. According to one, the Divine Farmer invented the market when, 'at midday, he brought together all people under Heaven and assembled together all goods under Heaven. They exchanged [their goods] and then retired, each obtaining what he wanted' (*Zhouyi*, 'Xici'). Such descriptions present the market as a natural flow of people and goods with everything in perfect balance: surplus evens out shortage so that everyone is self-sufficient; and all actors are in control of the market forces linked to their own produce. In times of economic crisis, calls for a return to the utopian market of natural exchange were sometimes voiced at court. As late as the first century BCE, the moneyless society, an age before coinage and currency encouraged dishonesty and speculation, was proposed to the Han emperor as a solution for some of his economic woes.

Few thinkers, however, believed in the natural market of a utopian past. They were quick to realize that, in reality, there is nothing natural about the market. Mencius recollects the days when markets required only light supervision. He then explains that taxation came about in response to sordid profit-making:

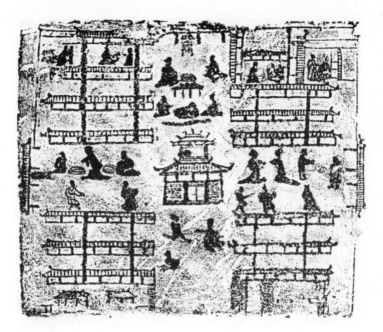

Figure 8.3
Market scene.
Ink rubbing of a Han brick; Pengzhou, Sichuan.

In antiquity, the market was for the exchange of what one had for what one lacked. The authorities merely supervised it. There was, however, one despicable fellow who always looked for a vantage point and, going up on it, gazed into the distance to the left and to the right in order to secure all the profit in the market for himself. The people all thought him despicable and, as a result, they taxed him. The taxing of merchants began with this despicable fellow. (*Mencius* 2B.10)

In an ideal world, the ruler should only have to conduct inspections without having to levy taxes (*Mencius* 2A.5). Yet, in reality, taxation proves indispensable as a moral corrective to prevent hoarding and the accumulation of wealth in the hands of a few.

A real concept of taxation did not emerge in China until around the time of the Warring States and the age of the city state. Taxation was closely linked to military obligation. In the totalitarian state of Lord Shang, all adults were subjected to at least three forms of taxation: conscript labour, military service and a land tax to be paid in grain. Prior to this, status and ritual obligation drove the transaction of goods, land and labour: the ruling classes derived their income through the rights and privileges they held over land and those who worked it. ('I owe you' meant 'I return income from work on landholdings granted temporarily to me by you'). The right to buy and sell plots of land and establish ownership over them emerged around the time of the first empire. Yet owning land in ancient China was not an inalienable right: actual control of a given plot of land, not legal definitions or proprietorial rights, mattered more. Poor farming households – that is, the majority of the working population – relied on the state for loans of tools, draft animals and advances in grain. The Han empire would be well established (around the mid second century BCE) before the rationale for taxation in China began to be fully based on economic grounds. Military obligation was gradually overtaken (but not replaced) by obligations in cash or kind, and wealth and goods were discussed on their own commercial and economic terms. In addition to revenues from agriculture, the Chinese empire's treasury would depend on the court's ability to cream off revenue from trade through state monopolies.

As the commentary to *The Great Learning* remarks,

'accumulating wealth is the way to scatter people (away from the ruler); scattering wealth among them is a way to gather the people (around him)'. Regulating inheritance was another important means of preventing wealth being concentrated in the hands of a few. The principle that a father's estate must be divided equally among his sons was introduced by Lord Shang to break up the hereditary nobility. Although the concept has been interpreted very freely over the centuries, the division of wealth between siblings remained a mainstay of Chinese law throughout imperial times. It was the family's duty to split resources. Given the importance of the family, even today, one might conceive of inheritance tax levied by the state as violating the integrity of the family.

Who regulates the market, and how? *The Master Guan* includes extensive discussions on the issue in a set of chapters that mostly date to the first two centuries of the Han dynasty. The text expresses a range of views, but it offers clear outlines of economic theory and policy. Master Guan gives the ruler vital interventionist responsibilities: he directs the cyclical pattern of storage and circulation of goods by stocking up in good times and distributing in times of shortage. The ruler's role is to ensure a correct balance between production (farming) and commerce (trade). This requires him to intervene to prevent extreme price fluctuations and stabilize the market by storing up grain and hoarding reserves of bronze and gold coin, since 'grain moves to wherever the price is highest just as water flows downhill' (*Guanzi* 74). There is a firm acknowledgement that markets are in a state of constant flux: 'To maintain a proper balance, one must allow prices to go up or down; it is impossible to keep them constantly steady' (*Guanzi* 81). Thus economic policy is presented as managing change and keeping an eye on the invariables that sustain production. *The Master Guan* summarizes it as a process of monitoring the constant shifts between 'what is light and what is heavy', 'cheap or expensive', 'unimportant or important'. In practice this means that those in power should oversee the relationship between money versus goods, supply versus demand, production output versus taxation rates, surplus versus shortfall. In its desire to sustain a rural market economy, the Chinese state has been interventionist since its conception. According to *The Master Guan*, it must patrol fluctuations in the economy with fiscal and monetary policies to ensure that 'wealth issues from a single outlet' – that is, the ruler or state (*Guanzi* 73).

Unlike Mozi's insistence on thrift, *The Master Guan* recommends a good balance between consumption and frugality. Excessive spending is detrimental to the welfare of society, but so is extreme frugality. For the first time in Chinese economic history, in an essay entitled 'Extravagance in Expenditure' (*Guanzi* 35), *The Master Guan* puts forward the idea of increasing public spending in order to stimulate the economy: encouraging consumer desire for luxury goods, lavish temples and costly festivals and funerals can be a good way to provide employment. Indulging the rich therefore is a way to create work for the poor. (This timeless argument is still heard today in bids by developing countries and cities to host mass spectacles such as international sporting events.)

The marketplace in ancient China, like the agora in Greece or forum in Rome, was more than simply a commercial space. Markets were walled and access to them through gates was tightly patrolled. One modern Chinese word for town or city, *chengshi*, may be literally translated as 'walled marketplace'. This facilitated the collection of fees and control of goods but also ensured that trading was visually separated from other activities. The market thus offered an alternative social venue, a place away from both the court and the domestic sphere dominated by the rules of the family and the prying eyes of the ancestors. The market provided a venue for unlikely en-counters, a social space where ideas converged, and one of few public spaces where criminals and honest men operated simultaneously. Markets are zones of inclusion and exclusion, indispensable yet also morally objectionable, socially innova-tive as well as subversive. In the words of one Han chancel-lor: 'If you stir up the markets and empty out the jails, evil men will have no place to stay and will cause you trouble elsewhere' (*Shiji* 54). In imperial China's capitals, urban plan-ning followed cosmology. Markets tended to be located to-wards the north of the city, the direction associated with the dark *yin* energies. Hence the market was where the bodies of executed criminals could be exposed to the public. There were at least two distinct types of trader: those who traded at market stalls where they were registered and paid a toll; and travelling merchants who peddled their goods outside the marketplace along roads and waterways, to the frustra-tion of the tax collector.

The market (which could be held up to three times a day) could be a theatre for bribery and corruption. Unsurprisingly, we find the Confucius figure paraded as a moral influence on the market. Xunzi notes that before the Master took up office as minister of justice in his home state of Lu, sheep and cattle traders would give their animals water to drink on the morning they were to be sold in order to increase their weight; animals intended for sale at market would be groomed to fetch a higher price (*Xunzi* 8.2). Once Confucius was in post, however, prices in the market were no longer artificially inflated; the natural economy, if you remember, requires no laws, simply good behaviour (*Huainanzi* 20.9). Government officials were tasked with collecting levies, clamping down on fraud (rogue traders, counterfeit coins, weights and measures) and overseeing general management of the market (including the disposal of dung and night soil). Night markets, a feature of many Chinese towns today, were the exception as they fell outside the control of the traditional curfews. Calendars suggest that some traders consulted diviners for good luck in business: certain days would be deemed auspicious or inauspicious for 'importing or exporting goods', 'bringing in valuable goods' and 'trading on the market'.

Market supervisors assured the quality of goods and detected fakes and forgeries. Price labels were attached to articles bought or sold at market; cloth had to be sold in the correct widths. The origins of goods had to be certified by engraving or labelling them with the names of the workshop, the artisans and their overseers. Quality-control officials could add their names as a mark of certification. When products fail to meet certain standards, 'the artisan must be punished so as to get to the bottom of the true nature of his deception' (*Lüshi chunqiu* 10/1.5). The laws of Qin and Han suggest that the marketplace was strictly controlled by the authorities. Stalls were laid out along lanes depending on the goods they sold. Hawkers were grouped in teams of five and made mutually responsible for reporting on each other's activities. Those who failed to pay their duties had their goods confiscated by the government. Trademark and trading standards had to be upheld, and accounts had to be correct. Stolen goods were valued at the fair-market price from the time the thief was apprehended, and merchants and traders could be banished for cheating. Ideologically, the market in ancient China does not appear in a wholly favourable light, but as a tightly supervised space where the prospect for profit and gain was constantly overshadowed by the potential for disorder and misdemeanour, and where the lure of greater returns constantly tested principled human behaviour. In many ways, it is an image that still endures. Confucius's reticence to speak publicly about profit-making may well have been grounded in a conviction that there is hardly any market that does not deviate from the Way.

Poverty

Most people dislike poverty and are driven to seek material comfort or wealth. Yet, like wealth, poverty can be interpreted in different ways. One may define it as being deprived of something or being denied access to a resource; alternatively, one can explain poverty as possessing a smaller share of the available wealth, which is how one Han-period dictionary defines the Chinese character for 'poverty' (*pin*). For some Chinese thinkers, to be poor represented an absolute and unacceptable failure on behalf of the individual or society – a self-inflicted condition. Others conceived of poverty in relative terms and saw it as a lesser evil; they argued that it is better to be poor than to lack moral standards.

Confucius acknowledges that poverty is relative and hard to quantify. A ruler of a state or a head of a household should not worry that his people are poor, but that wealth is unevenly distributed. Similarly, it is not the number of subjects in a community that determines its strength, but whether or not they get on with each other. If wealth is equitably distributed, there is no poverty (*An.* 16.1). Just as Confucius refuses to secure honour and wealth by immoral means, poverty too should be remedied only by ethical methods: 'Poverty and disgrace are things that all people hate; yet unless they are avoided following the proper way, I will not discard them' (*An.* 4.5). Given the choice between indulgence and thrift, the latter produces the better person: 'Extravagance leads to immodesty, while frugality leads to scruffiness. Yet it is better to be scruffy than immodest' (*An.* 7.36). So there is pleasure to be found in drinking water and having a modest meal (*An.* 7.16). The virtuous pauper Yan Hui, Confucius's smartest disciple, embodied the idea that there can be dignity in poverty. In the end, neither poverty nor riches should derail a person from the moral path. The gentleman, when poor, still delights in the Way and, when wealthy, will still observe the rites (*An.* 1.15). Confucius refuses to condone poverty; it is a moral shortfall of a ruler who fails to look after his people: 'When the Way prevails in a state, it is a disgrace to remain poor and without rank; in a state where the Way does not prevail, it is a disgrace to be wealthy and of noble rank' (*An.*8.13). Poverty results from political failure and profligate rulers. Sages, by contrast, live modestly.

For Confucians, there can be no moral victory attached to material depravation. Mozi in fact accuses them of aggravating poverty as they overspend on rituals, music and funerals. Mencius notes that hunger and thirst will cloud any ambition of the human mind and stifle good judgement: 'Those who are hungry find any food sweet, while those who are thirsty find any drink sweet' (*Mencius* 7A.27). For the Confucian, lacking material means is less to do with individual hardship than preventing people from performing their social and ritual duties. Without resources, it is harder to be a filial son and support one's parents. If you are unable to feed yourself, how will you feed your ancestors through sacrifices? (One of the most sensitive indicators of abject deprivation in Chinese historiography is the selling, and cannibalism, of children as it subverts both the notion of parental love and the expectation that children sustain their parents in old age.) Yet in the end virtue will trump poverty as the accomplished person does not get worn down by material shortage, even if starting from rags requires more courage: 'To be poor without harbouring grievances is difficult; to be rich without showing arrogance is easy' (*Da Dai Liji*, 'Wu Di de').

Showing charity and compassion was considered a duty and generally supported, although some railed against what they regarded as a corrosive effect on society. *The Master Guan* advises that when a ruler enters a new capital he should show nine forms of compassion: honour the elderly; care for the young; have sympathy for orphans; support the disabled; bring together those who are lonely; inquire after the sick; keep track of the destitute; offer relief to those in distress; and continue sacrifices that were left off (*Guanzi* 54). Yet some objected to this principle. For the Legalists, poverty represents a personal failure resulting from one's own choices and cannot be blamed on the authorities, who cannot prevent people from acting in a certain way, but only reward or punish them retrospectively. It follows, then, that charity can be construed as a means of rewarding those who fall short and do not work, and that poverty relief can be seen as counterproductive. Han Fei takes a firm stance against the idea that one should tax the rich to take care of the poor:

> When the educated classes of today talk about governing, many say, 'One should give land to the poor and destitute in order to compensate for their lack of resources.' Now if there are people who, having the same opportunities as everyone else, are able to keep themselves fully supplied even without the benefits of a good harvest or some additional source of income, it is either because they work hard or because they are frugal. If there are some people who, having the same opportunities as everyone else, still fall into poverty and destitution even without the misfortunes of famine, sickness and natural disasters, it is either because they are wasteful or because they are lazy. Those who are wasteful and lazy become poor, while those who work hard and are frugal become wealthy. Now if a superior imposes taxes on the rich in order to redistribute their wealth among poor households, this is stealing from those who work hard and behave frugally and giving to the wasteful and lazy. If a ruler does this and then expects his people to be industrious in their work and frugal in their expenditures, he will be disappointed.
> (*Han Feizi* 50)

An argument along similar lines was that charity could be used as an excuse or cover-up for a ruler's failure to provide the means for a regular and constant livelihood. To that end, *The Master Huainan* argues that it is better for a government to distribute resources to the people on a regular basis, rather than engage in irregular bouts of charitable giving:

> When a ruler favours charitable giving, he will lack a fixed standard for distributing [resources]. When there is no fixed distribution coming from above, resentment will not cease below. If he increases taxes to fill the storehouses with surplus, the people he is helping will despise him. If he appropriates little and gives much, the quantity of his surplus will not be sufficient. Thus, to be fond of charitable giving is a method that will only give rise to resentment. (*Huainanzi* 14.37)

Despite the rise of the fiscal state and an empire that drew its revenue from taxation, the Chinese understanding of human economic behaviour remained deeply influenced by customs and conventions that originated in the ritual economy. The historian Sima Qian wrote that people do not need to be taught the desire for wealth; it is an integral part of human nature. The various debates in ancient China on the virtues and vices of profit and the material aspects of life create the impression of gradation in the Chinese concept of wealth: the means by which one secured a living were wrapped up in different moral packaging. Sima Qian concludes that there are three types of wealth: 'The most superior form of wealth is that which is based upon agriculture, the next best is that which is derived from secondary occupations, and the worst form of wealth is that which is acquired by evil means' (*Shiji* 129). What he did not mention was that there is a fourth way to think about material wealth: consider it immaterial! That is how the hedonist Yang Zhu described his own lust for life: 'Those who are good at enjoying life are not poor, and those who are good at freeing themselves from care do not get rich' (*Liezi* 7).

CHAPTER 9
Food for Thought

Let us conclude this book with a Chinese meal. At first sight, culinary habits and cuisine seem far removed from the world of philosophy or politics. Few among us will have the Dao on our minds when picking up a Chinese takeaway, or think of sweet as more *yang* than sour – Confucius was a chef of ideas, not a cook. It is no small irony, then, that, for many of us, our first or most frequent encounter with the Chinese world is through its food. Where the brain may be slow in adjusting to new ideas, our palate often does the job for us.

Few cultures put more emphasis on the central role of food preparation and consumption than the Chinese in both a secular and religious context. This fascination with food, past and present, speaks to Chinese sensitivities, and to the Chinese way of life in general: human cultures experience and explain the world by tasting and digesting it (I eat and feed, therefore I am). Chinese thinkers make frequent reference to butchers, cooks and food: there is a Dao that runs through the stomach. Cooking and dining make for an instructive social laboratory. Not only is eating (and drinking) the most recurrent and essential activity of the day, but it is also one of the most ritualized activities we submit ourselves to – we observe table etiquette, and, on most occasions, eat in company with others. In short, food is medicine, pleasure, skill, sustenance, ethics, politics and economics rolled into one. It shapes who we are, or in Mencius's version of 'we are what we eat': 'A person's surroundings transform his *qi* just as the food he eats changes his body' (*Mencius* 7A.36).

The Chinese were, and generally remain, less carnivorous than their European counterparts. A meal consisted chiefly of staples combined with greens, tubers, fruits and, where available, fish. Meat tended to be reserved for elites or consumed on special occasions. Dairy products were not an integral part of the diet. The main staple during the age of the philosophers was grain. As is still the case today, northern and southern diets reflected two distinct agricultural traditions: the dryland cultivation of cereals (millet, barley, wheat) in the north; and wetland rice agriculture in the south. Noodles are first mentioned around the turn of the first century CE but were probably consumed much earlier. We can be reasonably confident that Confucius never drank a bowl of tea since the earliest reliable evidence of tea drinking dates only to medieval times. However, the Master may have caught sight of chopsticks. They began to be commonly used by the late Warring States period, alongside the hands and spoons that had been reaching for the platter for centuries. Han Fei even claims that the last Shang king already used a pair of ivory chopsticks.

The cultural history of Chinese cuisine (of itself fodder for several separate volumes) is too broad a subject to discuss in one short chapter. 'In eating it is best not to fill up; in thinking it is best not to overdo' (*Nei ye* 11.4). The question of interest here is why comments about cooking, diet and

eating were so prevalent in the vocabulary of Chinese statesmen and philosophers. Chinese thinkers discovered in culinary culture a cornucopia of analogies and metaphors that
they could draw from to illustrate their core ideas in a more
or less instantly recognizable way. Cooking offered the perfect image for concepts such as balance, measure, proportion, frugality and harmony. Furthermore, deeply ingrained
in Chinese thought was the notion that persons of authority
(rulers, sages), or those aspiring to ingest and appreciate the
world around them on a profounder level, needed to be carefully catered for because diet not only influences us physically,
it also affects us psychologically and morally, with a profound effect on everything we think and do.

Blending a stew

In an interview in March 2013, China's president Xi Jinping
intimated that a leader should never be slack or careless; he
should work hard, day and night, since 'governing a large
country is like frying a small fish'. Xi was quoting *The Classic of the Way and Virtue* (DDJ 60). In that Daoist classic, the
image is used to suggest that too much meddling with the
state will make it fall apart, like a small fish in a frying pan
that is poked too much. The following year, in a speech delivered at UNESCO headquarters in Paris (on 27 March 2014),
Xi talked about cooking soup to illustrate the idea of 'harmony in diversity' ('Who would eat soup if we used water to
bring flavour to it?'). Here he was alluding to a sixth-century
BCE adviser, Yanzi, who once told his lord, Duke Jing of Qi,
that the art of government can be compared to cooking and
seasoning a well-balanced stew. To soothe the temper and

calm the emotions of the duke, Yanzi advised that he should be nourished with a harmonious mixture of ingredients:

> Harmony may be compared to a stew. You have water, fire, vinegar, mince, salt and plums, with which to cook the fish and the meat. It is brought to the boil by means of firewood. Next the cook blends the ingredients, equalizing the stew by means of seasonings, adding whatever is deficient and carrying off whatever is in excess. Then his lord eats it and thus brings his heart at ease. (*Zuozhuan*, Lord Zhao 20)

In a multipolar world of different nations and traditions, Xi proposed 'supplementing each other with flavourings, drawing on advantages and conscientiously blending in case the flavour is too bland or [too] strong'. In other words, good politics resembles the art of mixing a stew into a harmonious blend so as to 'eliminate contradictions and divergence'.

In availing himself of millennia-old culinary analogies, China's most powerful politician (or his scriptwriter) continued a practice dating back to the dawn of political rhetoric in China. Indeed, in ancient China the art of cooking, also known as 'harmonizing flavours', was regularly linked to ministerial talent. 'Be to me as the yeast and the malt in making sweet spirits; as the salt and the prunes in making a harmonious stew,' Shang king Wu Ding (*c.*1200 BCE) is alleged to have said when inviting instruction from his minister (*Shangshu*, 'Yue ming'). The Legalist thinker Han Fei, too, notes that ministers are like cooks who 'blend the five flavours' to serve to their lord (*Han Feizi* 37).

Cooking provided the perfect metaphor for governance: a cook does with food what a ruler does with his populace. He manipulates individual ingredients for the benefit of a harmonious mixture, just as the monarch guides individuals to blend in with the collective. Mixed together in just the right combination, ingredients are transformed into a blend that is more powerful (flavoursome) than its separate components: no single flavour stands out, yet their right mixture enhances the dish. In Chinese, the word for 'harmony' (*he*) even doubles up as a verb for 'mixing' or 'blending' (*huo*). During the opening ceremony of the 2008 Beijing Olympics, 'harmony' was the Chinese character that was choreographed to appear from movable-type printing blocks during a drum dance performed by actor-singers dressed to represent Confucius's disciples, each waving a bamboo-slip scroll of the *Analects* and chanting quotes from the Master (see Figure 9.1).

Like the cook, the butcher, too, possesses a knack for fairness and balance as he slices meat into even portions. When a future chancellor to the Han court garnered praise for the equitable way in which he shared out meat after a sacrifice, he replied: 'Alas, if only I were the Steward for All under Heaven, I would be [as equitable] as I have been in [distributing] this meat' (*Shiji* 56). From carving meat in a village to a post as prime minister in the capital, 'cutting meat and cutting words is one and the same thing' the philosopher Wang Chong once commented (*Lunheng* 80). In ancient China, the steward or cook, who originally acted as an assistant at banquets, hunts and sacrifices, enjoyed a close bond with his superior. Cooks emerge as confidants and wise counsellors in the ruler's inner circle, like the personal butler or chef who travels everywhere with his rich or famous employer.

Figure 9.1
The Character for 'harmony'.
(Beijing 2008 Olympics Opening Ceremony).

The cook is a powerful figure as he gains access to his master's mind via his stomach. He influences his master's well-being with nutrition that affects both body and mind. (He is also able to poison him!) Only proper nourishment can ensure mental alertness: 'Flavour serves to promote the circulation of *qi*. *Qi* serves to give fullness to the mind, the mind is used to fix words and words are used to issue commands' (*Zuozhuan*, Lord Zhao 9). So the cook is also a physician. The boundaries between food as nutrition and food as medicine were blurred in China. *The Rites of Zhou* refer to an official known as the 'dietary physician' (no specific mention of medicine is made in his job description). He blends ('harmonizes') ingredients for his king and does so according to a seasonal logic:

In general, for the regular preparation of [vegetarian] foodstuffs, he follows the season of spring [that is, he uses seasonal spring produce]; for the preparation of the stew, he follows the season of the summer; for the preparation of sauces, he follows the season of autumn; and for the preparation of drinks, he follows the season of winter. In all cases when he blends [harmonizes], in spring he uses a higher quantity of sour ingredients, in summer bitter, in autumn pungent and in winter more salty. He mixes them with soft and sweet ingredients ... (*Zhouli*, 'Shi yi')

However, having such influence cut both ways: cooking could be a matter of life and death. A master chef too good at the job might end up entombed with his lord to cook for him in the afterlife. Those who got it wrong could end up in their own grave for as little as a slice of undercooked liver or a hair in the soup.

So for those in power it pays not to judge a person only by his words, but by the way he or she cooks. China's most famous cook-turned-minister, Yi Yin (seventeenth century BCE?), gained a post with the founding Shang king because of his cooking ability, not on account of skilful arguments or verbal artistry (though, judging by later accounts, he possessed some of those talents too) (*Han Feizi* 3). What happens in the cooking pot can happen to the world and ourselves, he claimed, if only we succeed in blending life's gifts and challenges into the right mixture: 'The transformations within the cauldron are quintessential, marvellous, refined and delicate. The mouth cannot express this in words, the mind cannot illustrate it by analogy' (*Lüshi chunqiu* 14/2.4). Joy and fulfilment are like the satisfaction we feel when tasting an exquisite dish – impossible to put into words.

We judge people on the basis of how they conduct themselves around the dinner table. We judge the host by the food and wines being served, the other guests who have been invited, the strategic seating plan and the conversation that is fostered during the course of the meal and post-prandial proceedings. The etiquette of the dinner table can serve to mask the effects of direct confrontation, or tempt someone to drop their habitual guard and share their secrets. Conviviality can be genuine or contrived. Formal dinners offer the perfect palliative for keeping up appearances (if only speech balloons could reveal what lies behind the forced smiles of heads of state as they toast each other on such occasions).

In ancient China, the banquet offered a venue for the judgement of human character, a setting where social skill and political dexterity came into play. Entertainments and feasts were laid on to 'inculcate reverence and frugality' or 'demonstrate kindness and generosity' (*Zuozhuan*, Lord Cheng 12). For the host, the banquet provided a means of showing prestige and impressing an imagined community of allies. An accomplished lord 'displays his ritual vessels and arranges feasts in order to promote harmony and friendship' (*Guoyu*, 'Zhou yu'). Matters of political and military honour could be settled during a banquet; by contrast, a lack of generosity on the part of the host could have dire political consequences. The meal provided an opportunity for subtle political manoeuvring, a platform for self-aggrandizement or a forum where the conduct of a ruler or superior could be evaluated. Duke Wen of Wei (r. 445–396

BCE) once organized a banquet at which he encouraged all his great officers to give assessments of him; unexpectedly, the one guest who candidly criticized him was permitted to stay at the party and was later promoted (*Lüshi chunqiu* 24/3.5).

Banquets and drinking parties could be organized as a ploy to trick, humiliate or eliminate political opponents. Guests could be assassinated, detained or poisoned, and character contests in song or verse during a meal could invite vengeance or reprisals by attendees. Banquets were rule-infested gatherings. Knowing when and how to decline an invitation could save your life, as could acting drunk and leaving early (as did the founder of the Han dynasty who famously had to escape from a banquet that had been set up by his rival as a trap). To snub a host on the grounds that a feast was beneath or above one's status could be a mark of personal integrity or a diplomatic tactic – culinary diplomacy at work. One sixth-century BCE envoy from Confucius's small home state of Lu agreed to remain at the party only when his host had consented to remove any surplus dishes (*Zuozhuan*, Lord Zhao 7). This clearly did not set a precedent, however. Party officials in China today have only recently been told to cut down on extravagant hosting and food wastage.

Guidelines on dining etiquette were meticulously detailed. They ranged from rules on how to welcome and seat guests and on how to lay out dishes to directions on the order and sequence of service. There was even guidance on how to eat, drink and generally comport oneself during a meal:

> Do not roll rice into a ball; do not bolt down the various
> dishes; do not swill down [the soup]. Do not make a noise

in eating; do not crunch the bones with your teeth; do not
put back fish you have been eating; do not throw bones
to the dogs; do not snatch [at what you want]. Do not
spread out the rice; do not use chopsticks when eating
millet. Do not gulp down broth, nor add condiments to it;
do not keep picking your teeth, nor bolt down sauces ...
(*Liji*, 'Qu li').

However, no protocol ever succeeds in preventing drunk and
rowdy behaviour. Zhuangzi strikes a note of realism here when
he states that 'those who drink following etiquette start off
in an orderly fashion but invariably end up in unruliness'
(*Zhuangzi* 4.2). Moralists made their point by referring to
the ancients, who were exemplars of temperance. Thus the
same Yanzi encourages his lord to moderate his drinking by
reminding him that, in the good old days, guests toasting more
than five rounds would be executed (*Yanzi chunqiu* 1.3). *The
Ritual Records* hints that rituals were instituted to curb excessive drinking: 'With one toast, a host and his guests are
obliged to salute each other numerous times. Thus one can
drink for the whole day without becoming drunk' (*Liji*, 'Yue
ji'). Anyone who has had to sit through a marathon Chinese
banquet as a guest of honour might have found some solace
in the ritual classics!

Tasting the world

Unsurprisingly, as the ultimate model of measured sobriety,
Confucius praises those who avoid overindulging in culinary extravagance. Yet the *Analects* also portray the Master as

someone with a sensitive palate: 'He did not object to having his grain finely cleaned, nor to having his minced meat cut up fine. He did not eat grain that had been damaged by heat or damp and turned sour, nor fish or flesh that was gone. He would eat nothing that was discoloured or smelled strange, nor anything that was not properly cooked or out of season. He did not eat meat that was not cut properly, nor what was served without its proper sauce …' (*An.* 10.8). Still, the aim here is not to portray Confucius as a distinguished gourmet, but rather as someone able to cultivate himself through a sense of balance and proportion. The Confucian gentleman is able to pace himself: once a sage, never a glutton.

To command the world, one should eat it. Yet power and strength do not derive from being able to gorge on everything within reach, but from the ability to control one's inner self through a dietary regime that holds the middle between excess and starvation. The smooth circulation of *qi* through the organs is essential:

> As a general rule, do not eat rich and fatty foods, nor highly spiced flavours, nor strong wines. These are said to cause the onset of illness. When one can eat at regular intervals, the body is certain not to suffer calamitous influences. Generally the Dao of eating involves neither going hungry nor engaging in gluttony. This is called 'comforting the Five Viscera'. The mouth must find the taste sweet. Keep your vital essence in harmony and your bearing correct. Guide them with spirit and *qi*. Make the hundred [i.e. many] joints of the body relaxed and comfortable, so that they can all

receive nourishment from *qi*. When drinking, be certain
to take small sips; hold yourself upright and avoid abrupt
movements. (*Lüshi chunqiu* 3/2.5)

Thus, just as in China's imagined geography, its rituals, ethical theories or political philosophy, her sages stress the importance of holding on to the mean even in their diet. Do not overindulge, Mozi advises, but, like the ancients, 'stop when you have replenished the void left by hunger, when your breathing becomes regular again, your limbs are strengthened and ears and eyes become sharp' (*Mozi* 21.3). If the Son of Heaven sticks to a balanced diet, he secures cosmic stability for the world at large. A healthy ruler makes the body politic function smoothly: 'Calmly, he occupies the centre and controls the four quarters. At dawn he takes a meal: this is the beginning of lesser *yang*. At noon he takes a meal: this is the beginning of greater *yang*. In the afternoon he takes a meal: this is the beginning of lesser *yin*. In the evening he takes a meal: this is the start of greater *yin*' (*Baihutong*, 'Li yue'). During times of crisis (such as a famine or drought), the ruler moderates his own diet and economizes on the sacrifices offered to the spirits. During times of plenty, he partakes more generously of his meals and shares this generosity with his subjects; in times of austerity, he substitutes feasting with symbolical acts of abstention.

There is a reason why a Chinese emperor fed well (other than because he could): the Son of Heaven's mealtimes marked the passage of time and the alternation of *yin* and *yang*. As the link between Heaven and Earth, his well-balanced and accurately timed meals were a ritual that was vital to the well-being of the cosmos and hence the welfare of all. Ritual calendars suggest that feeding the Son of Heaven was a giant catering operation. For China's early emperors our knowledge of this is limited to guidance in ritual texts, but more records are available for late imperial China. For example, palace records from the eighteenth century reveal the resources and expense that went into feeding the Forbidden City. (The cost for the year 1757 has been estimated at 9,540 ounces of silver.) Thousands of menus are preserved that give us an insight into what pleased the palate of Emperor Qianlong (r. 1735–96). At times, imperial menus featured more than ninety dishes. In 1779, the emperor got through a hundred and forty ducks and chickens in one month. Luckily he did not have to eat his way through everything himself. 'Leftovers' were shared with concubines and sent off following a protocol to princes, princesses, officials and dignitaries. Often the emperor would only symbolically 'touch' the food before it was passed on to his court. However, food was first assembled as a whole in front of the emperor before it was divided up and shared out. The symbolism behind these incredible daily displays of food brings us back to the status of the Son of Heaven as the linchpin of the universe, as articulated in the ancient ritual texts. Ruling over a vast territory that stretched beyond the walls of his court, the Son of Heaven ritually sampled the products from every corner of the empire. He had a cosmic meal that included all flavours 'under Heaven'. As with all dignitaries on a tour of their realm (or politicians during election campaigns), it is good politics to sample the local delicacies.

The Art of Cook Ding

One of the most widely quoted passages from *The Master Zhuang* is the tale of Cook Ding that appears in a chapter tellingly entitled 'Essentials for Nourishing Life' (*Zhuangzi* 3.2). It takes the form of a dialogue between a nobleman, Duke Wenhui of Wei (r. 369–319 BCE), and his cook, Ding, who is butchering an ox while his master looks on. Cook Ding is fully engrossed in his job as he carves away. 'As his hand slapped, shoulder lunged, foot stamped, knee crooked, with a *hiss!* with a *thud!* the brandished blade as it sliced never missed the rhythm …' The duke is impressed: 'How wonderful that skill should attain such heights!' Then Cook Ding puts his cleaver down and tells his lord that what he truly cares about is the Dao, which is something that goes beyond mere skill:

> When I first began to carve oxen, I saw nothing but oxen wherever I looked. Three years more and I never saw an ox as a whole. Today, I am in touch with the ox through the spirit in me, and do not [even] look at it with my eyes. My senses now know where to stop, and my spirit runs its course as it pleases. I follow the natural grain, slice along the main seams, and let the blade be guided by the main cavities. I follow the inherent structure [of the ox] so my cleaver never meets with the slightest obstacle even where the ligaments and tendons join, not to mention when it encounters a solid bone. A good cook changes his cleaver once a year, because he hacks. An ordinary cook changes it once a month, because he smashes. Now I have had this cleaver for nineteen years,

and have dissected several thousand oxen, but the edge is as though it were still fresh from the grindstone.

Cook Ding continues to describe how he dissects his ox with effortless ease, by steering his blade through the open spaces between the joints and, when needed, by focusing his spirit on the occasional tough joint so that, with one flick of the cleaver, the meat drops off the bone. By concentrating on the Dao and going with the flow and natural anatomy of things, he has learned to navigate the complex carcass of life without encountering the slightest resistance or exhausting his vital energies. He is a true master of life and much stronger than his patron, who enjoys all the trappings of aristocratic status (including the beef stew!) and who, normally, would not set foot in an abattoir or take a tutorial from a menial servant. 'Excellent!' Duke Wenhui concludes. 'Listening to the words of the cook, I have learned from them how to nourish life.' Again, the cook emerges as the real philosopher, this time with the message that if we wish to live on the edge of a knife that is never blunted, we should be roaming between the joints. To breathe out, one must first breathe in; to master the complexities of the external world, we should aim to strengthen our internal vital energies.

The idea of the Chinese philosopher conceiving of his trade as butchery or cookery might raise an eyebrow. Nevertheless, I believe some things ring true in the metaphor. The dividing line running through ancient China's intellectual landscape was not one between rationalists and idealists, or between those who believed or disbelieved in the forces of the supernatural; it was not between adherents of logic or advocates of

Figure 9.2
Butchers and cooks at work.
Ink rubbing, Wuliang family shrine, Shandong; 2nd century CE.

intuition, or between those who developed theories of know-ledge and those sceptical of it. 'To carve or not to carve' was the question that exercised the thinking minds of ancient China. The point of departure for most intellectual traditions we have encountered in this book lay here: do we gain more from life by cutting up the world into units or categories we can control, manipulate and (pretend to) understand, or is human existence better served if we leave the world intact to operate following its own internal and spontaneous logic? Is it better to alter or adapt, be in or out, engage or withdraw? Is our inner self best left untouched, like an uncarved block (*DDJ* 19, 28), or should we work and sculpt it? And when we fashion ourselves and society around us, what shape should it take? Crucially, through it all, how do we preserve the harmony of the whole and the integrity of the one: the self, the family, the state, the monarch, the empire, Heaven, the cosmos, the Way? To most, then, thinking Chinese meant focusing on society, politics and the ethics of the here and now. The shape of the cleaver mattered little as long as it could cut. Perhaps not much has changed.

Notes and Further Reading

For translations of primary source texts, where available, I have drawn on or adapted existing scholarly translations that have stood the test of time. Otherwise, translations are my own. Details of primary source translations are given here for the chapter in which the original work features most prominently. For a brief description of the original Chinese source, see 'Primary Source Texts'. Some spellings/romanization of Chinese authors/titles below may differ from those in the main text, where pinyin is used throughout.

CHAPTER 1: CHINA IN TIME AND SPACE

I refer to Wolfram Eberhard in his *A History of China from the Earliest Times to the Present Day*, 2nd edn (London: Routledge & Kegan Paul, 1960), p. 1. References to *The Master Huainan* follow and/or modify the translation by John S. Major, Sarah A. Queen, Andrew S. Meyer and Harold D. Roth, *The Huainanzi: A Guide to the Theory and Practice of Government in Early Han China* (New York: Columbia University Press, 2010). Yuri Pines is quoted from Pines, Lothar von Falkenhausen, Gideon Shelach and Robin D. S. Yates (eds), *Birth of an Empire: The State of Qin Revisited* (Berkeley and Los Angeles: University of California Press, 2014), p. 227. Feng Youlan is quoted from Fung Yu-lan, *A Short History of Chinese Philosophy*, ed. Derk Bodde (New York: Macmillan, 1960), p. 12.

The most comprehensive guide to the study of Chinese history is Endymion Wilkinson's *Chinese History: A New Manual*, 5th edn (Cambridge, MA: Harvard University Asia Centre, 2017). Good surveys of the period include Michael Loewe and Edward L. Shaughnessy (eds), *The Cambridge History of Ancient China* (Cambridge: Cambridge University Press, 1999); Mark Edward Lewis, *The Early Chinese Empires: Qin and Han* (Cambridge, MA: Bellknap Press, 2007); and Li Feng, *Early China: A Social and Cultural History* (Cambridge: Cambridge University Press, 2013). For the archaeological record, see Lothar von Falkenhausen, *Chinese Society in the Age of Confucius (1000–250 BC): The Archaeological Evidence* (Los Angeles: Cotsen Institute of Archaeology and University of California Press, 2006), and Gideon Shelach-Lavi, *The Archaeology of Early China: From Prehistory to the Han* (Cambridge: Cambridge University Press, 2015). For extracts on the First Emperor from Sima Qian's *Historical Records*, see Raymond Dawson (trans.), *Sima Qian: The First Emperor*, with a preface by K. E. Brashier (Oxford: Oxford University Press, 2007). Most of the one hundred and thirty chapters of the *Historical Records* are now accessible in English translation (in multiple volumes). I recommend Burton Watson, *Records of the Grand Historian*, rev. edn, 3 vols (New York: Columbia University Press, 1993), and William H. Nienhauser Jr et al., *The Grand Scribe's Records* (Bloomington: Indiana University Press, 1994–). On the role of monarchical rule, see Yuri Pines, *The Everlasting Empire: Traditional Chinese Political Culture and Its Enduring Legacy* (Princeton, NJ: Princeton University Press, 2012).

On the Great Wall, see Arthur Waldron, *The Great Wall of China: From History to Myth* (Cambridge: Cambridge University Press, 1990), and Julia Lovell, *The Great Wall: China Against the World, 1000 BC–AD 2000* (London: Atlantic Books, 2006).

On the institutions of empire, see Michael Loewe, *The Government of the Qin and Han Empires: 221 BCE–220 CE* (Indianapolis: Hackett, 2006). On the Five Classics, see Michael

Nylan, *The Five 'Confucian' Classics* (New Haven, CT: Yale University Press, 2001). For a translation of the *Book of Odes*, see Arthur Waley, *The Book of Songs* (New York: Grove Press, 1996). The *Shanhaijing* is introduced and translated by Anne Birrell, *The Classic of Mountains and Seas* (Harmondsworth: Penguin, 1999). On Chinese writing, see William G. Boltz, *The Origin and Early Development of the Chinese Writing System* (New Haven, CT: American Oriental Society, 1994). The most accessible dictionary for the language of the period is Paul W. Kroll, *A Student's Dictionary of Classical and Medieval Chinese* (Leiden: E. J. Brill, 2015).

For Simon Leys's take on Confucius, see the introduction to his *The Analects of Confucius* (New York: Norton, 1997). Among the many translations of the *Analects*, I recommend D. C. Lau, *The Analects* (Harmondsworth: Penguin, 1979; in multiple reprints); Roger T. Ames and Henry Rosemont Jr, *The Analects of Confucius: A Philosophical Translation* (New York: Ballantine Books, 1998); and Edward Slingerland, *Confucius: Analects, with Selections from Traditional Commentaries* (Indianapolis: Hackett, 2003). On the history of scholarship on China, see David Honey, *Incense at the Altar: Pioneering Sinologists and the Development of Classical Chinese Philology* (New Haven, CT: American Oriental Society, 2001), and Norman J. Girardot, *The Victorian Translation of China: James Legge's Oriental Pilgrimage* (Berkeley, CA, and London: University of California Press, 2002). Legge's (now dated) translations of the Five Classics and Four Books have appeared in multiple reprints. Some (or parts of them) were first published by him in Hong Kong and then in London as *The Chinese Classics: With a Translation, Critical and Exegetical Notes, Prolegomena, and Copious Indexes*, 5 vols (Hong Kong and London: Trübner, 1861–72). Other works (including *The Book of Rites* and *The Book of Changes*) and parts of works appeared in Max Müller's *Sacred Books of the East* series (Oxford: Clarendon Press, 1879–).

CHAPTER 2: THE WAY (DAO) AND ITS WAYS

Among the hundreds of translations of *The Classic of the Way and Virtue*, D. C. Lau's translation in the Penguin Classics series, *Lao Tzu Tao Te Ching* (Harmondsworth: Penguin, 1963; in multiple reprints), still stands as one of the better ones. *Inner Training* is studied and translated in Harold D. Roth, *Original Tao: Inward Training (Nei-yeh) and the Foundations of Taoist Mysticism* (New York: Columbia University Press, 1999). For *The Master Zhuang*, translations follow and/or modify Victor Mair, *Wandering on the Way: Early Taoist Tales and Parables of Chuang Tzu* (Honolulu: University of Hawai'i Press, 1994) (references follow the paragraph division in Mair). On *The Book of Changes*, see Edward L. Shaughnessy, *I Ching: The Classic of Changes* (New York: Ballantine Books, 1996) (this also contains a translation of the *Ersanzi wen*); on its fate around the world, see Richard J. Smith, *The I Ching: A Biography* (Princeton, NJ: Princeton University Press, 2012). On correlative thinking and cosmology, see Angus C. Graham, *Disputers of the Tao: Philosophical Argument in Ancient China* (La Salle, IL: Open Court, 1989), pp. 313–70, and Robin R. Wang, *Yinyang: The Way of Heaven and Earth in Chinese Thought and Culture* (Cambridge: Cambridge University Press, 2012). A version of the 'Monthly Ordinances' calendar is preserved in *The Spring and Autumn Annals of Mr Lü (Lüshi chunqiu)*. References to this text follow and/or modify the translation by John Knoblock and Jeffrey Riegel, *The Annals of Lü Buwei* (Palo Alto, CA: Stanford University Press, 2001).

CHAPTER 3: THE ART OF GOVERNMENT

On military strategy, including full translations of the *Sunzi bing fa*, see Roger Ames (trans.), *Sun-Tzu: The Art of Warfare* (New York: Ballantine Books, 1993) (quotation from p. 41), and

Ralph D. Sawyer (trans.), *The Seven Military Classics of Ancient China* (Boulder, CO: Westview Press, 1993). On the notion of 'positioning', see François Jullien, *The Propensity of Things: Towards a History of Efficacy in China* (New York: Zone Books, 1995) (quotation from p. 49).

On Confucius's sayings and anecdotes, the composition of the *Analects* and the different personae of Confucius, see Michael Nylan and Thomas Wilson, *Lives of Confucius* (New York: Doubleday, 2010); Michael Hunter, *Confucius Beyond the Analects* (Leiden: E. J. Brill, 2017); and Paul R. Goldin (ed.), *A Concise Companion to Confucius* (Hoboken, NJ: Wiley-Blackwell, 2017). Translations from *The Master Xun* (and in-line references) follow and/or modify John Knoblock, *Xunzi: A Translation and Study of the Complete Works*, 3 vols (Stanford: Stanford University Press, 1988–94). For an alternative translation, see Eric Hutton, *Xunzi: The Complete Text* (Princeton, NJ: Princeton University Press, 2014). *The Doctrine of the Mean* is introduced and translated in Roger T. Ames and David L. Hall, *Focusing the Familiar: A Translation and Philosophical Interpretation of the Zhongyong* (Honolulu: University of Hawai'i Press, 2001).

A translation of *The Master Mo* is available in the Penguin Classics series as *Mo Zi: The Book of Master Mo*, trans. Ian Johnston (London: Penguin, 2013) (in-line chapter and paragraph references follow Johnston). A more scholarly, informed translation is John Knoblock and Jeffrey Riegel, *Mozi: A Study and Translation of the Ethical and Political Writings* (Berkeley, CA: Institute of East Asian Studies, 2013). For a recent study, see Chris Frazer, *The Philosophy of Mozi: The First Consequentialists* (New York: Columbia University Press, 2016). For the texts associated with 'Huang-Lao' philosophy and politics, see Robin Yates, *Five Lost Classics: Tao, Huang-Lao, and Yin-Yang in Han China* (New York: Ballantine Books, 1997), and Leo S. Chang and Yu Feng, *The Four Political Treatises of the Yellow Emperor* (Honolulu: University of Hawai'i Press, 1998).

My translations from the *Shangjun shu* follow Yuri Pines (ed. and trans.), *The Book of Lord Shang: Apologetics of State Power in Early China* (New York: Columbia University Press, 2017) (quotation from p. 97). On Shen Buhai's thought, see Herrlee G. Creel, *Shen Pu-hai: A Chinese Political Philosopher of the Fourth Century B.C.* (Chicago and London: University of Chicago Press, 1974). References to the *Shenzi* follow Creel. References to the Shen Dao *Shenzi* follow Paul M. Thompson, *The Shen Tzu Fragments* (Oxford: Oxford University Press, 1979). For Graham's characterization of legalism, see *Disputers of the Tao*, pp. 267 ff. On the thought of Han Fei and the book named after him, see Paul R. Goldin (ed.), *Dao Companion to the Philosophy of Han Fei* (Dordrecht: Springer, 2013). For translations of *The Master Han Fei* and *The Master Guan*, see W. K. Liao, *The Complete Works of Han Feizi* (London: Arthur Probsthain, 1959); Burton Watson, *Han Fei Tzu: Basic Writings* (New York and London: Columbia University Press, 1964); and W. Allyn Rickett, *Guanzi: Political, Economic, and Philosophical Essays from Early China*, vol. 2 (Princeton, NJ: Princeton University Press, 1998). I quote Benjamin I. Schwartz from his *The World of Thought in Ancient China* (Cambridge, MA: Harvard University Press, 1989), p. 92. For a full translation of *The Stratagems of the Warring States*, see James I. Crump, *Chan-kuo Ts'e* (Oxford: Clarendon Press, 1970).

CHAPTER 4: THE INDIVIDUAL AND THE COLLECTIVE

The *Mencius* is translated by D. C. Lau in the Penguin Classics series as *Mencius* (Harmondsworth: Penguin, 1970) and, more recently, by Irene Bloom as *Mencius* (New York: Columbia University Press, 2009); I generally follow Bloom. For a thematic study, see Kwong-Loi Shun, *Mencius and Early Chinese Thought* (Stanford, CA: Stanford University Press, 1997). For a complete translation of *The Zuo Tradition*, see Stephen Durrant, Wai-yee Li and David Schaberg (trans.), *Zuo Tradition/Zuozhuan: Commentary on the 'Spring and Autumn Annals'*, 3 vols (Seattle: University of Washington Press, 2016). References to the Qin legal statutes follow Anthony F. P. Hulsewé, *Remnants of Ch'in Law* (Leiden: E. J. Brill, 1985).

On the social stages of life, see K. E. Brashier, *Public Memory in Early China* (Cambridge, MA: Harvard University Press, 2014), especially part 2. On childhood, women and mothers, see Anne Behnke Kinney (ed.), *Chinese Views of Childhood* (Honolulu: University of Hawai'i Press, 1995), and her translation of the *Lienü zhuan: Exemplary Women of Early China: The Lienü zhuan of Liu Xiang* (New York: Columbia University Press, 2014); Lisa Raphals, *Sharing the Light: Representations of Women and Virtue in Early China* (Albany, NY: State University of New York Press, 1998); and Robin Wang, *Images of Women in Chinese Thought and Culture: Writings from the Pre-Qin Period to the Song Dynasty* (Indianapolis and Cambridge, MA: Hackett Publishing, 2003). For Ban Zhao and the *Admonitions*, see Nancy L. Swann, *Pan Chao: Foremost Woman Scholar of China* (New York: Russell and Russell, 1932). On foot binding, see Dorothy Ko, *Cinderella's Sisters: A Revisionist History of Footbinding* (Los Angeles: University of California Press, 2005).

On filial piety, see Alan K. L. Chan and Sor-hoon Tan (eds), *Filial Piety in Chinese Thought and History* (New York: RoutledgeCurzon, 2004), and Keith N. Knapp, *Selfless Offspring: Filial Children and Social Order in Medieval China* (Honolulu: University of Hawai'i Press, 2005). For a translation of *The Classic of Filial Piety*, see Roger T. Ames and Henri Rosemont Jr, *The Chinese Classic of Family Reverence: A Philosophical Translation of the Xiaojing* (Honolulu: University of Hawai'i Press, 2009). The only full translation of *The Ritual Records* in English remains James Legge's *Li Ki* (1879–91), in Max Müller (ed.), *Sacred Books of the East*, vols 27 and 28 (Oxford: Oxford University Press, 1926; reprinted 1960). I quote Nivison in Michael Loewe and Edward

L. Shaughnessy (eds), *The Cambridge History of Ancient China* (Cambridge: Cambridge University Press, 1999), p. 767. *The Master Lie* is translated by Angus C. Graham as *The Book of Lieh-tzu: A Classic of Tao* (London: Mandala, 1991). *The Great Learning* is introduced and translated in Andrew H. Plaks, *Ta Hsüeh and Chung Yung (The Highest Order of Cultivation and On the Practice of the Mean)* (London: Penguin, 2003).

CHAPTER 5: BEHAVING RITUALLY

Discussions of ritual theory that (partly) draw on the Chinese tradition include Catherine Bell, *Ritual Theory, Ritual Practice* (New York and Oxford: Oxford University Press, 1992); Adam B. Seligman, Robert P. Weller, Michael J. Puett and Bennett Simon, *Ritual and Its Consequences: An Essay on the Limits of Sincerity* (Oxford: Oxford University Press, 2008); and Michael Ing, *The Dysfunction of Ritual in Early Confucianism* (Oxford: Oxford University Press, 2012). On *li* in its historical context, see Yuri Pines, *Foundations of Confucian Thought: Intellectual Life in the Chunqiu Period, 722–453 BCE* (Honolulu: University of Hawai'i Press, 2002), Chapter 3.

The Book of Etiquette and Rites is translated by John Steele, *The I-Li or Book of Etiquette and Ceremonial*, 2 vols (London: Probsthain & Co, 1917). No full English translation is as yet available for *The Rites of Zhou*. For studies, see Benjamin A. Elman and Martin Kern (eds), *Statecraft and Classical Learning: The Rituals of Zhou in East Asian History* (Leiden: E. J. Brill, 2009). For thematic studies on Xunzi's philosophy, including his views on ritual and music, see Paul R. Goldin, *Rituals of the Way: The Philosophy of Xunzi* (Chicago and LaSalle: Open Court, 1999), and Eric L. Hutton (ed.), *Dao Companion to the Philosophy of Xunzi* (New York: Springer, 2016).

On music, see Kenneth DeWoskin, *A Song for One or Two: Music and the Concept of Art in Early China* (Ann Arbor: Center for Chinese Studies, University of Michigan, 1982); Roel Sterckx, 'Transforming the Beasts: Animals and Music in Early China', *T'oung Pao* 86 (2000), pp. 1–46; and Erica F. Brindley, *Music, Cosmology, and the Politics of Harmony in Early China* (Albany, NY: State University of New York Press, 2012). For theories of the emotions, see Curie Virág, *The Emotions in Early Chinese Philosophy* (Oxford: Oxford University Press, 2017).

The most comprehensive studies of the legal codes of the Qin and Han with extensive translations and commentary are Anthony F. P. Hulsewé, *Remnants of Ch'in Law* (Leiden: E. J. Brill, 1985), and Anthony J. Barbieri-Low and Robin D. S. Yates, *Law, State, and Society in Early Imperial China: A Study with Critical Edition and Translation of the Legal Texts from Zhangjiashan Tomb No. 247*, 2 vols (Leiden: E. J. Brill, 2015). References to Qin laws follow Hulsewé. For a good survey, see also Mark Edward Lewis, *The Early Chinese Empires*, Chapter 10. A solid introduction with translation of the Tang legal code is Wallace Johnson, *The Tang Code*, vol. 1: *General Principles* and vol. 2: *Specific Articles* (Princeton: Princeton University Press, 1979 and 1997). Later imperial legal codes are accessible in Jiang Yonglin (trans.), *The Great Ming Code* (Seattle: University of Washington Press, 2005; paperback 2014); and William C. Jones et al., *The Great Qing Code: A New Translation* (Oxford: Clarendon Press, 1994).

CHAPTER 6: SPIRITS AND ANCESTORS

Max Weber is quoted from his *The Religion of China* (Toronto: Free Press, 1951), pp. 156–7. For Mozi's position on ghosts and spirits, see Roel Sterckx, '*Mozi* 31: Explaining Ghosts, Again', in Carine Defoort and Nicolas Standaert (eds), *The Mozi as an Evolving Text: Different Voices in Early Chinese Thought* (Leiden: E. J. Brill, 2013), pp. 96–141. Lin Yutang is quoted from *The Importance of Living* (Singapore: Cultured Lotus, 1937;

reprinted 2001), p. 17 (2001 edn). Charles O. Hucker is quoted from his *China to 1850: A Short History* (Palo Alto, CA: Stanford University Press, 1978), p. 16.

The best study of the ancestral cult is K. E. Brashier, *Ancestral Memory in Early China*, Harvard-Yenching Institute Monograph Series 72 (Cambridge, MA: Harvard University Press, 2011). See also Miranda Brown, *The Politics of Mourning in Early China* (Albany, NY: State University of New York Press, 2007). Accessible studies of religion include Poo Mu-chou, *In Search of Personal Welfare: A View of Ancient Chinese Religion* (Albany, NY: State University of New York Press, 1998), and John Lagerwey and Marc Kalinowksi (eds), *Early Chinese Religion: Part One: Shang through Han (1250 BC–220 AD)*, 2 vols (Leiden: E. J. Brill, 2009).

The *Chuci* is introduced, annotated and translated by David Hawkes as *The Songs of the South: An Ancient Chinese Anthology of Poems by Qu Yuan and Other Poets* (Harmondsworth: Penguin, 1985). On views of the afterlife, see Michael Loewe, *Ways to Paradise: The Chinese Quest for Immortality* (London: George Allen & Unwin, 1979), and *Chinese Ideas of Life and Death: Faith, Myth, and Reason in the Han Period (202 BC–AD 220)* (London: George Allen & Unwin, 1982). On the material culture of tombs, see Wu Hung, *The Art of the Yellow Springs. Understanding Chinese Tombs* (London: Reaktion Books, 2010), and Lai Guolong, *Excavating the Afterlife: The Archaeology of Early Chinese Religion* (Seattle, WA: University of Washington Press, 2015). For a concise discussion of the relationship between religious traditions and the state, see Anthony C. Yu, *State and Religion in China: Historical and Textual Perspectives* (Chicago and La Salle: Open Court, 2005).

On sacrifice, see Roel Sterckx, *Food, Sacrifice, and Sagehood in Early China* (New York: Cambridge University Press, 2011; paperback 2015). For studies of almanacs, see Donald Harper and Marc Kalinowski (eds), *Books of Fate and Popular Culture in Early China: The Daybook Manuscripts of the Warring States, Qin, and Han* (Leiden: E. J. Brill, 2017). Still very useful as an entry into

Han religion is Derk Bodde's *Festivals in Classical China:
New Year and Other Annual Observances During the Han Dynasty,
206 B.C.–A.D. 220* (Princeton, NJ: Princeton University Press,
1975). The philosophy of Xu Gan is collected in his *Balanced
Discourses*, trans. John Makeham (New Haven, CT, and London:
Yale University Press, 2002). I quote Graham from Angus
C. Graham, *Chuang-tzu: The Inner Chapters* (London: Hackett,
2001), p. 176.

An excellent survey of the history of the period of disunion
following the Han dynasty is Mark Edward Lewis, *China Between
Empires* (Cambridge, MA: Harvard University Press, 2007).
On neo-Confucian philosophy, see Daniel K. Gardner, *The Four
Books: The Basic Teachings of the Later Confucian Tradition*
(Indianapolis: Hackett, 2007); Peter Bol, *Neo-Confucianism in
History* (Cambridge, MA: Harvard University Press, 2008); and
John Makeham (ed.), *Dao Companion to Neo-Confucian Philosophy*
(New York: Springer, 2010). A good selection of neo-Confucian
writings is available in William Theodore de Bary and Irene Bloom
(eds), *Sources of Chinese Tradition: From the Earliest Times to 1600*,
2nd edn, vol. 1 (New York: Columbia University Press, 1999),
chapters 19, 20 and 21 (for the Western Inscription, see p. 683).
On the civil service examination curriculum and its role in the
politics and society of early modern and late imperial China,
see Benjamin A. Elman, *Civil Examinations and Meritocracy in
Late Imperial China* (Cambridge, MA: Harvard University Press,
2004), and Hilde de Weerdt, *Competition over Content: Negotiating
Standards for the Civil Service Examinations in Imperial China
(1127–1279)* (Cambridge, MA: Harvard University Press, 2007).
On the Confucian movement underway in today's China, see
Sébastien Billioud and Joël Thoraval, *The Sage and the People: The
Confucian Revival in China* (Oxford: Oxford University
Press, 2015).

CHAPTER 7: THE WORLD OF NATURE

I quote Derk Bodde from his *Chinese Thought, Society, and Science: The Intellectual and Social Background of Science and Technology in Pre-modern China* (Honolulu: University of Hawai'i Press, 1991), p. 263. References to *Chunqiu fanlu* follow the translation by Sarah Queen and John S. Major, *Luxuriant Gems of the Spring and Autumn* (New York: Columbia University Press, 2015); Lin Yutang is quoted from *The Importance of Living*, p. 47 (2001 edn).

On medicine, see Paul U. Unschuld, *Medicine in China: A History of Ideas* (Los Angeles: University of California Press, 1985); Donald J. Harper, *Early Chinese Medical Literature: The Mawangdui Medical Manuscripts* (London and New York: Kegan Paul International, 1998) (this includes, among others, *Prescriptions Against Fifty-Two Ailments* and *Conjoining Yin and Yang*); Vivienne Lo, *How to Do the Gibbon Walk: A Translation of the Pulling Book (c.186 BCE)* (Cambridge: Needham Research Institute Working Papers, 2014); and Miranda Brown, *The Art of Medicine in Early China: The Ancient and Medieval Origins of a Modern Archive* (Cambridge: Cambridge University Press, 2015). For studies and annotated translations of the *Huangdi neijing* texts, see Paul U. Unschuld, *Huang Di Nei Jing Su Wen: Annotated Translation of Huang Di's Inner Classic – Basic Questions*, 2 vols (Los Angeles: University of California Press, 2011), and Unschuld, *Huang Di Nei Jing Ling Shu: The Ancient Classic on Needle Therapy*, 2nd rev. edn (Los Angeles: University of California Press, 2016). Chunyu Yi and his case stories are studied in Elisabeth Hsu, *Pulse Diagnosis in Early Chinese Medicine: The Telling Touch* (Cambridge: Cambridge University Press, 2010).

Malraux is cited from *The Temptation of the West*, trans. Robert Hollander (Chicago: University of Chicago Press, 1961; reprinted 1989), pp. 63–7 (1989 edn). On the animal world, see Roel Sterckx, *The Animal and the Daemon in Early China* (Albany, NY: State University of New York Press, 2002), and Roel Sterckx, Martina

Siebert and Dagmar Schäfer (eds), *Animals through Chinese History: Earliest Times to 1911* (Cambridge: Cambridge University Press, 2019). The best survey of botany is Georges Métailié, *Science and Civilisation in China*, vol. 6, part 4: *Traditional Botany – An Ethnobotanical Approach* (Cambridge: Cambridge University Press, 2015). For a translation of *Yanzi chunqiu*, see Olivia Milburn, *The Spring and Autumn of Master Yan* (Leiden: E. J. Brill, 2016).

Useful surveys of China's environmental history include Mark Elvin, *The Retreat of the Elephants: An Environmental History of China* (New Haven, CT: Yale University Press, 2006), and Robert B. Marks, *China: Its Environment and History* (Plymouth: Rowman and Littlefield, 2012). On water and floods, see Sarah Allan, *The Way of Water and the Sprouts of Virtue* (Albany, NY: State University of New York Press, 1997), and Mark Edward Lewis, *The Flood Myths of Early China* (Albany, NY: State University of New York Press, 2006). Environmentalist readings of China's philosophers and religious traditions include Mary E. Tucker and John Berthrong (eds), *Confucianism and Ecology: The Interrelations of Heaven, Earth, and Humans* (Cambridge, MA: Harvard University Center for the Study of World Religions, 1998); Norman J. Girardot, James Miller and Liu Xiaogan (eds), *Daoism and Ecology: Ways Within a Cosmic Landscape* (Cambridge, MA: Harvard University Center for the Study of World Religions, 2001); and James Miller, *China's Green Religion: Daoism and the Quest for a Sustainable Future* (New York: Columbia University Press, 2017).

On astronomy, see Daniel P. Morgan, *Astral Sciences in Early Imperial China: Observation, Sagehood, and the Individual* (Cambridge: Cambridge University Press, 2017), and Christopher Cullen, *Heavenly Numbers: Astronomy and Authority in Early Imperial China* (Oxford: Oxford University Press, 2017). Joseph Needham's *Science and Civilisation in China* (*SCC*) series (1954–) is published by Cambridge University Press. Needham founded the Needham Research Institute at Cambridge. I quote the Needham question as it appears in *SCC*, vol. 1: *Introductory Orientations*, pp. 3–4. The only full (and rather antiquated) English translation of the *Discourses in the Balance* (*Lunheng*) is Alfred Forke, *Lun Heng: Philosophical and Miscellaneous Essays of Wang Ch'ung* (*Part I and II*), 2nd edn (New York: Paragon Book Gallery, 1962).

CHAPTER 8: WORK AND WEALTH

On Quesnay and his contemporaries, see Lewis A. Maverick, *China: A Model for Europe* (San Antonio, TX: Paul Anderson, 1946). For the technical history of farming, see Hsu Cho-yun, *Han Agriculture: The Formation of Early Chinese Agrarian Economy* (*206 BC–AD 220*) (Seattle and London: University of Washington Press, 1980), and Francesca Bray, *SCC*, vol. 6, part 2: *Agriculture* (Cambridge: Cambridge University Press, 1984). On the political philosophy of agriculture and commerce, see Roel Sterckx, 'Ideologies of the Peasant and Merchant in Warring States China', in Yuri Pines, Paul R. Goldin and Martin Kern (eds), *Ideology of Power and Power of Ideology in Early China: Studies in Early Chinese Political Thought* (Leiden: E. J. Brill, 2015), pp. 211–48. On the work and life of craftsmen, see Anthony Barbieri-Low, *Artisans in Early Imperial China* (Seattle, WA: University of Washington Press, 2007).

The most up-to-date survey of Chinese economic history is Richard von Glahn, *The Economic History of China: From Antiquity to the Nineteenth Century* (Cambridge: Cambridge University Press, 2016). See also Tamara T. Chin, *Savage Exchange: Han Imperialism, Chinese Literary Style, and the Economic Imagination* (Cambridge, MA: Harvard University Press, 2014), and Elisa Sabattini and Christian Schwermann (eds), *Between Command and Market: Economic Thought and Practice in Early China* (Leiden: E. J. Brill, forthcoming).

CHAPTER 9: FOOD FOR THOUGHT

On food and philosophy, see Roel Sterckx, *Food, Sacrifice and Sagehood in Early China* (New York: Cambridge University Press, 2011; paperback 2015), and Roel Sterckx (ed.), *Of Tripod and Palate: Food, Politics, and Religion in Traditional China* (New York: Palgrave MacMillan, 2005). References to speeches by Xi Jinping are drawn from his *How to Read Confucius and Other Chinese Classical Thinkers*, trans. Zhang Fengzhi (New York: CN Times Books, 2015), pp. 24–26, 41–2 and 257–9. Surveys of diet and cuisine include Chang Kwang-chih (ed.), *Food in Chinese Culture: Anthropological and Historical Perspectives* (New Haven, CT: Yale University Press, 1977); Eugene N. Anderson, *The Food of China* (New Haven, CT: Yale University Press, 1988); and Thomas O. Höllmann, *The Land of the Five Flavors: A Cultural History of Chinese Cuisine*, trans. Karen Margolis (New York: Columbia University Press, 2013). For technical aspects, see Huang Hsing-tsung, *Fermentations and Food Science*, in Joseph Needham, *SCC*, vol. 6, part 5: *Biology and Biological Technology* (Cambridge: Cambridge University Press, 2000). On the history of chopsticks and tea, see Q. Edward Wang, *Chopsticks: A Cultural and Culinary History* (Cambridge: Cambridge University Press, 2015), and James A. Benn, *Tea in China: A Religious and Cultural History* (Honolulu: University of Hawai'i Press, 2015). On ritual and diet under the Qianlong Emperor, see Angela Zito, *Of Body and Brush: Grand Sacrifice as Text/Performance in Eighteenth-Century China* (Chicago: University of Chicago Press, 1997).

Primary Source Texts

Listed below are the primary source texts that have been cited in the main text. Published translations of them, where available, are listed in 'Notes and Further Reading'. References in the main text are usually to the Chinese title of the work and the relevant chapter number, followed, where possible, by a number for a sub-section (e.g. *Xunzi* 9.14). Alternatively, a chapter title is given in transcription after the name of the work (e.g. *Shangshu*, 'Kang gao'). References to *Zuozhuan* are by name and year (thus 'Lord Zhao 1' refers to the first year in the chronicle of Lord Zhao). The texts listed below are the most important received texts, *Analects* being abbreviated in references to *An.* and *Daodejing* to *DDJ*. Any additional sources, including archaeologically recovered manuscripts, are introduced where relevant in the main text.

Analects (*Lunyu*), abbreviated to *An.*: collected sayings attributed to Confucius (551–479 BCE) in dialogue with his disciples; compiled by multiple hands from around 400 BCE and possibly as late as the second century BCE. As the most important text associated with the figure of Confucius, it was classified as one of the **Four Books**. See Chapter 3 for more detail.

Baihutong (*The White Tiger Hall Discussions*): a state-sponsored compendium dealing with rituals, matters of government, nature and religious and philosophical concepts; purportedly compiled or edited by Ban Gu (32–92 CE) as an account of a conference held in 79 CE.

Chuci (*The Songs of the South*): an anthology of poetry and poetic prose with mythical allegories and themes linked to shamanism. Some pieces are attributed to Qu Yuan (fourth century BCE) and his disciple Song Yu (third century BCE), while others are of unknown provenance.

Chunqiu (*The Spring and Autumn Annals*): a concise historical chronicle set in Confucius's native state of Lu for the period from 722 to 481 BCE. It was classified as one of the **Five 'Confucian' Classics** in the second century BCE.

Chunqiu fanlu (*The Luxurious Gems of Spring and Autumn*): a philosophical text attributed to Dong Zhongshu (*c.*179–104 BCE) but also containing writings of his disciples and critics; it presents a vision of history, kingship and cosmology through the ethical and political principles found in the ***Chunqiu*** and its *Gongyang Commentary* (*Gongyang zhuan*).

Da Dai Liji (*The Record of Rites by Dai the Elder*): a heterogeneous collection of essays on ritual matters assembled in the name of the ritual scholar Dai De (first century BCE).

Daodejing (*The Classic of the Way and Virtue*), abbreviated to DDJ: Daoist classic also known as *The Laozi*, consisting of eighty-one short aphorisms; although attributed to the semi-historical figure of Laozi (Master Lao; *fl. c.* sixth century BCE?), its authorship is unknown; a version of the text existed at least from the fourth century BCE onwards.

Daxue (*The Great Learning*): Confucian essay preserved as a chapter in the ***Liji***, possibly dating back to the third century BCE, and later attributed to Zengzi, a disciple of Confucius. It was classified as one of the **Four Books**. See Chapter 4 for more detail.

Five 'Confucian' Classics (*Wu jing*): a set of canonical classics that became part of the curriculum at the Imperial Academy established in 124 BCE. See ***Chunqiu***, ***Liji***, ***Shangshu***, ***Shijing*** and ***Zhouyi***.

Four Books (*Si shu*): a set of Confucian texts classified by the neo-Confucian philosopher Zhu Xi (1130–1200 CE) and his followers, comprising the **Analects**, **Daxue**, **Mencius** and **Zhongyong**.

Guanzi (*The Master Guan*): an extensive compilation of texts on self-cultivation, political philosophy and economics; the text is named after Guan Zhong (d. 645 BCE), a famous minister from the state of Qi, but contains many chapters datable to the Han period; collected and edited by Han imperial librarian Liu Xiang (79–8 BCE). It also contains the *Nei ye* (*Inner Training*), a poetic treatise on the workings of the mind, meditation and breath control.

Guoyu (*The Discourses of the States*): accounts of the speeches and dialogues of important rulers and figures from eight states during the Spring and Autumn period (eighth to fifth century BCE); compiled from the mid fifth to the late fourth century BCE.

Han Feizi (*The Master Han Fei*): major work of political philosophy that developed a theory of state power and a vision of the role of the ruler; mostly written by the Legalist thinker Han Fei (*c.*280–*c.*233 BCE). See Chapter 3 for more detail.

Han shi waizhuan (*Outer Commentary to the Book of Odes by Mr Han*): collection of around three hundred anecdotes, attributed to academician Han Ying (*c.*200–*c.*120 BCE), with moral lessons illustrated and supported by quotations from the **Shijing**.

Hanshu (*The Dynastic History of the Former Han*): a historiographical work compiled by Ban Gu (32–92 CE) and covering the history of the Han dynasty, starting with its founder Liu Bang around 210 BCE down to the fall of Wang Mang in 23 CE.

Hou Hanshu (*The Dynastic History of the Later Han*): the official history of the Han continuing from the period covered by the **Hanshu** until the end of the dynasty (*c.*220 CE). Compiled by Fan Ye (398–446 CE).

Huainanzi (*The Master Huainan*): a twenty-one-chapter anthology compiled under the auspices of an imperial kinsman, Liu An (?179–122 BCE), and presented to Emperor Han Wudi in 139 BCE as a comprehensive synthesis of all contemporary knowledge. See Chapter 7 for more detail.

Huangdi neijing (*The Inner Canon of the Yellow Emperor*): a foundational medical classic consisting of dialogues between the legendary Yellow Emperor and one of his ministers; the authorship of its four constituent texts is unknown; dating to the late Warring States and Western Han period. See Chapter 7 for more detail.

Lienü zhuan (*Biographies of Exemplary Women*): a collection of 125 life stories of famous and lesser-known women grouped according to the virtues they display; compiled towards the end of the first century BCE by the Han imperial librarian Liu Xiang.

Liezi (*The Master Lie*): a classic of Daoist philosophy presented through lively stories, sayings and parables; the book is named after the sage figure Master Lie (or Lie Yukou; *fl. c.*400 BCE), a figure of doubtful historicity, but no received version exists before the fourth century CE.

Liji (*The Ritual Records*): one of three main ritual anthologies describing ceremonial practices and prescriptions; its contents are miscellaneous, with many sections of unknown origin and date. The text was classified as one of the **Five 'Confucian' Classics** and is also known as one of the so-called **Three Ritual Classics**.

Lunheng (*Discourses in the Balance*): a polemical compendium on history, natural phenomena, philosophy, popular religion, literature and politics written by Wang Chong (*c.*27–*c.*100 CE).

Lüshi chunqiu (*The Spring and Autumn Annals of Mr Lü*): a comprehensive philosophical encyclopaedia completed around 239 BCE under the patronage of Lü Buwei (d. 235 BCE).

Mencius (*Mengzi* or *The Master Meng*): text containing the sayings of the Confucian thinker Mencius (Meng Ke; 372–289 BCE).

It was classified as one of the **Four Books**. See Chapter 4 for more detail.

Mozi (*The Master Mo*): the basic text of Mohist thought, attributed to its historical founder Mozi (Mo Di; *c.*479–381 BCE) but written and developed by his followers. See Chapters 3 and 4 for more detail.

Nei ye (*Inner Training*): see ***Guanzi***.

Nü jie (*Admonitions for Women*): the first extended text in China written by a woman, Ban Zhao (*c.*48–116 CE), and addressed to women.

Qianfulun (*Comments of a Recluse*): a text comprising thirty-six essays by Wang Fu (*c.*90–165 CE); it covers miscellaneous topics, ranging from economics to the interpretation of dreams.

San zi jing (*The Three Character Classic*): Confucian primer made up of three-character lines; composed during the thirteenth century CE, it is attributed to Wang Yinglin (1223–96). See Chapter 4 for more detail.

Shangjun shu (*The Book of Lord Shang*): the foundational text of Legalist philosophy originating in the state of Qin; attributed to Lord Shang (Shang Yang/Gongsun Yang; d. 338 BCE), with portions composed long after his time. See Chapter 3 for more detail.

Shangshu (*The Book of Documents*): a compilation of variously dated chapters mostly focusing on political philosophy in the form of speeches and instructions from ruler to ministers and the people; the text is also known as *The Classic of History* (*Shujing*) and was classified as one of the **Five 'Confucian' Classics** in the second century BCE. It includes the *Yu gong* (*The Tribute of Yu*), an early geographic treatise.

Shanhaijing (*The Classic of Mountains and Seas*): a description of the world, its rivers and mountains, plants and animals, monsters and spirits; attributed to the legendary Yu the Great but of uncertain authorship.

Shen Dao *Shenzi* (*The Master Shen*): text preserved in fragments only and associated with the Legalist thinker Shen Dao (*c.*360–*c.*285 CE).

Shenzi (*The Master Shen*): text preserved in fragments and associated with the Legalist thinker Shen Buhai (d. 337 BCE).

Shiji (*The Historical Records*): a history of China from its mythical past down to the second century BCE, the time of its author Sima Qian (*c.*145–*c.*86 BCE).

Shijing (*The Book of Odes*): a classic work of poems, airs and temple hymns consisting of 305 pieces dating between 1000 and 600 BCE, allegedly collected by Confucius. The text was classified as one of the **Five 'Confucian' Classics** in the second century BCE.

Shuowen jiezi (*Explaining Graphs and Analysing Characters*): China's first comprehensive character dictionary, compiled by Xu Shen (30–124 CE).

Sunzi bing fa (*Master Sun's Art of Warfare*): the most important military classic and treatise on strategy to survive from ancient China, compiled over the course of the fifth and fourth centuries BCE. See Chapter 3 for more detail.

Three Ritual Classics (*San li*): a term used by the commentator Zheng Xuan (127–200 CE) and later scholars to refer to a body of texts on ritual brought together during the Han period and comprising the *Liji*, *Yili* and *Zhouli*.

Xiaojing (*The Classic of Filial Piety*): a short text expounding the virtues of filial piety (respect in the service of parents and the elderly), largely in the form of answers by Confucius to questions posed by his disciple Zengzi. Compiled or circulating shortly before the Qin dynasty.

Xin xu (*New Arrangements*): an anthology of moral anecdotes and historical tales compiled or written by the Han imperial librarian Liu Xiang.

Xunzi (*The Master Xun*): a work containing the thoughts of the Confucian philosopher Xunzi (Xun Qing; *c.*335–*c.*238 BCE). See Chapter 4 for more detail.

Yantie lun (*Discourse on Iron and Salt*): record of a court debate ordered by imperial edict in 81 BCE, compiled a few decades after the event.

Yanzi chunqiu (*Master Yan's Spring and Autumn Annals*): a collection of 215 anecdotes containing moral counsel and political remonstrations by Yanzi (Yan Ying; *fl.* 547–489 BCE) primarily to his lord, Duke Jing of Qi (r. 547–489 BCE). Compiled by the imperial Han librarian Liu Xiang.

Yili (*The Book of Etiquette and Rites*): one of the **Three Ritual Classics**, with chapters on topics such as capping (to mark a boy's coming of age) and nuptial rites, drinking and banqueting, archery meetings and mourning attire. It includes material possibly going back to the fifth and fourth centuries BCE, but not assembled until the Han period.

Yu gong (*The Tribute of Yu*): see **Shangshu**.

Zhanguo ce (*The Stratagems of the Warring States*): a collection of stories centred on political strategy, warfare, persuasion and manipulation, set at the courts of the Warring States period; compiled by Han imperial librarian Liu Xiang.

Zhong lun (*Balanced Discourses*): a collection of philosophical essays by Xu Gan (171–218 CE).

Zhongyong (*The Doctrine of the Mean*): a core treatise on Confucian self-cultivation transmitted as a chapter in the **Liji** and attributed to Confucius's grandson Zisi (483–402 BCE). It was classified as one of the **Four Books**.

Zhouli (*The Rites of Zhou*): a text describing the idealized structure and administration of the royal state of Zhou; credited to the Duke of Zhou but compiled in the Han period; also known as one of the **Three Ritual Classics**.

Zhouyi (also *Yijing* or *The Book of Changes*): a divination text, with parts originating in the Western Zhou period (tenth to eighth century BCE). The text is organized around sixty-four variations of six solid or broken lines known as hexagrams, and was classified as one of the **Five 'Confucian'**

Classics in the second century BCE. See Chapter 2 for more detail.

Zhuangzi (*The Master Zhuang*): a literary masterpiece of Daoist philosophy attributed to Zhuangzi (Zhuang Zhou; *c.*369–286 BCE) but containing material from different authors. Completed around 300 BCE with some parts possibly over a century later. See Chapter 6 for more detail.

Zuozhuan (*The Zuo Tradition*): a lengthy work of historical narrative and speeches, completed around 300 BCE, and organized as a commentary on the **Chunqiu**.

Pinyin Pronunciation Guide

Rather than arranging transcribed sounds alphabetically, the list below follows the convention of separating initials and finals (e.g. *h* + *uang*) and grouping cognate sounds together (e.g. unaspirated and aspirated *b*/*p*, *d*/*t*).

b	as in *boat* or *bee*
p	as in *stop* or *point*
m	as in *mum* or *mole*
f	as in *fit* or *fast*
d	as in *down* or *dear*
t	as in *task*
n	as in *name*
l	as in *luck* or *lamp*
g	as in *good* or *girl*
k	as in *kiss* or *curb*
h	the *ch* in *loch* or *Bach*
j	as in *jeep*
q	the *ch* in *cheese* or *cheers*

x	the *sh* in *sheep* or *ship*
zh	the *j* in *Joe* or *juice*
ch	the *ch* in *cheap* or *chat*
sh	the *sh* in *shoe* or *shark*
r	the *re* in *pleasure*
z	the *ds* in *woods* or *kids*
c	the *ts* in *cats* or *rats*
s	as in *see* or *sense*
(y)i	the *ea* in *eat* or *flea*
(w)u	the *oo* in *room* or *u* in *plume*
yu	*yew*
ü	as in German *über*
a	as in *ah-hah* or *father*
(w)o	the *oa* in *moat* or *oi* in *soil*
e	the *u* in *huh* or *er* in *hers*
(y)e	the *eah* in *yeah*
ai	*eye* or as in *why*
ei	as in *weigh* or *spray*
ao	as in *trout* or *cow*
ang	as in *angst*
eng	the *ung* in *hung*
ong	the *ung* in German *Achtung*

ou	as in *oh* or *dough*
an	as in *pan* or *fan*
en	the *un* in *under* or *en* in *Wendy*
er	the *ar* in *car*
hai	*high* or *hi*
ia	as in *media*
ian	*eeh-en*
iang	*eeh-ahng* as in *young*
iao	as in *miaow* or Italian *ciao*
ie	*eeh-eh* as in *ear* or *here*
in	as in *bean* or *fin*
iu	the *eo* in *Leo* or *ay-o* in *Galileo*
ua	as in *suave* or *guava*
uan	as in *swan* or *Don Juan*
uang	*wan* (as in *wander*) + *-ng* (as in *wong*)
ui	*way*
un	*won*
uo	*wore*

Map and Figure Credits

Maps 1.1–1.3: Wu Huiyi and Xie Dan.

1.1. The First Emperor. Facsimile reprint from *Sancai tuhui* (*Assembled Illustrations of the Three Realms*; 1609).

1.2. Cang Jie, inventor of the Chinese character script. Facsimile reprint from *Sancai tuhui* (1609).

1.4. James Legge, translator of the Confucian Classics. Image from *James Legge: Missionary and Scholar*, by his daughter, Helen Edith Legge (London: Religious Tract Society, 1905).

1.6. Fragment from a text entitled 'Black Robes' ('Zi yi') held at the Shanghai Museum. From Ma Chengyuan ed., *Shanghai bowuguan cang Zhanguo Chu zhushu*, vol. 1 (Shanghai: Shanghai guji chubanshe, 2001), p.46.

3.1. A statue of Confucius at Clare College, Cambridge, by the contemporary sculptor Wu Weishan. Photo by Nigel Brown. Courtesy of the Master and Fellows of Clare College.

6.1. The Queen Mother of the West. Line drawing from a mural, Yinan tomb, Shandong province, Eastern Han period. After Hayashi Minao, *Kandai no kamigami* (Kyoto: Rinsen shoten, 1989), supplementary plate 2 (left register).

6.2. Jade burial suit of Zhao Mo, King of Nanyue (d. 122 BCE). Courtesy of the Nan Yue Wang Museum, Guangzhou.

6.3. Confucius meets Laozi. Drawing based on an ink rubbing, Wuliang family shrine, Shandong province, second century CE. Courtesy of the Needham Research Institute, Cambridge.

7.1. Reconstruction of the 'Guiding and Pulling Chart' (c.168 BCE) from Mawangdui Tomb no. 3 in Changsha. Courtesy of Wellcome Images.

7.2. The winged doctor Bian Que, legendary inventor of acupuncture, treating a patient. Ink rubbing of a fragment of an Eastern Han tomb relief, Shandong province. Courtesy of Huang Longxiang.

7.3. Illustrations of birds from an early Chinese dictionary. Song-period block print edition of the *Erya yin tu* by Guo Pu (276–324 CE). Courtesy of Wellcome Images.

7.4. Reconstruction of Zhang Heng's seismograph. Courtesy of the Needham Research Institute, Cambridge.

8.1. Divine Farmer (Shennong) holding a two-pronged spade. Ink rubbing, Wuliang family shrine, Shandong province, second century CE. Courtesy of the Needham Research Institute, Cambridge.

8.2. Working the fields. Drawing based on an ink rubbing, Sichuan province, Eastern Han period.

8.3. A market scene. Ink rubbing of a Han brick, Chengdu, Sichuan province. Image courtesy of Hajni Elias.

9.1. The character for 'harmony' as portrayed in the opening ceremony at the 2008 Beijing Olympics. Photo: Xinhua.

9.2. Butchers and cooks at work. Ink rubbing, Wuliang family shrine, Shandong province, second century CE. Courtesy of the Needham Research Institute, Cambridge.

Acknowledgements

My students, past and present, at Cambridge and elsewhere, have been my greatest help and inspiration. Without them this book would never have been conceived. I am deeply indebted to Eamonn O'Ciardha for combing through a version of the entire manuscript, alerting me to countless errors. Imre Galambos, Boping Yuan, Emma Wu, Adam Chau, Romain Graziani, Wu Huiyi, Hajni Elias and John Moffett were generous with tips and assistance whenever I needed it. My editor at Penguin, Casiana Ionita, provided expert guidance throughout, as did Kate Parker during the copy-editing process. For insight I owe much to scholarly work by colleagues; for any oversights and inaccuracies I take sole credit. I thank Cheng Eng who, as always, cares and encourages; and Leon, for persuading me that Chinese philosophers are no match for cows and superheroes.

Index

(Numbers in italic indicate an illustration of, or relating to, the entry in question.)

PELICAN BOOKS

PELICAN BOOKS

PELICAN BOOKS